P9-DFQ-836

The
HOUSE
THAT
Ruth
BUILT

The HOUSE THAT *Ruth* BUILT

A New Stadium, the First Yankees Championship, and the Redemption of 1923

ROBERT WEINTRAUB

LITTLE, BROWN AND COMPANY
New York Boston London

Little, Brown and Company
Hachette Book Group
237 Park Avenue, New York, NY 10017
www.hachettebookgroup.com

First Edition: April 2011

Little, Brown and Company is a division of Hachette Book Group, Inc.
The Little, Brown name and logo are trademarks of Hachette Book Group, Inc.

The publisher is not responsible for websites (or their content) that
are not owned by the publisher.

Library of Congress Cataloging-in-Publication Data

Weintraub, Robert.
   The house that Ruth built : a new stadium, the first Yankees championship, and the
redemption of 1923 / Robert Weintraub.
      p. cm.
   ISBN 978-0-316-08607-3
   1. New York Yankees (Baseball team) — History — 20th century.   2. Yankee Stadium
(New York, N.Y. : 1923–2009) — History — 20th century.   3. Baseball — New York
(State) — New York — History — 20th century.   4. Ruth, Babe, 1895–1948.   I. Title.
   GV875.N4W46 2011
      796.357′64097471 — dc22   2010048633

10   9   8   7   6   5   4   3   2   1

RRD–IN

Printed in the United States of America

For my mother, Judith Weintraub, who always said,
"I think you have a book in you."

The scar is still upon my heart from 1922
The blight is still upon my soul for what I failed to do
But now once more the battle cry comes sweeping down the plain
And I come with lifted mace to wipe away the stain...
For though I fell as Lucifer in last year's jamboree
They'll find another "Babe" at bat in 1923.

Grantland Rice, *"The Babe Speaks,"*
New York Tribune, *October 8, 1923*

Contents

The

HOUSE
THAT
Ruth
BUILT

Preface:
The Ungrateful Houseguest

JOHN MCGRAW NEVER learned to drive. Baseball's greatest manager usually got around the city by automobile, driven by his
chauffer, James Thompson. But October 10, 1923, was a mild Indian
summer morning, pushing sixty degrees just before eleven when the
leader of the New York Giants stepped onto the sidewalk outside the
Polo Grounds. McGraw's destination was only a short stroll from
here, five or ten minutes at most, so he waved Thompson away and
decided to walk.

McGraw's players emerged from the ballpark behind him, hauling the tools of their trade—gloves, bats, spikes—and jumped into
a fleet of waiting cabs, two or three men to a car. They were ready
for action, especially since today's matchup was the first game of the
1923 World Series. But it was not a home game. For the first time in
three seasons the Fall Classic wasn't being played entirely on the
sporting green of the Polo Grounds.

McGraw wore a tailored suit rather than his uniform. All summer
he had worn the flannel togs, but come fall he switched to civvies.
He was quite warm as he walked the short, steep distance up to

Eighth Avenue. The cabs bearing his players sped past. The Polo Grounds sat in Coogan's Hollow, a swale of land under Coogan's Bluff, a ridge overlooking the Harlem River and named for James J. Coogan, the onetime Manhattan borough president who owned the land until his death in 1915. The park was at the corner of West 155th Street and Eighth, putting it on the northeastern edge of Harlem. Immediately to the west, the posh neighborhood known as Sugar Hill (Duke Ellington's destination in "Take the A Train") was just beginning to show the fruits of the epoch known as the Harlem Renaissance, thanks to a boom in black artists, writers, thinkers, and (perhaps most significantly) organized gamblers. Known as "bankers," they had just introduced a craze called the "Numbers" that was sweeping the area like wildfire.

As McGraw walked through Harlem, he would likely have heard from windows and storefronts the hottest recording of the year, Bessie Smith's "Downhearted Blues":

I got the world in a jug, the stopper's in my hand,
I'm gonna hold it until you meet some of my demands.

As McGraw walked toward the 155th Street Viaduct, he encountered a bustling city swept up in the ethos of the day: making money and enjoying life. The Great War was over, as was the postwar recession that had hamstrung the national economy. Salaries had caught up to cost-of-living increases that had grown exponentially after the war, and New York's (and the rest of America's) mood grew more joyous as a result. The '20s had just begun to roar. Earlier in the year, the *Sporting News* called it "a fast age, and we're doing time in jazz, not goose step," and French psychologist Émile Coué had recently introduced an affirmation that was sweeping the United States: "Every day, in every way, I'm getting better and better!" It appealed to a nation that fairly leapt out of bed each morning, eager to attack the day.

New York City, as ever, was at the forefront of that attack, setting the tempo for the rest of the country. Prohibition was the law of the land, but it was merely a fanciful notion in New York—the saloons, speakeasies, and corner delis were full of drinkers of both sexes, a new and welcome development. The capital of fashion, media, shipping, and entertainment, New York was emerging as the foremost city in the world, especially with Europe still prostrate from the previous decade's destruction.

The center of New York power, then, as now, remained downtown, in the Financial District. But uptown had the Giants, for the past two decades the nation's most potent sporting brand. These two critical elements of New York's cultural engine—sports and money— were merging rapidly. The ad salesmen at the big newspapers had taken it as gospel that baseball fans—an unserious rabble with little taste, in their eyes—didn't constitute the buying public, but that changed in the '20s. *Literary Digest* noticed the new climate: "We have no hesitation in declaring that if an accurate poll were taken of the attendance at any big-league ball game the ratio would be around 80 per cent of business officials, office employees and men of leisure to 20 per cent of the actual 'laboring class.'" A little relaxation at the ballpark was expected after a day spent frantically selling or dealing in the rarefied air of high finance.

Stock and real estate speculation was the Big Thing on Wall Street, and the deal making continued in the Polo Grounds grandstand. As one player said, "I'd go to the ballpark and get stock tips from turnstile men and bootblacks and peanut butchers and newspapermen. Everybody was going to be a millionaire. It was a little confusing." The Giants started home games at three thirty p.m. in order to better allow the moneymen to travel north after a day of wheeling and dealing to watch McGraw and his team dominate the National League.

But today's contest was starting earlier, at two p.m., and it most certainly wasn't a home game for the Giants. As McGraw turned toward the water on the 155th Street Viaduct, passing over the Harlem River Speedway, built for horse and carriage but now crammed with automobiles, the enemy's fortress came into view. McGraw scowled. The building in front of him, just across the river in the Bronx, would be the scene of today's game and the cause of much of the manager's agita — the brand-new Yankee Stadium.

Despite its proximity to Manhattan, the Bronx definitely had an outerborough feel to it (expressed neatly in a headline in that morning's *Daily News:* "Bronx Landlords Count Dogs as Added Tenants"). Under ordinary circumstances, a sneering McGraw would have paid as much attention to a Bronx baseball park and its *American League* occupants, the Yankees, as he would to something stuck to the bottom of his shoe.

But this was no ordinary time. Thanks to the deep pockets of the men who had bought the team in a deal brokered by McGraw himself, the Yankees had emerged as dangerous rivals to the Giants for the hearts and minds of New York baseball fans. And thanks to the team's superstar — to McGraw, a mighty ape with intellect to match — the Yankees had not only challenged the Giants on the field but outstripped them at their own gate. Since 1912, the two teams had shared the Polo Grounds, with the Yankees as tenant and the Giants as landlord, so this development hit the Giants and McGraw, who owned roughly a quarter of the team, right in the wallet. But it was a situation McGraw and Giants majority owner Charles Stoneham had thought they could rectify — by evicting the Yankees.

They did, kicking the Yanks out of the Polo Grounds and essentially forcing them (*daring* them) to build a home of their own. So the bickering Yankees owners, Jacob Ruppert and Til "Cap" Huston, responded by going all-in. They put aside their own differences long enough to construct this gigantic palace of sport within shouting distance of the Polo Grounds. It had opened six months earlier on April 18, to enormous fanfare and great critical and popular reception.

Money was at the heart of this competition, and the Yankees suddenly had more of it—and with the Stadium they now had the means to increase revenue exponentially. But McGraw and the Giants could still win where it counted most—on the field.

Separated by a thin slice of the Harlem River, Manhattan and the South Bronx look like jigsaw pieces left slightly apart. At 155th Street, McGraw traversed the gap by means of the four-hundred-foot swing span of the Macombs Dam Bridge. And as he made landfall in the Bronx, the boisterous crowds hoping to attend the first World Series game ever at the Yankee Stadium came into view. This new monstrosity held an enormous number of fans, upwards of sixty thousand, and it seemed like twice that number were milling outside the Stadium on 161st Street, on River Avenue, and on the unpaved section of Doughty Street (to be renamed Ruppert Place in 1933) near the Elevated train, hoping to buy tickets. McGraw despaired momentarily, wondering how he would get through the logjam, when a policeman recognized him and organized a flying wedge, leading McGraw to a side entrance.

Once inside, McGraw wrinkled his nose and stepped into the visiting clubhouse. His players were inside, quietly awaiting batting practice. Unused lockers surrounded the team—and they'd remain empty. Such was McGraw's distaste for the Yankees and their new home that he had refused to allow the Giants to change inside the Stadium. Thus the team had met at the Polo Grounds, put on their uniforms, and headed over the river. McGraw might have to play the World Series here, but he didn't have to spend any more time as guests of the Yankees than absolutely necessary.

Much has changed on the Manhattan side since the days when McGraw strolled through the area. Next door to the former site of the Giants home field is Rucker Park, where the fabled summertime Rucker Tournament attracts the best playground basketball players in the city and beyond. One Hundred Fifty-fifth Street abuts the northern edge of another park, one named for a New York baseball player—Jackie Robinson, who played in Brooklyn! Eighth Avenue today in this stretch of Harlem is now called Frederick Douglass Boulevard. But perhaps the greatest change, at least from a baseball perspective, is that the Polo Grounds no longer exists. A large public housing project stands where the diamond and seats once did, and the entire area is in thrall to the great new Yankee Stadium across the river. Everywhere one turns in the summer months, the familiar Yankees "Top Hat and Bat" emblem (which didn't exist in 1923) winks out from memorabilia stores, makeshift parking lots, and pre- and postgame watering holes. It is a turn of events that would have eaten at John McGraw.

The New York Yankees are the preeminent sports franchise in the United States, if not the world, and the club's résumé is well known to most fans—twenty-seven World Championships (as of 2010), by far the most of any team in any sport. But in 1923 this dominance didn't yet exist. As that year's World Series opened, the Yankees had yet to win a single championship. And in the previous two seasons, it had lost the Series, decisively, to its mighty rival— the New York Giants.

The Yankees rose to prominence on the broad slugging shoulders of Babe Ruth. He is by general consensus the most important and greatest player in the game's history. As we look back from the perspective of nearly a century, the Babe's extraordinary career appears to be an unchecked litany of achievement and triumph. But in 1921 and 1922, Ruth had failed to deliver a World Series to New York. He had been an important component of three championship teams in Boston, but as a pitcher, not an everyday player expected to carry the team on his back (Ruth was one of many stars in Beantown). Since switching to the outfield and moving to the biggest city in the country in 1920, Ruth had come up short in the Fall Classic.

In the spring of 1919, while Ruth was still in Boston, the Sox played a traveling series of exhibitions with the New York Giants, and during an early game at Plant Field in Tampa, Florida, Ruth gave a glimpse of the immediate future of the National Pastime. Newly a full-time outfielder, the Babe launched a stupendous blast, later estimated at 587 feet, carrying far past a cordon of automobiles that surrounded the playing field. Players on both sides watched slack-jawed, as though an alien vessel had just appeared from the sky and landed at home plate. In contrast, Ruth stayed casual. "I don't think anyone went to shake his hand, they were so dumbfounded," recalled teammate Harry Hooper. "Babe? He didn't think he had done anything wonderful. To him it was just another wallop."

But one witness to the colossal home run remained unimpressed — John McGraw, who sneered, "If he plays every day, that bum will hit into a hundred double plays." Since then, the enmity between Ruth and McGraw had only grown. The Babe may have stolen the hearts of New York baseball fans with his unprecedented slugging, but McGraw had gotten his last laughs in the World Series, when it mattered most.

He designed a strategy used to attack Ruth's hitting style and called every pitch from the dugout, baffling the slugger and rendering him the "Swatless Sultan." "A man of a thousand successes, the Babe has since his ascendancy as a home run hitter been a World Series jest," wrote Arthur Robinson in the *New York American* following Ruth's collapse in the 1922 Series, where he was held to a measly two hits in seventeen at bats, and such was the prevailing wisdom. Ruth was labeled "an exploded phenomenon" in the *New York Sun* and a "flat failure" by the Associated Press. The Babe's homers were great for the box office, but when it came to winning, the Scientific Baseball perfected by John J. McGraw still ruled.

Ruth suffered through a miserable 1922 even before the Series. A new contract was paying him, in his matchless phrase, "a grand a week," $52,000, but the giant salary was hardly earned. Ruth was suspended for the first six weeks of the season for taking part in an illegal barnstorming tour, and he fought with umpires, fans, and teammates. "Your conduct…was reprehensible to a great degree—shocking to every American mother who permits her boy to go to a game," said AL president Ban Johnson after Ruth viciously cursed an umpire. "A man of your stamp bodes no good in the profession.…It seems the period has arrived when you should allow some intelligence to creep into a mind that has plainly been warped."

Drink played an outsize role in Ruth's troubles. He had started the epic elbow-bending in spring training, which the Yankees perhaps unwisely held in New Orleans. The Babe guzzled cocktails every night at the Little Club, right across the street from the team's hotel, joined by many of his teammates. "Yankees Training on Scotch" accused one newspaper headline. He had other poor habits. Joe Vila, a sportswriter who worshipped McGraw and reviled the Babe, gleefully wrote about Ruth spending too much time at the racetrack and refusing to take morning batting practice while suspended.

Ruth also warred with his manager, Miller Huggins, whom the Babe loathed. At one point, exhausted by his star's behavior, Huggins yelled at Ruth, "If you don't want to play ball, why don't you go home?" Ruth responded, "You go home! If you don't like the way I play ball, why don't you fire me?" Huggins didn't, but given Ruth's puny 1922 World Series batting average of .118, he might as well have.

The opprobrium from the heretofore worshipful sporting press, particularly the New York writers, blindsided Ruth, rendering him a "stunned hippopotamus." He confessed (admittedly in a ghostwritten column) to "lying awake, thinking about his problems." So in a little-known subplot to his sprawling career, Ruth spent the winter of 1922–23 in isolation on his Massachusetts farm, working out and, at least publicly, swearing off the destructive distractions that had caused his tumble. "Nothing but ice water for me," he told astounded newsmen one evening the following spring. "I haven't had a drink all winter."

Ruth responded with his greatest overall season, one well shy of his most prodigious home-run totals but compensated for with outstanding all-around play—at the plate, in the field, on the base paths, and in the locker room. He was rewarded with his first and only MVP Award, and the Yankees followed him all the way to an easy pennant.

A redemptive World Series victory would cap a season that had started on a forbidding yet glorious April day in the Yankees' new home. But defeating the rest of the American League was the easy part. Ruth and the Yankees still had to best their bitter rival, John McGraw and his two-time-defending-champion Giants. The manager held the world in a jug and was demanding a third consecutive championship, his most desired and elusive goal.

Introduction:
Opening the House —
April 18, 1923

IT WAS A Wednesday morning, overcast and blustery. In retrospect, the opening of the Yankee Stadium, as everyone was calling it, seemed to demand a sun-splashed afternoon, but early spring in New York is fickle, and the baseball gods hadn't yet made up their minds about the new palace in the South Bronx.

The night before the first game at the Stadium, Babe Ruth stayed at his Upper West Side apartment in the Ansonia Hotel on Broadway, between 73rd and 74th. The seventeen-story, fourteen-hundred-room residential hotel had dominated the West Side skyline since its opening in 1904, and it featured Beaux Arts decorations, rounded corner towers, and a healthy supply of gargoyles, which earned the Ansonia the nickname "the Wedding Cake." Built to resemble a nineteenth-century French resort, the Ansonia was the latest word in customized comforts, with Turkish baths, the world's largest indoor swimming pool, expensive basement shops, and several in-house restaurants, serving mainly French cuisine. A garden on the roof provided fresh flowers and vegetables. It was a fitting home for New York's foremost sporting superstar. Among the tenants were

Enrico Caruso, Flo Ziegfeld, Igor Stravinsky, and, for a short while, well before Ruth arrived, Arnold Rothstein. The gambling kingpin known as "A.R." would later meet in the lobby with other conspirators to discuss how best to profit from the coming World Series fix of 1919.

Ruth was awoken at nine that morning by a phone call from Bill Slocum, a reporter for the *New York American*. The paper paid Ruth $1,500 for the exclusive rights to his "column," which Slocum was charged with ghostwriting, and now the reporter needed some material from the Babe for the afternoon edition. Ruth would later say Slocum "knew how he thought" better than anyone. Slocum asked if anything unusual had happened in the last couple of days that could be worked into the column, and Ruth mentioned that his business manager Christy Walsh's friend "Van Looneytune," or whatever it was, had given him a lucky silver dollar. "You mean Hendrik van Loon?" asked Slocum. The Dutch historian had written a bestselling book for children, *The Story of Mankind,* in 1921. Ruth confirmed that was who he meant.

That worked for Slocum—he passed along the tale to the readers, who breathlessly followed the Babe's every deed. Ruth was so popular that papers across the country printed his stats—not his team's but his alone. Before hanging up, Slocum told Ruth that huge crowds were likely to gather at the Stadium, and he should leave for the Bronx early.

The Babe wasn't too worried. They weren't going to start without him.

When Ruth looked into the bathroom mirror that morning at the Ansonia, he saw a tall, broad, strapping man with a burly torso stuck on top of famously thin ankles. His head was enormous, making him easy to pick out even from the farthest reaches of the ballpark. In contrast, his bright brown eyes were small, deeply sunk into his skull. His eyebrows were extremely bushy. Ruth's nose was flat, pushed in as though he had been in one fight too many. His hair was deep brown, practically black, with crisp curls. He wasn't classically handsome, surely, but he exuded an unmistakable charisma that lured the opposite sex like deer to a salt lick.

His backstory was well known to the sports fans of the day. "If it wasn't for baseball, I'd be in either the penitentiary or the cemetery," he once said. Ruth didn't even know his date of birth until years later. The Babe was born George Herman Ruth in Baltimore, Maryland, but it wasn't until he applied for a passport after he became a famous ballplayer that he discovered he'd been born on February 6, 1895, making him a shade past twenty-eight on the morning of April 18, 1923.

There wasn't much birthday cake in the Ruth home. It was a life of squalor and neglect. His father, also named George, and his mother, Catherine, struggled to control their wild son almost immediately. George Ruth Sr. was a taciturn saloonkeeper in the southwestern part of the city, and he showed little patience with his namesake. Little George stole from the saloon till, chewed tobacco, and drank unfinished beer from patrons' glasses—all at the tender age of six.

He was tough, and a bully. When a knock was heard at the door in the Ruth home, it was often the parent of a classmate of George's, there to show Mr. and Mrs. Ruth "what your George has done to my son." "I have the same violent temper my father and older brother had," Ruth said from the distance of adulthood. "Both died of injuries from street fights in Baltimore, fights begun by flare-ups of their tempers." Once, he stole a dollar from the saloon and bought ice cream for the neighborhood kids. His father found out and horse-whipped him silly. The next day, George did it again—just to show his father he wouldn't give in.

A short time later, just after turning seven, George was declared "incorrigible" and shipped off to St. Mary's Industrial School, a home for orphans and wayward boys. Over the next couple of years,

George Sr. and Catherine repeatedly retrieved their son from the school and tried to make him a part of their home. All attempts at domesticating little George failed, and he was permanently returned to St. Mary's in 1905, just as he turned ten years old.

At the school, Ruth met his father figure and baseball tutor, a Xaverian priest from Canada named Brother Matthias. Matthias taught George how to read and write, and how to be a part of decent society. Over the years he put Ruth to work building cabinets, rolling cigars, and making shirts. Mostly he taught George the game of baseball. He did it so well that at the age of eight Ruth was playing on the team for twelve-year-olds.

Aping Matthias's huge uppercut swing, the strapping teenage Ruth was an obvious prospect for area teams. He could hit farther than anyone else on his squad, and he showed excellent control and speed as a left-handed pitcher. He starred for local semipro and sandlot teams when he wasn't playing for St. Mary's. In February 1914, Jack Dunn of the Baltimore Orioles, then a top minor-league team, signed Ruth to his first professional contract. "Who's the big fella?" someone asked early in Ruth's time with the Orioles. "He's Jack Dunn's baby" came the reply, and thus was George Ruth forever renamed "Babe."

At noon, the gates were opened at the Yankee Stadium for the first time. A smallish crowd, perhaps five hundred souls, gathered around the still-shuttered ticket windows. But in less than an hour, that changed dramatically. By one o'clock, a churning sea of humanity had formed around the new Stadium, descending on the thirty-six ticket booths that ringed the Stadium, even though the first pitch wasn't until three thirty. About fifteen thousand tickets had been presold, leaving the majority up for grabs at one p.m., when the shutters opened on the booths with a loud clatter.

Reserved seats for this first game in the Yankees' new home sold for $3.50, grandstand seats for $1.10, bleacher seats for $1.00. A pair of scalpers—Abe Cohen of Brooklyn and Sebastian Calabrese of East 27th Street—were arrested by Inspector Andrew O'Connor for selling $1 seats for $1.10. They were unable to post $500 bail, and so spent the evening in night-court jail. Most of the huge throng had walked or come by train, including Commissioner of Baseball Kenesaw Mountain Landis, who took the Interborough subway to the Bronx. "No ball fan rides to the game in a cab," said the commissioner, though he was caught up in the crowd, necessitating a police rescue. Still, the two thousand parking spaces for automobiles were full long before game time, despite the fact that gasoline distillate was an outrageous sixteen cents per gallon. Cars were up on curbs, parked haphazardly on nearby streets, and many drivers got out and started walking from at least a mile away. The *Boston Globe* estimated that 8,500 cars were parked in the vicinity.

At 2:10, all the ticket windows slammed shut, except for the bleacher seat windows—and at about 3:05, the last ticket was sold. It was left to the New York Police Department to inform the disappointed crowds that they should go home. Somewhat surprisingly, there was no violence, no shoving, just some grumbling. In all, an estimated 25,000 fans had been turned away.

As for the lucky fans who got a seat, the team's co-owner, Colonel Jacob Ruppert, bet sportswriter Damon Runyon a suit of clothes that there were more than 71,000 paying customers. The Yankees officially reported an astonishing 74,217, a record number the papers faithfully passed along. It wasn't until May that the true number of fans who clicked through the forty turnstiles was discovered. A boxing match was staged for the Milk Fund charity, and ten thousand extra seats were put in place on the field. The total number of tickets printed was seventy thousand—thus, some alert reporters deduced, the Stadium could hold only about sixty thousand for baseball. When confronted, the Yankees' business manager Ed Barrow admitted he had added standing-room-only fans to the original estimate, and was forced to amend the number to about 62,200, probably still exaggerated, but nevertheless by far the largest crowd in the sport's history.

Damon Runyon never did collect his new suit from Colonel Ruppert.

There were a few snafus, as would be expected on a new stadium's opening day. Yale basketball coach Joe Fogarty had reserved a box for himself and several other minor dignitaries, but when they showed at 1:15, Fogarty found his seats had been sold. He demanded an audience with Barrow, who was harried with a thousand last-minute details. "There's nothing doing," roared Bulldog Ed, and a nearby cop ushered the coach out of the Stadium.

Peanuts and Cracker Jacks cost a nickel; soda pop, fifteen cents. The game program, with team owners Jacob Ruppert and Til Huston on the cover, not Ruth, cost fifteen cents. Ushers wearing tuxedos and bow ties welcomed fans to a park that the *New York Evening-Telegram* said smelled of "fresh paint, fresh plaster and fresh grass," and the large breezeways allowed for the masses to find their proper sections with little difficulty. A pair of announcers, one down each line, took up their positions, megaphones in hand. Never before had two in-crowd announcers worked a game, but then this place was too damn big for just one man, no matter how loud. Jack Lenz wore his hallmark derby on the first-base line. George Levy, a regular announcer at the Polo Grounds, worked the third-base side. His megaphone was noticeably smaller than Lenz's.

A heavy tarp had protected the field for the past week, but early in the morning Yankees groundskeeper Phil Schenck ordered it removed, revealing a perfect, gleaming green. New ballparks traditionally had poor fields for months until the combination of sun and regular usage alchemized them into playing condition. Not so this field. Schenck had been the original keeper at Hilltop Park, the Yankees' home when they were known as the Highlanders, or, to some, the Hilltoppers. But when the team moved into the Polo Grounds,

Schenck was made redundant. For ten years he was the "groundless groundskeeper," a jolly, beloved figure among team officials but one with no field of his own to seed, sod, and mow.

Schenck had clearly not lost his touch while the Yanks toiled at the Polo Grounds—the field was a masterpiece. In an unusual move for the era, the areas encompassing home plate and the on-deck circles were entirely grass, save for a strip of dirt that connected home with the pitching mound. As was common, the foul lines ran past home, forming an *X*, with the dish marking the spot. The Yankees had held the field's first workout the morning before, and judged it unrivaled in the league. Now it stood ready for its initial contest.

Back at the Ansonia, Ruth made his way through the lobby. He passed a newsman selling papers that noted the Berlin riots had dropped the deutsche mark to 33,000 to 1 U.S. dollar, heralded a pledge by Alma Cummings to stage the first one-hundred-hour dance marathon in Toronto (beyond the reach of the "Stop-the-Dance" law), and reported on the sensational testimony in the big police-bootlegging scandal of the moment, during which Mary Castro claimed to have bribed Robert "the Sprinting Detective" McAllister $600 to let her go free after he arrested her for violation of the Volstead Act. "Lie! It's a frame-up!" screamed the accused constable from the gallery.

Beyond the front page, a Macy's ad predicted, "It is apt to be a bit chilly during the opening game of the baseball season....So wear a newly arrived topcoat ($27.50–$54.75). Or perhaps a cap ($1.88), or a Lansdowne hat ($4.89)." Another ad suggested the sporting fan "take along plenty of smokes, and we suggest the following items to add to your enjoyment of the National Game: Tampa blunts ($2.49 for a can of fifty), made with Havana filler and Havana wrapper; Italian briar pipes (.39 apiece); or Three Castles cigarettes, packed in airtight tins of fifty each (at $1.88)." The arts section advertised the latest movie offerings around town, including Harold Lloyd in *Safety Last,* Lionel Barrymore in *Enemies of Women,* and Marion Davies in *Adam and Eva.*

Perhaps most important, the *Times* and the *Herald* and the *Daily News* and the *Post* and the *Tribune* and the *World* and the *American* and all the other broadsheets and tabloids published during this golden age of newspapers provided directions to the grand new ballpark at 161st and River Avenue in the South Bronx.

Autoists could cross the Harlem River at 138th, 145th, 155th, or uptown at 181st. Those without cars could ride the subway, taking either the east side Jerome Avenue Line to the newly refurbished and expanded 161st Street station or the Elevated train to the Jerome and Anderson Avenue stop and walk two blocks. A trip from Grand Central Terminal to the Yankee Stadium was estimated at sixteen minutes.

Ruth, of course, would drive, and just before noon, he stepped out to his new Pierce-Arrow. He also owned a sporty Stutz Bearcat for when he really wanted to feel the wind in his hair, and would later favor cherry-red Packards, ones with his monogram etched into the driver-side door. His teammates nicknamed his ride "the Ghost of Riverside Drive." He'd roar up to the Stadium parking lot, his space nearest the entrance always left available, his radiator cap missing and water spouting and steaming up like Old Faithful.

Policemen sent by Ruppert were waiting to escort the Babe to the Bronx. Ruth stopped to sign a few autographs for waiting children and spontaneously invited a few to be his guests at the big game. They hopped in his car. Ruth often picked up young fans en route to games. "Just be sure the bottom of your pants is clean," he'd warn. The cops led him up the east side and across the Harlem River via the Macombs Dam Bridge at 155th Street. Around the Stadium, dust swirled in the wind from the recently leveled streets that were yet to be paved.

Another phalanx of officers waited at the main entrance to the

Stadium. The convoy stopped, and a uniformed bodyguard, who ensured him a clean path through the mob, accompanied Ruth. Ruth took down a list of policemen on duty to give to Barrow, who would procure tickets for all. And he wrote a note on one of his personal cards for the kids to take to the ticket booth. Then he strolled into the Yankee Stadium for the first time to play an official baseball game.

He bounded up the flight of wooden steps on the third-base side to the spanking-new clubhouse. "Nice of you to join us, Jidge!" yelled a few players, using the locker room shorthand for George. He was the last man in, as usual.

The Babe hung his perfectly tailored suit in the shiny maroon locker with RUTH stamped on it in metal letters. For the first time in his career, he had a locker that actually locked. Like his parking spot, it was right next to the entrance, making for quick and easy egress. In time, however, the area would become jammed with mementos that fans sent as tokens of their admiration.

A pay phone had been installed in the clubhouse just for him. In the future, whenever it would ring, the other players would dive for the phone, assuming the caller was a woman or a celebrity they could rib. "Ruth had twenty-four secretaries," said fellow Yankee Waite Hoyt, referring to his teammates. Ruth also had a separate trash can next to his locker, where he pitched scads of letters from fans, business come-ons, and assorted invitations—he even called the waste bin his "mailbox." Doc Woods, the Yankees trainer, once pieced together six thousand dollars' worth of checks Ruth had simply torn up unseen.

Now the Babe called over the clubhouse boy, handing the kid his 1918 championship ring (which he would wear until he earned one with his new team), his gold watch, and a chain, and told him to put them in the massive safe that had been with the organization since its inception and trundled with great effort across the river. Ruth's goods were placed in the slot designated for Jack Chesbro, the original star of the New York Highlanders. In exchange, the club-house kid handed the Sultan two hot dogs.

Ruth then went through his usual pregame ritual, starting with a rubdown. He scarfed the franks, took a big swig of bicarbonate of soda ("My milk," as Ruth referred to it), and belched loud enough to turn heads. Now he was ready to play some ball. He slipped into the team's brand-new white home uniform and readied to take the field.

As the Yanks dressed and the crowd pressed the gates, the Boston Red Sox, New York's historically appropriate opponents on this day of days, were hiking across the Macombs Dam Bridge. They had been warned that getting to the Stadium was going to be difficult, and unlike the Babe, the Sox didn't rate a police escort.

So manager Frank Chance—former Yankees headman and "Peerless Leader of the old-time Cubs, returned now to lead the Red Sox out of the baseball wilderness"—and his team took cabs from the Ansonia, where they stayed a floor below Ruth. They made it to within a mile and a half of the Stadium, then lugged their equipment and a change of clothes across the river into the Bronx. Howard Ehmke, Boston's bony ace pitcher, would have the task of slowing Ruth and the two-time American League champs. While ambling toward the Stadium, Chance told Ehmke to simply walk Ruth if need be—concentrate on the table setters; don't worry about the Big Ape. But Ehmke had a superb changeup that had retired the Babe in the past. And anyway Ruth was in a funk. Everyone had seen the World Series the previous fall...

In the *New York Telegram* of April 17, Fred Lieb assessed the new Yankee Stadium. Lieb noted the short porch down the right-field line, combined it with the Babe's ability to bring fans to the park, and coined an eternal nickname for the place: "The House That Ruth Built." Now Ruth led his team out onto the field for the first time in "his" park. "Some ballyard!" he exclaimed. The Stadium was jammed, even though first pitch was still more than two hours away. According to Damon Runyon, "The heads were packed so closely that Al Goullet, the six-day bicycle rider, could have ridden his bike around the stadium on the track of their hats." The ramps and passageways were crushed with fans. The refreshment stands were jammed, with huge lines of people trying to get a frank and a near beer before the festivities started. A large number of workers swarmed the interior, the construction project that raised the Stadium from nothing still ongoing.

The Red Sox had played a series of exhibitions before coming to New York. The crowds had been sparse. So the huge throng at the Stadium was a financial windfall. As the visiting team, Boston collected a quarter for each head that passed through the gates. The $15,550 hardly made up for the sale of the Babe three years earlier, but it was a tidy sum in owner Harry Frazee's pocket.

Yes, the Yankee Stadium was cozy straight down the right-field line, but otherwise the dimensions were far less conducive to Ruth's slugging power than the Polo Grounds had been. The Babe had attended the team's workout at the Stadium the day before. His first reaction to his new home was "I'll never hit sixty homers here." It may have been just under three hundred feet to right, but that was still a good forty feet farther down the line than in the Polo Grounds. And the power alleys and center field were miles away. Ruth squinted through the mist that had begun to appear. For a park supposedly created to accentuate his power, this was no picnic. This was a Stadium built for grandeur and maximum profit, not necessarily for Ruth home runs.

Fred Lieb shared none of the Babe's doubts. He also coined the short porch in right "Ruthville."

First pitch was scheduled for 3:30, but the festivities began well before that. Dignitaries wearing their Sunday finest lined the box seats, which were the only ones in the Stadium not bolted down.

Each box had room for several chairs, and if an invited guest arrived to find no room, another seat could be brought into the box to accommodate him. They were also the only seats in the Stadium not painted green.

The dugout benches were also green, as were the columns that held up its roof. The dugouts were the most comfortable in the sport, with a cushioned bench and a wooden floor. Equipment bags, gloves, and caps hung from metal hooks. There were no bat racks—players laid out their bats on the dirt in front of the dugout, despite the risk to fielders tracking foul pop-ups.

On the field, Ruth posed with Huggins, Chance, Ruppert, Huston, and Landis for a variety of photos to mark the occasion. The pop of the flashbulbs and the resulting smoke mixed with the misty conditions to form a surreal vision in front of the Yankees dugout. It was something out of a Civil War battle, all smoke and noise and confusion and clashing uniforms.

After the photos, a group of men in fancy mohair coats approached the Babe. They carried a long wooden box. "Your bat, sir," one said to Ruth, and opened the box to reveal a special lumber carved just for the occasion, to be used by the Babe during this game only. A glass frontage on the box displayed the specifications: a fifty-three-ounce bat, built for the Babe and paid for by the *Los Angeles Mirror*. By arrangement, after the game the bat would travel in its own train car to L.A., where it would be awarded to the winner of a charity home-run contest for area youth.

Ruth swung the bat a few times to get the feel for his new ash. The L.A. contingent dispersed, replaced by a smiling Al Smith, the governor of New York. "Remember me, Babe?" asked the dapper, white-haired Smith. Bronx borough president Henry Bruckner paid his respects, as did several lesser pols. Notably absent were New York City mayor John "Red Mike" Hylan, who claimed sickness, and AL president Ban Johnson, who had come to loathe Ruppert and Huston.

"Root, Root!" called Colonel Ruppert in his Bavarian twang from his box. Ruth ambled over to the co-owner. Ruth had a formal, if friendly, relationship with the colonel, nothing like his palling with Huston. But he respected the beer baron and had spent many evenings sampling his product. Ruppert never called the Babe anything but "Root." Judge Landis was standing there too. Ruth winked and intimated he wouldn't cause the commish any more trouble this year. Landis scowled in reply, his face assuming the lean, pinched countenance of a moray eel.

Just then, the distant sound of thunder was heard. No, not thunder—it was a band. The March King himself, John Philip Sousa, was leading the Seventh Regiment Band around the park, playing his classics: "Stars and Stripes Forever," "The Liberty Bell," "Semper Fidelis," and his newest composition, "Nobles of the Mystic Shrine." Sousa led the seventy-five-piece orchestra around the outfield, sporting "only a few gross of his medals."

In 1923 baseball, not football, was the sport associated with military might. Now, with postwar pride still gripping the nation, a full military display was held honoring the doughboys. The American Legion had a full brigade on the field. Representatives of the Veterans of Foreign Wars announced a new president had been elected to lead the group: Colonel Huston, half owner of the Yankees. The superintendent of West Point, F. W. Sladen, was on hand, as was his adjutant, Captain Matthew Ridgway, who would go on to fame on the battlefields of World War II and Korea.

But there was one snag. This new Stadium was so vast that all of the pageantry—even Sousa's marches—was swallowed up. The *New York Post* observed "the Regiment Band worked hard in the left field corner, while only snatches of the tunes reached the crowd near the home plate. It was like hearing the music of a parade on Fifth Avenue from the window of an office on a cross street." Sousa pressed on and led the band to the flagpole in center field, where the players marched out to meet the musicians, single file. Managers

Chance and Huggins tugged at a rope, raising the 1922 AL pennant along with Old Glory while the national anthem played. The resulting roar from the crowd "carried across the Harlem and far beyond," noted the *Times*.

The teams formed parallel lines and marched back to the infield. The Yankees wore their new white uniforms, sporting the pinstripes the team would become famous for, but not the interlocking *NY*—that had been removed in 1917. The players draped gray sweatshirts over the uniforms. The Red Sox sported gray, but the rest of the ensemble was "a symphony of red"—the caps, the stockings, and the sweatshirts, which were a bright scarlet. "Luckily, their concrete dugout was fireproof," wrote one wag.

The umpires originally slated to call the game were William Evans and "Ducky" Holmes, but at the last moment Tom Connolly, who umpired the first game in New York Highlanders history, was handed the nostalgic assignment of calling balls and strikes. The game was thus officiated by three umps. Connolly took George Levy's smaller megaphone to announce the day's batteries: Ehmke and Al DeVormer (who had been traded to Boston from the Yankees over the winter) for the Sox, Bob Shawkey and Wally Schang for the home team. Few in the crowd could hear Connolly. Few fans without binoculars could see him either, unless they were at field level. Barrow was upstairs and took in the fans' complaints. He made a mental note to start selling binoculars at games.

There was a steady, mountainous roar in the place as game time approached. It was as though a tsunami were rolling up the Harlem River. The players could hardly hear themselves think. "It was like a battleship cannonade," said Shawkey, who had been in the navy during World War I.

Governor Smith was awarded the honor of throwing out the first pitch in Yankee Stadium history. From his box, "Smilin' Al" tossed a strike, to the great surprise of the press corps—after all, "Tradition demands that the thrower miss the objective by several feet. Old-time baseball men considered it a distinct social error." The governor waved to the crowd and shook hands with, among others, his whip-smart young assistant, an ambitious city planner named Robert Moses.

As the Babe tossed his final warm-up throws with center fielder Whitey Witt and left fielder Bob Meusel, Ruth couldn't avoid feeling the enormity of the situation. This was not just any ballgame, not even any other opening day. Ruth was used to all eyes being on him, but not such jaundiced ones. Since melting down in the World Series the previous fall, the Babe had been at the center of a torrent of criticism.

"There are no excuses for the lamentably weak hitting of Babe Ruth," opined *Baseball Magazine* in the wake of the 1922 Series, voicing a common opinion. "Ruth entered the Series in excellent physical condition and was shown up by the [New York] Giants pitchers in a way that amazed the fans." The superb writer W. O. McGeehan noted, "It is a delicate thing, that co-ordination of brain, eye, and muscle that Jack Dempsey has and Bill Tilden has and the Babe used to have to a superlative degree. It has to be guarded jealously. Even then it disintegrates gradually, but surely it should be retained for a longer time than apparently Ruth has been able to retain it. Is it leaving Ruth? Or can he get it back?"

Critics had questioned his vision, his swing, even his mental state. Small wonder Ruth muttered to his teammates upon leaving the clubhouse this afternoon, "I'd give a year off my life to hit one today." The Babe was on trial, and he knew it better than anyone else.

As game time approached, the sun popped out from behind the clouds, drawing a cheer. Many fans still shivered—the temperature barely scraped fifty degrees. After all the pomp, the first actual baseball game in the Yankee Stadium was about to be played. The Yanks spilled out of their dugout on the third-base side (hard as it is to picture for modern fans, the team occupied the left dugout until 1946) to take the field. Yankees starting pitcher Bob Shawkey, wearing his hallmark red sweatshirt under his uniform, was easy to pick out, even from the distant bleachers. He finished his warm-up tosses and stared in at his catcher, Wally Schang. Chick Fewster, Boston's shortstop, stepped into the batter's box. At 3:31 p.m., Shawkey began the first game ever at the House That Ruth Built with a ball outside.

On the third pitch, Fewster skied one into the stands, the first foul ball hit into the crowd, and a fan made a wonderful one-handed stab, earning a nice round of applause. Fewster eventually grounded out, and Shawkey set the side down in order. Now Ruth was coming up third and eagerly awaiting his first at bat in his House. Howard Ehmke heeded his manager's advice by retiring Witt and Joe Dugan in front of the Babe. Then the Sox hurler, utilizing his tricky hesitation delivery that usually managed to throw off the hitter's timing just enough, tossed a softy to the plate. Ruth whipped his fifty-three-ouncer through the zone but just missed a solid connection, flying out harmlessly to left.

With one out in the top of the second, George Burns, Boston's first baseman, collected the first hit in Yankee Stadium history, a clean single to right. Burns was promptly thrown out stealing, and the game remained scoreless until the third. One of two men inside the manually operated scoreboard in right-center field turned over another 0. The scoreboard itself was a marvel, with room for twelve innings of scoring from every game in major-league baseball. Unfortunately, fans sitting behind home plate struggled to read the out-of-town scores due to the immense distance. The scoreboard interrupted the steady stream of ads that festooned the fences around the outfield. Ever-Ready sterilized shaving brushes and Gem razors were among the sponsors with billboards along the field.

Aaron Ward started the bottom half with a base hit. Everett Scott sacrificed, but Ward was nailed at third on Shawkey's comebacker to Ehmke. Then the Yanks mustered a two-out rally. Witt walked, and Dugan singled in a run, the first tally in Stadium history. That put two on, and it was the Babe's second chance for a hit.

Sun battled cloud for supremacy of the sky as Ruth sauntered to the plate. "Be smart here, George, two men on," yelled Huggins from the bench. Ehmke threw a curve for a strike, then a fastball outside. Ruth waved his club back and forth, trying to think along with Ehmke. Two more pitches went by, a ball and a strike. The count was 2–2. *Be smart here, George.* He remembered his first time up and sensed that the super-slow ball was coming. Sure enough, Ehmke sidearmed a crawler.

Ruth took two quick steps forward in the box to meet the pitch and uncoiled a mighty whack. The sound carried much farther around the ballpark than did Sousa's band. The ball rose on a high parabola toward the right-field wall.

The roar from the crowd practically flushed birds from trees all the way to the Connecticut border. Ruth lost sight of the ball as it rocketed toward the white frieze atop the Stadium, but he knew from the moment he made contact that it was too much for the park—any park—to hold. Ehmke did too. He dropped his head, resisting the urge to watch the ball sail away. "The revelry became riot," wrote the *Daily News,* as "people tore up programs, smashed canes, and launched all manner of foodstuffs" into the air. As the ball settled in the stands, straw hats sailed into the sky, some landing on the field. Fortunately for the cleanup crew, it was too chilly for most people to have braved going out in straw, and felt hats were too pricey to toss away.

The Babe had done it! Ruth had risen to the occasion once more, and with one mighty clout, all the doubts, all the ill tidings, all the failure from the season before, washed from his shoulders. He trotted around the bases through the mist, enveloped by the overwhelming noise from the crowd.

The Stadium press box was located in front of the mezzanine behind home plate (unlike at the Polo Grounds, where the reporters worked from the lower deck, fifty feet from the batter's box). More than 150 writers crammed in to cover this day of days. Grantland Rice's account of the Babe's shot in the *New York Tribune* rivaled his famous story the following year chronicling the Four Horsemen of

Notre Dame, and was written in the same press box. "A white streak left Babe Ruth's 53-ounce bludgeon in the third inning of yesterday's opening game at the Yankee Stadium. On a low line it sailed, like a silver flame, through the gray, bleak April shadows, and into the right field bleachers, while the great slugger started on his jog around the towpaths for his first home run of the year." Rice thought the shot had induced "the greatest vocal cataclysm baseball has ever known."

Hendrik Willem van Loon, the man Ruth had called "Van Looneytune," was a guest of Ruth's business manager, Christy Walsh, that day. He later remembered, "The fans were on their feet yelling and waving and throwing scorecards and half-consumed frankfurters, bellowing unto high heaven that the Babe was the greatest man on earth, that the Babe was some kid, and that the Babe could have their last and bottom dollar, together with the mortgage on their house, their wives and furniture."

Ruth was mobbed in the dugout by backslapping teammates wearing broad grins. He took it in stride, though his face lit up when he saw five-year-old Ray Kelly jumping up and down. Kelly was the team mascot, having been spotted by the Babe playing catch with his dad on Riverside Drive at age three. Ruth told Ray and his father, "I'm taking Little Ray with me to the Polo Grounds tomorrow. He's going to be my mascot." Kelly was in the dugout for most home games ever since, and his young face now reflected unbridled ecstasy.

Seventy-five years later, the ball Ruth hit into the right-field seats was sold at auction for $126,500. That was tip money compared to the bid for the bat that smashed the homer. In 2004 a collector paid $1.265 million for the ash, inscribed TO THE BOY HOME RUN KING OF LOS ANGELES, "BABE" RUTH. Said "Boy Home Run King" was named Victor Orsatti. After he died, his caretaker sold the lumber, with some of the proceeds going to open an orphanage in Mexico. The homer was the 198th of Ruth's career. Lost amid the hoopla and the roar of the crowd and the frankfurters flying through the air was the fact that it was now 4–0, New York. That was plenty for

Shawkey. He fired a three-hitter, and the Yanks won comfortably, 4–1. As for Ehmke, he had wised up—the next two times the Babe appeared at bat, Ehmke walked him.

In the fifth inning, the clouds had thickened, and a sizable portion of fans left the Stadium before the last pitch. "Even the band tore out," reported the *American*. Joe Harris hit a fly to right, and Ruth juggled it, once, twice, a third time, and then the ball fell to the ground. It turned out to be a harmless error, though the Yanks, particularly Aaron Ward, teased the Babe mightily over it. As the game neared its finish, a large group of fans hopped over the wall and surged onto the field in right, surrounding the Babe.

It took some time to clear them, and as the delay mounted, the Sox dugout called for a forfeit. Finally the throng was prodded back into the stands, and the final innings were played. As the game ended, there was another field invasion, and several Yankees had trouble getting to their dugout. Ruth was surrounded by roughly five hundred kids, who grabbed for his jersey, his cap, and his glove. "Babe had smashed out a home run and once more he reigns in the kingdom of boyish Bronx minds," reported the *Bronx Home News* on the melee. The last out was officially recorded at 5:36, meaning the game had lasted a taut two hours and five minutes.

The winning clubhouse was merry. Ruppert and Huston shook hands and slapped backs all around, conspicuously on opposite sides of the room at all times. Huggins had been suffering from a painful toothache but shrugged it off in the joy of the moment. Wally Pipp and Bob Meusel engaged in a playful wrestling match.

Ruth belatedly made it to the clubhouse after extricating himself from the riot on the field and ambled over to his locker. Telegrams of congratulations sat in a pile, and more were coming in, but Ruth ignored them. His watch, chain, and ring were returned, and he dressed quickly. The raccoon coat went over his mammoth shoulders, his hat rakishly tilted at a cool angle. He looked every inch the part of the triumphant '20s superstar.

The Babe offered Dugan and some others a ride back to Manhattan. A spin in the Babe's Pierce-Arrow, with cops clearing the way, sounded better than hailing a cab in the mess outside, so the players threw on their clothes and chased after the big man through the side door. Ruth took out his customary enormous black cigar, shoved it between his teeth, and roared away, past hundreds of waving and cheering fans who were headed for the Elevated train.

Many observers had feared that the grand new Stadium would be impossible to leave, considering the sea of humanity clogging the exits, but it held up well under the pressure of opening day. Double ramps allowed the crowds to depart without delay. Fans from the bleachers and far ends of the grandstand poured out onto the field and were swept through the gates in left. Exits on Doughty Street and 157th, on the south side of the new Stadium, also eased the traffic flow. Major Thomas Birmingham, one of the head engineers on the Stadium construction project, timed the departing crowd. The ballyard was abandoned in eleven minutes. "It was emptied yesterday...in quicker time than the Polo Grounds ever was," reported the *New York Times*.

Outside, there were few problems. The Jerome Avenue station was clogged with fans, requiring police to take charge. Otherwise the trains ran smoothly. Auto traffic cleared rapidly. There were no businesses or attractions in the surrounding neighborhood to keep many fans in the vicinity. By six o'clock, the streets around the Stadium were empty.

The previous two and a half hours provided a subtle but apparent altering of the city's pecking order. Suddenly the Yanks were on equal footing with John McGraw and his world champions, even if they couldn't seem to beat the Giants on the diamond.

The *New York Tribune* captured the moment:

Our battling colonels dreamed a dream on the eve they were about to be dispossessed.... On the dream they gambled. Sometimes dreams come true.

Winter

Early on the morning of Tuesday, December 26, 1922, a plain truck with DAILY BROTHERS stenciled on the side pulled up to a vast work site at 161st and River Avenue in the South Bronx. A man stepped out into the frosty air. He worked for a subcontractor of White Construction Company, the firm building the giant new Yankee Stadium. And the project was behind schedule.

The subcontractor's job that chilly morning was to reopen a pit to expose a water main for inspection by the city. It was a typically frustrating delay in what was proving to be a winter of discontent for the builders. Visible breath spewed from the workman's mouth as he huffed away, digging out the water main. He worked quickly, keen to escape the bitter cold and icy wind. He finished with his labor and was about to leave when he surreptitiously tossed something into the pit, hiding it under some loose dirt. The next day, the city inspector okayed the main, and the pit was closed, sealing the item inside.

What, exactly, the man threw into the open pit that would soon be filled by the most famous sporting ground in the country isn't known. But, as noted in Harry Swanson's informative work *Ruthless Baseball,* the worker did write, in the margins of records he submitted to White Construction, that he had buried something in order to bring luck to the Yankees. He didn't elucidate on what it was. A horseshoe? A religious amulet? A Baby Ruth candy bar?

Whatever it was, it worked.

A few years before the anonymous worker dropped his totem into the pit, baseball had undergone a tectonic shift. The time before Babe Ruth became a New York Yankee in 1920 is known in retrospect as the dead-ball era. Practitioners and press at the time called the prevalent style Scientific Baseball. Runs came at a premium, earned with difficulty through cunning, aggression, and patience. They weren't so much scored as crafted. The sacrifice hit, the stolen base, and the hit-and-run play were the pillars on which the game rested. So too the spitball, taking the extra base, and sliding with spikes raised. It was the baseball equivalent of the trench warfare going on in France. Nothing came easily.

Then along came the Babe. Ruth's power at the plate combined with new rules that emphasized offense. After the Black Sox Scandal of 1919, which left eight Chicago White Sox players suspended permanently from baseball for conspiring to fix the World Series, the sport moved quickly to offset the bad press by enacting fundamental changes, with an eye toward attracting fans with a punchier, gaudier show. New, more tightly wound baseballs were produced. Smudged, dirty balls were tossed out immediately in favor of whiter balls that were easier for the hitter to see. Trick pitches that required foreign substances, like the spitball, the emery ball, and the mud ball, were banned. Fans were no longer required to throw balls back from the stands to be reused.

Taken cumulatively, the effect was explosive. As with the introduction of the forward pass in football or the twenty-four-second shot clock in basketball, baseball's changes altered the game utterly. In 1918, the eight American League teams combined to hit ninety-eight home runs. Two seasons later, in 1920, Ruth alone hit fifty-four, more than all but one other major-league *team*. Ruth hit fifty-nine home runs in 1921, a display heretofore incomprehensible. But by now the long ball wasn't solely a Ruthian phenomenon—seven other teams hit more than the Babe, and while no single player approached Ruth, five hit more than twenty. In 1922 the league topped one thousand combined homers for the first time. "The home run fever is in the air," wrote prominent baseball chronicler F. C. Lane. "It is infectious." With one big wallop, sluggers like Ruth could plate enough runs to win a game in a single blow.

And the crowds followed. The style of play embraced by the likes of McGraw, Ty Cobb, Honus Wagner, and the other big stars of Scientific Baseball had excited few but the most hard-core fans. And after World War I and its trench-warfare horrors that included modern "advances" such as the machine gun and mustard gas, the very concept of "science" had taken on a negative connotation.

And, of course, the fans dug the long ball. In 1919 the Giants easily outdrew the Yankees at the park they shared, the Polo Grounds. But once Ruth arrived in New York in 1920, the crowds streamed through the turnstiles when the Yankees were in town, eager to witness the slugging sensation in person. The Yanks drew nearly 1.3 million fans in 1920, about 350,000 more than the Giants. In 1921 and 1922, the Yankees easily topped one million fans, while the Giants were drawing 973,477 and 945,809, respectively. The Babe was "as much a tourist attraction in New York City as the Statue of Liberty, Grant's Tomb, and the Fulton Fish Market," wrote baseball historian Lee Allen. "The sightseeing Pilgrims who daily flock into Manhattan are as anxious to rest eyes on him as they are to see the Woolworth Building," the *Times* noted.

This was an intolerable situation for the prideful Mr. John McGraw, who not only managed the Giants but held an ownership stake.

Sometime late in September 1920, McGraw and Charles Stoneham huddled in the owner's suite at the Polo Grounds. It was at this meeting that the two men decided to evict their uppity tenants. One of them said, "The Yankees will have to build a park in Queens or some other out-of-the-way place. Let them go away and wither on the vine." Most sources agree that McGraw is the one who said it, and it does sound like the crusty John J. But there is no definitive proof that it wasn't Stoneham.

Having a home to call their own was always the agenda of the co-owners of the Yankees. As soon as the pair bought the club in 1915, they tried to buy the Polo Grounds in order to raze it and build a monster, 100,000-seat stadium at the site. The plan was scotched. Nevertheless, the dream lived on, and the eviction notice was the prod to fulfill it.

Due to Prohibition, it was a difficult time for Ruppert—one of the biggest beer makers in the country, the purveyor of the popular Knickerbocker Beer and other fine concoctions—to plow enormous funds into any project. The temperance codes ate steadily at Ruppert's core business. The idea of a Yankee Stadium, a House That Beer Built, filled with fans drinking Jacob Ruppert Brewery products, had long been the colonel's fondest wish. Now he had the means and the impetus to actually build his dream palace—and no one could buy his beer. It was a maddening turn of events.

To his credit, Ruppert refused to let Prohibition alter his stadium dreams. He decided the long-term profits from building a successful new ballpark would outweigh immediate losses caused by construction costs. At the same time he fought against Prohibition as fiercely as anyone in the country. He wanted beer, at least, to be kept legal; if liquor had to be sacrificed, so be it. Real beer, that is—the new laws did allow beer to be sold, but at such a weak alcoholic content that it scarcely resembled what Ruppert considered a worthy product. In 1921 he sued the U.S. government in order to raise the alcoholic minimum in the near beer and was unsuccessful. In 1922 he made waves accusing federal agents of accepting bribes to allow several of his rivals to sell real beer. For the length of Prohibition, he lobbied intensely to be able to sell a decent bottle of brew — and by all accounts obeyed the letter of the law. Meanwhile, the brewery switched gears to crank out syrup, soda bottles, and various other sundries in order to stay afloat during the length of the Volstead Act.

While Ruppert fought the Man, he and Huston scoured the boroughs for an ideal spot to build their dream home. One site north of the Polo Grounds at 225th Street in Inwood was "in the family," having been purchased by previous Yankees owner Frank Farrell as a possible future home for the franchise. The land could be bought from Farrell — who was in ill health and in need of money — easily enough. But Ruppert thought the area too far a journey from the moneyed fan base on Wall Street and in midtown.

The owners looked at Queens next, surveying a site under the Queensboro Bridge (at 59th Street). This too was found wanting, leaving the borough baseball-free until the Metropolitans came to town in 1962. A downtown spot on disused Pennsylvania Railroad tracks was perfect — indeed, it would be discussed as a possible location for arena construction for decades to come. But before plans to build there got under way, the War Department nixed them. The site was to be used for antiaircraft emplacements to defend the city against the hard-to-figure possibility of aerial bombardment (the War Department was a bit dark about just who was threatening the United States by air in the early 1920s). Huston, a veteran of two wars and a man of influence in military affairs, burned up the telegraph lines lobbying his numerous military contacts in Washington, but he couldn't sway the generals. Downtown was out.

The closest the colonels came to building in Manhattan was at Amsterdam Avenue, between 136th and 138th (near the current location of P.S. 325 and its playground), on a lot owned by the Hebrew Orphan Asylum. The orphanage was a century-old home that held nearly two thousand Jewish children in a massive self-sufficient building. But it was steadily losing ground to orphanages that housed kids in small, rural cottages rather than urban monoliths. Selling the lot to the Yankees would enable the orphanage to regroup for the foreseeable future and build more up-to-date homes.

A contract was drawn up to secure the site. But the execs at the orphanage wanted to build on land in the North Bronx and couldn't get plans in order soon enough to guarantee a sale date to the colonels, who were eager to proceed. So the deal fell through, and Cap and Jake kept looking.

Time was running out on Huston and Ruppert. They needed to get the construction process started, or they'd be forced to beg the Giants to allow them to rent the Polo Grounds for another year—at no doubt usurious rates. Despair began to set in after the Hebrew Orphan Asylum deal fell through—Huston admitted to the *American* that he was "frustrated." Then, from out of the blue, their perserverance paid off. A large lumberyard in the South Bronx, almost directly across the water from the Polo Grounds, became available. Ruppert and Huston couldn't believe their luck. The land was an ideal spot to build a grand palace, right under the nose of John McGraw. McGraw scoffed at the project. "They are going up to Goatville," he snapped. "And before long they will be lost sight of. A New York team should be based on Manhattan Island."

2

THE LAND HAD originally been denoted as City Plot 2106, Lot 100 Farm, granted in the mid-eighteenth century to John Lion Gardiner, descendant of the first Englishman to be granted land in New York, Lion Gardiner (Lion Gardiner also founded Gardiners Island, off the east end of Long Island). John Gardiner is thought to have been the original owner of the Coogan's Bluff and Hollow area where the Polo Grounds sat, making him the aboriginal land baron of New York baseball.

By 1921 the estate of William Waldorf Astor (the only son of John Jacob Astor) owned the land. William had died in 1919, and the family was happy to unload the disused lumberyard. The Yankees paid $675,000 for just over twelve acres of boulder-strewn, unsightly dirt between 161st and 157th Streets going north to south, and between River Avenue and Doughty Street going east to west (while the Yankees bought a twelve-and-a-half-acre lot, the Stadium construction project itself used only ten acres of land). The site was asymmetrical; imagine a rough scalene triangle with two of the vectors not quite meeting up.

The nearby Macombs Dam Bridge, a swing bridge often improperly referred to as the 155th Street Bridge, connected the Bronx and Manhattan. It is the third-oldest bridge in the city, having opened in May 1895. The dam the bridge is named for was finished in 1814 by Robert Macomb to facilitate water traveling down from the Croton Reservoir to Manhattan and to create a millpond. Irish workers were mainly responsible for building both dam and bridge, and many settled in the Bronx, where they reverted to a rural existence. When the Yankees bought the land, farms were visible on the horizon.

But the area was also about to take off as an economic center. The nearby Grand Concourse was a fashionable thoroughfare, not quite Fifth Avenue swank but serving the needs of Bronx residents just fine, especially now that it was almost fully paved. The city, eager to halt the monumental waste of provisions that rotted at rail depots before it could reach the eating public, was building the Bronx Terminal Market underneath the Macombs Dam Bridge, in a small neighborhood known as Mott Haven.

Immigration and exodus from the tenement slums of Manhattan swelled the population of the Bronx. A significant number were Jews—by 1930, nearly half the Bronx's 1.2 million residents were Jewish. And, most pivotally, the expansion of the city's subway system during the war years to include the Bronx transformed the borough from rural backwater to an important slice of Greater New York City. Indeed, the Interborough Rapid Transit line practically passed through the Stadium site, emerging from its tunnel one block over on Gerard Avenue and curving to run on River Avenue. It would cost a nickel for fans to traverse the river and attend games. The new Stadium would play a major role in boosting the borough as well. "In the overall picture of the Bronx, the Stadium was unquestionably one of the major engines of change and development in the area," Lloyd Ultan, the Bronx borough historian, told the *New York Daily News*.

To house the new residents, a boom of apartment construction took place in the Bronx in the early 1920s, offering more amenities: the new buildings had elevators to ease top-floor access. Wide court-yards were built at the entrances, with shrubbery and, often, stone lions as decor. Jutting brickwork provided shadows on the surfaces of the buildings. Moorish- and Spanish-style architecture were the predominant motifs.

The land around the Stadium site included the tidal basin at the mouth of Cromwell's Creek, named for a local nineteenth-century dairy farmer. The basin had once been a favored spot for Bronx residents to ice-skate in winter, though the salty water of the Harlem River perennially threatened to cause perilously thin ice. The project forced skaters to the lakes in Van Cortlandt and Corona parks. The neighborhood to the north, Morrisania, was, appropriately (given Ruppert and Ruth's heritage), a mostly German enclave, and home to many breweries before the war and Prohibition took their toll.

Huston and Ruppert finalized the deal on May 16, 1921. Cap ensured the press that construction costs would be strictly contained—and that as an old and successful engineer, he would gladly take over the project himself if matters spiraled out of control. There was the small matter of getting permission to close two small streets that crossed the site: Cromwell Avenue, which ran from the prospective home plate out into center field, and 158th Street, which crossed Cromwell and ran between the dugouts. Huston doubted there would be much of a holdup. Playing the 1922 season in the new park was taken for granted.

The Bronx lumberyard may have been choked with sizable boulders, but it had some advantages. The earth bed was soft granite, good for construction. It was close to the water, so the enormous supply load could easily be transported to the site. And it wasn't hemmed in by other developments, which was fortunate because clearing the site required laborers to use steam shovels and horse-drawn wagons, both of which needed space to operate and, for the equine, graze. The colonels planned to convert the surrounding area into parking lots in order to accommodate automobiling fans living in Long Island, Westchester, New Jersey, and Connecticut.

Cap Huston enjoyed his life as a millionaire and member of New York's sporting elite. Prohibition may have been damaging his partner's bottom line, but it scarcely made a dent in Huston's social life. He was a drinking buddy of most of the press who covered his team, as well as of many of his players, especially Ruth. But there was more to Huston than bending his elbow. Cap had spent much of the last six years traveling the country, studying the construction of other ballparks and the plans for new parks, including one due to go up nearby at Columbia University. He was willing to draw the Yankee Stadium plans himself but decided to go with someone more expert in the art of stadium building.

The Osborn Engineering Company had designed stadiums across the country, including Fenway Park, Tiger Stadium, Comiskey Park, Sportsman's Park in St. Louis, and even the Polo Grounds. The firm would go on to build iconic structures such as Michigan and Notre Dame stadiums. Based in Cleveland, Osborn would also blueprint the monstrous Municipal Stadium on the shore of Lake Erie.

Founded in 1892, at the dawn of the Ohio Railroad boom, Osborn specialized in building bridges for trains. In the new century, it earned a reputation not only for quality sports arena design but also for unique flourishes. The Polo Grounds sported an ornate terra-cotta frieze of eagles. Cleveland's League Park was built with expansive exterior archways and rooftop cornices.

Huston came to Osborn looking for a masterpiece, one with "an air of dignity." And the firm went to work, pulling late-night shifts, the architects laboring into the wee hours, accompanied only by the sounds of whistles blowing as the freight trains crossed Osborn-built bridges nearby.

The company came up with an elegant monument to grandiosity, an aircraft carrier to the minesweeper across the Harlem River. It would be triple-decked, the first to be designed that way, and roofed all around—"impenetrable to all human eyes, save those of aviators," according to an Osborn press release. Ruppert didn't want play to be visible from train tracks or buildings, present and future, on River Avenue.

The interior works were to feature an astonishing "eight toilet rooms for men and as many for women scattered throughout the stands and bleachers." The team had stressed accommodating women to Osborn, intent on "making them as comfortable as possible," according to the *Times*. The latest comfort contrivance, an electric elevator, would connect executive offices with the main entrance (the team would relocate its offices from Times Square to the Stadium). Refreshments were to be provided by one main restaurant near the entrance, with several satellite stands dotted throughout the Stadium. While this is commonplace today, that was an unusual setup for the era. There were to be no stairs in the Stadium. Scissor ramps would lead to any deck or the mezzanine. And despite its grandeur, in one respect it was to be intimate—the box seats would be only thirty-six feet from the bases, ten feet closer than in the Polo Grounds. The fences behind home plate would be eighty-two feet away. The dish was to be clearly defined by surrounding it with grass, unlike in other parks which were completely dirt behind home.

The construction design called for the park to face away from the setting sun, so that when the first pitch came at 3:30, home plate would be in shadow, while the pitcher's mound would remain in sunlight, creating an advantage for the hurlers. The setup meant that during the summer months, left field would be the main "sun field," where the outfielder would have to battle the rays to pick up the ball. That virtually guaranteed that Ruth would play right field at the Stadium.

A terra-cotta panel of an eagle alighting on crossed bats was planned for the main entranceway. But the real eye-catcher would be the arched frieze that would encircle the top of the structure. It was an inspired touch, a true original, not an homage or copy of any other park. According to Osborn, the frieze was originally designed to be built of "Toncan metal," which referred to a copper-iron alloy, but in the end, it was pure copper. It would gracefully arc around the building, forming scalloped-shaped curves, sixteen feet wide at its fattest.

Most fans are familiar with the Yankee Stadium "facade." It is probably the most identifiable part of the structure, and the element that made the Stadium instantly recognizable and memorable. Just when and where the term "facade" replaced "frieze" in the Stadium lexicon isn't certain (with the advent of the new Yankee Stadium, an effort has been made to refer to the current model properly as a frieze). A critic who saw the blueprints wrote in *American Architect* that the frieze was "rather idiotic" but granted that it gave the place a "festive air."

From the first, the Yankees' new home was referred to not as a "park" or a "field" but a "stadium." The word derives from Ancient Greece, where a "stade" was a unit of measure (approximately six hundred feet) used to denote the length of footraces. Buildings where the races were held were called "stadiums" (or "stadia"), and the Yankees' new palace was certainly designed to invoke the classical period. It wasn't the first use of the word in America: a handful of football arenas used the term, and Griffith Park in Washington, the home of the Senators, had been renamed Griffith Stadium in 1921, minus any actual improvements. But the Yankee Stadium certainly was the first baseball field to *earn* the appellation.

And Jacob Ruppert was adamant about one detail. The new edifice was to be named for the team that called it home, not anyone involved in building it or inspiring it. Yankee Stadium, it would be called; until the 1930s, everyone naturally appended the prefix "the." Hence the ball park was referred to from birth as "the Yankee Stadium."

Huston and Ruppert were bowled over by Osborn's designs. The architects had conjured a modern coliseum that the Romans would envy. Now all they needed was someone to build the thing.

3

GAINING PERMISSION TO close Cromwell Avenue and 158th Street, thought to be small beer in the overall process, proved to be a sticky thorn in the colonels' sides. The owners had underestimated both McGraw's connections and his ire. In the short term, the Stadium construction project became a test of who held more sway with Tammany Hall.

The sun was setting on the Tammany machine in the 1920s, but it was still a force to be reckoned with, from the backstreets to city hall. Tammany headquarters was a three-story, large-windowed building on 14th Street, next to Tony Pastor's Theater. Everyone in municipal employ, from policemen to sanitation workers to politicians, had a hand extended, waiting to be greased.

Ruppert was a Tammany man dating back to the 1880s, when he served on the staff of Governor David Hill, a machine politician through and through. Hill had granted Ruppert the title "Colonel" during a stint in the New York National Guard's "Silk Stocking" Seventh Regiment (so called because many members were drawn from New York's social elite). It was a political, not a military, appellation. Nevertheless, Ruppert insisted he be addressed and referred to as "Colonel Ruppert" thereafter.

Through Hill, Ruppert made the right connections at Tammany, enough to ensure a successful run for Congress, where he represented the Upper East Side as a Democrat beginning in 1899. He served four terms, although at no time did lawmaking supersede beer making as a priority.

But McGraw and Stoneham had darker, and more recent, ties to Tammany. McGraw had long experience with the workings of the machine. In 1906 he opened a pool hall on Herald Square with well-known gambler and oddsmaker Jack Doyle. He moved it into a larger space across the street a couple of years later, this time backed by a more notorious, if silent, partner—Arnold Rothstein.

"A.R." would be better known as the gambling kingpin who helped to plot the 1919 World Series fix, and was immortalized as Meyer Wolfsheim in *The Great Gatsby*. In 1909 he was merely a hot pool stick adept at playing the Tammany game. Rothstein bested another pool shark named Jack Conway in a fabled thirty-hour match at McGraw's pool hall in September. The press blew the match up to enormous heights, and thereafter Rothstein's name came to define a sharp, slick gambler. He opened his own gambling parlor, which only drew him closer to the machine.

Until the "Big Bankroll" was gunned down in 1928, McGraw remained tight with Rothstein, giving him season tickets to the Polo Grounds in exchange for accepting his help with Tammany to ease the $300-a-month tab the police demanded for "protection" on his pool hall. Rothstein also had a legitimate business interest, an insurance company, to which Stoneham granted a contract to underwrite the Polo Grounds. The *Washington Post* reported that Rothstein, "New York's biggest gambler," had even "bought a big chunk of Giant Stock" (the Giants were listed officially as the National Exhibition Company and were occasionally referred to as such in the papers). Rothstein's right hand, fighter-turned-fixer Abe Attell, haunted the ballpark as well, often passing inside info on bent races to the manager.

So when the Yankee Stadium project was announced, McGraw and Stoneham likely turned to their buddy, and the expected approval to close Cromwell Avenue and 158th Street mysteriously never came. Repeated entreaties by Ruppert, Huston, and their attorneys were swallowed up by a bureaucratic black hole. There is no definitive proof of direct Rothstein involvement, but it seems probable that McGraw and Stoneham would have liked to delay the construction project in order to (a) humiliate the Yankees and (b) collect an exorbitant rent for the 1922 season. As a shadowy minority owner of the Giants and a longtime associate of McGraw and Stoneham, Rothstein had direct interest in anything that brought more cash into the National Exhibition Company coffers.

Rothstein not only held a firm grip on the New York underworld but had amassed the political patronage that would allow him such power. The Big Bankroll had the ability to bury the request for the street closings with one well-placed call to the proper committee—part of the Board of Estimate called the Sinking Fund Commission—and it would be difficult to trace his involvement, or McGraw's. But there were other delays. The Astor family owned much of the land in the immediate area of the closings outside the Stadium site, and the family had to grant permission for the changes. As the decision makers lived in England, the process took far longer than it would have otherwise. Whether nefariously or innocently, the Stadium project was smothered in its crib, and the Yankees had no choice but to play the 1922 season at the Polo Grounds. Stoneham and McGraw magnanimously welcomed the Yankees back—and jacked up the annual fee for renting the park from about $60,000 to nearly $75,000.

On March 22, 1922, the Board of Estimate at long last approved the street closings and sent word to the mayor's office. John "Red Mike" Hylan had risen to the city's top post through Tammany connections of his own. So it should have been no surprise that he took a week and a half more to "deliberate" on the closings before rubber-stamping the decision on March 31. The process had taken almost ten months. By contrast, most of the permits and variances that the Yankees applied for were granted in a matter of weeks.

The way was at last cleared, and the American Bridge and Taylor-Fichter Steel Construction companies already had been secured to establish the steel skeleton of the Stadium. The contracting firm that would be in charge of the rest of the construction had been likewise previously chosen by Ruppert and Huston, although not revealed to the public. Virtually every Tammany-connected construction firm had lined up to get in on the action. After all, Ruppert was a Tammany man too, just not at the level of Arnold Rothstein. But they underestimated the terrain the Stadium occupied in the colonel's mind. This was not to be a patronage project rife with cut corners and winks and nods. Ruppert planned this arena to be the world's finest, a monument to his team and his name.

Ruppert and Huston agreed on few matters, but when it came to the Stadium project, the two were in lockstep. It was more about professional craftsmanship to Huston—his engineer side blanched at the idea of second-rate work. So he hired his close friend, war buddy, and engineering confidant Major Thomas Birmingham to be his right-hand man. Birmingham was expected to liaise with Osborn's engineer on site, Bernard Green.

The owners placed classified ads soliciting construction bids. The most promising one came from an up-and-coming firm not in thrall to Tammany Hall. It was called White Construction Company, based at 95 Madison Avenue. "Let White Build It of Concrete" was its motto. Huston and Ruppert chose the firm over bigger and better-known bidders such as Turner Construction and Frederick T. Ley & Company.

In the spring of '22, with all bureaucratic delays behind them, the colonels penned a short letter of inquiry to White Construction Company:

We own a plot of land in the Bronx at 161st and River Avenue, containing about 240k square feet. We MUST play ball there next spring. The Osborn Engineering Co. of Cleveland, Ohio are preparing the plans and specifications for a stand that will seat about 75,000. The contractor that we will eventually select must furnish everything, even the "home plate" and the laundry equipment. We are going to let this business at a definite price — a lump-sum basis — and we must have the completed stadium by April 18, 1923. Are you interested?

Yes, they were. On May 3, 1922, the parties agreed on a construction contract worth just over $1.1 million. The work began two days later, on a drizzly, misty morning. There was no ceremony, no ribbon cutting, just a fleet of trucks and dozens of horse-drawn wagons clearing away the debris. There was no time left for pomp.

4

THE TEN ACRES of construction were a miasma of sound, sparks, and steel. A lumber mill and concrete mixer operated right on-site. Long wooden boards were placed on curbs to facilitate heavy trucks coming and going, and the echo of their wheels depressing the wood thrummed around the clock. Everywhere, men with screwdrivers and sledgehammers toiled, with clouds of dirt, sawdust, and iron flakes choking the men and reducing visibility. Cranes and derricks dotted the area, dipping and flexing from the moment first light crayoned the Bronx sky to well past the dinner hour. A billboard at the center of the hubbub announced the FUTURE SITE OF SECOND BASE.

The epic nature of the project soon became apparent. A battalion of five hundred workers swarmed the work site from dawn to dusk. Both Osborn and White set up shanties that served as headquarters in the middle of the fray. The grandstand foundations required a massive excavation of earth, roughly 25,000 square feet of it. Sixteen thousand square feet of sod were trucked in from Long Island, to be spread over 13,000 cubic yards of topsoil. That was a short commute compared to that of the lumber—some two and a half million feet of Pacific fir, shipped down the West Coast and through the Panama Canal.

The wood was used to create 10,712 upper grandstand seats, 14,543 lower grandstand seats, and the huge bleachers, crafted right on-site, that ringed the Stadium. They were bolted down by 135,000 steel casings and fixed to around 400,000 pieces of maple. Ninety thousand holes were drilled for the seats. More than one million screws kept it all together. Philip Goldrick & Sons of Kingston, New York, one of the largest brick companies in the United States, used barges to float in several tons of brickwork to the site. Then there was the truly heavy stuff. Thirty thousand cubic yards of concrete, poured into 140,000 bags by Thomas Edison's concrete company, Edison Portland. Twenty-five hundred tons of structural steel. One thousand tons of reinforced steel. Five hundred tons of iron. More than four miles of steel piping for handrails and fencing. The Yankee Stadium construction project was unprecedented in the Bronx and rivaled the largest to that point ever undertaken in the city.

The material was used to construct—in the words of internal White Construction Company documents—"more than a ball park. It is an office building—a main restaurant with several branches—a club house complete in itself—an athletic field subdrained by 25k running feet of clay pipe." White's original contract to erect this multiuse behemoth was for $1,136,604, with a projected profit of $69,419. The company hired some forty-three subcontractors to handle various aspects of the construction, including Otis Elevator Company; M. Limanti & Sons, to handle the delicate tiling and terra-cotta work; and Daily Brothers, to excavate the water mains, an employee of which added that little extra something to the project.

Almost immediately Huston, Birmingham, and the White Construction people tossed out the idea of the triple-decked, roofed design that left the field visible only from the air. The lack of sunshine on the grass and in the stands made this facet a nonstarter. Instead, there would be an upper and a lower grandstand sandwiching a narrower deck of seats to be called a "mezzanine." The word was an architectural term referring to an intermediate floor, and that's what this middle stand would be. It certainly wasn't grand enough to be a "grandstand." Those who called the Stadium the first triple-decked arena in the country were, technically, inaccurate—it was really two decks and a mezzanine. The distinction would be lost on awed patrons.

Ruppert wanted to sell Knickerbocker Beer to the contractors right on the premises. Thirsty workers enthusiastically approved, until they discovered that the city wouldn't let real beer be sold, only near beer, and, worse, that they would have to pay full price. The resulting outcry—the workers threatened to boycott the Jacob Ruppert Brewery—forced the colonel to abandon his plans.

It was the least of Ruppert's frustrations. At times it seemed the Stadium would never be finished. Dozens of change orders were sent to White, from the relocation of major sections of the office space to bumflufferies such as changing the location of the clubhouse radiators. The most problematic was Change Order #9.

The bleachers were, in the original design, meant to be temporary, movable wooden structures. But the colonels belatedly realized that, given the money that was being spent elsewhere, the bleacher section would be a comparative eyesore. So they doubled down, investing an additional $136,569 into the bleachers, which were originally budgeted to cost around $116,000. Concrete footings were poured, exterior walls were erected to match the rest of the Stadium exterior, and ramps, bathrooms, and refreshment stands were added to the bleacher area. Not only was Change Order #9 a major project in and of itself but it had a ripple effect on the rest of the construction, as contractors were pulled away from other details and the changes affected things such as the overall weight the concrete would have to support and how much flow the sewer lines would have to contain.

Other, outside delays were just as severe. A national rail strike in

July 1922 crippled any chance that the Stadium might be finished that year. The steel had been ordered weeks before, but delivery had been delayed. The colonels blamed White Construction. White claimed the fault lay elsewhere. It was just one of a series of disagreements between the parties, with Osborn also entering the mix. The three-headed command system was proving dysfunctional. Communication among the engineers, the builders, and the colonels was poor. At one point, a three-member arbitration panel was proposed to cut through the arguments over money and direction, but the sides couldn't even agree on who would serve on the panel. As more time slipped away, the idea was abandoned.

By the time the Yankees and Giants were facing off at the Polo Grounds in the 1922 Series, the Stadium was only about one-third finished. Privately (and separately), the colonels despaired of being able to finish in time for opening day.

Meanwhile, they were facing even larger problems. Across the river from the nascent Stadium, their star player, the Yankees' meal ticket, the man directly responsible for the necessity of a new Stadium in the first place, was suffering a World Series meltdown.

5

"NICE GOING, Two Head!"

The shout came from a dugout full of giggling New York Giants. It was directed at the burly gent at the plate, who had just swung at and missed a pitch from Giants pitcher Jack Scott so violently that he had dropped to one knee, practically screwing himself into the ground. Now infielders and bench jockeys alike were "taking him for a ride," in the parlance of the day, hammering Ruth with a torrent of insults. "Two Head" in particular incensed the Babe, the gibe attacking his unusually large melon.

It was Game Three of the 1922 World Series, the second straight contested entirely at the Polo Grounds between the two New York franchises that called it home. The Giants had won the opener, and Game Two had been controversially called due to darkness, ending in a tie. It was the fourth inning of Game Three, and the Giants were cruising behind Jack Scott, up 2–0. Ruth was now 2–9 for the Series and was frustrated. In his eagerness to pull the ball into the short right-field porch, he had grounded out weakly to the right side in his first time at bat. The bench jockeying from the Giants increased his anger, and the more Ruth flailed, the nastier the catcalls from McGraw's crew.

Now the strapping right-handed Scott delivered and plunked Ruth right in his gluteus maximus. "We couldn't miss that fat ass!" someone in the dugout shouted merrily. Sore and angrier than ever, the Babe trotted to first base. At least he was aboard. Wally Pipp struck out, bringing up left fielder Bob Meusel. Meusel rapped a grounder to second, which caromed off Frankie Frisch, the "Fordham Flash," and into short right field. Ruth rounded second like a runaway steer and barreled toward third. Frisch chased down the ball and whipped it to Heinie Groh, the diminutive third baseman who was crushing the Yankees pitching, en route to a .474 average in the Series (he would order a vanity license plate afterward reading "MR 474").

The throw beat Ruth by several feet. Refusing to slide, the Big Bam lowered his shoulder and powered into Groh, sending him head over heels toward the stands. Groh held on to the ball and showed it to the umpire, George Hildebrand, then dropped it and aimed an overhand right at Ruth's nose. Hildebrand intercepted the blow, so Groh went "cheek to jowl" with Ruth. "The Babe could have reached over and picked Groh up with one hand," judged the *Times,* "but the argument got no further than the verbal stage."

Ruth trotted off the field to a rousing chorus of hoots and moans from the crowd, and redoubled insults from the Giants. Among the epithets hurled his way was "nigger."

The game got worse for the Babe. He and Groh went at it again between innings as the Yankees took the field, and the crowd booed Ruth lustily. The Babe tipped his cap ironically at the jeering. Twice more he tapped out weakly to second base against Scott. The Giants completed a 3–0 victory, and held a hammerlock on the Series. Ruth was 2–11 and showed no sign of being able to solve the Giants pitchers, who were taking instruction on every delivery from John McGraw.

After the Game Three debacle, Ruth grabbed Meusel for backup and charged across the hall to the Giants dressing room.

"Where's [Johnny] Rawlings?" Ruth boomed, seeking out the runty Giants utility infielder and chief name-caller. Rawlings was nearby, putting on his socks at his locker. "Listen, you little shit—if you ever call me that again, I'll beat the hell out of you, I don't care how little you are."

A calm Rawlings replied, "What's the matter—can't you take it?"

"I can take it, but I won't take that."

Rugged Giants catcher Earl "Oil" Smith wandered into the fray, asking Ruth, "What did he call you?"

"He called me a nigger," huffed Ruth.

Opponents frequently harassed the Babe with off-color reference to his supposed African-American heritage. Ruth was often referred to as "Nigger Lips" and other such unpleasantries, and he once brawled with Ty Cobb over a similar insult. There is no truth to the notion that Ruth was even partly black, but it was typical of the times that he reacted with such violence to the very thought.

Smith grunted, "That's nothing," spat tobacco juice on his own clubhouse floor, and walked away. Then pitcher Jesse Barnes interjected, "You shouldn't mind that after what you called me yesterday."

"I didn't call you anything yesterday," said Ruth.

"You're a fucking liar!" thundered Barnes, yanking off his coat and squaring up to Ruth, ready for fisticuffs.

Just then, Hughie Jennings, the former Oriole great and longtime friend of McGraw who served as a Giants coach, emerged from behind a closed door. "What are you doing in here?" he demanded of Ruth.

Sputtered the Babe, "I came in to see Rawlings. He can't—"

"Get outta here! And you too, Meusel. You have no business here. Get out before McGraw finds you here." A chastened Ruth turned to leave, the idiocy of this invasion slowly dawning on him. But he couldn't resist a final commentary.

"Listen, fellas, I'm sorry this happened. I don't mind being called a cocksucker, an asshole, or a motherfucker. But from now on, none of that personal stuff!" The locker room erupted in laughter. A perplexed and deadly serious Babe at last departed. Meusel, never having said a word, followed in his wake.

"And no more of that football out there!" yelled Groh to Ruth's back as he left.

The Giants went on to complete a humiliating sweep of the Yankees, not counting the tie. For the second straight season, the Giants had defeated their tenants in the InterCity Series. They were champions of the world and, more important, New York City. In 1921, the Giants had won too — five games to three in the final best-of-nine Series ever played. Ruth had suffered a painful arm injury sliding into third base and missed a good chunk of the action, giving Yankees fans hope that 1922 would be different. It was worse.

"Clan McGraw," as they were called in the press, had administered a thorough whipping that left little doubt as to what team was the greatest in the land. The Giants had not only swept the favored Yankees but embarrassed the mighty Ruth, to the tune of two measly hits in seventeen at bats, a .118 average, with a solitary RBI and no home runs. McGraw's genius seemed unimpeachable. He had devised a pitching strategy for every Yankee, and the Pinstripes had been held to a feeble .203 team average with just two homers.

McGraw received most of the credit for the win. He was the almighty conqueror, living up to his nickname, the "Little Napoleon." Playing the part of a supine Europe was Babe Ruth. He had been rendered useless by McGraw's stratagems. He made things worse by tossing out a weak alibi: the Yanks had been idle for a few days before the start of the Series, and that had thrown them off their game. In reality, Ruth stunk. And there was no injury, no purely cosmetic positive moments, no legitimate explanation for what had happened.

Well, there was one explanation: the Babe was overrated, and his brand of power baseball was finished, a passing fad. Certainly no match for the mental mastery of Scientific Baseball as practiced by John J. McGraw. Joe Vila, a frequent Ruth critic in the pages of the *New York Sun,* reliably led the anti-Ruth charge: "There are no excuses for the lamentably weak hitting of Babe Ruth, now an exploded phenomenon. Ruth entered the Series in excellent physical condition and was shown up by the Giants pitchers in a way that amazed the fans. Leader McGraw had Ruth's number last year but Yankee partisans refused to believe it."

W. O. McGeehan called Ruth a "tragic figure." Grantland Rice grandly noted, "This has been a tough epoch for kings, but not even those harassed crowned heads of Europe ever ran into greater grief than the once-reigning monarch of the mace fell heir to this week.... He finished...the most completely subdued and overpowered star that ever had a coronet hammered from a clammy brow."

Baseball Magazine dismissed the Babe, wondering if George Sisler of St. Louis, 1922's Most Valuable Player, would be the new favorite of fans everywhere: "It is almost certain that Ruth can never be restored to anything like the position he held in the minds of the fans....Ruth is no longer a youngster, except in disposition, and bids fair to become a liability to the NY club instead of its best asset."

Ruth was labeled with that worst of all sports labels, "choker." He had come up short in the big show for the second straight season, this time so badly that all the king's men might not be able to repair him. This reaction to a lamentable World Series seems outsize, but, as the baseball writer John Tunis put it, "Losing is the great American sin." Sports can be a cruel mistress—regardless of the brilliance that came before, one poor performance on the big stage can forever tarnish an otherwise sterling legacy. As Rice wrote, "Fanatical memory is brief and fickle. The average fan recalls only the last few games. Heroes can be made and wrecked in a single Series."

Guts and rising to the occasion were key tenets of Scientific Baseball. Ring Lardner, who loved McGraw and small ball and loathed what the homer had done to his beloved game, wrote an ode to the 1914 "Miracle" Boston Braves after the 1922 Fall Classic that was little more than a slap at Ruth. "The kind o' men that can do their best in a pinch is the kind that's most valu'ble in baseball or anywheres else. They're worth more than the guys that's got all the ability in the world but can't find it when they want it." Ruth generally thrived as a showman, loved the stage and the knowledge that all eyes were on him. Now, it was generally acknowledged, that image had been proven a front—fine for exhibition games and barnstorming tours where he was expected to hit, but not for the World Series crucible where he *had* to hit. Ruth had not been simply defeated— he had been shown to be a fake.

Also in question was the future of the New York Yankees. The team had been 7–5 favorites to win the Series, fancied by the sharps around town for their supposedly superior pitching and the presence of the almighty Ruth. The squad was poleaxed by the defeat. Ruth had been terrible, but the rest of the team hadn't been far behind. "These four defeats inflicted by the Giants have humiliated the AL in a way that cannot be forgotten," said American League president Ban Johnson gloomily. "I freely admit that the Giants played wonderfully; but the mistakes of the Yankees were abominable, to say the least." The idea that this collection of pinstripes could ever win it all was roundly questioned.

After the final out of the Series, a disconsolate Ruth sat for a long time at his locker, unable to dress. One member of the training staff tried to buck up his spirits. "Shut up before I stick my fist in your trap," snarled the Babe. He kicked a trunk on his way out the door.

Ruth slunk out of the Polo Grounds and locked himself away at the Ansonia Hotel. Two days after the Series ended, Ruth slammed his automobile into another car at the corner of 86th and Broadway, vehicular battery that would land him in court and cost him $583. For the Babe, 1922 couldn't end fast enough.

6

AFTER THE 1922 Series, Ruth and Meusel headed west on a barn-storming tour, playing with and against local nines, the Babe earning a grand a game, his Yankee teammate $800—assuming certain attendance figures were met. Ruth couldn't conjure a scenario in which he wouldn't bring out the crowds—to cheer or to boo. One California writer sarcastically wondered if Ruth would hold forth after each game on "How I Made Those Two Hits in 1922's World Series."

A similar trip had cost the two men the first six weeks of the 1922 season. A rule left over from the dead-ball days stated that participants in the World Series couldn't make extra scratch by playing exhibition games around the country during the winter.

But if ever there was a codicil that Ruth was bound to ignore, it was this one. In early-'20s slang, it was "wet"—naive, unhip, yesterday. Anyone with half a brain and some gumption could see the sense in striking while the iron was hot. From a marketing standpoint, who else would the great masses living far from the major-league cities want to pay to see but the best in the game? Ruth may have been "wet" in some areas, but not when it came to making dough off his abilities to whack a baseball. So when a shifty promoter set up some dates in Buffalo; Elmira; and Jamestown, Pennsylvania, after the 1921 World Series, the Babe signed on.

Judge Landis warned Ruth not to go. Ruth had offhandedly told him about the coming tour during the Series, and Landis had taken the drastic step of visiting the locker room after Game Eight to advise the Babe against going. He gave similar admonishments to Huston, who took Landis far more seriously than did Ruth—by this point the Babe was convinced he *was* baseball, and who would argue differently?

"Tell the old guy to go jump in the lake," Ruth said to Huston, who had raced down to Grand Central in a final, futile attempt to talk his friend and star out of defying the judge. Landis instead banned teammates Ruth and Meusel for the first six weeks of 1922, saying, "This case resolves itself into a question of who is the biggest man in baseball, the commissioner or the player who makes the most home runs." Privately Landis asked, "Who does that big monkey think he is?" The judge answered his own rhetorical questions by relegating the superstar (and his cohort Meusel) to the dugout. Landis also docked Ruth and Meusel their 1921 World Series shares.

His point made, the commissioner quietly dropped the rule soon thereafter. Thus Ruth and Meusel were free to head west in late 1922. It was a backbreaking trip. The two Yankees schlepped across the Great Plains, beginning in a backwater town in Iowa called Perry. Despite an icy wind, eight hundred fans turned out to see the Babe. Similar conditions plagued stops in Lincoln and Omaha, Nebraska. In the aptly named Sleepy Eye, Minnesota, Ruth somehow clubbed two homers in a freezing sleet before five hundred paying, and shivering, customers.

Onward Ruth went. Sioux Falls, Deadwood, Scottsbluff, Sioux City—the logistics alone of getting from place to place were crippling: all-night train rides and perhaps a few hours' sleep before the next game in the next town. Still, everywhere he went he was cheered for his dogged goodwill and his drive to thrill fans who rarely if ever got to see him play—even if they had to pull the scarves from their faces to watch the game.

On October 22 Ruth reached civilization—Kansas City—where he played in a game against the Negro League Monarchs and stuffed himself with barbecue. He took some criticism in the local press for playing with the black ballplayers, but Ruth had never had an issue taking the field with Negro Leaguers and would do so for years to come. The long slog finally ended in Denver, where Ruth took advantage of the thin air to launch stupendous blow after stupendous blow in batting practice.

Ruth self-tallied his home-run count at an even twenty for the seventeen-game tour. When asked how much money he took in, the Babe replied, "I had a lot of fun," and left it at that.

He returned to New York in early November. But if he hoped the time away had made fans forget his miserable World Series, he was mistaken. One of Ruth's neighbors at the Ansonia greeted him by asking how McGraw had made him look so foolish. The press wrote snide asides alluding to his October failure. Ruth decided that the best thing for him to do was to blow town again, and he knew just the place to go—Home Plate.

That was the name Ruth gave his 190-acre farm on Dutton Road in Sudbury, Massachusetts. He supposedly bought the place while with the Red Sox to reconcile a quarrel with his wife Helen, although there is no definitive statement proving that supposition. It was a place to escape the confines of Boston when the city felt claustrophobic and was a relatively safe investment as well. Plenty of Ruthian high jinks took place in Sudbury, though—legend has it that the Babe once pushed a grand piano out onto nearby frozen Willis Pond for an alfresco concert, only to have it sink through the ice and drown. (In 2010 an expedition discovered parts of what might have been Ruth's piano at the bottom of the pond, thanks in part to the help of a psychic.)

The house might have been worth a whole lot more had Ruth's eye for decorating matched his eye at the plate. When he purchased Home Plate, it was stuffed with expensive furniture, antiques, and accessories that were worth as much as the price of the house itself. The Babe hired a bunch of movers to crate up the lot and haul it away, telling a flabbergasted Waite Hoyt, "It was just junk." Ruth remodeled the interior to meet his tastes, adding a couple of wings to give it some grandeur. The house had pale-green shutters, three chimneys, and all the latest interior furnishings. One remnant of the prior owner was a full set of Waverley Novels in the library, which Ruth kept, placing a number of trophies among them.

In the winter of 1922–23, Home Plate was to serve as a combination of Elba and Parris Island, at least in theory. Ruth wanted to cultivate the simplicity of life on the farm during the hard winter months, while at the same time forging his body like a blacksmith for the long road back to the top.

On his last night before decamping from New York, the Babe held a dinner at the Elks Club for the sporting press, the same shapers of public opinion who had been shoving stilettos in his flanks since the Series. Ruth's press agent, Christy Walsh, set it up. Walsh may have been even more emblematic of the go-go '20s than his client. He sniffed cash in the breeze like the mako shark smells a drop of blood in the ocean. A lawyer from California, Walsh first met the Babe by pretending to deliver a case of bootleg beer to his apartment at the Ansonia. He boldly asked Ruth how much he received for the ghostwritten articles penned in his name. "About five dollars each," replied Ruth. "What's it to you, anyway?" Walsh guaranteed him a thousand dollars in sixty days if the slugger hired Walsh to run his PR setup. Christy borrowed the money from a friend and gave it to the Babe thirty days later, and an impressed Ruth turned over his public affairs to Walsh. The press agent would go on to land a roster of sports' biggest names, including John J. McGraw.

Now Walsh sensed that he could set up his client for a boffo comeback story, complete with a theme of self-reliance straight out of Emerson. The Elks Club dinner that night championed the virtue of the farm, right down to the life-size cow statue that took up the center of the banquet room. The writers were invited to ask the Babe anything, and they didn't hold back, giving Ruth rougher treatment than he was used to.

New York State senator Jimmy Walker, a rising Tammany star who would soon earn fame as the fast-talking, fast-living, occasional-governing mayor of New York, gave the keynote speech. "Babe Ruth is not only a great athlete, but a great fool," he began. "His employer, Colonel Jacob Ruppert, makes millions of gallons of beer, and Ruth is of the opinion that he can drink it faster than the colonel and his large group of brewmasters can make it. Well...you can't! Nobody can."

It went on and on, a maudlin, sentimental monologue about Ruth's annus horribilis of 1922, how he had let the city down, how he had let himself down. "The cheers of yesterday have a short echo," Beau James reminded the Babe.

Mostly Ruth had failed America's children. Walker finished with an anecdote straight out of Dickens: "Babe, a kid just stopped me on the street and asked me for a dime. He wanted to make it to a quarter and buy a Babe Ruth cap. Don't you think you owe something to that kid and others like him? Or are you going to keep on letting those little kids down? Will you not, for the kids of America, solemnly mend your ways? Will you not give back to the kids their great idol?"

Walker's speech may have been over the top, but it hit home with its target. Writer Paul Gallico called it a "brilliantly phony" performance, and sure enough Ruth began weeping at the thought of disappointing all those "dirty-faced" children, as he himself had once been.

The Babe got up to speak, and you could hear a pin drop in the place. "I know as well as anybody else just what mistakes I made last season," he admitted. "There's no use in me trying to get away from them. But let me tell you something. I want the New York sports-writers to know that I've had my last drink until next October. I mean it. Tomorrow I'm going to my farm. I'm going to work my head off—and maybe part of my stomach."

The writers giggled at that, but if they thought the evening was headed in a lighter direction, Ruth proved them wrong. "Oh, maybe now and then I'll come down to New York to see the old town, but it won't be too often. I'm serious about this. I'm going to work hard. And then you just watch me break that home run record next year!" And the crowd of jaded, cynical ink-stained wretches applauded mightily.

The next morning, Ruth caught a train for his farm, and the long path to redemption.

The mythology angle is tantalizing—coddled star eschews the good life and goes spartan to regain the eye of the tiger. One can practically imagine Ruth as Rocky Balboa preparing to fight Ivan Drago, running through waist-high snows, lifting wheelbarrows in the barn, and chopping endless wood in order to wreak havoc come spring.

Actually, Ruth did chop some wood. There is pictorial evidence that the Babe did take the ax to at least a few logs, and wood-chopping was a common enough form of off-season exercise for ballplayers in those days. His caretaker (and later Sudbury town historian) Forrest Bradshaw told reporters that the wood Ruth chopped was mainly for the benefit of publicity rather than his batting stroke or keeping the house toasty, but the Babe did shovel more than his share of snow around the property.

As a working farm, Home Plate was a failure, despite the purchase of a thousand hens for a gleaming new chicken house. Most died before any eggs could be collected. Ruth's pigs, horse, Flemish giant rabbits, cows, and fowl added little to nothing to his fortune or dinner table. And the entire enterprise shut down a few years later when Ruth's dog, a vicious Great Dane, chewed the udders off a neighbor's prize cow, costing the Babe five grand. Still, Ruth enjoyed the country-gentleman aspect of the sabbatical, posing in a grouse-shooting kit, talking of raising fur animals, and doting on Helen and his newly adopted daughter, Dorothy. He joined the bowling club of nearby Waltham and the Thursday evening chess club, perhaps readying for the mental challenge of McGraw.

In early January, Ruth's friend and *Daily News* journo Marshall Hunt set out to have a look at life at Home Plate. It was an epic journey, as his directions in the *News* indicate:

First, get to Boston the usual way.

Then, accommodation train to South Sudbury.

Leave train at S. Sudbury and ask first living person where Babe lives.

Start out on foot, first purchasing pair hip boots.

When overtaken by horse-drawn sled conveying children to school, accept ride for one mile.

Walk another mile through drifts and then accept ride with farmer on milk sleigh.

Walk two more miles, then turn in at Ruth's gate, pass around to back door and knock.

Hunt's odyssey was for naught—when he got to the door, he was told by Ruth's cook, Fannie, that Ruth had gone to Boston the day before and wasn't home. Hunt noticed a "large blue limousine" in the barn and was told that the Babe had set off for Boston in it, but being unused to driving a car of that size, he had plowed into a snowdrift and burned out the clutch trying futilely to get out (why he was driving was never clarified). His usual chauffeur, named Walter, informed Hunt that Ruth was forced to borrow a neighbor's horse-drawn sledge to get to the train station.

The Babe would have been far better served to employ a full-time driver, as McGraw did. The Yankee brass often allowed players to drive their own cars to Boston, Philadelphia, and Washington rather than travel with the team by train, over manager Miller Huggins's strong reservations. But Ruth, whose driving record in the city was far from clean (and generally ignored by adoring police), was an extremely dangerous presence on the rudimentary roads of the Northeast. His twelve-cylinder Packards could attain 110 miles per hour, and he pushed the cars right to the edge of their performance envelopes, with disastrous results.

His most famous wreck, of many, came after a game in Philadelphia in 1920. He was driving late at night, headed to Washington, with Helen, teammates Frank Gleich and Fred Hofmann, and coach Charley O'Leary. At around two a.m., his passengers passed out from the night's revelry, the Babe sang "The Trail of the Lonesome Pine" at the top of his voice to keep himself awake. It didn't help his alcohol-impaired vision, however—outside Wawa, Pennsylvania, he skidded off the road and flipped several times before settling into a ditch. Amazingly, everyone was thrown clear and unhurt, save Ruth, who twisted his knee.

The car was towed to a nearby garage, where Ruth told the awe-struck mechanic to sell it and keep the profits. After a few hours of restless sleep, he called a cab and raced to DC. He arrived unaware that the newspapers were filled with stories of his death. It was the Fourth of July, and a sellout crowd of twenty thousand filled Griffith Stadium to pay their respects—only to see the undead Babe limp out to his position in left field, blithely ignorant of the fuss.

Ruth was never a bibliophile, but upon decamping for Massachusetts he swore off books for good. "Reading isn't good for a ballplayer," said Ruth. "Not good for his eyes." His eyesight was under surveillance by the press, who considered it a prime suspect in his Series downfall. PR man Christy Walsh used the Babe's peepers as an excuse for curtailing any vaudeville appearances in the foreseeable future. Ruth had teamed with a well-known singer-comedian named Wellington Cross and soloed on a song specifically composed for him called "Little by Little and Bit by Bit, I Am Making a Vaudeville Hit." The act failed to gain notice, although Ruth's singing voice was rated as fairly good. The floodlights were bothering his eyes, was Walsh's logic, providing a subtle though implausible explanation for his collapse in the Series. Ruth's mediocre box office was never mentioned as a reason for the hiatus.

Helen enjoyed the time at Home Plate more than George. She was so often a figure overshadowed by her immense husband. Helen Woodford had met the Babe when she was just sixteen, four years younger than Ruth, who was even more naive about the world than Helen. She was the first woman the Babe had talked to upon arriving in Boston, and to say he rushed into the marriage is an understatement. Away from the big city, in a rural setting far from the adoring masses, Helen was on a more equal footing, especially now that a baby had arrived.

Ruth's daughter was discovered, not announced. In the fall of 1922, Helen was spotted pushing a pram in and out of the Ansonia with a baby inside — and not a newborn. Helen insisted that little Dorothy, sixteen months old in September of 1922, was not adopted, but no birth certificate was ever found, and Helen's will referred to Dorothy as her adopted daughter. Years later, the truth came out. While on a trip to California, Ruth had fathered a child with a woman named Juanita Jennings. Jennings came to New York to deliver the child, and while she was still in the hospital Ruth took the baby and gave her to Helen to raise. Juanita slunk away into the shadows of history, presumably well compensated for her silence.

Up at Home Plate, the Babe ice-fished, went for long walks, and ate well without overindulging. He took no hard liquor, smoked less than usual, and chopped at least some wood. It wasn't a regimen that would seriously tax Rocky, perhaps, but for this left-hander, it did the trick. Mostly, Ruth kept his promise to stay away from the temptations of the city in favor of the "snow and seclusion of a little Massachusetts hamlet." While amid the drifts with shovel or fishing pole in hand, Ruth could do little but dwell on his Fall Classic failure, and imagine the upcoming campaign. This would be his most important season to date.

Since coming to the Big Town in 1920, Ruth had been one of a kind during the regular season, but in today's terms, he had yet to prove himself a "True Yankee," a designation that comes only with winning it all. Ruth had just one way back into the good graces of Yankees fans—beating McGraw and bringing the Yankees their first World Series.

7

On New Year's Day 1923, Wee Willie Keeler passed away in Queens at the depressingly young age of fifty-one. Keeler's death hit his former teammate and good friend John McGraw hard. "Hit 'em where they ain't," Keeler's pithy advice for baseball success, remains one of the game's most lasting epigrams, but it was uttered during a period when "where they ain't" meant in the field of play, not beyond it. Wee Willie, McGraw, and the rest of the Baltimore Orioles of the 1890s never conceived of a time when a player could regularly park balls in the distant stands. But that time had arrived. Keeler's passing was portentous—his style of play was on the way out too.

Revolutionary change is wrenching to those on the wrong side of history. That was particularly true for the man most identified with Scientific Baseball's speed, skill, savagery, and strategy. John J. McGraw was also the sport's foremost manager and tactician, and among the biggest names in baseball. And McGraw wasn't a man to give in without a fight. In fact, fighting was what he did best.

In Cuba, where McGraw spent many winters, they called it *béisbol de sangre*—"blood baseball." Baseball to the death. "I can think of no man whose name was more universally associated with the virile, competitive spirit of baseball than John McGraw," said Commissioner Landis. McGraw prized the hit-and-run, the stolen base, the double play. Mostly, he prized fundamental baseball, and built a career of more than four decades on learning and then teaching the right way to play the game. That did not, in McGraw's world, mean hitting home runs.

To McGraw, the home run was an abasement of the game he loved—a cheap, undignified method of scoring runs. It was unmanly, which may have been the opposite of what others thought of Babe Ruth, but this was how McGraw saw and treated him. To McGraw, Ruth was never "Babe," or the "Sultan of Swat," or the "Bambino," or any of two dozen other picaresque nicknames the press hung on the slugger. The manager referred to Ruth with studied derision. The "Big Ape," the "Big Baboon," "Monk," and various other primate-based monikers were McGraw's favorites, based not upon the well-traveled fiction that Ruth was partly black but upon the brute simian approach to baseball that Ruth embodied.

McGraw loathed Ruth. Bedrock differences in approach combined with turf battles to turn the men into warring gang leaders. Had circumstances been slightly different, however, McGraw might have found much common ground with the Babe. Like Ruth, McGraw traveled from Baltimore to New York and captured the heart of the Big Town. And as with the Babe, McGraw overcame long odds to achieve his place in the pantheon of the sport.

John Joseph McGraw was born on April 7, 1873, in the village of Truxton, New York, about twenty-five miles from Syracuse. He was the first of eight children. Like Ruth, John McGraw was named for his father, an Irish immigrant who had fought in the Civil War. The elder McGraw was a glorified coolie, working long, backbreaking hours fixing railroad cars and tracks for little pay. Food was as scarce as compassion in the McGraw home. Like George Ruth Sr., John McGraw Sr. was a heavy drinker, and beat his son.

The elder McGraw's mood blackened forever after the tragic winter of 1884–85, when a diphtheria epidemic claimed his wife, Ellen, three of his daughters, and one of his sons. Mr. McGraw, understandably perhaps, didn't handle it well. His alcoholism deepened, and he struggled to raise the four surviving children on his own. Instead of rising to the occasion, he turned his home into a house of fear. The father beat his eldest son with such severity that John Jr. moved out of the house and across the street, where he was taken in by a widow named Mary Goddard.

McGraw discovered baseball at age sixteen, and although he was a runt, barely a hundred pounds, he was an excellent pitcher and a ferocious competitor. Spurring his play was the knowledge that his father hated the game, considering it uncivilized, especially compared to soccer and rugby. John Jr. disagreed, although his style of play was hardly "civil."

He was no natural, out of Ruth's class both as an athlete and as a physical specimen. In McGraw's first minor-league game, he committed eight errors. But his teeth were sunk into the game, and he steadily improved. And when McGraw knocked three doubles in an exhibition game against the major-league Cleveland Spiders, the *Sporting News* recorded the feat for posterity.

While other players were taking a break from the game in the winter of 1891, McGraw went to play with a barnstorming outfit in Cuba. He became a fan favorite, earning the nickname "El Mono Amarillo" — "the Yellow Monkey" — due to his scampering style and the bright-banana-colored uniforms the team wore. He also fell in love with the Pearl of the Antilles and would return often. By 1892 McGraw was in the majors with the Baltimore Orioles, then in the National League and doomed to fold, only to be reborn as the minor-league outfit Ruth would star for two decades later. When Ned Hanlon took over as manager of the NL Orioles in mid-1892, he rescued McGraw from a place on the bench, installing him as his third baseman and leadoff hitter. Hanlon loved aggressive, smart players, and McGraw fit that description to a tee.

The Orioles were a machine in the days when players' mustaches were fatter than their paychecks, winning three straight pennants from 1894–96. The team was stocked with stars such as Wee Willie Keeler, Wilbert Robinson, Dan Brouthers, and Hughie Jennings. And it was a tight bunch — for a couple of seasons McGraw lived in a house with nine teammates, waking early to commandeer the hammock on the back porch to read the sports pages.

McGraw flourished, quickly becoming the league's best leadoff man. Though still woefully undersized (his first uniform, the smallest in the equipment trunk, was far too large — it fit a teammate five inches taller and forty pounds heavier), McGraw hit over .320 for nine consecutive seasons, and his career on-base percentage of .466 trails only Ted Williams and Ruth on the all-time list.

But it was as a schemer and innovator that McGraw truly found his calling. He adopted a batting method that involved placing his hands well up on the bat ("choking up") and slapping the ball wherever he chose. Often he would swing down on the ball, creating a high bouncer that couldn't be fielded in time to throw him out at first, a ploy that became known as the "Baltimore chop." He excelled at wearing out opposing hurlers by fouling off pitch after pitch with deliberate intent. "McGraw would run halfway up to the pitcher, swing hard, but late, check his swing, and cut fouls along the left field line for an indefinite period" was how the *Sporting News* described his method.

On the base paths, "he played a ripping, tearing, charging" brand of baseball. His angry style was exacerbated by another tragedy, the death of his wife, Mary (called "Minnie"), to appendicitis in 1899. Even before then, his size and Napoleon complex led McGraw to fight just about every opponent and umpire who dared cross him. Unfortunately for John, his diminutive size doomed him in most of the brawls.

Bill Klem, the legendary umpire who would battle McGraw throughout his career, said, "It is highly doubtful John McGraw ever won a fistfight. And it is without question that he never ducked one." One Philadelphia pitcher, weary of McGraw's taunting, walked off the mound and knocked him out with one punch. His own teammate Keeler once demolished him in a clubhouse brannigan while stark naked. One wag observed the "bunions on his back from bouncing off barroom floors." The man McGraw would make baseball's first coach in 1907, Arlie Latham, may have gone a little far when he said, hammily, "John McGraw eats gunpowder every morning and washes it down with warm blood."

His most famous fight came in Boston on May 15, 1894. McGraw tangled with Beaneaters first baseman Tommy Tucker after deliberately kicking the sliding Tucker full in the face. They brawled while an inferno blazed through the neighborhood, burning the South End Ballpark to the ground. Even as the right-field bleachers burned, fans were hurling beer bottles, garbage, and ill wishes at McGraw.

The surefire way to set off McGraw's temper was to call him "Muggsy" (sometimes spelled with a single G). McGraw hated the nickname because there was a roughneck ward politico in Baltimore named Mugsy McGraw, and the rumor got started that John was his illegitimate son. He was "Young Muggsy McGraw" at first, then just "Muggsy." Naturally, since John was unable to laugh it off, the nickname stuck forever. It described him too perfectly to go away.

When he wasn't getting on base or slugging it out with another player, McGraw was brainstorming new methods of eking out an advantage in the game. He, Robinson, Jennings, and Keeler would sit for hours, talking baseball and working out tactics and specific situational plays. The bull sessions resulted in timeless baseball stratagems such as the hit-and-run.

The Orioles and McGraw also stretched the legal boundaries of the game. "With us, only the written rule counted...and if you could think up something not covered by the rules, you were ahead of the slower-thinking opposition by at least a full season," McGraw wrote years later. "McGraw uses every low and contemptible method that his erratic brain can conceive to win a play by a dirty trick," wrote one reporter. Indeed, to go through accounts of late-nineteenth-century Orioles games is to get a sense of the rule book being hastily rewritten after every ploy by McGraw & Company.

Some maneuvers were more legit than others. The O's had their groundskeeper maintain a hard and fast infield, and create a slight, barely perceptible downslope between home and first, the better to suit the speedy team and its chopping methods. Less sporting was a gambit against the Giants in the late 1890s. Hughie Jennings hit a ground ball to short, and the infielder threw wildly to first. The ball skipped into the Baltimore dugout and through an open clubhouse door. An alert Oriole promptly locked the door. Jennings scored the winning run while the Giants first baseman tried in vain to get inside and retrieve the ball.

Late-nineteenth-century games were nasty, violent affairs. Liquor flowed freely, fistfights were common in the stands and on the field, and few women dared darken the ballpark gates. Baltimore had steady attendance figures, but most clubs had trouble drawing fans because of the seedy atmosphere. "The things they would say to an umpire were unbelievably vile, and they broke the spirit of some fine men," said late-century umpire John Heydler, who went on to become president of the National League.

But McGraw was no ruffian away from the diamond. He cut a deal with Allegany College (now Saint Bonaventure University) near Buffalo to coach baseball in the off-season in exchange for the chance to attend classes. McGraw's formal schooling had stopped in the sixth grade, but as a ballplayer, he immersed himself in the classics, mathematics, and science. He became enamored with Shakespeare and would quote the Bard to his dumbfounded teammates.

As the new century dawned, the game stayed rough, but there was a higher standard of professionalism. The players included college graduates, many of whom were trained in engineering, architecture, or law. Baseball provided a fantasy escape from the drudgery

of office life. It was not a means to an end. Players who didn't like
the atmosphere simply decamped for jobs that didn't require cleats.
And slowly but surely team owners began to wean the cruder elements out of the parks in favor of more women and families.

While the ugliness was being phased out, so too were the Orioles,
at least the NL version. The team was contracted out of existence in
1899, with many of its players handed to Brooklyn. McGraw adapted.
With the advent of the American League in 1901, he took over the
Baltimore franchise in the Junior Circuit (the AL being twenty-five
years younger than the Senior Circuit, or the National League). The
president of the new American League, Ban Johnson, had recruited
McGraw to be player-manager in order to convey some legitimacy
to the new league and its Baltimore team, but he then cracked down on
McGraw's antics and constant warring with umpires, setting off decades
of antipathy between the two men. So on July 16, 1902, McGraw
jumped to the New York Giants, taking over as player-manager. The
team was a distant last, and McGraw released half the players overnight. "On my team, I'm the czar," he told a stunned locker room.
He was twenty-nine years old.

In New York, back in the National League, McGraw found his
calling. He was still cantankerous, still an innovator. But as a manager, McGraw felt his most important duty was to teach the game
and to get young players to play the proper way, as he saw it. This was
the basis for one of the greatest managing careers in baseball history.

The "player" portion of "player-manager" didn't last that first
season of 1902. An errant throw by deaf-mute pitcher "Dummy"
Taylor (a favorite of McGraw's, likely because he couldn't talk back)
smashed in his nose, leaving a fountain of crimson gushing from
McGraw's face, his sinuses in tatters. The injury ended his days in
the field, but McGraw could better serve the team as a full-time
manager anyway. The Giants finished second in his first full season
at the helm, 1903, and the following year they won the pennant.
McGraw held such a deep grudge against Johnson and the American

League that the Giants refused to play the 1904 World Series against Boston, halting a one-year "tradition" in its tracks. McGraw soon sensed the money that could be earned by participating, however, and reversed course, taking part in the '05 Fall Classic and winning the Series over Philadelphia in five games.

McGraw went on to win four pennants in seven years between 1911 and 1917 by building a system, acquiring players that fit it, and never straying from his path. He wanted good defensive players, fast runners, and men who could follow his orders to the letter. Those who failed to do what McGraw wanted were swiftly punished. In 1905 a part-time player named Sammy Strang had instructions to bunt but saw a fat pitch, swung away, and hit a home run. McGraw fined him $25: "I permit no deviation from instructions," said the manager (Strang came off the bench to hit fourteen times "in the pinch" in 1905, thus becoming the first man to be called a "pinch hitter"). Many more were simply released or traded.

The team curfew was 11:30 p.m. sharp, and a Giants flunky knocked on doors at precisely that time to ensure the players were inside. The team ran or walked to and from the hotel during spring training, no exceptions. They were given a strict diet and were expected to follow it. All pitches were called from the bench, using an intricate system. McGraw held a decoy bat while making decisions verbally. The relay man, also holding a bat, would then signal the catcher by adjusting his hands. Fist closed on the end meant "take," both hands over the top meant "hit away," and so on. There were several relay men in the dugout, and the players had to know who was that day's choice. One of McGraw's Hall of Famers, Frankie Frisch, wrote the signs on a piece of tape and stuck it to his cap, there were so many. In this manner McGraw scripted every action his team made—what pitches were thrown, the defensive alignments, and the batting strategy. McGraw paid particular attention to the tiny details. He instructed his players on everything from where to plant a foot when pivoting for a double play to which fielder backed up bases in every situation.

In later years, other organizations would shorthand their brand of baseball as the "Dodger Way" or the "Cardinal Way" or the "Oriole Way." The "McGraw Way" not only predated these but was a profound influence on them. As the hundreds of players McGraw taught spread out and became coaches and managers and scouts and trainers, they passed along the Word of McGraw. His legacy can still be seen in the game—especially in his very own National League, where pitchers still hit (if McGraw turned his nose up at the Ruthian power game, it is difficult to comprehend what his take would be on the designated hitter).

McGraw preferred college-trained players who "had two years' jump on the town-lot boy." But the game was changing through the 1910s and into the 1920s. The college boys could make money in professions other than baseball. Country kids and farm boys, their options limited, increasingly made up the majority of rosters. McGraw found he could shape these raw lumps of clay through endless drilling and teaching. And they responded to his attention—decent coaching at the small-town level was often nonexistent. As Heywood Broun wrote of McGraw, "He made kids from coal mines and wheat fields walk and talk and chatter and play ball with the look of eagles."

McGraw taught pitcher Burleigh Grimes a new method for throwing curveballs in "five minutes," according to Grimes. "It was a simple adjustment; trouble was, I'd never thought of it before and neither had any of my other managers." McGraw shaped young talents such as Fred Merkle, Fred Snodgrass, and Freddie Lindstrom—anyone named Fred was a candidate, apparently—into ballplayers. Al Lopez, who caught against McGraw's Giants and was later a longtime manager himself, said, "When you played McGraw's teams, you always knew that you were playing the best. You could feel his hand everywhere." Said Grimes, "I worked for McGraw for only one year, but I learned more that season than in all the years before—or since. The science of pitching took on a new meaning."

McGraw lived by a simple dictum: "One percent of ballplayers are leaders of men. The other ninety-nine percent are followers of women." It was his calling to be in that top percentile.

As baseball analyst Bill James points out, McGraw's view of managing was essentially negative. Once he built his players up, he rid the team and the game of everything that could cost him a win. Control was of primary importance. He was obsessively afraid of losing and managed accordingly. Whereas today a hard-driving perfectionism is almost a prerequisite to coach professionally, in McGraw's day it was rare, almost unheard-of. Most of his competitors in the dugout were former players unequipped to teach the game. That gave McGraw a distinct edge.

McGraw still carried many of the same traits he had as a bantamweight Baltimore Oriole. He was still ornery—Bob Shawkey, who would pitch against McGraw's team in the Series of 1921–23, remembered the manager's epithets echoing across the field. McGraw once brawled with one of his own pitchers during an intrasquad scrimmage when the hurler, E. E. "Hick" Munsell, continued to throw curveballs despite McGraw's express desires. He even once pushed (some go so far as to say punched) a boy who was selling lemonade a little too close to the Giants dugout. "If players thought I was mean they should have spent a little time under McGraw," remembered Rogers Hornsby, who was as hostile as he was talented. "He'd fine players for speaking to somebody on the other team. Or being caught with a cigarette. He'd walk up and down the dugout and yell, 'Wipe those damn smiles off your faces!'"

McGraw was still innovating, if anything at a higher rate than when he was playing. He was the first manager to have his staff chart pitches. He was the first to call every pitch from the dugout. He was the first to sign players specifically to pinch-hit and pinch-run. He was among the first to use his bullpen for reasons other than the outright failure of the starter, calling in pitchers to close games and retire specific hitters. He was one of the first (if not the first—the issue is debated by baseball historians) to regularly platoon players, having two men share a position instead of naming a full-time starter. He was the first to deliberately alternate his left- and right-handed hitters in the batting order. He was the first to show his players films of previous games to correct mistakes and improve techniques. He was the first to incorporate sliding drills, even hiring a sliding coach, a Cuban star named Armando Marsans. And he was the first to leave the baselines and manage the game from the dugout. In the beginning, opponents rode him mercilessly for that, calling him a "quitter." But winning makes believers out of even severe skeptics, and soon every manager was on the bench.

McGraw was also among the last of a dying breed, the owner-operator. While Charles Stoneham was the majority owner of the Giants in 1923, having bought the team from John T. Brush in 1919, McGraw owned a large minority share. As such, he had an outsize voice in franchise affairs, most notably the acquisition of players.

Until the calendar flipped to 1923, all had been peachy in McGraw's universe. He was atop the baseball world, unquestioned in his genius, and he held his enemies, Babe Ruth and the Yankees, under his boot. But Keeler's death cast a pall on the good tidings. Soon after, another reminder of the old days took its toll. McGraw underwent surgery on his sinuses to clear up cartilage damage left over from Dummy Taylor's off-target throw in 1903. And the license plates were stolen from McGraw's car while it was parked in front of the Waldorf Astoria Hotel. The gloomy tidings convinced McGraw that the time had come for a well-earned vacation, and so he and his second wife, Blanche, sailed for Cuba and a restorative spell under the sun, even as the Babe was felling trees in a snowy New England wood.

March

8

THE BALL CAME in slow and fat and gleaming white. It was the kind of meatball the Sultan of Swat ordinarily hammered into mincemeat far into the distance. Instead, he took a halfhearted swing and missed. The heavy winter coat Ruth was wearing probably didn't help. Nor did the swirling snow flurries. The ball plopped into some accumulated snow behind Ruth, for there was no catcher.

The Babe was in New York for a few days before heading south to Hot Springs, Arkansas, where he would enjoy a short vacation in the resort town before spring training began in New Orleans. Marshall Hunt had taken Ruth to the Yankee Stadium to show him his new home. Even as construction went on furiously all around them, Hunt tossed Ruth a few balls, but the Babe could barely touch the writer, not coming close to knocking one over the fence to where the workmen toiled. Shivering, Ruth called it a session after a dozen or so lifeless swings. The *Times* was a bit harsh in reporting "the old eye has not improved during the Winter Sojourn at Sudbury."

Despite the poor weather, the construction crews couldn't seek shelter and enjoy some hot soup—there was too much to do. The

American League had agreed to delay the start of the season by one week to accommodate the Yankees, but even with the seven extra days, it would take a Herculean effort to finish in time for opening day. The workers put in double shifts under adverse conditions, ignoring the frigid temperatures, icy winds, and billowing snow of winter in order to complete the job. The concrete works, dependent on moderate temperatures, slowed to a crawl. Already finished concrete buckled in freezing weather. Heavy gloves and coats made nimble work difficult, while the cold caused every hammer blow to reverberate through a man's spine. A freak March snowstorm halted construction for more than a week.

Worse news than the weather was a note sent by White execs on March 14 to the Yankees offices. Opening day was a little more than one month away. And White Construction Company was essentially broke. Due to the endless delays, White had been unable to pay its subcontractors, and the entire project was about to come to an abrupt halt. Desperate, Ruppert and Huston huddled with their lawyers and accountants, and managed to work out a deal to front White $50,000 immediately to cover payroll.

Despite the delays, the Yankee Stadium rose. Inexorably, the building took shape. Til Huston was a raging presence throughout, pushing the project forward, spiting the headaches and delays with sheer force of will. Ruppert was overjoyed that his recalcitrant partner was proving so useful in this area. Overseeing an engineering project wasn't Ruppert's milieu, and he blanched at the idea of putting on a hard hat and digging into the nitty-gritty of building the place. He was quite happy to let Huston have free reign in the Bronx while he stayed comfortably ensconced in his Manhattan offices. Cap wore out the White Company foremen with questions and kibitzing. Even Major Birmingham began to wince when Cap shuffled over to the job office.

There is no doubting Huston's importance to the work, however. He oversaw the sinking of the foundation shafts, the pouring of the concrete, and the erection of the steel girders. Each of the three levels was held up by a series of centralized steel pillars, and the spacing and tensile strength of each one was crucial. The grandstand seats and bleachers were manufactured right there at the site, and Huston was right there ensuring consistency. He was evangelistic on the subject of exits — Cap insisted on creating egress points in the outfield and grandstand to alleviate crowds. He scarcely went to the Yankees offices in midtown, leaving Ruppert and Barrow to handle team business related to winning the 1922 pennant and building the 1923 version of the squad.

Perhaps Huston's greatest contribution was his insistence from the beginning that the Stadium be a multisport venue, not merely a baseball paradise. He wanted some way to pull in money during the winter months and when the Yankees were on the road. A full running track surrounded the playing field for athletics meets, although it served as a "warning track" only down the left-field line. The center- and right-field fences were a good thirty feet beyond the track — so the raised inside wooden berm that separated cinder from grass was built to be lowered into the ground during games, thus saving fielders from tripping. The track was a standard quarter-mile oval except for the hundred yards down the first-base line, where it was misshapen. A runner sprinting in from along the left-field part of the track would reach home plate and bank sharply toward first base, practically at a forty-five-degree angle. Nevertheless, the Amateur Athletic Union came to the Bronx in late March and certified the track so that times recorded during meets would be recognized. The track was also used for bicycle races.

A large storeroom was constructed in the bowels of the Stadium to store vast quantities of sports equipment for games other than baseball. Football yard markers, boxing-ring ropes, bicycle pumps, long-jump pits, gymnastics mats — virtually every competition was accounted for, just in case the Stadium was the chosen venue. And the Yankees collected rental fees from the various stagers of these events.

The most farseeing aspect was the vault that Huston ordered to be buried under second base. It was crammed with the latest electronic communications gear. The setup allowed for an ultramodern (for 1923) press area right on the field. More important, when boxing matches came to the Stadium, the ring could be placed directly on top of the vault, and the press could set up ringside and work (and broadcast) right from the infield. This brilliant touch could come only from the mind of a sportsman-engineer.

On the subject of vaults, there was one aspect of the new Stadium that wasn't new. The team had the aforementioned safe dating back to the Hilltop Park days into which players deposited valuables for safekeeping during games and road trips, and sometimes for longer durations if they didn't feel the objects were secure at home. The safe had individually labeled drawers, still emblazoned with the names of the members of the Highlanders from early in the century. Wee Willie Keeler had his name painted in gold on the black surface of the safe, as did Jack Chesbro, Clark Griffith, and numerous other, less-well-known players.

The Yankees took the four-hundred-pound safe with them when the team moved into the Polo Grounds, and now it was schlepped across the Harlem River to its new home. It wouldn't make the next move, however—when the Yankees transferred to Shea Stadium in 1973 during the renovation of the Yankee Stadium, the safe disappeared.

The vastness of the new Stadium practically required lopsided playing dimensions. Straight down the lines were ridiculously short porches, 281 feet to left, 295 to right. But the fences curved away from the hitters at a steep rate to create a spacious outfield with hard-to-reach power alleys. The left-field fence was 395 feet away, reaching 460 feet in left-center. Similarly, right field was 370 feet, while right-center was 429 feet. Dead center was a distant 490 feet away, a marker almost as impossible to reach as the center-field clubhouse in the Polo Grounds. The enormous stretch from left-center to dead center quickly and obviously became known as "Death Valley." Right smack in the middle of the expanse was a flagpole, and Old Glory, the pole, and the base were all in play. To the distant batter, it looked like the pin flag on a par-five hole.

Left-center field boasted the oddest geometric aspect of the Yankee Stadium. The lower deck curved around into the outfield, approaching the bleachers about sixty feet from the foul line. The exit onto River Avenue came first, however, creating an alley between the deck and the bleachers, which sat well behind. Here, the fence was actually farther away than in dead center, an impossible 500 feet from home plate, although this would change before the 1924 season, when home plate was moved up slightly. This would be the future site of the left-field bullpen, and would abut the monuments erected to Yankees greats. Theoretically, a batter could clout a ball over the edge of the left-center-field seats and have it land in the alley where the exit met the bleachers—in play. It required such a colossal blast, however, that it never happened, though had the Babe been right-handed, it would have been at least plausible.

The bleachers were laid out at right angles to one another, to better facilitate viewing of athletics meets and football games. The left-field bleachers were considerably farther away from home plate (460 feet) than the ones in right field. The disparity gave rise to the taunting phrase "out in left field," an idiom that likely began its life thanks to the Yankee Stadium and its discordant angles.

The distance to right field seemed to undermine the common conceit that this was truly a house built for Ruth. If anything, the Polo Grounds, with its lefty-friendly dimensions, was the park that best suited the Babe. "I cried when they took me out of the Polo Grounds," he admitted later. Besides, Huston and especially Ruppert, while obviously recognizing Ruth and his impact on supplying the funds that helped build the Stadium, were far more concerned about posterity. This was to be a Stadium that would host sluggers for decades, long past the Babe's sell-by date. "Babe Ruth is at best a temporary attraction," agreed F. C. Lane in *Literary Digest*. "A few seasons at the most and his great feats will be but a memory. The Yankee Stadium, however, is a permanent institution."

Ruth was not merely a slugger. He would have to play right field in the Yankee Stadium too, and it wouldn't be easy. Between the running track and the fence, a grass slope climbed toward the wooden bleachers (this is what passed for a warning track), and Ruth would have to master the hill to pull in fly balls. He was somewhat familiar with such obstacles—Fenway Park was notorious for "Duffy's Cliff," a ten-foot mound in front of the famous left-field wall that was in play. Sox left-fielder Duffy Lewis became so proficient at playing the hill that it was named for him. It wasn't unusual for ballparks of the day to have discordant dimensions and planes. The Polo Grounds outfield was sunken some eight feet below the infield, forming what was called a "turtleback." When John McGraw stood in the dugout, he could see only the top halves of his outfielders.

At the Yankee Stadium, Ruth would also have the "Bloody Angle" to deal with, a portion of the right-field fence between the bleachers and the foul line that jutted crazily out into the field, turning every ball struck into the area into a cheap home run—or, if the fielder misplayed it, a potential inside-the-park home run.

Long before its official unveiling, the Yankee Stadium was greeted rapturously by the press. Its unequaled size was a common theme. The *New York Telegram* wrote: "Approaching from the 155th Street Viaduct, one is impressed with its bigness." The *Times* called it "a skyscraper among ballparks." "The Yankee Stadium is indeed the last word in ball parks," read *Literary Digest*. "But not the least of its merits is its advantage of position. From the plain of the Harlem River it looms up like the great Pyramid of Cheops from the sands of Egypt." A Philadelphia paper wrote: "It is a thrilling thought that perhaps 2,500 years from now archaeologists, spading up the ruins of Harlem and the lower Bronx, will find arenas that outsize anything that the ancient Romans and Greeks built."

That assessment, while hyperbolic, was understandable given how the Yankee Stadium so thoroughly dominated the surrounding Bronx landscape. Everywhere one looked was sky and earth, with a scattering of low-slung homes and businesses. One couldn't compare it to a mountain, as there were no others in the range. It was a stand-alone wonder, a man-made testament to power (in every sense of the word).

And, like the pharaoh's honorific, the Stadium was a monument to great wealth. The *New York Evening World* conveyed the feeling of capitalist power that oozed from the building. It thought the Yankee Stadium had "the austere dignity of a bank. Money speaks there in the low, modulated voice that is more eloquent than the shouts of a mob storming the Bastille." The Stadium personified "big" and "rich," two of New York's elemental traits.

As such, it was immediately, quintessentially of the city. The Polo Grounds was a fine place to play ball but didn't fill visitors with awe—in part because it sat in the hollow of Coogan's Bluff. The Yankee Stadium, however, towered above its surroundings like the Eiffel Tower or Big Ben. "Travelers approaching New York from the sea are greeted by the lofty torch of the Statue of Liberty," wrote F. C. Lane.

> Visitors arriving from the north over the tracks of the New York Central or New Haven Railroads are confronted by the imposing pile of the new Yankee Stadium. The approaches to the world's metropolis are appropriate in either case. To the sojourner from Europe, New York means opportunity. To the visitor from other parts of America, New York is the amusement center of the continent. And that spirit of diversion finds fitting expression in the colossal monument of athletic sport.

Although the Yankee Stadium's awe-inspiring vertical size was breathlessly reported, what catches the modern eye is the horizontal space. Photos from 1923 taken inside the Stadium tended to capture not the three-tiered grandstand in its towering glory but rather the enormous expanse of the outfield and bleachers, which is less Everest than Sahara, impressive in sweep but low to the ground. Enhancing this impression is the lack of background buildings. The Bronx County Courthouse—which would eventually serve as a familiar backdrop to the Stadium, peeking over the stands from its position on the southern end of the Grand Concourse—wasn't built until 1933. Except for a handful of small homes and the Elevated train, there was nothing around to hem in the Stadium, so it appeared to stretch on and on into eternity.

With the Stadium just about complete, Cap Huston decided to show off the place to a chosen few. Standing high in the upper grandstand, he proudly displayed the astonishing vista with a flourish of his arm. "The Bronx are not so wild when you get used to them." He beamed.

Colonel Ruppert preferred a prophetic warning: "Yankee Stadium was a mistake, not mine but the Giants'."

9

RUTH HOPED TO begin his redemptive season with a quiet, productive spring. Unfortunately, the start to 1923 was anything but. "Ruth is a man of many infections," read the *Times* in January, cheekily working his sexual history into a routine notice that the Babe had had a boil lanced on his ring finger.

Before traveling to spring training, Huston visited Ruth during his New York convalescence and was wowed by the Babe's fitness. "He's not exactly sylphlike and willowy," said Til, "but he looks as if he is down to playing weight," which usually didn't happen for players of that era until the season started.

The Babe was in fighting trim, at 210 pounds, while playing a week of golf in Hot Springs, but on March 2, after a thirty-six-hole marathon, he started coughing up bile and collapsed. The diagnosis was influenza, not the deadly strain that had scythed across the globe in 1918, but serious enough. Ruth's temperature skied to 104, and rumors quickly circulated that he had died (no man has ever had more, as Mark Twain might say, greatly exaggerated death reports than Babe Ruth). He recovered but lost another twelve pounds in the process. Instead of being fit as a fiddle, he was weak and drawn when camp opened in New Orleans.

The bout with the flu was bad enough, but the Babe felt worse still when the papers filled with news that an underage (nineteen, when the legal age of the time was twenty-one) woman was claiming Ruth had fathered her baby. Someone named Dolores Dixon was suing the Babe for $50,000. Ruth had been served the papers on the very evening of his public scolding at the Elks Club in November, but he had hoped it would be dismissed, as he was sure this was a false claim—or was it? He thought he had never heard of or seen this Dixon woman before, but given his lifestyle, it certainly wasn't impossible that he had (another) illegitimate child. Helen, despite inwardly knowing a thing or two about the extent of Ruth's dalliances, laughed off the charges and publicly stood by her George.

It was a gesture of faith on her part, for the Babe didn't exactly consider his marriage sacrosanct. "Why don't you blow out of here!" he yelled at Helen on numerous occasions. "You cramp my style." His libido had raged unchecked while in Boston. "When they let him out of St. Mary's," recalled a Sox teammate, "it was like letting a wild animal out of its cage." Now that he was turned loose upon a city far larger and stocked with many, many more available women, Ruth's sexual scorecard rivaled his home-run rate. One teammate recalled, "He'd stick his thing into anything that had hair on it." Ruth once entered a crowded hotel room and yelled, "Anyone who doesn't want to fuck can leave now."

He generally preferred prostitutes, because he had neither the time nor the inclination to court properly. Hunt of the *Daily News* would accompany the Babe on adventures out into the wilds of the nation, in search of Ruth's two favorite targets: steak dinners and cathouses. Nothing suited Ruth more than a large meal followed by a trip upstairs to a whore's boudoir. Or vice versa. "Lots of times on the road Ruth had connections in rural places, really choice," Hunt recalled. Ruth once walked into a St. Louis whorehouse and announced he was going to have sex with every woman there. He did, then tucked into a large breakfast. In Hot Springs, Ruth would take writer Frank Graham driving in the Arkansas countryside, looking for farmhouses advertising "Chicken Dinners." "What he really wanted was the chicken-daughter combo, and he got plenty of them," recalled Graham.

Fred Lieb said Ruth was obsessed with the penis and not merely because he was famously well-endowed. His speech was peppered with phallic allusions, such as "I can knock the penis off any ball that ever was pitched." A large stack of mail was "as big as my penis." When he aged he confided to Lieb, "The worst of this is that I no longer can see my penis when I stand up." The female genitalia weren't left out. Asked "How's it going, Jidge?" he would respond, "Pussy good, pussy good."

Ruth and Bob Meusel often shared hotel suites on the road. One time Ruth brought home a woman, and they shared noisy relations, after which the Babe came out to the common room to smoke a cigar. The next day, Meusel asked how often Ruth had laid the girl. "Count the cigars," replied Ruth. According to Long Bob, there were seven butts in the ashtray.

Usually the Babe preferred the safety of numbers. Lieb noted that one woman was never enough for Ruth—only multiple women could leave him fulfilled. "Frequently, it took half a dozen."

Restraint would have been a difficult proposition for a man in his position. Ruth's effect on women was akin to the effect the Beatles would have forty years later—hysteria. Women offered themselves to Ruth constantly, even as he passed by on a moving train. At a strapping 6'2" and over two hundred pounds, he dwarfed most other players of the day, and despite his enormous intakes of food and drink, he was an excellent physical specimen during his early years in New York. Women wrote him propositioning letters by the sackful, but according to Waite Hoyt, since Ruth seldom opened fan mail, his teammates were the beneficiaries, snatching up the invites and arranging liaisons for themselves.

Occasionally there was blowback. In 1921, several reporters watched openmouthed as Ruth sprinted on board a train and raced down the passageway, chased closely by a woman wielding a butcher knife. The writers learned she was the wife of a Louisiana politician who thought *she* was the only one. That didn't wind up in the papers the next day, or ever. Neither did a Detroit incident in which an irate husband waving a revolver chased a near-naked Babe out of a hotel.

It wasn't a laughing matter. A turn-of-the-twentieth-century outfielder in Boston named Chick Stahl had killed himself after repeated harassment from a woman claiming a child out of wedlock, a tale that made its way to Ruth in his early days in the Hub. Not that it caused much of a dent at the time, but he was reminded of it now that this Dixon woman was making his life miserable.

In an ironic piece of public relations, Ruth invited photogs to his New Orleans hotel room and had his picture taken rocking his daughter to sleep. He impressed on gathered scribes how serious he was about changing his former wild ways. "I've been behaving myself for a long time," he said. "Seems that as soon as a fellow gets a little bit famous, he gets himself into a lot of hot water. I'll fight that case to the last ditch."

Dixon was claiming that she and Ruth went "automobiling" several times a week in that damnable year, 1922; that she and Helen had actually met for coffee; and that she had caught the Babe's eye while working as a shopgirl. Her lawyer, George Feingold, laid it on like blueberry jam. Ruth had sexually assaulted Miss Dixon, he claimed, "both in New York City and in Freeport [New York]." Shortly thereafter his client had found herself a mother-to-be, Feingold clucked, and her betrayer had instructed her to go to hell. This from a man who had once addressed her as "my little watch charm." Feingold sighed. "She has become sick and disabled and has suffered in body and mind."

Ruth exclaimed, "It's blackmail, nuthin' but a holdup game," and though he had the legalese wrong, Dixon's lawyer later admitted they were indeed aiming for a quick, tasty settlement. Instead, Ruth went to court, and the suit dissolved. There was no "Dolores Dixon" after all—it was an assumed name taken by a desperate girl out for some extortion money from what seemed an easy target.

Skinny and bruised by false accusation, Ruth went to New Orleans and couldn't buy a hit. Not much else either—the perpetually strapped Babe (he was forever shy on cash, despite his enormous earnings) borrowed $1,500 from Hoyt and Dugan, which he repaid at 6 percent interest after his first regular-season payday. His loss of form at the bat was more worrisome than his cash flow. Barrow chided him for playing too much of that "sissy golf," but that wasn't the culprit. Ruth had refrained from swinging, in the after-hours sense, all winter and spring. And he had swung a driver and an ax. But he had hardly swung a bat, and the rust was showing.

Worse, Ruth, for the first time ever, was tentative on the baseball field. The swagger was gone. Grantland Rice noticed: "The old time air of complete confidence that feathered his other spring trips has been missing to a large extent so far and his once-perfect timing has not been in evidence."

The Yankees left New Orleans to play fifteen games against Brooklyn, the two teams slowly working their way north. The Babe was struggling, delivering plenty of "windies," but the strikeouts showed more than rust—this was a bona fide slump.

"It would appear to one who has been analyzing the case for the last several years," wrote Hunt in the *Daily News,* "that if Mr. Ruth were drowning, someone would chuck him an anvil. Were he marooned on a desert isle and starving, the waves would wash up a book. An excruciating case." According to the *American,* "The Babe...seems to be worried. His attitude is different now from what it was." Large crowds still appeared to see him at every stop, but now many of them were booing. A boy who skipped school in Tulsa to see the Babe whiff four times lamented, "I expect I'll get the dickens from my teacher." Not letting down those "dirty-faced" children remained paramount. "I've been getting a lot of letters from kids who say they're rooting for me to come back," Ruth mentioned to a ghostwriter at the *American*. "They've been doing a lot of worrying about me." Ruth was struggling with more than baseball. The *American* went on to report that Ruth sang first bass in a quartet one evening on the train, and had "reached heroically for a high note and struck a sorrowful discord."

Another night, after the Babe had gone hitless in five at bats, the teams rode the train toward Tennessee. Manager Miller Huggins summoned Ruth to his dimmed Pullman car and had him close the door. As the darkened midsouth countryside whistled past, Huggins talked quietly, earnestly. He told Ruth that his game had slipped hugely and that he was letting the team down, and then he dropped this bomb: "You just might be through as a player, George." Noticing the Babe's angry look, Huggins explained hurriedly that Ruth was twenty-eight—lots of players lost it at that age.

Now, Hug was hardly above a little reverse psychology. He had tried many gambits to compel Ruth to toe the line, and this easily could have been another. He had his opening—Ruth's shocking failure in October and his spring ineptitude—and, in a tactic worthy of McGraw, maybe he tried to scare Ruth straight. Or, given his dislike for the Sultan and eagerness to twist the knife, Huggins may have been attempting to get under the skin of his nemesis. He may even have been sincere.

One thing is certain: Huggins got Ruth going. Great athletes throughout history have taken any slight, real or imagined, and used it as a motivational force. Ruth already had his legs taken out from under him in 1922. Now this little doorstop of a manager was telling the greatest slugger the sport had ever seen that he was a sack of tomatoes.

Well, *fuck him.*

Sure enough, Ruth began socking the ball, 1921-style. In Vicksburg, after getting into a car with a stranger to talk with a sick boy who worshipped him, he hit a pair of home runs. Two hits in Chattanooga, three more in Asheville, North Carolina. Many of the parks the teams played in were too small to handle the overflow crowds that turned out to see Ruth, so fans were allowed to congregate down the lines. The Babe lashed screaming foul liners into the throng, genuinely afraid he was going to kill somebody. But he was locked in, and it felt good.

The *Sporting News,* ever eager to romanticize the game, posited that the trip to see the sick boy is what relaxed Ruth and stopped him from pressing. He needed to become his "natural self." He certainly was winning back the fans. An old farmer had shown up in Knoxville, where the Yankees played the day before the Vicksburg game, and pounded on Ruth's door. He told the slugger about his ailing grandson, an orphan stricken with typhoid, who only wanted an autographed baseball. Instead, Ruth drove deep into the mountains with the man, sat with the boy all night, and left behind signed balls, gloves, and bats.

It wasn't the first time that spring that Ruth had gone AWOL to serve his public. Ford Frick, the future commissioner of baseball, remembered a hot, dusty game at the Pensacola Naval Air Station in Florida, after which the team hurriedly dressed, eager to get the hell out of town. But Ruth was extremely late to the train station. Huggins fumed, pacing up and down the depot, threatening that he was going to call the colonel and get Ruth suspended. The Babe finally rolled in, still in his grimy uniform.

"Where have you been, you big ape?" Huggins roared. "Don't you know we got a train to catch? I ought to—"

"Oh, Hug, don't get excited," Ruth said. "Someday you'll have a stroke if you're not careful. Some kids were playing ball outside the park, and they wanted me to manage one of the teams. I did and we won. You wouldn't want me to walk out on them, would you, Hug?" Wearing a shit-eating grin a mile wide, Ruth then boarded the train, and the Yankees chugged away.

In Muskogee, a game was stopped in the ninth inning when hundreds of local boys surrounded Ruth in right field "like a hive of bees in swarming time." They followed him to the team hotel, stayed outside in a driving rain while Ruth dined, and resumed their stalk at ten that evening, when Ruth walked to the train station. They waved and cheered until the last car had disappeared from sight.

10

THE 1923 YANKEES were mostly the same team that had fallen prostrate before the McGraw Machine the previous October. Wally Schang was a better than average catcher; slugging vet Wally Pipp held down first; steady Aaron Ward was at second; Everett Scott, team captain, was the shortstop. The Deacon had played in 986 consecutive games heading into the 1923 season, a record that the *New York Herald* declared "should last fifty years."

"Jumpin'" Joe Dugan (so called for his habit of "jumping," or leaving, teams due to homesickness throughout his early career) held down third. Dugan had been acquired during the pennant chase of 1922, coming over from Boston for a grab bag of players, including Chick Fewster and the talented Lefty O'Doul. The deal outraged baseball, especially St. Louis, locked as the Browns were in a race with New York at the time. As a result, a trade deadline was enacted to prevent late-season raids on bottom-dwelling clubs by the front-runners.

Although his 1923 season would turn out rather average, Dugan possessed a solid glove, a reliable bat, and a quick wit. During one contentious salary negotiation with Colonel Ruppert, the owner's cries of poverty led Dugan to ask, "Could you use a loan?" The sense of humor ran in the family. Dugan had nine siblings and cash was tight, so when the fabled Connie Mack came to his Connecticut door to sign Joe and laid five hundred-dollar bills on the kitchen table, his father exclaimed, "For five hundred dollars you can take the whole family!"

Miller Huggins loved Dugan, saying that spring, "In the list of present-day players, Joe Dugan is first, second, and third. He can run, catch, hit, and throw. Other than that he is practically useless." Dugan wasn't the most graceful of players. At the plate he resembled "a kangaroo ready for takeoff," and in the field "a toy jumping jack on a string." He is remembered more for his joie de vivre than his play, which underrates his importance to the first Yankees dynasty. He was solid and at times outstanding in the clutch, not unlike future Yankees third basemen Graig Nettles and Scott Brosius. A bizarre superstition separated Dugan from the others—he refused to throw the ball back to the pitcher from his position at third base. He would throw it to another fielder, or walk it over and hand it to the hurler, but never would he throw it over.

Whitey Witt, the hero of the 1922 pennant race, patrolled center. The Yankees had managed to slip past the St. Louis Browns late in the season, taking two of three to seize the pennant in a contentious series at Sportsman's Park in the Gateway City. Witt was hit in the head and knocked unconscious by a flying soda-pop bottle in the second game, and when he returned to dramatically knock in the winning run in the rubber game, New York was pennant-bound, finishing 94–60, one game ahead of the Browns. The excellent Bob Meusel was the nominal left fielder, but in actuality he would play almost as much right field as Ruth in 1923. The Yankee Stadium's tough sun field was to left, so Ruth played right. Most other parks in the AL, however, were sunny in right, so on those fields Ruth played left. In 1923 he would see eighty-three games in right field, seventy-eight in left field, and seven more in center field. It wasn't so much that

Ruth was incapable of picking up fly balls in the sun. But given the outsize importance of the Babe to the Yankees, relieving him of this small burden helped his overall morale and thus the team's.

Despite the presence of Ruth, the heart of the Yankees was the pitching rotation. New York possessed four solid right-handed starters: Bob "the Gob" Shawkey, "Bullet" Joe Bush, Waite "the Schoolboy" Hoyt, and "Sad" Sam Jones. Jones would pitch more than twenty years in the bigs, chalking up his longevity to never wasting energy on throws to first base. "There was a time there for five years, I never *once* threw to first base to chase a runner back," said Sad Sam. "Not once in five years. Ripley put that in *Believe It or Not!*" Another righty, Carl Mays, was also on the team, nickname-free, but was buried in Huggins's doghouse due to lingering suspicions stemming from a curious incident during the 1921 World Series.

The Yankees had won the first two games of that Series but dropped the third. In Game Four, Mays had been dominant for seven innings but came unglued in the eighth. Emil "Irish" Meusel, Bob's brother, led off for the Giants. From the bench, Miller Huggins signaled that he wanted Mays to throw a fastball. Mays tossed a slow curve instead, and Meusel cracked it over his brother's head and off the left-field wall for a triple. Huggins was furious, and later in the inning anger turned to distrust when Mays fell down trying to field a bunt. The Giants scored three times in the frame—runs that provided the winning margin.

The incident might well have been forgotten but for reporter Fred Lieb. That evening, he was approached by a well-known Broadway actor (whom Lieb never identified). The thespian said he had it on good authority that Mays had been paid to discreetly dump the game. He said that Mays's wife, watching from the stands, was the go-between—if she signaled that money had been passed to her, that meant Mays should ease up. Sure enough, claimed the actor, Mays's missus had waved a white handkerchief just before the eighth-inning meltdown.

Engaging in some activist journalism, Lieb brought the man to Til Huston's room in the Hotel Martinique to tell the Yanks co-owner the tale. Lieb and the actor found Huston and Boston Red Sox owner Harry Frazee, a theater impresario and prodigious drinker, passed out cold, fully dressed, liquor bottles everywhere. It was not an uncommon sight where Messrs. Huston and Frazee were concerned. But when roused, Huston sobered instantly at the news that the Series might not be on the up-and-up. In a scene that could have been from one of Frazee's Broadway farces, the quartet of writer, actor, and owners, all in varying states of inebriation, went to Judge Landis's room, even though it was nearly one a.m.

"What the hell do you fellows want at this hour of the night?" roared the semidressed commissioner at the door. When he was informed of Mays's possible subterfuge, Landis immediately sprung into action, assigning a detective to investigate. But no evidence was ever found, and Landis never took steps against Mays. Years later, on another occasion in which Huston found himself three sheets to the wind, a soused Cap began to tell Lieb of how his Yankees would have won the 1921 and 1922 World Series but for nefarious players on the take. Huston passed out before he could elaborate. Lieb could never get any more details from him but guessed he was referring to the Mays incident. For his part, Mays always claimed that he threw Meusel a curve because he had gotten Irish out on that pitch earlier in the game.

All the pitchers in the Yankees rotation but Shawkey had been brought in from Boston, part of a spree of sales and trades between the Sox and Yanks later known collectively as the "Rape of the Red Sox." Before the start of the 1923 season, Barrow went back to raid Frazee's roster once more. The Yankees rotation desperately needed a lefty for balance. Huggins had even pointed to the lack of a south-paw as a key reason the Giants overwhelmed his team the year before. So in January New York sent a trio of young prospects and $50,000 to Beantown in exchange for the "Knight of Kennett Square" (Pennsylvania), Herb Pennock.

Pennock was a true country gent, the kind Ruth played at being. He "rode hounds," raised foxes, and undertook other squirish activities appropriate to the well-heeled country where he was raised. He had been a teammate of Ruth's in Boston, and the two were close. That wasn't unusual—few who met Pennock disliked him.

He was a thinking pitcher, one who seldom threw the same pitch to a batter twice. His arm was exceptionally slender, "as thin as a high school girl's from shoulder to wrist," according to *Baseball Magazine.* "His biceps is conspicuous by its absence. In fact, his arm appears so frail that it would impress the observer as quite unsuited to the grilling labor of the hurling mound." Pennock delivered the ball with his limb in a hellacious twist, so that the curve began virtually from the instant it left his hand. He also snapped his wrist with such violence it could be heard from the dugout.

Pennock believed in a clinical approach to pitching. "The first commandment is observation," he said. "Look around. Notice the little quirks in the batter, and notice your own quirks. Your doctor never stops learning. The great pitcher imitates him." If Pennock had a knock, it was that he was a "whittler," a pitcher who threw extra pitches off the plate trying to entice the batter into swinging (a "nibbler," in modern slang).

Pennock's arrival would prove critical, but at the time the Yankees were criticized for making a shortsighted move. Pennock may have been well liked, but he wasn't exactly a stopper. His combined record in 1921 and 1922 was a miserable 23–31, and the press felt that New York had given up too much in exchange for a "passing veteran," as Joe Vila described him. The *New York World* thought the Yanks had been "gypped."

But in all the Yankees were a superb assemblage, one with few equals in either league. They were considered a favorite to capture another AL pennant, but the preseason analysis in the press didn't hand anything to them. The hangover from the team's flop in the '22 Series was impossible to quantify. And the experts felt the Yankees would be strongly challenged by a slugging Detroit squad that threatened to field nine .300 hitters, including player-manager Ty Cobb; by St. Louis, which had lost to the Yankees by a single game the year before and was still potent despite the crushing loss for the season of first baseman and batting champion George "the Sizzler" Sisler to a nasty case of sinusitis; and by Cleveland, led by the superb player-manager Tris Speaker. "Five AL clubs can win the pennant," said Ban Johnson.

In addition, there was one team that had already proven itself indisputably superior—twice. And with the Polo Grounds all to themselves, they were intent on winning a third straight championship, ideally at the expense of their former tenants and personal pigeons.

11

JOHN MCGRAW ARRIVED for spring training in San Antonio in early March after his vacation in Cuba (he would have happily trained the Giants in Cuba, but he feared the temptations of the island would ruin his efforts). McGraw spent almost every off-season there, maintaining friends from his days as El Mono Amarillo. He managed games in the Cuban League and let his thinning hair down at a racetrack and casino he co-owned with Charles Stoneham.

The first thing he noticed upon arriving by train in Texas was the absence of his prized acquisition, the man whose presence seemingly guaranteed another championship for the Giants.

If the Good Lord had to create the image of an ideal athlete, he could have done worse than to sculpt Jack Bentley. Bentley was a strapping two hundred pounds, a few hairs shy of 6' tall, with Atlas-sized shoulders and long, lithe legs. He spoke in a mesmerizing basso profundo, and surprised reporters and teammates with a quick, sharp wit. He was rakishly handsome, well dressed, and poised under pressure. Teammate Art Nehf summed Bentley up: "I never saw anybody who looked more like a major league ball player—or acted like one is supposed to act."

John Needles Bentley was also a war hero. In World War I, he fought with such gallantry with the 313th Infantry Regiment that he earned a battlefield promotion to first lieutenant. During the savage fighting at Montfaucon, where Colonel Til Huston was also exhibiting courage under fire, Bentley crawled through intense artillery shelling to cut the German wire, opening the way for his regiment to capture a key watchtower. He was gassed while fighting and won two commendations for bravery.

He had gone to war instead of joining the Red Sox and, upon returning from battle, spent some time in the minors. Bentley played with Ruth's old team Baltimore in 1922, where he became the Babe of the International League. He pitched and played first base, dominating the league on the mound and in the batter's box. He went 13–2 with a 1.73 ERA as a hurler, while cracking 22 homers with 128 RBI and hitting .350. He was the greatest drawing card the league had ever seen. A Baltimore tailor offered free suits to every Oriole who hit a home run in 1922. After collecting his eighth suit, Bentley offered the tailor a compromise—a suit for every *four* homers. "I didn't want to break the poor fellow," Bentley said.

McGraw may not have liked Babe Ruth or what he represented, but that didn't mean the manager would balk at signing what appeared to be a square-jawed, matinee-idol, war-hero version of the Babe. A bidding war with the Yankees and Reds drove up the price tag, and McGraw was forced to pay through the nose to get Bentley, wiring 65,000 "fresh and juicy mackerel" to Jack Dunn for his services. "I'm buying Bentley as a pitcher," insisted McGraw, who, like Miller Huggins, wanted a lefty starter.

But Bentley refused to go quietly. Players were chafing more and more against a system that paid them poorly and expected them to be treated like chattel by management, and a new National Baseball Players Association had sprung to life, promising a unified front when it came to getting the most out of new contracts. By early 1923, well over two hundred players had joined up, more than one-third of the total in both leagues. Talk of a players' strike surfaced and gained plausibility as spring approached.

The Giants were among the most active teams in the association. The *Times* reported that "practically every member" of the squad had joined up, with team captain Dave Bancroft assuming leadership duties. McGraw was incensed, both at the potential loss of control and at the "ingrates," his well-compensated players who weren't satisfied making top dollar to play baseball in the biggest city in the nation. "Except for Edd Roush and Rogers Hornsby, we have the twelve highest-paid players in the National League," claimed McGraw spuriously, though it was certainly true the Giants had the league's highest payroll. He moved to quash the nascent union activity in his clubhouse, barring any unsigned player from spring camp, among other tactics.

The players weren't ready to go to the mat as a group in 1923, and one by one the dozen or so holdouts filed into camp in San Antonio, chastened. The sheer tonnage of prospects McGraw had brought to Texas hurried many of them along—some forty players were on hand, an amazing number for the time. One was a tall first baseman from Memphis named Bill Terry. He had shocked McGraw when they met at the Peabody Hotel in Memphis by demanding the manager meet his salary at Standard Oil, where Terry worked in the off-season. The idea of ballplayers out for more money was hardly a new phenomenon, but as McGraw aged, it irked him more and more. So he blamed the problem, as he did most modern developments, on Ruth.

There was one player who didn't come crawling to San Antonio with his tail between his legs: Jack Bentley. Worldly, married, a father, learned (he studied philosophy and loved to discuss Socrates, Plato, and especially the Chinese philosophers), a war veteran— Bentley was exactly the type to notice he was worth sixty-five large to John McGraw and to wonder why he wasn't getting a piece. So he held out for a portion of his sale price, on top of his salary. So strong was Bentley's stance that he threatened to quit baseball rather than report without a share of the transfer fee.

McGraw's response was predictable: "The attitude of the younger players certainly has changed. In the days when I was an active player we first wanted a chance to prove that we could play ball. Not the young players—they want to be paid a bonus for giving a mild demonstration of baseball."

McGraw may have been insulted, but he wasn't above using Bentley's absence to have some fun. One day, the manager surreptitiously signed Bentley's name in the register of the St. Anthony Hotel, where the team stayed in San Antonio. He wrote "Room 802" in the book. Club secretary Jim Tierney noticed Bentley's apparent arrival and informed McGraw, who ordered Tierney to bring Bentley to his new manager, posthaste.

Of course, Tierney couldn't—Bentley was cooling his heels in Baltimore. When the secretary failed to find him, a *faux* outraged McGraw told Tierney to stay in the lobby until the wayward pitcher showed up. Hours passed. Finally, at about 2:30 a.m., McGraw called the lobby phone, asking for Tierney. Disguising his voice, the manager mumbled, "This is Jack Bentley. I'm over in [nearby] New Braunfels."

"What are you doing there?" asked Tierney.

"I'm in jail."

"What?" screamed the secretary.

"Yes—I came over here to see some friends of mine, and we were speeding, and a cop pulled us up. Then he found a couple of quarts of liquor on the floor of the car, and when he went to take it I slugged him and—"

A shocked Tierney started shrieking, "Wait till I tell Mr. McGraw!" Bentley/McGraw pressed him to get $500 in bail money over to the New Braunfels jail immediately. "You can rot in that cell for all time as far as I'm concerned!" yelled Tierney down the line. He hung up and raced to McGraw's room, where he encountered the manager having some drinks with Bozeman Bulger, Frank Graham, and a few other writers. They were in on the gag and wanted to play along, but at the sight of the red-faced, hysterical Tierney, the room exploded in laughter.

Before John J. could torment any more members of his staff, an agreement was reached. Both the Orioles and the Giants would kick $2,500 to Bentley as a bonus. The Next Ruth finally joined the club, and impressed McGraw with his batting prowess in a private workout when he arrived in San Antonio, held away from the prying eyes of the press, some of whom lingered outside the fence, hoping to at least hear what was going on.

Unfortunately it soon became apparent that Bentley enjoyed over-indulging at mealtime. He had reported twenty pounds overweight. "Two uniforms should just about cover him," noted the *Post*. An irate McGraw ran Bentley endlessly, before and after every workout, dressing him in heavy wool sweaters and rubber suits in the Texas heat. The regimen continued until the Giants reached New York. Sure enough, Bentley began the season in shape.

Jack wasn't a natural fit with the country boys in the Giants club-house. It didn't help that he showed up with a cocky attitude that didn't match his exploits, which at the major-league level were exactly none. And he was proving exceptionally sensitive to criticism. He didn't mind hearing it about his weight. But he didn't like to hear any-thing about his on-field failings, even from John McGraw himself.

Earning a compliment from the Little Napoleon was tough. Once, a player made a nice grab in the field and came back to the dugout making noise about it. McGraw fixed him with a firm look and said, "My boy, one small breeze doesn't make a windstorm."

The folks in Baltimore saw Bentley's struggles coming. One sports-writer, Chuck Foreman, had written, "[Bentley] has been pampered and petted so in the last few years he seems to imagine himself immune from criticism. With a losing club he could not get along, for the ragging of the fans would be too much for him and yet he, unable to stand the gaff, hopes to go to the majors."

The Giants weren't losers, but the manager and the fans demanded the best and were quick to let players know when they weren't living up to the team's standard. The incumbent first baseman, George "Highpockets" Kelly, knew all about it. The tall (6'4", hence the nickname given to him by Damon Runyon, based on how high Kelly had to reach for his shirt-pocket chewing tobacco), laconic Kelly had been McGraw's choice to replace the popular "Prince Hal" Chase at first base. After a slow start, Kelly was practically run out of town by Chase-loving Giants fans. But McGraw stuck with him. "I put you at first base because I thought you belonged there," he told the shaken Kelly one day after a particularly fierce riding from the fans. "I still think so. Just keep your mind on your job and in a short time the assholes who are yelling at you now will be yelling for you."

Sure enough, Highpockets won over the crowd with sterling defense and a steady bat. McGraw would claim later that Kelly got more key hits for him than any player he had ever managed. But the Polo Grounds was no place for the meek, and certainly no place for a bonus baby who couldn't cut the mustard in the National League. As Bentley struggled during the spring, the press piled on, and the crowds followed suit. McGraw began to wonder if his prize was going to pan out.

The *Sporting News* took note: "Bentley is suffering the penalty of delay in reporting to the Giants. He came into camp fat and it took all his time to reduce his belt line, without a chance to try out his arm. Now he is stamped with the fatal word 'lemon' and it will be a tough job for him to climb the grade."

McGraw needed Bentley to come through, for his pitching staff was now a question mark. The ace, Art Nehf, was fine, coming off a series of excellent seasons, and veteran Hugh "the Astoria Eagle" McQuillan was reliable. But Jesse Barnes and Jack Scott, two key contributors in 1922, were less so. Worse, to McGraw, they weren't taking the opportunity provided by the spring action to solidify their games. Instead, they were carousing, touring the Alamo City's pleasure spots. McGraw was particularly sour on Scott, whom he had gone out of his way to claim from the scrap heap the season before. He labeled Scott an "ingrate" and fined him $100.

Barnes, McGraw felt, was being led astray by "Oil" Smith, the rough-and-tumble catcher, who dragged Barnes along for excursions deep into the night. McGraw said of Smith, "He is an anarchist with no respect for law and order," making the illiterate catcher seem more like the Italian Luigi Galleani, whose followers carried out a wave of terror bombings a few years earlier.

Rosy Ryan filled out the rotation. Ryan was a newlywed—after a sterling performance in Game One of the '22 World Series, he proposed to his girlfriend, who accepted. Ryan had been a spitballer before the 1920 rules were enacted. He could have been allowed to continue throwing the spitter under a grandfather clause that let pitchers such as Burleigh Grimes and Stan Coveleski doctor the ball. But McGraw refused to name him on the grandfather list sent to the commissioner and insisted Ryan become a "real" pitcher. He taught Ryan the curveball, and the hurler carved out a decent career because of it. But he was no better than a third starter.

With such an uneven staff, McGraw needed all his wiles. His use of Claude Jonnard was an example. Jonnard was blind in his right eye but effective in short doses. McGraw used him as one of the game's first relief specialists. Although the "save" statistic had yet to be invented, a retroactive count has Jonnard leading the majors in saves in 1922, and he would again in 1923. He didn't have much competition—Connie Mack was the only other manager creative enough to see the opportunities in using a pitcher specifically to close out games. There was also a cultural element. In 1923, stamina was considered a moral quality in pitchers. The ability to go nine (or more) innings revealed the essence of the man, regardless of the quality of the pitching itself. McGraw's reputation was enough to overcome this stigma: if he said you were coming out and Jonnard was coming in, it meant nothing about your manhood—you were merely following orders.

Even with Jonnard, the Giants pitching staff had become the weak spot of the team. The unit had come up huge in the World Series the past two seasons, but could they stand up to another full pennant race?

Fortunately for McGraw, his team was certain to hit its way into contention, and catch just about anything hit at them. The "$100,000 infield" included three future Hall of Famers: Kelly at first; the "Fordham Flash," Frankie Frisch, at second; and Dave Bancroft at short. Heinie Groh, the hero of the Fall Classic, was the third baseman. He used a bizarrely shaped bottle bat, one with an enormous barrel and a sliver of a handle. Groh had gone to Spalding headquarters in Chicago and in the basement whittled a bat himself. "When we were finished it looked like a crazy sort of milk bottle or a round paddle—real wide at one end and tapering real quick to a thin handle," Groh told Lawrence Ritter years later.

A rival player named Ivey Wingo once said, "There are two types of catchers—those who think on their own, and those who wear the uniform of the Giants." McGraw's penchant for calling pitches meant the New York catchers were able to concentrate on hitting. The starter was Frank Snyder, who hit .343 in 1922. His backup was Smith.

The left fielder was the other half of New York's aforementioned sibling sensations, Emil "Irish" Meusel, Bob's older brother. McGraw had brought him to New York from the Phillies in part because he thought the warring-brothers concept might be good for some extra box office. The Meusels were German, not Irish, but a sportswriter in Philly had taken note of Emil's ruddy features and ebullient manner and deemed him "Irish," and the nickname stuck. Such was the power of the printed word during the era.

In right field was one of McGraw's favorite players, Ross "Pep" Youngs. The tiny Texan (Pep was a slight 5'8", 162 pounds) was a superb natural athlete, a daring base runner and a feared slap hitter. Of all the 1923 Giants, his style most closely approximated McGraw's during his Orioles days.

Center field was home to McGraw's experimental platoon system.

Bill Cunningham and rookie Jimmy O'Connell, a pair of Californians, shared the position with a former cabdriver from Kansas City named Charles Dillon Stengel. Casey, as everyone called him (thanks to his hometown), had come to the Giants in 1921 as a classic McGraw pickup, a savvy, prickly vet who knew the game and played it the John J. Way.

True, Stengel was a bit... *off.* In the Kentucky Bluegrass League, where he got his start, Stengel would trot in from the outfield and slide into the dugout. There was an insane asylum beyond the outfield fence, and his manager used to tap his own head, point out past the wall, and tell Stengel, "For you to wind up there is only a matter of time." McGraw didn't mind — on the contrary, he wanted someone to shake up the lethargy that sometimes set in on a winning team. "This is too dead a ball club," he said when acquiring Stengel. "I'd rather have someone with a little life — somebody that does things a little out of the way."

Stengel had come to New York in time for the 1921 Series and was granted a full share of more than $5,000 even though he didn't play in a game that October. "I made more money sitting with the Giants than I ever made standing with anybody else," he said. In 1922 McGraw used Stengel to perfection, giving him 250 at bats, mostly against right-handed pitching, and Casey repaid his manager by hitting .368. By '23, Stengel was thirty-two, with a weak arm, not much speed left, and a profound inability to hit left-handed pitching. But he was still smart. McGraw used him as a defensive replacement at all three outfield spots, due to Stengel's mastery of playing the sun field. Casey excelled at the fine art of tilting the peak of his cap and leaning over to spot the ball. McGraw, ever the stickler for fine details, was over the moon, even if that particular skill was about to become moot — that summer, former Pirates great Fred Clarke patented the first flip-down sunglasses for use in the sun field. "It's fit for autoists too," said Clarke.

One steamy spring afternoon in San Antonio, McGraw sidled up to Stengel. "I'm taking an interest in you," the manager said bluntly. "Would you like to be a coach on this club in later days?" The surprised Stengel mumbled, "Sure," and wound up coaching the Giants B team that spring. The man who would later be deemed the "Old Perfessor" learned his trade at McGraw's side. He would play only seventy-five games in 1923 and would spend the rest of the season apprenticing under the master.

Of course, had John J. known that Casey would use his tutelage to lead the hated Yankees to a spate of titles beginning in 1949, he'd have had Stengel shipped out of town on the next train. Casey would put to use McGraw tactics such as dedicated relief pitchers, using the full roster, and, most notably, employing the platoon system in which Stengel was himself a pioneer. Stengel paid close attention during the season, earning a PhD in managing.

McGraw didn't like his players, even his best ones, to rest on their laurels, so he brought in a host of youngsters to push veterans at several positions. Two other notable buys in the winter of 1923, in addition to Jack Bentley, were Travis Jackson and Jimmy O'Connell. O'Connell, a gangly, friendly kid with dirty-blond hair and a uniform to match, cost McGraw $75,000 and got time in center field. O'Connell's career ended almost before it got started—in 1924, he was implicated in a bribing scandal and banned from the game for life by Judge Landis. In the spring of '23, however, he was a sensation, smashing line drives all over the place. McGraw gave him little advice, save to say, "I paid seventy-five thousand for you, but I don't expect you to give it back to me in base hits your first week, your first month, or even your first year.... If you get off to a slow start, don't worry."

Travis Jackson was a more interesting case. He was given little chance to compete at shortstop, where team captain Dave Bancroft held sway. Fans in Little Rock, where Jackson had played the year before, agreed. Jackson was an atrocious fielder, committing a whopping seventy-three errors in 1922. "A lot of those were double errors—two on the same play, a boot and a wild throw," Jackson

The Yankee Stadium, April 18, 1923. (National Baseball Hall of Fame Library, Cooperstown, New York)

Before the House That Ruth Built was constructed on City Plot 2106, Lot 100, a lumber mill belonging to the estate of William Waldorf Astor occupied the site. (National Baseball Hall of Fame Library, Cooperstown, New York)

The construction of the Yankee Stadium was held up by suspicious bureaucratic delays, but the actual building was completed in only 284 days. Note the sign marking the future site of second base amid the chaos. (National Baseball Hall of Fame Library, Cooperstown, New York)

The Yankee Stadium a few days before opening day. While the Stadium's vertical size captured most of the press notice, the vastness of its horizontal planes are equally impressive. At its deepest point, the fence is five hundred feet from home plate. (Diamond Images / Getty Images)

The Yankee Stadium was built in close proximity to the Polo Grounds. The bridge on the left over the Harlem River is the Macombs Dam Bridge. The Giants, at McGraw's insistence, changed at the Polo Grounds and crossed the Macombs Dam Bridge in full uniform rather than dress at the Yankee Stadium. (National Baseball Hall of Fame Library, Cooperstown, New York)

Ruth ponders his miserable season during his annus horribilis of 1922.
(Transcendental Graphics / theruckerarchive.com)

McGraw and Ruth shake hands through gritted teeth before hostilities begin at the 1922 World Series. McGraw would humiliate Ruth during the Giants' sweep, calling pitches that held the Babe to a .118 average.
(© Corbis Images)

Ruth is feted at an Elks Club dinner for the New York sportswriters. The night's theme is the "Rural Life"—note the cow. Later in the evening, the Babe would be reduced to tears by a shaming speech from Jimmy Walker, future mayor of New York City. (Transcendental Graphics / theruckerarchive .com)

Home Plate, Babe Ruth's farm in Sudbury, Massachusetts, where Ruth spent the winter of 1922–23, far away from New York and his October failure. (National Baseball Hall of Fame Library, Cooperstown, New York)

While Ruth's workout regimen in Sudbury may have been for the benefit of the media, exercises such as chopping wood and carrying cut logs through heavy snow couldn't have hurt, even if done only occasionally. (Library of Congress)

Ruth leads his team out onto the Yankee Stadium field for the first time, April 18, 1923. (AP / Wide World Photos)

Red Sox manager Frank Chance raises the American flag over the new Yankee Stadium. Moments later, Yankees manager Miller Huggins would raise the 1922 pennant on the same pole. (National Baseball Hall of Fame Library, Cooperstown, New York)

Yankees co-owners and bitter rivals Jacob Ruppert and
Tillinghast L'Hommedieu
"Cap" Huston flank
Commissioner of Baseball
Kenesaw Mountain Landis
before the first game at the
Yankee Stadium. It was one
of the rare occasions when
a photographer caught Huston without his hallmark
derby hat. (National Baseball Hall of Fame Library,
Cooperstown, New York)

The Yankee Stadium grandstand and left-field bleachers are packed on
opening day. Note the grassy hill in the foreground, a hazard that the outfielders had to negotiate. (National Baseball Hall of Fame Library, Cooperstown, New York)

remembered. "The people in the first base stands and right field bleachers knew me. When the ball was hit to me they scattered. 'Watch out! He's got it again!'"

Jackson had been involved in a frightening collision late in the season, slamming into center fielder Elmer Leifer with such force while chasing a pop fly that Jackson fractured his skull and Leifer lost his left eye from the damage. A dented shortstop who couldn't field would hardly seem to be a candidate for a spot with the two-time champs, but McGraw saw something special in the shy, skinny Jackson. His manager at Little Rock was Kid Elberfeld, one of many of McGraw's cronies now spread across the country, working in baseball. Elberfeld felt that Jackson had the raw elements to make an excellent player: he was fast, smart, and one of the best bunters Elberfeld had ever seen. That appealed to McGraw—here was a prototype for his scientific style. If he could only be taught to catch the damn ball.

McGraw with a mission was a McGraw full of pep and vinegar. Every day in San Antonio he was on the field in uniform, and he was everywhere—slapping thousands of grounders to his infielders, hitting fungoes to the outfielders, demonstrating techniques to his pitchers. He gave extra-special attention to Jackson, essentially teaching him to play shortstop from the ground up. He hit grounder after grounder to Jackson, correcting the tiniest details in the youngster's form. By the time the team broke camp, McGraw could see the glimmerings of what would become Jackson's Hall of Fame career.

Even though his club had achieved the pinnacle of success over the last two seasons, McGraw attacked the spring as though he had taken over a last-place team. Despite his advancing age and burgeoning waistline, he was the first on the field and the last to leave every day. He drilled his team relentlessly into tip-top condition, in stark contrast to the Yankees, who were sluggish, the players mostly left to their own devices. The *Daily News* noticed the difference: "The systems are quite the antithesis of each other. Watching this year to see which produces the better results will be...interesting."

April

12

THE GIANTS BEGAN April by playing in a ten-game exhibition series across the south with the Chicago White Sox, much as the Yankees and Dodgers were doing. McGraw, still enjoying the buzz from training camp, celebrated his fiftieth birthday on April 7 in Memphis, blowing the roof off several Beale Street establishments during the merriment. This was hardly unusual for the hard-partying McGraw, whose position in the social whirl of New York belied his reputation as baseball's Richelieu.

Before the Sultan of Swat arrived, the undisputed prince of the city was John McGraw. "John McGraw *is* baseball," proclaimed *The New Yorker.* "In his personality he reflects everything there is of the street kid, up to the ponderous and precious Babe Ruth." "Jawn J." was what everyone called him, Lawd of Noo Yawk. New Yorkers have always enjoyed a pugnacious, take-no-prisoners mentality, and that was McGraw, a man whose "very walk across the field in a hostile town was a challenge to the multitude."

Yet his fiery personality was offset by generosity away from the park. He was an inveterate check-grabber and cultivated a penchant for entertaining stories and evenings out. There was always a crowd around him at dinnertime. In other towns he was reviled but always made a show of going to swank eateries, taking over the back rooms, hiring the best piano player in town, locking the doors, and wining and dining late into the night. He was also a soft touch for old ballplayers, fighters, writers, or gamblers in need of a few bucks. One of his good friends and a coach on his staff, Hans Lobert, said in wonderment, "No one would believe me if I told them how much money he gives away. But, on the level, it's nothing for him to hand out two hundred and three hundred dollars a day. I try to keep a lot of those fellows away from him, but it looks to me as if he goes out of his way to meet them."

This duality proved irresistible to all manner of sportsmen, society types, gamblers, show folk, and politicians. They were drawn to the short, stocky, square-faced manager from Nowheresville who had parlayed a little bit of talent and a lot of will into the greatest gig in town. A first-generation American, he shook the upper-class gentry out of their civility, made them admire his endless struggle for victory. As much as anyone in early-twentieth-century New York, McGraw brought the classes together through the sheer force of his personality. Al Jolson, Ethel and Lionel Barrymore, George M. Cohan, Sam Shubert, Oscar Hammerstein, "Gentleman" Jim Corbett—all were huge Giants fans. McGraw and his team were the toast of the town.

"The only popularity I know is to win," McGraw once said, and in his achieving the latter, the former became self-fulfilling. The Giants *were* New York to the rest of the nation. "It's great to be young and a Giant" were the immortal words of Larry Doyle, a star second baseman for McGraw in the heyday of the Giants dominance. McGraw was the center of gravity, the brilliant sun around which all of New York sports revolved (a fact Doyle, the team captain and loyal *kohai* to McGraw's sensei, discovered the hard way: he was traded the instant McGraw found someone better).

The manager was very well-off by the standard of the day. For most of his career, he was the highest-paid figure in baseball, and it took a long time for even Ruth to catch up (in 1923 McGraw would make $65,000, not including stock dividends from his roughly 25 percent share of the Giants. The Babe got $52,000). McGraw dressed the part of the important New Yorker, wearing custom-made shoes and shirts from Havana, and suits tailored to his unusually short arms. He often journeyed abroad with his good friend, the great pitcher Christy Mathewson. The two embarked on a grand tour of the globe after the 1913 season, returning to the States on the *Lusitania* fifteen months before she was sunk by a German U-boat.

But McGraw wasn't about to become a swell. He loved boxing and was a fine judge of fistic talent. Even more than the Sweet Science, McGraw loved the ponies. An inveterate gambler, he bought into a racetrack in Cuba, and decamped from New York City as often as possible for Belmont Park. The Yankees batboy in 1923, John Horgan, who had served the Giants in the same capacity for the previous three years, remembered his time with McGraw: "My principal duty was to find out who won what race. I ran back and forth to the clubhouse. If his horse won, I would wave a white sweatshirt. If he lost, I would wave a red sweatshirt McGraw kept for just that purpose." John J. was ejected from more games than any other manager in history until his record was broken by Bobby Cox in the twenty-first century, and many times McGraw got himself tossed merely so he could get to the track.

Gambling was never far from McGraw's mind. Back in Baltimore he and Wilbert Robinson had opened a gaming house, the Diamond Café, to augment their baseball income, popularizing and possibly inventing duckpin bowling in the process. When McGraw came to New York, billiards drew him in.

He was a hustler too, besting pigeons in checkers, cards, and drinking contests. He once hustled a few marks out of $2,300 in Hot Springs by pitching silver dollars into a basket in a hotel lobby. One enraged loser called the cops, who arrested McGraw.

Somehow there were no consequences when he won $400 by betting on his Giants to win the 1905 World Series. His motto was "Never tip off a sucker," and he lived up to that adage both on the field and off.

The two worlds he inhabited, the genteel and the seedy, sometimes collided violently. McGraw belonged to several supper clubs, including the Lambs Club, a theatrical hangout turned upscale drinking establishment thanks to Prohibition, where McGraw palled around with the likes of actor John Slavin and songwriter George M. Cohan. One sultry August night in 1920, McGraw brawled in the grillroom of the Lambs with renowned actor William Boyd, who whacked the manager over the head with a water carafe. Later that evening, McGraw and Slavin took a cab uptown to McGraw's apartment at 109th and Broadway. What happened on the street well after midnight isn't known, but Slavin was found unconscious with a broken jaw, and when police arrived at Jawn J.'s door to interview him, the manager had a shiner over one eye and multiple cuts on his face.

The cops found a bottle of whiskey in McGraw's apartment, so they hauled him in for violating Prohibition. The manager's friend and prominent lawyer William "the Great Mouthpiece" Fallon defended McGraw at trial and won easily, thanks to stirring testimony from McGraw, who hobbled to the courthouse on crutches, having twisted an ankle at the Polo Grounds. Slavin forgave him the apparent assault, and even Boyd became a friend.

McGraw had remarried back in 1902, shortly before taking over the Giants. His second wife, Blanche Sindall, would remain loyally at McGraw's side until his death, traveling with him and accompanying him on his forays into the city's nightlife. McGraw spent a good deal of disposable income on the missus, showering her with expensive jewelry and perfumes. Unlike her husband, Blanche could drive, but generally the couple was chauffeured from hot spot to hot spot.

Sportswriters were constant companions, and they pumped up

McGraw's image on and off the diamond. His foremost champion in the press was a man named Bozeman Bulger, who wrote for the *New York Evening World* and the *Saturday Evening Post*. Bulger was the clown prince of Gotham sportswriters, playing practical jokes in the press box and keeping up a witty prattle throughout games—often to the detriment of his focus on the contest itself. Once, while designated the official scorer, Bulger noticed he was a hit short in the box score. He arbitrarily assigned the hit to Doyle, figuring that "if anybody got it, he did." And Bulger once broke his leg while hook sliding on a waxed floor during a drunken debate with McGraw. The reporter grew close to McGraw and became his Boswell, ghostwriting hundreds of articles as well as an autobiography under the manager's name.

Bulger was hardly alone in McGraw-worship among the typing class. Ring Lardner, who wrote a syndicated sports column, and Joe Vila of the *New York Sun* were writers who loved McGraw and loved Scientific Baseball, and they were only too happy to defend John J. to the end, which often meant lashing out at power players, namely the Babe. But McGraw did have detractors. One longtime baseball writer, Sid Mercer, took Muggsy to task for needlessly intimidating and humiliating a young colleague of Mercer's at the *New York American*. Although McGraw made a rare public apology after Mercer's rebuke, the writer never forgave the manager for it. Still, Grantland Rice spoke for most of his contemporaries when he said in 1920, "John McGraw was without doubt the most picturesque figure in the past twenty-five years of baseball, bar nobody. More than any other man, he came to personify New York—the Big Town."

McGraw may have been ebullient away from the park, but the form of the Giants as they made their way north darkened his mood. The team struggled against the mediocre ChiSox, splitting the first nine games 4–4, with a tie. In Jackson, Mississippi, before the tenth and final game, McGraw reamed out his players, warning them of dire consequences should they lose the game and thus the series to an—*ack*—American League team, and a pretty sorry one at that.

Duly chastened, the Giants went out and destroyed the Sox 9–2 to "win" the ten-game series. The manager, if not the team, was already in midseason form.

13

THE GIANTS ARRIVED at Penn Station by train just after midnight on April 14, 1923, ready to begin the new season. The Yankees pulled in about twenty-two hours later, at around ten o'clock p.m. The day before, Cap Huston had led the New York print media on an official tour of the new Yankee Stadium. To say they were impressed by the new park's size would be an understatement. John Kieran wrote in the *Tribune* that "standing in the back row of the upper stand it looks like a three-day fall into the infield and two weeks' voyage to the center field bleachers." Damon Runyon had a similar take: "The upper tier of the stand juts out over the field like a hanging cliff, with a sharp downward shoot.... It would be a long fall from the top seat to the ground. A man would have time to think over a lot of things."

At one point, Major Birmingham interrupted the tour to tell Huston that someone had accidentally broken two windows in the team office. "I'm not surprised," joshed Til. "I invited some newsmen to meet me there today."

Huston had come a long way in his relationship with the media since he first appeared on the scene in New York in 1915, a virtual unknown, especially in contrast to his well-connected partner, Jacob Ruppert. Only a single photograph of Til was known to exist at the time he bought the club, a dated military portrait that Cap hated. He ducked all attempts to get a shot of him during the negotiations, wishing to remain private. Finally, after much entreaty once the sale went down, he consented. "Take the doggone thing," he grumbled. But Huston warmed very quickly to the life of owning a New York baseball team.

He is a key figure in New York Yankees history, but today he is almost totally forgotten. It would seem unlikely that a man with a name as epic as Tillinghast L'Hommedieu Huston could fall down the memory hole, but indeed Jacob Ruppert's partner for the years 1915–23 is little remembered.

Huston was born in Buffalo on July 17, 1867, making him all of three weeks older than Jacob Ruppert. He was the third of seven children born to his father, Richard, and mother, Mary Elizabeth, a schoolteacher from Kentucky. Like John McGraw's father, Richard Huston emigrated to the United States from Ireland, leaving behind the cruel ministrations of his own Anglican minister–father. Despite his harsh upbringing, Richard apparently couldn't put the old man out of his mind completely—L'Hommedieu, or "Man of God," is a clear homage to his father. Richard was born in 1825, the same year the Erie Canal opened, and when he settled in western New York, the grand simplicity of the nearby canal no doubt influenced his decision to become a civil engineer, concentrating on the growth industry of the day, railroads.

Early in Til's life, the Hustons moved to Cincinnati to be closer to Mary Elizabeth's family across the state line in Kentucky. Til followed in his father's footsteps, studying engineering even though Richard's success in the field was modest at best. The Hustons weren't as destitute as the McGraws, but money was tight enough. Til loved baseball but, due to his portly girth, seldom played.

Til worked alongside his father for several years on the Louisville and Nashville Railroad. Father and son both knew Til possessed the superior mind, and Richard encouraged his boy to strike out and put his brains and energy to use. Til was a hard worker, spending long hours at the office and putting in weekends on odd jobs around Cincinnati. He made friends easily, and his work ethic caught the attention of city officials.

Huston had thus worked his way up to the position of city engineer of Cincinnati in February 1898. When the USS *Maine* exploded and sank under suspicious circumstances in Havana Harbor, Huston was swept up in the call for revenge spurred by the Hearst newspaper syndicate. The Spanish-American War broke out soon after, and Til volunteered. Using his office as a conduit, he recruited engineers from the Midwest and South, creating an engineering regiment essentially by himself. He and the 2nd U.S. Volunteer Engineers shipped out for Cuba in April 1898.

His record in Cuba was extraordinary. His most important feat was the rebuilding and sanitizing of the infamous leper hospital at San Lazaro. The colony was situated at the southern edge of Havana, on a muddy, neglected spit of land. Huston led Company C of the 2nd U.S. Volunteer Engineers to the hospital, where the sick lay in makeshift cots under deplorable conditions, even by leper-colony standards. Most Cubans gave the area a wide berth, believing anyone who ventured there would be stricken.

Huston's men rode up to the hospital early in the morning, and for a long moment there was inaction. It seemed no one wanted to test the Cubans' belief in the strength of the leprosy contagion. Finally Huston dismounted, stripped off his jacket, grabbed a shovel, and began to dig away the muck that surrounded the hospital. Shaken from their stupor, his men joined in. Soon, Company C had completely remade the hospital to modern standards of construction.

Huston never hesitated to touch the lepers that watched his progress. None of his men fell ill.

Til's feat earned him an honor for courageous service and made him one of the most famous men in Cuba. The San Lazaro construction would be a crucial development for Huston—it led directly to the securing of contracts that would make him a very rich man. His next job was to similarly bring up to standard the largest orphanage in Cuba, the Casa de Beneficencia. Once it was complete and gleaming in the Caribbean sun, Huston and his men built sewage-disposal systems all across Cuba until the conflict ended in late 1898. Til attained the rank of Captain, and "Cap" became his peacetime nickname.

Huston was fond of the island and its people, and more important, the hustler in him sensed there was much business at hand. So when most Americans returned home at the cessation of hostilities (in fact, yellow fever had forced the withdrawal of much of the American Expeditionary Force months before), Huston and several of his engineers remained. He was favored within the new Cuban government for his work at San Lazaro and was well liked by the U.S. military command at Guantánamo Bay. Huston parlayed these connections into a rich contract to dredge Havana Harbor. When that huge job was completed successfully, he quickly secured contracts to do similar work in Santiago de Cuba, Matanzas, and Cienfuegos. In addition to harbors, Huston built seawalls, public buildings, private residences, and railroads and wagon trails.

By this point, Til had long since stopped putting on work boots and getting his back into a dig. "Never do anything you can hire someone to do for you" was his new maxim. "It's the one who tells the other fellow what to do who reaps the profits." And the profits came, faster than Huston could spend them. He talked little of money, and there was a certain clandestine nature to some of his Cuban work, but even a conservative estimate put his personal wealth in the multiple millions.

Til spent a decade and a half in Cuba and became a regular at posh spots such as the Havana Country Club, as well as at the gaming tables around town. He passed a good deal of time playing faro and roulette with another inveterate gambler: John J. McGraw. The two first met in New York in 1911, when Huston traveled to see McGraw's Giants compete in the World Series. McGraw returned the visit, coming to Cuba later in the year, and the pair became fast friends. The manager recognized in Til something of his own battling persona, and for Huston, McGraw provided a connection to the game and country he missed. It wasn't long before Til started asking McGraw about buying a major-league team.

Back in New York, the manager happened to have a baseball-crazy rich man constantly pestering him about purchasing the Giants—Jacob Ruppert. McGraw, ever the sharp middleman, brought his two friends together to buy the city's American League franchise, a team that had been officially called the "Yankees" for only two seasons when Ruppert and Huston bought it. Before then, they were the New York Americans, popularly known as the Hilltoppers—a reference to Hilltop Park, the team's home. Situated on Broadway in Washington Heights, between 165th and 168th Streets (the current site of the Columbia-Presbyterian Medical Center), the upper Manhattan locale engendered the franchise's other nickname, the Highlanders. (The fact that the team president was a man named Joseph Gordon enabled the press to partake in some wordplay, riffing off the fabled Gordon Highlanders Regiment of the British Army.)

The Hilltoppers played deep in the shadow of the Giants. That changed somewhat on April 11, 1911, when a massive fire burned the mounds of peanut shells under the bleachers at the Polo Grounds. The conflagration destroyed the ballpark, leaving the Giants with little option but to rent Hilltop Park. Suddenly the hugely popular Men of McGraw were sharing space with the stepsister ball club from the juvenile American League.

Then–Giants owner John T. Brush rebuilt the Polo Grounds with concrete and steel, and the team returned to 155th and Eighth in late June. And at the end of the 1912 season, Brush was in a position to return the favor. The Highlanders' lease at Hilltop Park expired, and the team moved into the Giants' home, paying rent every month to Brush and McGraw.

The press occasionally used the term "Yankees" to represent these American Leaguers, mainly to describe their trips north from spring training in the south (the first appearance came in the *New York Evening Journal* in 1904), and the nickname was printed on some baseball cards in 1911. Now, with the team no longer at Hilltop Park or particularly high up on Manhattan Island, the New York Yankees were officially born.

The move to the more spacious Polo Grounds did little to improve the team's fortunes on the field. The owners, Frank Farrell and William Devery, were former bartenders who used corrupt connections in Tammany Hall and the police department to punch above their weight and become owners of a baseball team. They were usually broke, thanks to tastes for liquor, (slow) horses, and prostitutes, and forever on the verge of indictment for one dubious scheme after another. They were convinced to sell the team by Ban Johnson, who wanted more from his league's entry in the nation's flagship city.

Huston and Ruppert met for the first time at Claridge's restaurant in June 1914. John J. sent along a mutual friend named William Fleischmann to get the conversation started. Huston and Ruppert swiftly bonded over their mutual love of the game and agreed to a partnership that would protect their wealth should the venture take a turn for the worse.

Huston and his family moved to New York, into what the press called a "magnificent home" on Riverside Drive, and decorated it with as many reminders of Cuba as he could (he also kept a home in Havana). Til was married to Lena Belle Gladhart, a Kansan who met Huston when she came to Cincinnati to visit relatives in 1890. She was content to stay home in Ohio while her adventurous husband made his fortune. Mama Lena, as everyone called her, lost two children in infancy, and although the Hustons had three healthy children, two girls and a boy, the tragic losses haunted her thereafter. The heartbreak did serve to further bond Til to McGraw, who knew something about untimely deaths in the family.

There was one other thing Huston and Ruppert agreed on that night: neither was interested in the Yankees. The AL franchise was too small-time, and the league itself too nouveau to be considered by gentlemen such as themselves. Certainly the Junior Circuit was gaining ground, and perhaps sharper men would have taken note of the fact that AL teams had won six of the ten World Series played by the summer of 1914. And many of the game's best players, including Ty Cobb, Tris Speaker, and Nap Lajoie, were American Leaguers. But the AL had existed only a little more than a decade at this point, and Ruppert in particular embraced the stability and peerage of the NL. And, more important, both Ruppert and Huston were enamored of John J. McGraw. McGraw and the Giants *were* baseball, and his two friends wanted to compete with him, not simply rent the Polo Grounds from him.

But John J. went to work on them. He flattered the rich men, convincing them that the Yanks were a slumbering behemoth, merely requiring the time-honored pillars of money and baseball acumen to build them into something grand. "I am sure you are just the men to go ahead and get the necessary material," trilled McGraw. They might never become the Giants, mind you, but the franchise would be worth the time and effort of two titans such as Til and Jake. To a point, McGraw wanted the Yankees to be successful, especially if they could capture the pennant and set up a boffo InterCity Series. But he doubted this could be accomplished in short order, and even if it could, in his mind his Giants would have little to fear. After all, who would compete with the classy winners McGraw managed? It is also unproven but long rumored that McGraw took a cut of the sale price. After all, he was the middleman, putting together a deal using his contacts and savvy. A businessman of McGraw's ilk would have demanded to dip his snout.

The entire act was vintage McGraw. The ultimate control freak couldn't abide the idea that an unknown entity would take over the Yankees. Telling Huston and Ruppert that the Yanks had great potential wasn't just propaganda—John J. had to know that any team in New York with serious money behind it would be a force. Installing friends in the owners' box, men who owed their presence in the game to McGraw, seemed like a shrewd maneuver typical of the Little Napoleon. Unfortunately he couldn't foresee the changes coming just over the horizon and the monster he was about to unleash.

McGraw's whispering worked, and in the back half of 1914, Ruppert and Huston negotiated with Farrell and Devery for the sale of the team. Ban Johnson, eager to get a flagship franchise going for his American League, sat in and tried to goose matters along. There were two sticking points: beer and ballplayers.

A crucial component of this deal was the prospect of thousands of captive customers to whom Ruppert could sell Knickerbocker Beer. Ruppert always viewed owning a baseball team as a natural extension of his core business. The colonel was far ahead of his time when it came to recognizing the synergy between beer and baseball. Trouble was, another foresighted man named Harry Stevens had locked up catering at the Polo Grounds. Stevens invented stadium concessions as a business and held a ten-year contract. Despite repeated attempts, Ruppert could find no way to evict Stevens. So Ruppert decided to build his own stadium one day, where the Jacob Ruppert Brewery would hold sway.

Huston was more concerned with the Yankees roster. The 1914 team was a collection of mediocrities, names like Boardwalk Brown, Birdie Cree, and Lute Boone, forgotten to history. Only the short-stop, a young player named Roger Peckinpaugh, was anything but replaceable. Indeed, Peckinpaugh, at the age of twenty-three, had actually taken over the club as player-manager for the final twenty games of 1914.

Huston and Ruppert insisted on an upgrade if they were to invest in the team. Johnson, never above manipulating matters to his best advantage, agreed—he had a stake in the success of a New York team too. But working out exactly who would become a Yankee under the Huston-Ruppert ownership took months to decide, far longer than anyone had hoped. "What in the world could four men [including Farrell] find in the Yankees to talk about all day long?" asked the *Times*. It didn't help that Ruppert periodically left, unannounced, for vacations in the resort town of French Lick, Indiana, leaving negotiations at a standstill.

Finally a deal was struck in the early days of 1915. Five players would be moved from Rochester, including a powerful first baseman named Wally Pipp. And Huston and Ruppert would pay $450,000 to become the new owners of the New York Yankees. The team was, in Ruppert's own words, "an orphan ball club, without a home of its own, without players of outstanding ability, without prestige."

That had changed dramatically in eight short years. Now, another milestone approached: the opening of the new Stadium that Ruppert had dreamed of. There was still work to be done on various parts of the superstructure, mainly in the team offices, but the Stadium was ready for action. The project had amazingly come together in only eleven months, despite the holdups and financial agita. Even with all the change orders and delays, actual construction took only 284 days, an astoundingly short slice of time. Cutting through the red tape surrounding the street closings had taken longer than erecting the entire Stadium. The $1.1 million construction budget was exceeded by $126,000, according to tax returns. The final cost to Ruppert and Huston, including the land and various other outlays, was $2,196,888.54. Office equipment, legal fees, and other quasi-related expenses ran the cost up to nearly $2.5 million.

After his tour, Huston held a box of polish while Ruppert ceremoniously applied the last dollop on the brass doorknobs of the main Stadium entrance. Tickets for opening day were due to go on sale April 11 at the team offices at 226 42nd Street, at the nearby Winchester sporting-goods store on 42nd near Madison, and at the Spalding store downtown at 126 Nassau Street. But a huge influx of checks and money orders to cover ticket costs had slowed the team's accounts department to a crawl, necessitating a one-day delay.

Meanwhile, the players who would call the new palace home played a final tune-up game on the fifteenth, a couple of boroughs over at Ebbets Field in Brooklyn. Ruth, his spring trial now well behind him, was phenomenal. Joe Vila had barbecued the Babe in the *Sun* the morning before the game, writing, "Ruth...is no longer a wonder. The baseball public is on to his real worth as a batsman and in the future, let us hope, he will attract just ordinary attention." Ruth showed Vila his vision of the future. Despite the biting cold and a steady rain, the Babe singled, walked twice, scored all three times he was aboard, made a sensational running catch on a line drive, and drew loud cheers when he executed a perfect hook slide into third base.

Those cheers were dwarfed by the roar following his heroics on opening day at the new Yankee Stadium three days later.

14

FORTUNATELY FOR JOHN McGraw's bile duct, the Giants were out of town while the Babe was christening the new Yankee Stadium in such style. The team was in Boston, having opened their season the day before against the Braves, on a "sharply cold" afternoon in front of eighteen thousand. The pregame festivities had a distinctly military bearing. Several top brass were in attendance, and the marines and army performed a mock drill and advance under smoke screen, mimicking the infantry charges they had done under far different circumstances in Germany and France. McGraw made for an interesting doughboy as he attempted to keep the cadence while marching behind the troops.

Governor Channing Cox threw out the first pitch from the mound, not his box, which was the general custom. And he tossed it not to a player but to Mayor James Curley, who crouched behind the plate in his three-piece suit. The "umpire" in this strange threesome was none other than Commissioner Landis, his shock of white hair giving away his identity, although he wore an umpire's mask. He called the pitch a strike.

The Giants eased past the "Codfish Clan," as the Braves were mysteriously called, 4–1, behind Hugh McQuillan, who tossed a four-hitter. They won the next day too, and the next. Then they went to Brooklyn and pummeled the Robins. Casey Stengel won a game with a ninth-inning hit, and Frankie Frisch had three safeties (two of them infield hits) and stole a pair of bases in a clinical display of Scientific Baseball in the fourth game of the set. In all, New York won seven of eight to start the season, all on the road, before coming home to open the Polo Grounds on April 26.

When Charles Stoneham truly understood the scope of the new park that the Yankees were building, he heard the bell tolling. Almost instantly he announced plans to expand the Giants field to hold 54,000 fans. The outfield bleachers were given the wrecking ball, and the double-decked grandstand was extended across most of the field. It then veered directly back, giving the grounds much more of a football-field look. Some noted its resemblance to a bathtub.

The extension of the second deck allowed for even easier home runs straight down the lines, with the overhang swallowing pop flies that might otherwise settle into fielders' gloves. But at the same time the work caused the distances in the power alleys to become even more extreme. Dead center field was now an enormous expanse, the fence measuring 483 feet from home plate. The Giants spun the expansion as an anti-Ruth maneuver, saying they wanted to encourage more inside-the-park home runs, "the most exciting play in baseball." *Sure,* McGraw seemed to be saying, *Ruth can hit them out, but that's boring! Speeding around the bases and sliding under the relay throw is more exciting.* The Babe took a look at the new dimensions and decreed he could still reach the fences.

A new clubhouse was built over old standing-room bleachers in center field. The clubhouse was farther from the dugouts than it had been, so the players had farther to walk after painful losses. One aspect remained unchanged: the Eddie Grant Memorial, dedicated to an infantryman and former Giants infielder killed in the Argonne Forest in 1918, was still in play at the base of the clubhouse wall.

Next to Grant's memorial had been a green curtain used as a hitter's background by the Giants and Yankees. The home team had raised it only when up at bat, then lowered it so as not to give the same advantage to enemy batsmen. That wouldn't come into play in 1923—Judge Landis outlawed the curtain after the 1922 World Series.

Construction wasn't finished in time for the first home stand of 1923 (a doubling of the workforce ensured the park was completed for the Giants' return to Manhattan in May). The area under the clubhouse structure in center field was just a vast chasm (and in play). Workers toiled away on the grandstands right through the eight games against Boston, Brooklyn, and Philadelphia. Perhaps distracted by the clamor, New York lost four of eight.

The Giants won the home opener, though—7–3 over the Braves. A recovered Mayor Hylan threw out the first pitch. The stands held thirty thousand fans, not even half the crowd that appeared in the Bronx for opening day. They gave Christy Mathewson, New York's fabled pitcher and future Hall of Famer, and now the Braves manager, the biggest ovation of anyone, even McGraw. And then the Giants were issued their 1922 World Championship rings, massive gold affairs with a ball diamond for a seal and a diamond inset.

Art Nehf allowed one hit, and the Giants exploded for six runs in the eighth. The team flashed some leather as well—Highpockets Kelly tied his own record with twenty-one putouts for the game. The two-time defending champs were 9–1 and clearly had picked up where they left off after whipping the Yankees in the 1922 Fall Classic.

While the '22 Series represented Babe Ruth's nadir, it was John J. McGraw's greatest triumph. The 1922 Giants had a balanced lineup and were defending champs, but they seemed to rely mainly on the wits of their manager, who couldn't hit or pitch. John J. sure had the book on the Babe, though. In the 1921 Series, Giants pitchers had whiffed Ruth eight times in twenty-one trips to the plate. McGraw felt that he had nothing to fear from the Mighty Monkey. He would call every pitch from the dugout, and provided his guys executed his orders to perfection, there was no way the Giants could lose.

McGraw had studied the Babe carefully during a ten-game exhibition series between the Giants and the Yankees played before the 1920 season. As the teams made their way north, McGraw felt he had spotted a weakness, even as Ruth was swatting tremendous home runs in towns across the south and mid-Atlantic. Slow curves and even slower change-of-pace pitches stymied the free-swinging, heavy-club-wielding Cro-Magnon. Instead of challenging his opponent's manhood, McGraw would use Ruth's forcefulness against him in a sort of hardball jujitsu.

That was one half of the plan. The other was a psychological-warfare campaign aimed at deflating Ruth's aura of invincibility. As McGraw's hurlers delivered, the manager would scream from the dugout, "Lay it over for him! He can't hit it even if you tell him what's coming!" The taunts doubled after every swing and miss. "Why in hell should Ruth worry me?" John J. wondered before the 1922 Series. "Why all this excitement about him?"

Despite McGraw's confidence, most betting favored the Yankees, 7–5, on consensus. But it was the Giants who drew first blood, scoring three eighth-inning runs to win the opener 3–2. Game Two was one of the more bizarre afternoons in New York baseball history.

Lord Louis Mountbatten was among those at the Polo Grounds that afternoon, and he hit the concessions as though he'd been at sea for months, consuming six ice-cream cones, two bags of peanuts, and four soda pops while "rooting for Babe Ruth until he was hoarse." He saw a game that ended in controversy. At 4:43 p.m., with the score tied at three after ten innings, umpire George Hildebrand mysteriously called the game on account of darkness, although there was still a good forty-five minutes of daylight left. It was a tie. The rules of the day said there would be no replay—the day's proceedings had been for naught.

The players were astonished, but most laughed off the inconvenience of having wasted the afternoon. "It was crazy," recalled Jumpin' Joe Dugan. "The people were milling around, yelling. They were mad at everybody. They could have played another inning or two anyway. It was broad daylight." The fans went bananas. Most blamed Landis, who sat glumly in his box, dumbfounded. Several thousand surrounded him, yelling, "Fake!" One fan shouted, "Barnum was right, and we're the suckers." It was an ironic turn of events—the man baseball had looked to in its darkest hour to tidy its sullied name was now being accused of cheating the game for money, just as the Black Sox had done.

"My goodness, Judge, but they are giving you the bird," noted Mountbatten, who sat nearby. The police attempted to escort Landis out, but he refused. "I'm not afraid of any crowd in New York. I'll make my own way from the field."

Most believed there was a conspiracy afoot to rake in another day of profit at the expense of the fans. The court of public opinion forced Landis to order the dispersal of the day's take to various charities. Behind closed doors, he gave Hildebrand the reaming of a lifetime for prematurely calling the game.

Game Three occasioned a signature triumph for McGraw. Starting pitcher Jack Scott had been out of baseball after a miserable, injury-plagued 1921—the Reds had released him. He went home to North Carolina, where his uninsured tobacco farm promptly burned to the ground. With no crop to harvest, Scott began throwing again, and at midseason felt strong enough to return. With his last bit of savings, he came to New York and told McGraw he wanted back into baseball. Intrigued, McGraw stashed Scott in the city, loaned him some walking-around money, and let him pitch himself into game shape. Then he unleashed his new weapon on the NL. Scott won eight of ten decisions down the stretch and was a key reason the Giants won the flag. He shut out the Yankees 3–0 on four hits, culminating in Ruth's aggrieved visit to the Giants clubhouse.

After the clarification from the Babe, the Giants knew exactly which insults were kosher. And after Game Four—another Giants victory, another Ruth failure—the Babe was hearing it from all sides. A four-run fifth put the Giants ahead. Ruth had another hitless afternoon. In the eighth, a moment of truth appeared—4–3 Giants, the Babe up, tying run on second. The jawing from the Giants and the crowd was deafening. An intentional walk to the game's greatest slugger appeared mandatory, but it never crossed McGraw's mind. He knew he had Ruth flummoxed. The hurler, McQuillan, delivered changeups and big round curves, and on the fifth pitch, Ruth swung hugely and popped out. The Yanks never threatened again and trailed 3–0 in the Series.

Game Five was played despite intermittent rain. "This series wins the brown derby," mused one older fan. "First they call a game in broad daylight and then they play another in a cloudburst." The tenants of the Polo Grounds led their landlords 3–2 in the eighth in Game Five, desperately trying to avoid a humiliating sweep. No thanks to Ruth, who was hitless again, striking out in the fourth, tapping back to the pitcher in the sixth, and—*yes*—even sacrifice bunting in the first.

In the Giants' half of the eighth, with two out and runners on second and third, Pep Youngs faced Bullet Joe Bush. The Giants star was dangerous, but Bush felt as though he could get him out. Then Miller Huggins yelled from the dugout to intentionally walk Youngs. Bush, no fan of the manager, shouted back, "What for, you stupid oaf?" and threw a strike. Huggins repeated the order, with some flowery language attached. Bush obeyed this time and added a colorful retort to his manager.

George "Highpockets" Kelly came up with the bases loaded and ruined Hug's strategy with a rap to left to put the Giants ahead for good. The pitch was a medium-speed fastball, and to his dying day, Hug felt Bush allowed Kelly to get the winning hit to show up his manager, especially as the Series was as good as lost anyway.

The Giants were champs again, and their manager reaped the credit. "I signaled every pitch to Ruth," crowed McGraw. "In fact, I gave the sign for practically every ball our pitchers threw. They wanted it that way. You could see [our catchers] turn and look at me on the bench before signaling the pitcher. We pitched only nine curves and three fastballs to Ruth during the entire Series. The rest were slowballs [changeups], and of twelve of those, eleven set him on his backside." McGraw had a "book" on attacking the Yanks hitters that was published in the press months later. The line for Ruth read "low on the inside, nothing fast." McGraw had stuck with the plan, and his pitchers had made no mistakes.

After the final out of Game Five, adoring fans rushed onto the field of the Polo Grounds, trying to get a piece of the genius manager. McGraw emerged from the dugout to have his hat knocked off, his back pounded, and his cheek kissed by Giants rooters.

There was a huge clot of celebratory fans outside the gates on Eighth Avenue, waiting for the winners. McGraw came out to a deafening ovation, after which he thanked the crowd. One elderly woman managed to push her way through the crowd to McGraw, and the manager shook her bony hand with a smile. "I can go home now," she told a reporter from the *Times*. "I've seen the greatest manager in baseball."

The nation's sporting press was as awestruck as the old woman. "Behind these latest triumphs of the Giants the directing genius of John McGraw shone more brilliantly than ever before," opined the *Times*. "There is none to dispute his right to the title of greatest manager in baseball history. His record stands alone and unchallenged. He is the outstanding figure among all the managers in the history of the game."

The *Sporting News* wrote: "We yield to none in acknowledging the Napoleonic qualities of McGraw." A Detroit paper thought, "McGraw came as near to perfection in his strategy as man probably ever will come in baseball." "John Joseph McGraw is sitting on the top of the world," wrote the *Tribune*. "Not even Miller Huggins begrudges him his high estate. The world's championship for the Giants was won by a stout gentleman with a serge suit on the left end of the dugout. He was the best hitter and runner on the team."

McGraw traditionally took a suite of rooms at the Waldorf Astoria Hotel during the World Series. That night, celebrants in his suite partied until dawn. Guests poured in and crammed the adjoining hall. In attendance were gamblers "Diamond Jim" Brady and "Bet-a-Million" Gates (who, despite his nickname, had won only a few thousand on the Series); actress Lillian Russell; the new heavyweight champion of the world, Jack Dempsey; his manager, Jack Kearns; boxer Mickey Walker; and just about every sportswriter in town—Grantland Rice, Damon Runyon, Westbrook Pegler, Frank Graham, Ring Lardner, F. C. Lane, Bozeman Bulger, Heywood Broun, and of course McGraw's champion Joe Vila.

There was no Prohibition at the Waldorf that evening. The rye and scotch flowed. Pegler later wrote that guests emerged "hurtling, bruised and disheveled, like bums out of a barrelhouse." It was one of the greatest nights of John J. McGraw's life.

15

THE IDEA THAT the Yankee Stadium was an instant success is valid. The myth that the Stadium was filled to capacity for every game that first season is not. The very day after the grand opening, only 12,500 fans made the trip to the Bronx, roughly 50,000 fewer than the day before, a figure that gave McGraw and Stoneham a brief glimmer of schadenfreude.

Meanwhile Babe Ruth was discovering that his new house wasn't going to be quite as welcoming as the drama of opening day indicated. In the season's second game, Ruth crushed a drive 475 feet to left-center. It wasn't deep enough to clear the fence in the new Stadium, and Ruth settled for a triple. He also singled and walked twice in an 8–2 romp. The next day, the Babe walloped two shots beyond the track that encircled the field. The first went for three bases; the second for two, but it was the game-winning hit as the Yanks beat Boston again, 4–3. Ruth had hit four balls more than 450 feet and had only one homer to show for them.

The Yanks swept the four-game set, and then Washington came to the Bronx for the first-ever Sunday game held at the Yankee

Stadium. The capacity crowd returned. More than sixty thousand saw the Yanks lose for the first time, 4–3, to the Big Train—Walter Johnson, pitching in the seventeenth season of his storied career. The Yanks were handcuffed on Monday as well, losing to Cy Warmoth, who made only his second start in the bigs. His first came at the end of 1922, when he shut down the Yankees on five hits. This time it was three hits. Unfortunately the lefty had to pitch against the rest of the league, not just New York, and was relegated to the bullpen by June.

So Tuesday, April 24, saw Ruth—who still had hit only the one home run—and the Yankees trying to end a mini-slump against Washington. They would do so in front of a special guest: President Warren G. Harding, a tremendous baseball fan who had attended opening day in Washington during the first two seasons of his administration.

Harding was perhaps the president most steeped in the National Pastime. He had been part owner of a team in Marion, Ohio, his hometown. While there he took a personal interest in developing two star players, Jake Daubert and Wilbur Cooper, both of whom he shepherded to the majors. Upon his election to the highest office in the land in 1920, he returned to Marion for a charity game. He played first base, hit a single, and jammed his finger in two innings of play.

He had welcomed Ruth to the White House on several occasions, the men swapping baseball stories and helping themselves to large quantities of the bootleg liquor the president kept stocked at 1600 Pennsylvania Avenue. He was a massive Senators fan, to the point where sportswriter Thomas Rice wrote that Harding "was the sort that gloomed and did not enjoy his supper at the White House if he had seen the Washington team lose. On the contrary, he felt it was a pretty good world, and things would soon come out all right in Europe or elsewhere, if he had seen the Senators win."

The game was delayed while the presidential limousine and its police escort circled the Yankee Stadium track. Harding chatted with the Babe before the game. The Sultan wasn't exactly a follower of politics, unless you counted his famous line about getting paid more than President Hoover in 1930: "Why not? I had a better year than he did." But he enjoyed Harding's enthusiasm for baseball, and of course his reverence for the Babe.

After meeting with the Big Bam at his box, the president sent for the Big Train. Johnson distinctly remembered the moment years later. "As we shook hands he said, just as informally as possible, 'Well, Walter, I came out to root for Washington,'" recalled Johnson. One might think he'd be more circumspect about his rooting interest in Ruth's house, but then this is the president who once said, "I never saw a game without taking sides and never want to see one. There is the soul of the game."

The president threw out the first pitch from his bunting-bedecked box, bouncing it in front of Joe Dugan. He sat with Postmaster General Harry New, Chicago Cubs co-owner Albert Lasker (later considered the father of modern advertising), and Ruppert. Harding kept score as usual and chain-smoked throughout the contest.

The president was treated to a milestone game, a 4–0 Yankees victory and the first shutout in Stadium history, courtesy of Sad Sam Jones. Sam was actually a rather happy-go-lucky fellow. W. O. McGeehan of the *Times* had coined the nickname because he thought Jones looked melancholy while playing. As quoted in *The Glory of Their Times*, Lawrence Ritter's classic oral history, Jones said this was due to the fact that "I would always wear my cap down real low over my eyes. And the sportswriters were more used to fellows like Waite Hoyt, who'd always wear their caps way up so they wouldn't miss any pretty girls." The pitcher sure looked happy after the last out, slinging catcher Wally Schang over his shoulders and carrying him into center field.

Harding also witnessed something he likely valued far more than a win, Senators fan or not: a Ruth home run. The Babe was in a small slump, having gone hitless over the last three games. Ruth snapped out of it in front of the president, with three hits and three RBI. In the fifth, Ruth crushed a solo homer to right-center, and Harding applauded rapturously.

"If it had been Europe instead of the U.S., you might have thought that the Ruthian drive was by Royal command," reported the *Times*. "It seemed like a prearranged part of the program. . . . The President wanted to see Ruth hit a home run, and Ruth hit one."

Harding congratulated Ruth in the clubhouse after the game and went back to DC, where he continued his tradition of taking in the Sens home openers at Griffith Stadium. Inspired by his presence, Washington beat Philadelphia, 2–1. It was the last game Harding would ever see.

The Yankees finished out the month alternating wins and losses, culminating in a 17–4 bashing of Cleveland. Pipp and Meusel, hitting fourth and fifth behind Ruth, each collected four hits and combined for eleven RBI. Ruth walked three times in the game. A pattern was taking shape. The Babe's batting eye was sharp—he was taking pitches and hitting to all fields and was thus walked early and often. Pipp, Meusel, and Schang, the usual batsmen who hit behind the Babe, were seeing all kinds of fat pitches with at least one man consistently on base. New York trailed Cleveland by 1½ games at the close of April, but the offense was beginning to stir ominously, especially as the hitters began adapting to the Stadium.

Ruth had just the two homers at the close of April, at least in official contests. But in an exhibition game against the Doherty Silk Sox in Paterson, New Jersey, he gave a foreshadowing of the power to come. He slugged a titanic shot some 515 feet, the ball clearing the "bleachers, a sixty-foot street, a barn and two fences," according to the *New York World*. As Ruth rounded the bases, hundreds of kids stormed from the stands and tried to lift him aloft. Despite his winter slimming, the Babe was still too heavy for the children. He clattered to the grass, and his teammates rushed out and cordoned him off with their bats.

May

16

ARTIE NEHF WAS usually death for lefties. He had handled the most feared lefty slugger of them all, the Babe, in two straight World Series wins for the Giants. But on this muggy afternoon of May 4, at the Baker Bowl in north Philadelphia, another big hitter from the port side had just cracked a towering fly ball over the right-field wall, which was a mere 280 feet away from home but towered 60 feet over the field (by contrast, Fenway Park's famous Green Monster is 37 feet tall). The three-run homer broke a 4–4 tie and chased Nehf from the game in the bottom of the second. The "Organist" trudged slowly off the field as he made the walk of shame to an early shower.

The man rounding the bases, Cy Williams, was physically the diametric opposite of Ruth. Cy was rail thin—6'2" and 180 lean pounds. He was built much like his namesake, Ted Williams, the "Splendid Splinter"—a slight sylph of a man. His hairline receded like an ebb tide. His face creased and rumpled with wrinkles and crow's-feet. His teeth were rotting. And his pale skin burned easily. Valentino, Cy was not.

What he was, was the most terrifying slugger of 1923 who didn't play in New York City. Long before opponents began playing Ted Williams to pull the ball to right field using a stratagem called the "Williams Shift"—where the shortstop was positioned between first and second base, and the third baseman in the shortstop's spot— Cy Williams received the same treatment. Cy started to encounter the original "Williams Shift" in the early 1920s, when the new hitting rules, the short right-field fence at Philadelphia's Baker Bowl, and Cy's ferocious line drives combined to make him one of the NL's most feared hitters. "I couldn't hit a ball to left field if my life depended on it," Williams admitted. In 1923, it scarcely mattered. He would power forty-one homers to lead the National League (and match Ruth's AL-leading total) at the age of thirty-six. He had hit forty-four homers in 1921 and '22 combined.

A multisport star at Notre Dame, Cy played on the same football team as Knute Rockne (both were backup ends) and ran track. He turned down the chance to compete in the 1912 Olympics in the long jump (where he would have challenged Jim Thorpe) in order to sign with the Chicago Cubs. Traded to Philly, Williams toiled fruitlessly on a series of terrible Phillies teams. The "Baker Wall" was adorned with a mammoth advertisement for Lifebuoy soap, setting up the inevitable tagline—"And the Phillies still stink!" Losing wore on Williams—he never inured himself to the losses. Incredibly Phillies manager Art Fletcher (a McGraw disciple) was Williams's twelfth manager in his twelve years in the big leagues. In July 1923 *Sporting Life* wrote a long profile of Williams, praising him for playing so hard for such an awful team through the long, hot summer. Friends counseled him to ease up, but Williams wasn't capable of doing so. "More power to him" was the Babe's take on Cy's rage at the dying of the light.

Cy hung on until 1930, when he played twenty-one games at age forty-three. He retired rich, having invested heavily in Florida real estate and having sold at the top of the 1920s boom. Williams moved to Wisconsin, where he fished regularly for walleye and muskie with another ballplayer turned angler—Ted Williams.

The Giants came from behind to win the game on May 4, 11–9, in thirteen innings, kicking off a stretch of torrid ball by New York, who won sixteen of nineteen to begin May and establish themselves as front-runners. Included in the streak were seven straight wins over the Phillies. Philadelphia was ticketed for the bottom of the league—they would finish 50–104, the worst record in baseball. Williams couldn't be blamed—he had a fifteen-game hit streak at the beginning of May, a bountiful two weeks during which he hit eleven homers, knocked in twenty-nine runs, and accumulated sixty-five total bases. The Phillies were 2–13 in the stretch. One of the wins was a 20–14 embarrassment to pitching against St. Louis on May 11. In the game, Williams tied the existing major-league record with three home runs.

If there was a player who matched Williams in May, it was New York's Frankie Frisch, who scored twenty-five runs in the month and was near the league lead in batting. In a span starting on April 24, the switch-hitting Frisch had a hit in sixteen of seventeen games, and in all but five he had at least two hits. Frisch was batting .410 after rapping three hits against Pittsburgh at the Polo Grounds on May 13, a 9–0 Giants win. He also was playing a sterling second base. The "Fordham Flash" had another distinction besides his on-field excellence. He was among the very few to openly defy his manager.

Frisch was a bluff, blunt kid from the Bronx, which alone may have been enough to set off McGraw. He went to PS 8 Briggs Avenue Academy, just off the Grand Concourse, roughly forty blocks north of where the Yankee Stadium would be built. There he met the woman he would eventually marry. Frisch was a spectacular natural athlete, which likely prevented a torrent of school-yard taunts about his prominent nose. He stuck close to home after high school, choosing to attend Fordham University despite entreaties from McGraw, who didn't want him to waste time and risk injury playing other sports. But Frisch loved basketball and football and track, and played them all at Fordham. He earned the moniker the "Fordham Flash" for his great speed on the fields of Fordham and perhaps for his ability to get from one practice to another.

After four years of collegiate stardom in the Bronx, Frisch came over to Manhattan, joining the Giants without playing a single game in the minors. His talents were obvious: he could switch-hit; he was fast and nimble, and had great hands in the field; and he was brainy, with a natural feel for the game. Frisch possessed a keen batting eye—he rarely struck out (only twice in seventeen full seasons would Frankie strike out more than eighteen times). And he was versatile enough to play multiple positions. Still, McGraw drilled him relentlessly. He hit "thousands upon thousands" of grounders to Frisch, tried (not always successfully) to get him to stop sliding head-first, and taught him how to hit without crossing his hands. The manager always had something to teach a player, no matter how gifted he was. In some ways, the more talented the player, the more McGraw enjoyed breaking him down and imparting the McGraw Way from the ground up. But he picked the wrong man to try to bully in Frank Frisch.

The number of college men in baseball may have been dwindling, but in other aspects, Frisch was emblematic of the "new man" of the 1920s who saw the postwar era as a time for individual achievement and not for blind obedience to the old methods. He was independent and proud and didn't tolerate tongue-lashings. As Donald Honig writes in *Baseball America:*

A more complicated man had emerged from the brutality of a triumphant world war, from the radical ideas of the intellectual marketplace, from the contempt for Prohibition, from the whirligig pace of the decade. The will of John McGraw was losing its capacity to break the spirits of men who were playing in front of larger, noisier, more adulatory crowds, and some of those spirits were as rock-hard and unyielding as his own.

When it came to his manager, Frisch stood as firm as Gibraltar. Their relationship was defined early in Frisch's career, at his first training camp in 1919. McGraw would have his players run several miles each day at the field, then walk a few more back to the hotel as additional exercise. Frisch tired of the regimen quickly and one day hitchhiked his way back to the hotel. McGraw caught wind of that and confronted his rookie in the hotel restaurant, bellowing at top volume, "You son of a Dutch merchant! You rockhead! Next time I catch you riding anywhere I'll fine you five bucks a mile! You know what legs are for—baseball!" Frisch glared right back at McGraw, snarling, "You won't be getting a dime out of me," and walked away.

Where others would take McGraw's abuse with a bowed head, Frisch would answer back tartly. The two men exchanged insults like gunfire. Freddie Lindstrom, who started his Hall of Fame career in 1924 with the Giants, remembered, "You could *feel* it when they got together. The name-calling became vicious, and I can remember McGraw finally roaring at him, 'You're through!'" It wasn't pure loathing, though, at least on the manager's part. As with Stengel, McGraw saw something of himself in the defiant Frisch. It was almost a familial battle, with Frisch as rebellious prince fighting the old and entrenched king to become his own man. McGraw even named Frisch captain in 1921, if only to blame him directly when things went wrong. Attacks on Frisch's wallet continued unabated— McGraw once fined the player $25 for suntanning at a beach when he should have been thinking about baseball.

"Times were changing and McGraw was unable to adapt," Lindstrom told Honig. "You see, his style of dealing with someone who made a mistake on the field was to chew them out unmercifully. He could be brutal. He thought nothing of humiliating a man in front of the whole team. For years he was able to get away with it. But Frisch wouldn't take it.... It ate [McGraw's] craw to have anyone talk back to him, to challenge not only his authority but his expertise. But it was a different caliber of man now and tactics that had been successful before were no longer applicable."

Babe Ruth making a mockery of the game he loved was bad enough—here was another star disrespecting McGraw right in McGraw's own clubhouse. But unlike Ruth, whom the manager considered crass and boorish, Frisch, in McGraw's mind, had toughness and a willingness to stand up for his principles. When they weren't hollering at each other at top volume, McGraw enjoyed conversing with Frisch on topics unrelated to baseball. The manager was a firm believer in education and liked to have learned people around, and Frisch was smart enough to be accepted at Fordham. It was a complicated relationship—one that ultimately exhausted McGraw. To use a modern cliché, John was *too old for this shit.*

The constant battles wore out the older man, and when Frisch jumped the team in the early summer of 1927 after a vicious tongue-lashing by McGraw, an incensed John J. reluctantly traded Frisch to the Cardinals for another problem superstar, Rogers Hornsby. Frisch became a key cog in the Gashouse Gang Cards that won several pennants. Hornsby lasted only a year with McGraw before being dealt again. Many years later, McGraw was still unable to get Frisch out of his mind. "I despised him, I despised him. But God I hated to see him go." Frisch later remarked that he had never had any problems with anyone else in a quarter century in baseball. But he also called McGraw "the greatest manager I ever saw in action."

McGraw certainly had a good first two months of 1923. The Giants closed May at 30–11, 5½ games up in the NL standings. It helped that New York spent virtually the entire month at home. In all of May, only a four-game set in Philadelphia was played anywhere other than the Polo Grounds. Clan McGraw went 16–7 in the stretch, winning in every manner possible. On May 19, Hugh

McQuillan tossed a three-hitter to best Cincinnati, 1–0. The next day, the Giants exploded for fourteen runs in squashing St. Louis.

On Saturday the twenty-sixth, Claude Jonnard, McGraw's relief specialist, made his only start of the season. "This time, Claude finished his own game, not somebody else's," noted the *Times,* also reporting that Jonnard showed "a lack of steadiness and control that was the result, doubtless, of too many afternoons spent on the bench." Nonetheless, Jonnard held the Phillies to three runs, and a tie game was broken up on consecutive pitches in the eighth. Pep Youngs doubled and came in to score on a triple that Kelly "smacked on the solar plexus."

The Giants finally dropped a couple of games at month's end to the Robins, but it scarcely seemed to matter. McGraw's men were well out in front and appeared to be galloping toward another pennant.

17

Yankees shortstop Everett Scott, known as the "Deacon" for his perpetually sour expression, played in his one thousandth consecutive game on May 2. Second place on the all-time list was Fred Luderus of Philadelphia, with 533. The Yanks were in Washington that afternoon, and Secretary of the Navy Edwin Denby came to Griffith Stadium to present Scott with a gold medal. The Deacon was a navy man who had played ball for the service during the war. A group of marines paraded in his honor before the game, and they saluted Scott with the choicest epithets they could muster, sotto voce, for a navy puke. The reticent Scott ignored pleas for a speech from the gathered throng.

The Deacon had earned his medal. There were many occasions when his streak seemed certain to end. Scott suffered throughout his career from boils, and before a 1920 game he developed one in his left eye that sat him down — but the game was rained out, and when the weather cleared, so had his eye. He was once knocked unconscious by a Waite Hoyt fastball — but played the next day.

His closest call would come in September 1922. Scott got off his

Chicago-bound train to visit some relatives in Fort Wayne before a series against the White Sox. Later in the day, a wreck on the tracks delayed his scheduled train to the Windy City. Scott hired a local farmer to drive him over backcountry roads to South Bend, where he caught a trolley to Gary. He hired another car, a fast one, to get him to Chicago. The farmer had called the local papers to alert them to Scott's race to the field, and thus he picked up a police escort on the outskirts of Chicago that whisked him to Comiskey Park. He arrived in the seventh inning of the game. Huggins chewed him out but inserted him right away, and the streak continued. Less than a week before the '23 season got under way, Scott was carried off the field after gruesomely spraining an ankle on a slide during an exhibition game in Springfield, Missouri. The press reported the end of his streak as a fait accompli. "Mishap Will Keep Scott from Record of 1,000 Games," read the headline in the *New York American.* But the Deacon would not be denied.

Scott struggled mightily in the World Series in 1922 (2–14, with one RBI), but that hadn't brought him national criticism as it had Ruth. It did, however, make the Yankees question whether they should go forward with the thirty-year-old as the shortstop and team captain. Rumors flew throughout the winter that Scott would be dealt, but here he was, in pinstripes, playing. He would play 307 more in a row before finally ending the streak. Scott then retired to Fort Wayne to run a bowling alley, where he rolled more than fifty perfect games.

This game was hardly perfect for Scott and the Yankees — they were shut out by Walter Johnson, 3–0, the one hundredth shutout of his career. A couple of days later, Ruth had his worst day of the season — indeed, his worst in more than a year.

In that game, less than a week after Ruth and Meusel were reinstated to the Yankees lineup following their six-week suspension to open 1922, Ruth stroked a single and tried to take second, where he was called out by umpire George Hildebrand (the same ump who would later call Game Two of the '22 Series due to "darkness"). Ruth popped up with a fistful of dirt, which he flung at the astonished ump. "From the grandstand it seemed that the dust spattered over Hildebrand's face and neck," reported the *Times*. "Some of it seeped down his collar and the rest fell on his arm and the front of his uniform."

Ruth was duly tossed from the game. On his way to the dugout to collect his gear, he sarcastically tipped his cap. A pair of Pullman train employees sitting near the Yankees dugout hurled epithets at Ruth. Suddenly the Babe jumped on the dugout roof and made for the porters, clambering through rows of startled fans to get there. The Pullman men retreated as the enraged Ruth approached, managing to keep a row or two of fans between predator and prey. Fans yelled, "Hit the big stiff"—even Polo Grounders had turned on Ruth. But there was no actual violence.

Ruth told the press he had been called a "low-down bum" and "other names that got me mad." When asked if he feared further action against him by Landis or Ban Johnson, Ruth replied, "I don't see why I should get any punishment at all. I would go into the stand again if I had to." Johnson fined Ruth $200 and stripped him of his team captaincy (given to Scott even though it was his first season in pinstripes).

Now, on May 5, just over eleven months after the imbroglio with the Pullmans, fans turned on Ruth once again. This time, it was due to poor play, mainly a halfhearted jog after a fly ball that turned into a triple for Philly outfielder Wid Matthews. The day before, Ruth had "nearly broke the royal neck," as the *Times* put it, tumbling into the stands chasing a fly ball, so his reticence on this pop down the right-field line was perhaps understandable. The Babe also fanned twice (once with the bases loaded) and went from first to third on a single—only to discover Joe Dugan standing at third already, a baffled look on his face.

The series with Philadelphia drew 110,000, a new record for a three-game set. The big crowds that weekend were aided by seven new ticket booths that had been added to the Stadium to ease the crush—four on Doughty Street, two on 157th Street, and one at the corner of 157th and River Avenue. The 35,000 at the Stadium this Saturday afternoon let the Babe have it. "The fans stood up, groaned, hooted, jeered, and gave a creditable imitation of a cat calling to his mate" when Ruth came to bat for the final time.

The episode showed that Ruth still had some ground to make up with the New York fans after his embarrassing 1922. Ironically, that evening was "Babe Ruth Night" at the Bijou Theatre. The entire team was invited to be feted before the performance of the show *Uptown West*. Only a handful showed, and Ruth wasn't one of them.

It was one of the rare times during May that Ruth didn't produce. The Babe stole home on the first of May against the Senators, a moment of dash and bravery that contrasted with his thuggish, home-run-or-bust image. Later in the year he would be standing at third against Washington and fake another steal of home. The nervous pitcher balked him in. The day after Scott's landmark game, Ruth sealed a 3–2 victory by gunning down a runner at third on a throw from deep right field. He made a scintillating catch on the fourteenth to rob Ty Cobb of extra bases, and on the twenty-fourth got a Philadelphia crowd roaring for an opponent with a series of defensive gems, including another outfield assist and a fine running catch of a line drive.

Meanwhile, the power that wasn't there in April returned in force. The Babe clubbed nine home runs in May, as the Yankees seized control of the AL with a 21–6 burst. One home run was a monster blow in Detroit, a day after a marker had been erected commemorating a tape-measure shot by Harry Heilmann, the Tigers batting ace. Heilmann's was the longest homer ever hit at Navin Field, and less than twenty-four hours later, Ruth had outdistanced that home run by a good twenty feet. The marker disappeared overnight.

It was outstanding play that impressed all, except perhaps John McGraw. His autobiography, *My Thirty Years in Baseball,* was published in the spring of 1923. It was a rarity of its time, a sports memoir (only McGraw's pal Christy Mathewson had had a successful release, the classic *Pitching in a Pinch*), as baseball fans weren't considered a bankable—or literate—audience by publishers of the day. Bozeman Bulger did the actual writing. In the book, McGraw named his "All-American Team," a lineup of the best players he had seen in his three decades in the game. Babe Ruth was conspicuously absent from the starting nine. "I have to smile when I realize that I have picked a team for the American League and, in my opinion, have made it so strong as to necessitate keeping Babe Ruth on the bench as a utility outfielder," wrote McGraw.

Others were more impressed, including the songwriting duo of A. Atkins and Harry W. Trout, who gave the world the song "Babe Ruth: He Is a Home Run Guy" in May of 1923.

Babe Ruth, Babe Ruth,
He will lose that ball and that's the truth

The song was actually written the week before opening day at the Stadium but was not released until May. It described Ruth's dramatic blast in Chicago on May 22. In the fifteenth inning of a 1–1 game, the Babe was gripping his bat in the dugout when Mark Roth, the Yanks traveling secretary, voiced a concern that the endless game was threatening to make the team miss a scheduled train to Philadelphia, the next stop on the itinerary. "Take it easy, I'll get us out of here," Ruth assured him, and proceeded to launch a two-run game winner to right.

That particular contest was significant for a more lasting reason: it was the first game the Yankees played under the sole ownership of Jacob Ruppert. He and co-owner Cap Huston had parted ways. Many wondered how they had lasted this long.

18

THEY WERE OBVIOUSLY different right from the beginning. On January 15, 1915, the two millionaires met in Ban Johnson's office in Manhattan to purchase the American League's New York franchise. Ruppert had been immaculately dressed, with an expensive suit, top hat, and monocle. He looked every inch the captain of industry that he was. Ruppert arrived for the sale accompanied by a phalanx of lawyers and assistants. He carried a monogrammed letter of acceptance written on personal stationery. He pulled from his pocket a cashier's check for $225,000, his half of the $450,000 sale price, and handed it with great pomp to Johnson.

Huston entered the room a few minutes later. He bore little resemblance to a man with the means to buy a baseball franchise. His suit was rumpled and creased, in dire need of pressing, likely because he had worn it for several days. His hat was in even worse shape, a dirty derby that he wore every day without exception. He arrived minus any entourage. He reached into his pocket for his portion of the money owed and produced 225 thousand-dollar bills, held together by a dirty rubber band. He tossed the bundle on Johnson's desk.

With that, the New York Yankees belonged to this original Odd Couple.

Unlike Babe Ruth and John McGraw, Jacob Ruppert had never lived an impoverished day. The second of six children, he was born into wealth on August 5, 1867—like Ruth and McGraw, he was named after his father. Jacob Sr. was himself the second generation of Rupperts to run a brewery. His father, Franz, was Bavarian, and he brought the region's passion for beer to New York when he emigrated to the United States.

Franz had run a small operation, but his son built a new brewery and set out to sell five thousand barrels a year. The Jacob Ruppert Brewery sat on several blocks of the Upper East Side, between 90th and 92nd Streets and Second and Third Avenues (now the site of the Ruppert-Yorkville high-rise towers, the construction of which ironically ended the neighborhood's lower-middle-class-German tradition).

Jacob Sr. was a natural salesman, and in his first year he hit his five-thousand-barrel mark. Sales rose steadily, in large part because of Ruppert's fine craftsmanship. He joined several German-American organizations that were often singing societies. He didn't have much of a voice, but he always brought refreshments.

Ruppert Sr. essentially invented small-scale beer marketing. He was one of the first in the business to thoroughly train his salesmen, including lining their pockets with expense money to lavish on potential customers. He also supplied them with an assortment of stories and jokes to enhance their sales spiel.

Young Jacob was close to his father but wasn't pushed in any way toward making beer a career. Instead, Ruppert Sr. wanted his son to be an engineer. Jacob took the entrance exams at Columbia's School of Mines, but the lager that flowed in his blood was too strong to ignore. He joined his father at the brewery at age twenty and never left.

Ruppert had always liked sports, and baseball was the first of his passions. Trouble was, he was no good at it. He wasn't physically small or even particularly uncoordinated. He just didn't have much aptitude for the game. Nevertheless, he was elected captain of his first youth team, mainly because he got his father to pay for the uniforms.

In 1890, at age twenty-three, Ruppert took over day-to-day operations of the brewery, and under his stewardship, sales grew exponentially. The company soon was selling half a million barrels of Knickerbocker and Ruppert's Beer per year. Remembering his father's modest dream, Jacob told associates his goal was to "sell five thousand barrels per day." After expanding the plant's capacity and hiring close to a thousand workers to service it, Ruppert easily surpassed that goal.

There was no income tax in fin de siècle America, and the huge profits on the sales of Knickerbocker made Ruppert truly wealthy. He emulated his father by joining every civic group he could. His entry into politics and the four terms in Congress were a natural offshoot of Ruppert's ability to work a room.

Upon returning full-time to New York, Ruppert moved into a grand mansion on Fifth Avenue at 93rd Street, not far from his father's home (down 93rd at Lexington Avenue) and close enough to the brewery to walk to work each day. It was a twelve-room penthouse fit for an aristocrat, with a butler, maid, valet, cook, and laundress on hand to cater to Ruppert's every need. There were peach and apple orchards in the backyard, and local kids, including a young Harpo Marx, routinely hopped the wrought-iron fence to steal the fruit.

While in Washington, Colonel Ruppert had begun to dress more and more dandified. He cut a dashing figure in his youth, with exquisitely tailored suits and a perfectly trimmed mustache. As he aged and became a closely followed society figure, he dressed in the latest fashions, adding to his wardrobe a chesterfield coat, a classy derby hat, and a monocle. He was the picture of wealth and luxury, in his later years resembling no one so much as Rich Uncle Pennybags, aka Mr. Monopoly, the well-heeled figure who graces the cover of the board game.

Despite the fact that Ruppert was a second-generation American and lived in New York his entire life (save his time in the House of Representatives), he spoke with a heavy Bavarian accent, in part because of the large Germanic presence in the Yorkville area at the turn of the century. Colleagues and friends at times struggled to make out what he was saying, especially in times of stress, such as late in a tense ball game. Ruppert supported and donated to German causes right up to the outbreak of World War I, but he was quick to denounce the aggression of his grandfather's homeland and distanced himself from his German roots thereafter (at least as much as he could while still muttering, *"Ach, du lieber Gott,"* at every frustration).

Ruppert also maintained a country estate up the Hudson in Garrison, New York, and he filled both homes with evidence of his passions. He collected antiques, fine jades, and porcelains. He loved monkeys and kept a troop of them—five capuchins and two rhesus monkeys—at his Garrison estate, where they "hobnobbed with the elite of the sporting world," according to the *Times.* He also let several peacocks run loose on the grounds. With his accent, foppish appearance, and capuchin monkey perched on his shoulder, the colonel on occasion could strike an extraordinarily eccentric mien.

He owned a large stable of horses, many of which were trained for professional racing, including Counter Tenor, the winner of the 1906 Metropolitan Handicap. Ruppert was a regular at the racetrack and a member of the Coney Island and Brooklyn Jockey clubs. He also owned greyhounds and bred Saint Bernards for show. One, Oh Boy, is still considered among the finest show dogs ever. Another rich man's hobby that Ruppert enthusiastically pursued was yachting. He cruised Long Island Sound in his ninety-foot yacht, *Albatross,* and was a member of the New York, Larchmont, and Atlantic yacht clubs. Science and exploration captured his fancy. Later in life he would richly fund expeditions, including Admiral Richard Byrd's second trip to Antarctica. Byrd's flagship was rechristened the *Jacob Ruppert* in recognition of the colonel's backing.

By 1914 the Jacob Ruppert Brewery was a key cog in the city's economy, and its workers pounded out double shifts as Americans bought and drank more beer than ever. His fortune was estimated at $70 million (approximately $1.5 billion in today's dollars). But Ruppert's life away from the kegs was more and more unfulfilling. He tired of yachting, his horses took a long hiatus from the winner's circle, and the war blunted his ability to import his prized Saint Bernards. A lifelong bachelor, Ruppert claimed men married only because they needed a housekeeper. He squired ladies in and out via a private elevator, but the swinger lifestyle wasn't satisfying either, especially as he neared fifty.

Increasingly it was baseball that pulled at him. Through McGraw's Giants, Ruppert had reconnected with the game of his youth, and now, with money dripping from his pockets, he wanted nothing more than to buy a major-league team. Ruppert liked the idea of someone to share the risk and capital required. So did a fellow down in Cuba whom John J. had mentioned.

Upon buying the Yankees, Ruppert was mostly concerned with changing the name of the team again. Few were calling for preservation of the name "Yankees," and the colonel wanted to advertise his product. But "Knickerbockers" didn't fit comfortably across a uniform, so he reluctantly agreed to keep the team name.

Jacob Ruppert Sr. passed away in 1915, dying of the most likely cause imaginable—cirrhosis of the liver, brought on by decades of drinking his own concoctions. He left an estate worth more than $6 million to his children. The colonel was named the sole entity in charge of the brewery and the family fortune. The drums of temperance were sounding across the nation, and despite his wealth, Ruppert faced a trying period—his business threatened by a sudden and shocking morality, his father gone, and his new baseball team inept.

Meanwhile, Ruppert and Huston were disproving the old maxim that opposites attract. The two men clashed almost from the first moments of their partnership, less over specifics than the hugely disparate natures of their personalities. Ruppert was classy, reserved, cautious. Huston was gauche, loud, rumpled. Cap was a meddler, suddenly believing he was an expert in all manners baseball. Ruppert deferred decisions to his baseball men. Huston, fancying himself a scout, lusted after a pitcher for Indianapolis named Dan Tipple. Cap journeyed to Indy to watch Tipple for several starts, looking over scout Joe Kelley's shoulder at his notes, making no secret that he thought Tipple couldn't miss. Indeed, the pitcher had won ten straight games to open 1915 and had tossed a no-hitter. But Kelley had reservations about Tipple's delivery and mental makeup.

Huston pressed onward, signing Tipple and rushing his prize to New York. "Rusty" Tipple started three games in 1915, winning one and losing one, and pitched nineteen innings altogether—and was never heard from again.

There were other, more frivolous differences between the owners. The superstitious Huston wore his absurd derby hat every single day, a habit that grated mightily on the fashion-conscious Ruppert. Even when temperatures soared past a hundred degrees, Huston refused to take the damn thing off. One of his pals in the press, W. O. McGeehan of the *Times,* labeled Huston the "Man in the Iron Hat." Ruppert also resented Huston's close relationships with the players and the writers.

For his part, Cap loathed the fact that Ruppert went around calling himself "colonel" when the beer baron had never been close to combat. Huston, though not exactly an infantryman, was justifiably proud of his war record and thought Ruppert a dilettante who laughably clung to a meaningless title.

War and rank would become a greater issue in 1918, when World War I at long last enveloped America. Huston enlisted once again, joining the 16th Engineers of the U.S. First Army. This brought him into regular contact with a different John J.—General "Black Jack" Pershing, commander of the First Army. Cap's battalion built roads and railways under intense German shell fire behind the British lines and during savage fighting at Montfaucon, France. They also constructed forty hospitals for the American Expeditionary Force.

During this stretch of action, Huston was promoted twice, from captain to major and then to lieutenant colonel. He was now equivalent in rank with his co-owner, Jacob Ruppert. Huston had always sneered at Ruppert's honorific title, and now the experience of coming under fire exacerbated his contempt. *How dare that fop! Running around calling himself "colonel" while the real thing was dodging artillery in the War to End All Wars!*

The issue that pushed the Ruppert-Huston relationship to the breaking point was not martial but managerial. Ineffectual manager "Wild Bill" Donovan was pushed out as the Yankees skipper after 1917. Ban Johnson, for whom the Yankees were a key project in creating equal footing for the American League, wanted someone with more grit and skill to lead the New York AL franchise than the avuncular but mediocre Donovan. Johnson had consulted the editor of the *Sporting News,* J. G. Taylor Spink, and Spink gave Ban a name. Johnson then began whispering the name in Ruppert's ear: *Miller Huggins.*

Huggins had managed the St. Louis Cardinals for the previous five seasons, with the team finishing third twice, including in 1917, when the Cards surprised the NL by playing good hustling baseball. But the Cards were sold during the 1917 season, a move that blindsided Hug, who thought he would be a partner in the new ownership group. Instead Branch Rickey was installed as the man in charge of baseball operations, and he wanted nothing to do with Hug. Rickey hired Jack Hendricks as the skipper after the season (Hendricks and the Cards would finish last in 1918, and Rickey would take over as manager himself).

Huggins was available, but he was also sure of one thing: he didn't want the Yankees job. He had told Johnson as much during the season when Ban first quietly sounded him out about moving to New

York. Hug didn't know or like the American League, and the short, quiet Midwesterner wanted nothing to do with New York City, where the citizenry demanded some *color* from their sportsmen. But at Johnson's repeated entreaties, he agreed to meet with Ruppert.

The colonel was less than impressed with Huggins at first glance. Few were—Hug was scrawny, ugly, half grown. Ruppert the Dandy sniffed at Huggins's working-class clothes and cap. He thought Hug drab and unfit to lead his proud franchise (at least the one he envisioned was coming soon) into battle. But Johnson worked on Ruppert. Taking a manager of Huggins's reputation away from the National League would be a coup. Eventually the colonel was convinced that Hug was the man to bring his crucial New York franchise up to snuff. Ruppert may have been a snob, but he was also willing to listen to others, especially in areas unrelated to beer and Saint Bernards. He was new to baseball and relied on Johnson's guidance.

Cap Huston had his own ideas about the next manager of his team. And Miller Huggins was decidedly not on his short list. Cap wanted to install his drinking buddy, Wilbert Robinson, another McGrawista. Robinson was the manager of the Brooklyn Robins—so called in honor of the helmsman himself. Robinson was a jolly fellow, true to his "Uncle Robbie" nickname. But he wasn't just good humor—Robinson had prodded Brooklyn to the World Series in 1916, an achievement that wowed Huston.

Writers dubbed the team under Robbie the "Daffiness Boys," owing in large part to a spring-training incident in 1916. Cubs catcher Gabby Street had recently caught a baseball that had been dropped—in a moment of PR-gone-wild—from the top of the Washington Monument. Robbie thought he could do one better. He had watched the female aviatrix Ruth Law performing at a nearby Florida beach and had the idea that he could catch a ball dropped from a moving airplane. He approached Law, who was willing to do anything for some publicity, and the stunt was arranged. The team placed their bets.

Law took to the sky and dropped an object from four hundred feet high. Robinson circled it, got directly under it—and found himself hurled to the ground by the impact of it hitting his chest. His torso was covered in a sticky wet liquid, which he took to be his own blood. "My God, I'm dead! The damn thing has exploded!" he screamed.

Unbeknownst to Robbie, one of his scheming players, a wacky outfielder named Casey Stengel, had prevailed upon Law to drop a grapefruit instead of a baseball. Robinson thus was covered not in blood but citrus. He knew he was very much alive when the team, led by Stengel, broke up laughing.

Despite his occasional buffoonery, Robinson was the man Huston wanted in charge of the Yankees. Unfortunately for Cap, events and geography conspired against him. He was in France building airfields while Ruppert and Huggins were meeting and Johnson was stage-managing events.

Huston let his feelings be known from the other side of the Atlantic Ocean. He fired off telegrams at a furious pace, disparaging Huggins and insisting Ruppert remember that Huston was co-owner of the team. But Ruppert would not be swayed. Out of a sense of obligation, he did meet with Robinson. But Robbie had no sooner sat down than the colonel growled, "Sorry, you're too old," and ushered the furious manager out the door. He then took Johnson's advice and hired Huggins, for reasons even he couldn't fully elucidate, and on October 25, 1917, Ruppert inked Huggins to a contract at nearly twice the salary he had been making in St. Louis.

Huston's explosion of anger drowned out the nearby war. Ruppert's brusque treatment of Robinson had gotten back to Til, who was incensed that he had been so easily outmaneuvered. Huston obliquely retaliated by sending numerous letters to newspapers demanding the sport be shut down and every player drafted into the war effort. It was a puny scheme, serving only to irritate his partner, who couldn't fathom Huston's utter distaste for his new skipper. The hiring of Huggins was a fait accompli, and Cap couldn't stop it, so he resigned himself to undermining Ruppert's man at every opportunity.

When Ruth came to New York in 1920, Huston allowed him to run roughshod over Huggins, waving off fines administered by the manager for the slugger's misbehavior or paying them himself. Other players also knew Huston had their backs and ignored Hug's attempts at discipline. The simmering situation exploded in the immediate aftermath of the 1922 World Series. Huston stormed out of the Polo Grounds following the final game, making a beeline for the Commodore Hotel and the pressroom bar. He dramatically swept a row of cocktail glasses from a table and yelled to one and all, "Miller Huggins has managed his last game for the Yankees!" He then disappeared into the New York night. One writer saw Huston head downtown, and extrapolated. "Cap Huston's famous Iron Boiler [his derby hat] was taken to the Brooklyn Bridge and tossed into the roaring torrent below," he wrote. "It required great persuasive arts to get Cap to take his head from under the iron hat before the tossing began." But Ruppert refused to consider firing Huggins, saying, "I won't fire the man who brought us two straight pennants."

The owners also fought over how best to donate the funds from the suspended Game Two of the '22 World Series. Commissioner Landis had ordered all profits dispersed to charity, and Ruppert wanted to spread the money over several different organizations. Huston, perhaps conditioned by this point to say "up" whenever the colonel said "down," wanted the entire pile to go to his pet charity benefiting war veterans. The more they argued about it, the more intransigent each man became. "This observer was an innocent bystander at one of those battles and can testify that the firing was heavy in both directions," remembered writer John Kieran.

Yankees business manager Ed Barrow drove the final stake into the heart of the partnership. "The Yankee Colonels were the strangest pair of men I have ever known in baseball," Barrow recalled. "When they agreed to buy the Yankees...it must have been the only time they ever did agree." Barrow was a two-fisted businessman who built the first Yankees dynasty. He personified not the later, bloodless Yankees of the midcentury but the rough-and-tumble Ruthian team. The strapping business manager was decidedly uncorporate, happy to come over the desk to fight a player who angered him with contract demands. In 1930 Barrow was briefly demoted after attacking the sportswriter Bill Slocum, one of Ruth's favorite ghostwriters, over a negative article. Ed's nickname, "Bulldog," was a window on his personality.

He was raised in corn country, mainly in rural areas of Iowa and Ohio that were essentially unsettled spaces between small towns. Before he got into baseball, Barrow lived an interesting, peripatetic life, boxing professionally, working as a city editor on a newspaper, running an inn, even managing a roller rink. He prized his excellent penmanship, perhaps because many people who grew up in the fields couldn't write at all.

He bounced around the minors as a fairly successful manager before getting his first shot in the majors, with Detroit. In 1918 he took the Boston job and won the World Series in his first season. He was unafraid of the team's star, once challenging Ruth to a club-house fight after the Babe had missed curfew (Barrow discovered him at six a.m. fully dressed under his hotel bedcovers). Ruth wisely backed down.

Barrow was ruthless with a dollar and unfeeling in his relations with players. His instant and infamous reaction upon hearing of Lou Gehrig's diagnosis of ALS was to tell Lou's wife, Eleanor, that the first baseman should "look for another line of work" as he was no longer of much use to the team. Mrs. Gehrig never forgave the "old bastard" for that one.

After the 1922 World Series, as Ruppert and Huston volleyed harsh words over Miller Huggins through the press, Barrow, weary of the drama, went to the colonel and threatened to quit. The business manager operated with little fear of his boss—earlier in the season, he had demanded Ruppert stay out of the clubhouse after games, as he was wont to demand of Huggins why his team didn't win by more runs. Now the situation was becoming intolerable. Barrow had no interest in working under split management, where his every move might be undermined, critiqued, and even overturned because of the rift in ownership. He also had a soft landing spot in mind. Barrow's name was being bandied about in important circles as a possible replacement for Ban Johnson as head of the American League. Ruppert begged Barrow to stay. The business manager agreed on one condition: Cap Huston must go.

Ruppert tried to throw money at the problem. He appeared to succeed in December 1922, when Huston agreed to a buyout. But in early January, the deal was called off. Some speculated that Huston had reconsidered, and surely he wanted to see the Stadium project through to its completion. But there was also a legal hitch. Ruppert's lawyers, fearing Huston would buy a controlling share in another club, attempted to insert a clause into the sale contract that forbade Cap from reentering baseball for ten years. Insulted, Huston refused to sell.

The great triumph of opening day was a short-lived joy for the Yankees co-owners. The men returned almost immediately to their mutual loathing by day two of the Yankee Stadium's official existence, and perhaps even earlier than that: on the night of the opener, Huston had thrown a celebratory bash at his usual spot, the Hotel Martinique at 32nd and Broadway. Ruppert and Barrow dropped by—for about thirty seconds, long enough to salute the other guests and insult Huston by leaving immediately after.

By spring, Cap reopened negotiations with Ruppert on selling out. He explored offering his half of the team to someone else, but the colonel didn't want another potential feuding partner and nixed the idea.

Ruppert's most important goal was to prevent Cap from taking his new wad of cash and buying another team—especially Boston.

Rumors abounded that Huston had his eye on the Sox, and the idea made plenty of sense. Cap would sever from the partner he disliked, buy a rival franchise from his good drinking buddy Harry Frazee, and remake them as a winner, knocking out Ruppert's team in the process. And given Cap's relationship with Ruth, a triumphant return to Boston by the Bambino wasn't out of the question. What a story that would make!

But it didn't come to pass. Huston never seriously entertained buying the Sox, though he wasn't above using the rumors to negotiate an extra hundred grand to be tacked on to Ruppert's buyout offer. Ruppert agreed to drop the legalese banning Huston from buying another club, and the sale went through. The deal was officially made on May 21, 1923, with the colonel giving Cap $1.25 million for his half of the club. Some of it was paid in cash, the rest in notes to be paid later, with the deal to be closed by June 1. The total represented a 550 percent return on Cap's initial investment, and the deal cemented the Yankees' position as the wealthiest franchise in all of sport (worth $4 million by some estimates), but even by 1923 standards, the Yankees seemed to be worth more than what Cap got for his half of the team.

Cap told the press he was retiring to "do some tall resting." Certainly Huston had to know in his heart of hearts that he was turning his back on real money. He had been present nearly every day as the Big Ball Orchard in the South Bronx went up. He had envisioned the massive grandstands filled with paying customers and seen the team become World Series contenders. Now, with his baby filled to its brim, there would be only a daddy's pride for Huston rather than financial remuneration. It wasn't a huge blow in and of itself—Cap walked away with plenty of cash. Still, for an army vet and the head of engineering projects for decades, the loss of control had to take some getting used to.

The colonel threw a directorship Cap's way as a sop, but there was no power and no money in it. More important to Huston was his new post as national commander of the Veterans of Foreign Wars, an honorary position he intended to devote his full attention to. And after completing the construction project to end all construction projects, Huston seemed to believe there were no worlds left to conquer. Earlier that year he had told a reporter, "I'm old and tired. The Yankees are a good team and the Stadium is nearly finished. It looks as if my work is about done."

His immediate plans involved pleasure. He told the *Times* of a trip to California to tour the state, a "vacation I've been promising myself for many years." He vowed to remain a great fan of the team, saying, "I'll probably enjoy it more if I have to pay my $1.50 at the box office." He didn't cut the cord entirely—Huston invited reporters to visit him at his new office at 30 East 42nd Street, which had been the Yankees business office until operations moved to the Bronx. But Cap seldom darkened the doors in Times Square.

As we look back from a distance, Huston seems less like the tired good soldier and more like Stu Sutcliffe, the "fifth Beatle" who left the band when it was on the cusp of superstardom. Huston, who agonized after the World Series losses of '21 and '22 due to an unslaked thirst for victory, sold out mere months before the franchise took its first step toward becoming *The Yankees,* sport's most renowned brand name. The owner who loved making the scene as the moneyman behind a pro baseball team was denied this great pleasure.

Instead of having a monument in his name in the Stadium that he did so much to build, Tillinghast L'Hommedieu Huston has become, instead, a mere footnote to history.

Ruppert, whose monument would later be erected in center field, put out a statement that papered over the hard feelings the two owners shared: "I am sincerely sorry to see Colonel Til go. For nine long years, we built the Yanks from the weakest club in the American League into the strongest. But Huston wanted a rest from baseball, and I think he had it coming to him."

The *Sporting News* gave it to him, all right—right between the eyes: "The disorganization of the Yankee team...has been charged to his meddling with the management and his discouragement of discipline....He has been a bull in a china shop....Mr. Huston, here is your well-known iron hat, and goodbye!"

Before the game in which Ruth homered in Chicago to send the Yankees to their waiting train, Ruppert sent a telegram to the visiting clubhouse that said it all: "I am now the sole owner of the Yankees. Miller Huggins is my manager."

19

BABE RUTH AND Miller Huggins had a love-hate relationship—in 1923 it was mostly love. The two would always be at odds, as only a fun-loving, uneducated, big-boned jock and a diminutive, nervous bookworm who lived with his sister could. But Ruth didn't make waves. For the moment, he had made peace with the situation and was intent on proving to Huggins and everyone else that he most assuredly was *not* through. And Huggins could now relax. "I wouldn't go through [that] again for all the money in the world," he told his sister, Myrtle. But that phase was over now. He had the full backing of Ruppert and Barrow, and now even Ruth was compliant.

Huggins would later actually thank Til Huston, saying the constant criticism spurred him on. There was another benefit. "[Huston] said I was so rotten, and said so in so many columns so many times, that nobody expected anything of me," said the manager.

Huggins and Huston were, oddly, homeboys, sharing Cincinnati as a hometown, though of course Huston was a decade older. Huggins yearned to be a drum major as a child, and even after becoming a major leaguer, he would snag an umbrella and strut around the clubhouse as though leading a marching band. It was a strange passion for a boy who grew up on the tough streets of Cincy's Fourth Ward.

Miller's father was a strict Methodist who disapproved of playing sports on Sundays. He didn't like baseball much either, preferring cricket. Miller gravitated toward the game (at first playing under the name Proctor to throw Dad off the trail) as it was the sole sport in which a stripling like him could compete. Huggins was 5'6", max— other measurements put him at 5'3". And he was puny too, just under 150 pounds at his heaviest, usually closer to 135 or 140. But he was quick and smart and passionate about baseball. He was called the "Mighty Mite" and "Mr. Everywhere" on the field—had he not played baseball, the nicknames might have been nastier.

At his father's insistence, Miller studied law at the University of Cincinnati. In the summer he played in the American Association. Soon he was faced with a choice: the game or the bar. He sought advice from his professor, future president William Howard Taft. "You can become a pleader or a player, but not both," Taft told him. "You seem to like baseball better." Huggins would later say, "I gave up the law for baseball because . . . it is more than a game, for the real ballplayer employs his brains as much as the shrewdest businessman."

In 1904 he joined the hometown team, the Reds, and took over at second base. He played literal small ball—crouching to draw walks, bunting, making contact, and running, running, running. His defense was first-rate. He was dealt to St. Louis in 1910 and became player-manager in 1913.

Hug was only 346–415 in five years managing the Cards. Nevertheless, his performance at the helm in St. Louis caught not only Ban Johnson's eye but John McGraw's as well. Both credited him with building a skinny shortstop named Hornsby into the magnificent Rajah, one of the game's all-time greats. McGraw never had a bad word to say about Hug. That might have been a tactical bit of buttering up, or perhaps sympathy for a fellow skipper who had to deal with Babe Ruth on a daily basis. The Arch City press had thought well of Huggins too. The "Little Miracle Worker of the West," they called Hug.

The manager knew New York would be an ill fit for him, and he was right. Huggins had spent his entire life in pleasant midwestern cities that were considerably smaller than the Big Town. The size and pressure of the city wore on him, and Hug was dour in a place that prized flamboyance. He was nervous and irritable, an insomniac—a neurotic. He had false teeth, and they didn't fit properly into his gums. He was forever suffering from sinus headaches, eye strain, and indigestion.

"New York is a hell of a town," he complained. "Everywhere I go in Cincinnati or St. Louis it's always 'Hiya, Hug' or 'Hello, Hug,' but in New York I can walk the length of Forty-second Street and not a soul knows me." He wasn't a good "mixer," not one to buy rounds for the press gang at the saloon or charm his way into some positive press. "I wish I had the knack of solving newspapermen," Huggins told *Baseball Magazine.* "But I haven't and that's all there is to the story. I work and if my work won't speak for me why I guess I shan't make much of a holler myself."

He also suffered in comparison to the great John McGraw. In contrast to the twitchy, tiny Huggins, the now sturdy McGraw *looked* like a topflight manager. His mere presence commanded men to his will. Meanwhile an umpire once mistook Huggins for the batboy. Ruth called him the "Flea," and Hug was once shut out of a banquet because the security guard wondered how "a little twerp like you could be Babe Ruth's manager." Huggins said, "McGraw and I could enter a crowded room at the same time and be introduced… and in two minutes the crowd would be all around McGraw and nobody would know I was there."

One New York paper put its finger on why: "Huggins lacks the dominating personality of McGraw. No one could imagine Hug saying to his players, 'Get in there and do such and such a thing and if it goes wrong I take the blame and if it goes right I also take the credit.' That is the doctrine of McGraw—definite, clear-cut, and forceful."

From the start, Ruth and Huggins clashed. The manager was in an impossible position, trying to enforce discipline on the most undisciplined athlete in sports, with a team owner who nulled any attempts to hit Ruth in the wallet. The Babe could barely stand to look at Huggins, off-put by the wrinkles and the awkward smile and the nervous tics.

Nineteen twenty-one and '22 were particularly tough. The Series losses left bitterness all around. Huston whispered into existence a campaign in the press to make Ruth player-manager, a role for which he was about as suitable as becoming leader of the temperance movement. Hug laughed that one off, noting, "Those fellows after my job hitched their wagon to the wrong star." The team was unruly and often liquored up. In spring training in 1922, a group of players gathered under Hug's hotel-room window and serenaded him: "Oh, Hug, your ball club is cockeyed drunk again! Miller, come get your drunken ball club."

Even when the Yankees won, Ruth and the players got all the credit—Hug was the scrawny midget who happened to be around. After the 1922 loss to McGraw, the *Sporting News* wrote: "Perhaps never in the history of the game has a manager been so flouted, reviled, and ridiculed."

To cope, Huggins went straight home after games to the Manhattan apartment he shared with his sister, Myrtle. Neither brother nor sister ever married. They were each other's sounding board. Hug would complain that the job was too frustrating to deal with and that he was about to chuck the whole thing. Myrtle would talk him down. "Stick it out," she'd say. "Don't let them be able to say that you quit when under fire." Hug would retreat to his room, smoke a pipe, and be up half the night.

But now, with Huston gone and Ruth on his best behavior, the worm had turned. Led by the Babe, the offense was rolling. The pitching staff was deep and talented. No team played better defense. Even the perpetually pessimistic Huggins could feel good about this Yankees season.

Meanwhile the Babe had met someone. He had been married to Helen for nine long years, an epoch of epic philandering with only occasional glancing blows of matrimonial fidelity. Not that the marriage was a total fiction. "Babe tried to make it work, wanted it to work, but they were just going in different directions," said Marshall Hunt.

His life changed during a series with the Senators in early May. Ruth was standing near the batting cage, waiting to take some practice swings, when his friend James Barton, a well-known actor, approached with a sparkling honey in tow. She was named Claire Merritt Hodgson, a southern belle and model-actress from Athens, Georgia (her ten-year-old cousin over in Demorest, Georgia, was a pretty fair ballplayer named Johnny Mize, who would go on to star for both the Yankees and the Giants). She was twenty-six and tiny, 5'2" and barely scraping past a hundred pounds. Her accent was pure southern honeysuckle, and her hair the color of dark chestnut. She and Barton were costarring in an awfully punny play called *Dew Drop Inn,* at the moment being staged in DC, and Barton invited Ruth to see the show that night.

The Babe had no interest in the play, but he sent Eddie Bennett, a team batboy, over to the National Theatre with a note for Claire, inviting her to his hotel suite. He assured her that single ladies would be safe — as always with Ruth, mobs of people were shuttling in and out of his room.

Claire wasn't particularly impressed by the ballplayer. "His banter was not up to a twenty-nine-year-old man's by a decade," she wrote in her autobiography. "His face and stomach were fat, his legs like a chorus girl's." But she warmed to Ruth as he talked frankly about his fears fostered by the nightmare of 1922. As the Babe put away drink after drink, he wondered aloud if he was indeed finished, as all the pundits had said after the World Series. He was afraid '23 would be another dark season, and he worried that people hated him, as he hated himself.

"You drink too," Claire said lightly. "It's not good for you."

"You sound like Miller Huggins," Ruth said. This was something new—a "dame" who tsk-tsked the Babe for his alcoholic intake. Most women he ran with would happily pound down the drinks right along with him.

The next night, Ruth and reserve catcher Benny Bengough saw *Dew Drop Inn* and visited Claire backstage. Ruth was smitten. He cared not a whit that she had married at age fourteen and had a child at sixteen—then abandoned them both in 1920 to come to New York and pursue her dream of stardom (in time, her daughter, Julia, would become Ruth's adopted daughter). He also ignored her reputation around the majors as a "Charity Girl," a promiscuous woman frequently seen in the company of ballplayers. No surprise there, although one man she was rumored to have had an affair with was her fellow Georgian and Ruth's bête noire, Ty Cobb.

She lived at West 79th Street, and the Babe spent a good many of his nights there. His teammates averted their eyes—it certainly wasn't their place to pass judgment on Ruth. He was playing good ball. So long as that continued to be the case, he could sleep with First Lady Florence Harding for all they cared. It wasn't as though his relationship with his wife hadn't been tested before. As Claire put it, "I was not breaking up a home. It was broken."

The Yankees began May 1½ games behind the Indians in the American League pennant chase. Come June, they led Cleveland by seven games, having gone 21–6 as the flowers bloomed at the New York Botanical Garden and perambulators strolled along the newly opened boardwalk at Coney Island. Ruth was the main force behind the stellar play, but he had plenty of help. Long Bob Meusel knocked in twenty-three runs in May—on the thirty-first, he and Ruth were tied for the league lead with thirty-three, one more than another Yankee, Wally Pipp. Oddly Meusel and Ruth were also tied atop the AL in times caught stealing with eight apiece, a bizarre number for the third and fifth hitters in a lineup. It was as though the doubts sown by their defeat in the '22 Series had led the slugging Yanks to a brief and futile flirtation with Scientific Baseball.

Leadoff man Whitey Witt was the beneficiary of the deep lineup behind him. He had forty-two hits and scored twenty-one times in May, often getting the Yanks on top early with a first-inning run (New York would outscore the opposition 122–67 in the first innings of games in 1923). Witt was born Ladislaw Waldemar Wittkowski in 1895, and at the time of his death in 1988 was the last living member of the 1923 Yankees. A Lilliputian lefty, the 5'7", 150-pound Witt batted with a crouch, making his already small strike zone practically disappear. He led the majors in walks in 1922 and was an adept table setter.

Bullet Joe Bush went 6–1 in May, Herb Pennock 5–0, Waite Hoyt 3–0. Bush and Shawkey led the league in strikeouts with forty each. The Yanks outscored opponents 156–96 in May, the widest margin of any month all season. It was a club firing on all cylinders. And the home fans witnessed hardly any of it. Just as the Giants spent nearly all month in Manhattan, the Yanks barely saw the Bronx. New York played only four games at their new home in all of May, losing two of three to the A's before embarking on a long western trip. The Yankees were a middling 11–7 when they shuffled aboard a train bound for Cleveland. They made stops in Detroit, St. Louis, Chicago, Philly, and Washington before finally coming home. Astoundingly they went 17–3 on this tour of the American League, including nine straight wins. The first of that streak was a thriller in Detroit on May 14. All was fine for the Hugmen as they built a 7–0 lead, but the Tigers rallied to tie the game at 8–8 with five in the ninth off

Shawkey and Bush. In the twelfth inning, Pipp's grand slam keyed an eight-run uprising, and the Yankees finally won, 16–11. The game lasted well over three and a half hours, an eternity by 1923 standards.

The Yanks won the next eight after that. On the nineteenth, Ruth homered in the first inning off Hub Pruett in St. Louis, Aaron Ward slugged one out in the eighth to tie the game at four, and Carl Mays, getting a rare start, tripled in two runs in the tenth to win it. Mays was so exhausted from his sprint to third that he was unable to pitch the bottom half of the inning. Hoyt finished up to earn his lone save of the season. During a six-game spree to close the month, the Yankees banged out more than seven runs a game.

And as if the lineup wasn't potent enough already, a man who would become one of the game's greatest hitters was about to join the team.

June

20

ON THE MORNING of June 11, 1923, a young prospect took the subway to the Bronx from his home in Morningside Heights, his glove, spikes, and hat rolled up in newspaper. He looked better suited for football than baseball, with broad shoulders, the arms of a stevedore, and an ample lower body, a girth that would earn him the nickname "Biscuit Pants." By the time his career was over, he would be known by a better sobriquet—the "Iron Horse."

Lou Gehrig's talents were no secret to baseball men in the city. McGraw had fallen in love with the strapping teenager while he was still attending Commerce High School (now Brandeis High School). Gehrig had played in a prep all-star game at Wrigley Field while the Giants happened to be in town. Lou clubbed a pitch onto Waveland Avenue, which got the manager's attention. McGraw may have been a critic of the mindless power game, but that didn't mean he would pass up an obviously special slugger.

So in 1921 Gehrig took his tattered, ancient first baseman's glove to the Polo Grounds for a workout. He was eager to meet McGraw, whom he idolized, but the irascible manager was in a foul mood, thanks to a Giants losing streak. When Gehrig let a slow roller dribble between his legs, McGraw barked from the dugout, "Get this fellow outta here! I've got enough lousy ballplayers without another showing up!" John J. stomped to the locker room and told the clubhouse manager, Fred Logan, to tell Gehrig to go home.

One of McGraw's scouts, Art Devlin, didn't give up so easily. He talked McGraw into letting Gehrig play under an assumed name in Hartford. Gehrig had by this time accepted a scholarship to play football and baseball at Columbia, and he refused McGraw's contract offer on eligibility grounds. The manager gave the kid a conspiratorial chuckle. "Everybody in your position uses a fake name," said McGraw, making Lou feel "wet." "Nobody will blow the whistle on you." So Gehrig signed with the Giants under the name "Lou Lewis" and went to play with Hartford of the Eastern League.

It didn't take long for word to filter down from the insurance town to the big city that Columbia's star recruit was jeopardizing his free ride. Andy Coakley, the Columbia baseball coach, traveled up to Hartford and demanded of Gehrig, "What are you doing in that uniform?" Coakley convinced Lou to leave Hartford and come back to school. The coach went before Columbia's board of trustees, who were preparing to strip Gehrig's scholarship, and talked them into giving Lou another chance. Coakley stressed that the innocent schoolboy had been hoodwinked by the nefarious genius of the Little Napoleon, and the trustees agreed.

The episode soured Gehrig on McGraw for the rest of his days. "In 1921 McGraw was a sophisticated, experienced baseball man, and I was a dumb, innocent kid," Gehrig told Fred Lieb. "Yet he was willing to let me throw away a scholarship as though it was a bundle of trash."

The manager wasn't too fond of Lou either. McGraw felt he had gone out of his way to give Gehrig a second chance that literally hundreds of other players hadn't gotten. To then walk out on McGraw after the manager had stuck his neck out for the kid? Unforgivable.

So Gehrig spent the spring of 1923 on the playing fields of the Ivy League rather than the Eastern League. On April 18, 1923, while the Yankee Stadium was opening its doors for the first time, Columbia University took the field against Williams College at South Field on 115th and Broadway. Gehrig, now a sophomore, was the starting pitcher and hit third in the lineup. He had two hits and struck out seventeen enemy batsmen but lost 5–1. Paul Krichell, the ace Yankees bird dog, went straight to Ed Barrow's office and said, "I think I've seen another Babe Ruth."

Krichell is among the greatest scouts in Yankees history, having discovered Tony Lazzeri, Mark Koenig, and several other building blocks of the great teams of the era. He had delivered players for Boston for years before that. When he burst into Barrow's office telling tales of another Babe, it was an opinion to be taken seriously.

Barrow advised Krichell to make sure, so the scout went over to Columbia two days later and saw Gehrig blast a homer entirely out of South Field and onto the corner of 116th and Broadway, a blast covering about 450 feet. It was the longest shot ever hit at South Field, until Gehrig launched one even farther three weeks later, a 500-foot behemoth that clattered off the steps of the Journalism School, a landing spot that guaranteed a write-up in the papers.

Krichell had seen enough. The Columbia baseball team didn't have a proper clubhouse, so the players dressed in a room in the Furnald Hall dorm. The scout pushed his way into the mobbed space and introduced himself to the muscular youngster. Krichell told Gehrig to come up to the Yankee Stadium the next day to talk contract.

Barrow offered Gehrig a $2,000 contract for the season, plus a $1,500 signing bonus. Lou wanted to finish his education, but both his parents, whom he worshipped, were in ill health, and the family needed the money. Gehrig sought the advice of a professor at Columbia named Archibald Stockder. "Lou, you've been in my class for almost a year," the professor told him. "I think you better play ball."

In reporting the signing, the *Times* called Gehrig the "best college player since George Sisler." Lou was pulverizing the Ivy League, hitting .444 with seven home runs. On hearing of the signing, Miller Huggins congratulated Barrow erroneously for finding a Jewish ballplayer.

Gehrig was a nervous wreck on the morning of his first trip as a Yankee to the new baseball palace in the Bronx. He was a timid man in general, a loner, born to similar poverty as Ruth, although he was doted upon as the sole surviving infant of four born to Heinrich and Christina Gehrig. Yet while Ruth grew to enjoy every second of his success, Gehrig was a depressive, with painfully low self-esteem. He could hardly bring himself to believe others liked him or found him worthy.

Huggins, Krichell, and Coakley met Lou in the clubhouse. There, in his undershirt, big as life, was the Babe, sitting at his locker working on his glove. "Hiya, Keed," growled Ruth when Gehrig was introduced to him (Ruth called everyone "Keed"). Several other players milled about, played cards, or smoked idly. After Lou got a tour of the Stadium, Hug escorted him out onto the field, where several players, including Ruth, were clumped around the batting cage. Pipp was taking his swings when Huggins chirped, "Hey, Wally, let the kid hit a few."

Gehrig hadn't brought a bat of his own, so he picked the biggest one he saw off the ground—a forty-eight-ounce monster belonging to one George Herman Ruth. Babe either didn't notice or didn't care that some rook was using his lumber. Gehrig was practically trembling as he stood in to take his swings, and he swung and missed a couple of times, then finally made contact, only to dribble one weakly toward first. But then Lou found his stride, launching a half dozen balls over the right-field fence, directly into Ruthville. Gehrig continued to line shot after shot to the deep reaches of the Stadium until Huggins yelled, "That's enough," and Gehrig ran over to first to field some grounders. One thing was crystal clear to everyone present: the new guy was a keeper. "We all knew he was a ballplayer in the making," said Waite Hoyt. "Nobody could miss him."

Gehrig stayed with the team for a few weeks in June and July. He saw little action, getting only five at bats. His father, despite his poor health, came out to the Stadium to see a game, assuming his son was the star performer, given the king's ransom he'd been paid. Instead, Gehrig didn't get off the bench. "They pay you to be a bummer," Gehrig père said. "You do nothing. What kind of business is this?" Lou's first professional hit finally came in St. Louis on July 7, a single off the fantastically named Elam Vangilder.

It was a miserable time for the future Yankee immortal. He was immeasurably raw, "one of the most bewildered recruits anyone had ever seen," according to a later *New Yorker* profile. He hated to feel overdressed, so he never wore a hat or coat. He hardly spoke, both because he was a rookie—and rookies were supposed to be seen but not heard—and because he was an urban college kid who had little in common with the older country types on the Yankees. Hunting and fishing were popular hobbies among the teams, and Gehrig, a son of German immigrants from Yorkville, had only occasionally seen a tree.

Mercifully, Gehrig was sent to the minors—back to Hartford, ironically enough. Finally given a chance to play, Lou stunk out the joint. After going two weeks without a hit, he pondered quitting and heading back to school. Paul Krichell was in South Carolina on a scouting journey when he heard about Gehrig's struggles, and he raced north to talk his player into sticking it out. "Don't fear failure," Krichell counseled. "That's baseball."

Sure enough, Gehrig improved—rapidly. He tore the cover off the ball for much of the summer and would be called back to the Yankees in September. Two years later, he would take the first-base job and keep it for 2,130 straight games.

The man Gehrig would take the job from, Wally Pipp, was having a decent 1923 season to that point. Pipp led the AL in runs batted in at the end of June with fifty-four, thanks mainly to hitting cleanup behind Ruth. He hovered around the .300 mark as well, though his power was off, with only three homers in three months. Today Pipp is a punch line, a cautionary tale. Anyone taking a sick day is advised not to get "Wally Pipped"—to allow his job to be usurped for mild medical reasons. His legendary headache that supposedly gave Gehrig his chance at the everyday gig is among baseball's shibboleths. Therefore, it should come as no surprise that little of the story is true. Like a host of fine ballplayers from Fred Merkle to Bill Buckner, Pipp was a very good player whose career was completely overshadowed by a single negative moment. In Pipp's case, it wasn't even a bonehead play or a failure of nerve. He simply was replaced by an all-time great.

In 1923 Pipp was a crucial part of the Yankees offense. He was known in the clubhouse as "Pipp the Rainmaker" for his slugging ability. He led the AL in home runs in 1916 and 1917. He was also a forerunner to Gehrig in another sense: from 1915–25, he appeared in more games than any other Yankee. He played a quality first base and ranks second on the Yankees all-time putouts list, behind only Gehrig.

Pipp was the backbone of the original "Murderers' Row," a nickname applied to the 1919 Yankees by Robert Ripley of *Believe It or Not!* fame, long before the Babe donned pinstripes. "Murderers' Row wasn't named for me, as many people think," said Ruth. "I just joined the Row when I joined the Yankees." There was Pipp, Frank "Home Run" Baker, Roger Peckinpaugh, Ping Bodie, and Duffy Lewis. In retrospect the lineup seems unworthy of the appellation because of what was to come, but at the time it was considered fearsome.

Ruth and Pipp were good friends for most of Wally's Yankees tenure, and they roomed together for a time, although they had a few brawls along the way. Pipp was a large man, and he knocked Ruth out on two occasions, according to Tom Pipp, Wally's son. Wally had grown up tough, the son of a poolroom owner in Chicago (and later Grand Rapids, Michigan).

During his career, Pipp was a prominent spokesman for Buick

and drove the latest models around town. He amassed a tidy sum but after his playing days went almost completely broke in the crash of 1929, living off the largesse of others until he found a job selling small parts to automobile companies. Money was always at the front of his mind. In 1922 he had picked up some extra scratch scouting for the minor-league team in Indianapolis. He watched a kid clout the ball around the Columbia campus. He thought Lou Gehrig was an excellent hitter but wasn't sure he could field well enough for the majors.

Fast-forward to 1925: The Yankees are struggling without Ruth, who is suffering from the "Bellyache Heard 'Round the World." Huggins benches several starters, including Pipp. On June 1, Gehrig pinch-hits for Pee-Wee Wanninger, beginning his streak. On June 2, Pipp tells Huggins that the kid should be in the lineup: "Tell [Gehrig] I have a headache or something." A few weeks later, Pipp gets beaned in batting practice, bringing actual head trauma to the "headache" tale. Add Gehrig's streak to the forces of time, and a great legend is born: Wally Pipp's headache cost him his job.

In actuality Pipp knew he was through. He was thirty-two in 1925, in his thirteenth season, and he had suffered through several injuries, hitting a mere .230. He was dealt to Cincinnati in the winter. He saw Gehrig's excellence and manfully gave the kid a chance for the betterment of the team.

Pipp would cross paths with Gehrig again, on May 2, 1939. Wally took son Tom from Lansing, where they lived, to Detroit. The Yankees were in town, and Pipp breakfasted with Gehrig. Over coffee at the Book Cadillac Hotel, Lou confessed that he wasn't feeling well and was going to sit out that day. Sure enough, Gehrig ended his streak that afternoon and soon revealed that he was suffering from amyotrophic lateral sclerosis. Pipp said, "The breakdown of Gehrig reminds me of the collapse of [Everett] Scott," who also had little in the tank after his streak ended at 1,307. "Playing day after day for a record in a book. It takes too much out of a man."

21

THE 1923 YANKEES were just getting to know their future tragic figure, but the 1923 Giants started theirs in right field. Ross Youngs was batting .363 on the day Gehrig took his first batting practice at the Yankee Stadium. He was a slashing, dashing favorite of New York fans, writers, and teammates. None loved him so blindly as his cantankerous manager. John McGraw once said he wouldn't trade Youngs for the Babe straight up, and he meant it. Like Gehrig, Youngs would fall far too early from a disease little understood at the time. Those who knew McGraw best said Youngs's death broke his heart and hastened his departure from the game.

Ross's nickname, "Pep," was as appropriate as Ruth's. Just as the Babe personified youthful exuberance and desire, Pep represented passion and vinegar. He crowded the plate, daring the pitcher to hit him and put him on base. He held the bat with his hands several inches apart and liked to creep up on the pitcher as he delivered. He was a master at punching the ball to all fields. His defining moment may have been a game in 1920, when he hustled out three triples against the Reds, tying a major-league record.

Ross Youngs liked speed. Sportswriter Sam Crane wrote of Youngs's daring: "Quick as a flash to take advantage of a momentary fumble by an opponent, he is off like the wind to stretch his hits." Not only was he among the fleetest players in the majors but he loved the fast automobiles pouring off the Michigan assembly lines: he owned several sports cars. Curiously, while he was a masterful base runner, he wasn't a great base stealer, getting thrown out far too often for someone with his speed. "Base stealing is one thing that you have to learn," he explained. "A man is born with a good batting eye. There is a certain fielding sense which seems to come naturally to some, although of course, it may be greatly developed. But base stealing is by no means a thing of speed alone." In 1923 he went out of his way to prove that: he was nailed nineteen times in thirty-two attempts.

Youngs was born in a dusty East Texas crossroads called Shiner, best known for the town brewery. He was an exceptional athlete despite his slight build, one of those kids who immediately dominate every sport they attempt. Pep was a star football player and was good enough at golf to win several amateur tournaments. He would later be known throughout baseball as the best golfer in the game. Youngs was a decent point guard on the basketball court, an avid hunter, and even an outstanding dancer.

Ross's mother, Henrie, raised Youngs and his two brothers herself— Stonewall Jackson Youngs had departed when Pep was ten. Henrie ran a boardinghouse, and Ross's early life was filled with strangers carrying suitcases and weary expressions. Early photos of Ross at track meets and football games show that he was misidentified as "Young" from a tender age—he said later that he stopped correcting people in his teens.

Baseball, not football or golf, was where the money was, so he attacked the game full tilt, becoming good enough to play with the Sherman Lions of the Western Association while still in high school. Scout Dick Kinsella spotted Youngs and notified McGraw of a second baseman who played the game much as he had. The Giants signed Youngs for $2,000 in 1917. McGraw tagged him as "Pep" in his first spring training, then sent him to Rochester for seasoning, where he hit .356 and became an instant cult hero. One fan wrote "An Ode to Pep Young [*sic*]."

He had a weakness, however: he couldn't make the short throw from second to first without gunning the ball, usually errantly. McGraw quickly had him moved to the outfield, where his live arm was an asset, not a threat, and Youngs cracked the Giants lineup by 1918.

Like many players, he exploded offensively in 1920, batting .351, good for second in the NL behind only Rogers Hornsby, while slugging .477. It was the first of five brilliant seasons at the plate. During the stretch, he averaged .341, and his slugging percentage never dipped below .446. His élan on the bases and in the field added to his reputation. Though he was short and stocky, his speed made him a superb outfielder—he ran down drives others let fall for extra bases. "He played the carom off the right-field wall in the Polo Grounds as if he'd majored in billiards," according to Frankie Frisch.

Pep was immensely popular among the fans and the press because he played every game as hard as possible. "He was the hardest-running, devil-may-care guy I ever saw," said Frisch. "The best at throwing those savage cross-blocks to break up a double play." That would become a point of contention come October 1923, but mostly Youngs's die-hard style was lauded. When complaints arose about the power game supplanting Scientific Baseball, often the underlying sentiment was about *effort*. The home run just seemed too easy in the sense that something as precious as a run should be earned over the course of several batters, not merely in one quick jolt. The least the players could do was work hard, and Pep did—demonstrably so.

The press also saw themselves as working-class stiffs and, except for the occasional star (like Heywood Broun, for example), were paid that way. They collectively worshipped Youngs. Sure, they loved Ruth, the King of the New York Streets, but as much if not more for his penchant for producing copy and selling papers as for his style of play. The home runs may have been exciting, but they weren't all-out, hustling baseball. Sportswriter Ford Frick, later the commissioner famous for putting an asterisk next to Roger Maris's sixty-one home runs for daring to break Ruth's single-season homer record, would write of Youngs: "Everybody has Cobb, Ruth, and Speaker on his all-time outfield. But, somehow, I've got to find a place for Pep Youngs. Don't ask me to take one out, I've just got to put Pep in there somewhere."

By 1924 Pep was an established star, and after another stellar season (including ten homers, a career high), he signed a three-year contract. One New York paper reported that McGraw promised Youngs "on the expiration of his contract he would be given another calling for a salary equal to or larger than that of any player in the game."

Pep wouldn't live to see the end of the contract.

In 1925 Youngs began to suffer from headaches, indigestion, and repeated viral infections. His all-out style was curtailed, and his batting average fell off dramatically. His health deteriorated in 1926. Pep lost considerable weight and missed almost half the season with various ailments. He still managed to hit .306 in ninety-five games, but it was the final flicker of a brilliant career. Doctors were unable to produce a diagnosis to encapsulate the multitude of symptoms. Pep's face puffed up badly, sometimes restricting his breathing. Back- and stomachaches were severe. His urine was bloody.

Dick Kinsella went to visit him early in 1927. "What I saw made me want to weep," Kinsella said. "I do not think he will ever play baseball again. The hand of fate is heavy upon him. From a player who weighed 170 pounds he is down to 120 pounds. He has had numerous blood transfusions. He divides his time being carried from his home to the hospital.... Baseball's slashing terror [has been] transformed into its most helpless individual."

It wasn't until Youngs had dipped below a hundred pounds that a kidney inflammation called Bright's disease was fingered as the culprit. Today it would be called nephritis and would be treated with antibiotics. At the time there was no cure, although warm baths and laxatives were thought to help. Some speculated that Pep's hard-core style had come back to haunt him, that his kidneys were injured in a collision with an outfield fence or another player. The disease had felled President Chester Arthur, Emily Dickinson, and, in 1924, Cincinnati Reds manager Pat Moran. On October 22, 1927, it took Pep Youngs.

His funeral in San Antonio drew thousands, including most of his former teammates and, of course, John McGraw. "He was the greatest outfielder I ever saw on a ballfield," McGraw said during the eulogy. From that point, the manager kept a framed photo of Youngs in his office, alongside one of Christy Mathewson. They were the only two players so honored in McGraw's long career.

A plaque in Pep's honor was laid at the Polo Grounds. It read:

A brave untrammeled spirit of the diamond, who brought glory to himself and his team by his strong, aggressive, courageous play. He won the admiration of the nation's fans, the love and esteem of his friends and teammates, and the respect of his opponents. He played the game.

The Yankees came home from their long road trip and hit a wall, going 13–12 in June. Perhaps it was the lame post-Huston moniker given to the team by the press: the "Ruppert Rifles." The dreary month also saw Ruth's lone escapade into 1922-esque off-field shenanigans.

After all that May power, Ruth managed only three dingers in June, although his batting average shot up thirty points. Of the Babe's twenty-nine hits for the month, twenty-one were singles, which may in part have been a result of a foot injury that became public by accident. The Yanks had scheduled an exhibition in New Haven on an off day, a common practice at the time. The Babe, who took the free day to travel to Sudbury to see his family, was a no-show, much to Hug's annoyance—and Ruppert's, as the team had to refund nearly a thousand tickets that were sold based on Ruth's participation. Ruth blamed an epic traffic jam. But the alibi didn't hold up. Huggins had called Home Plate in desperation, and a caretaker answered. The man quickly said that Ruth had "hurt his foot" and then hung up. Repeated calls got no answer.

The Babe had apparently overslept and missed his train. In his haste to get to his car and drive to New Haven from Sudbury, Ruth had missed a stair and wrenched his foot. It was painful but ultimately not serious. The Sultan of Singles didn't miss any time, and though his stance was slightly different, he played well, one of the few Yanks to have a strong first month of summer.

By this time, it was apparent that whatever ailed the Babe in '22 had vaporized. The league's pitchers took notice. Ruth began to accumulate intentional walks at a dizzying rate. On June 11, Sherry Smith of Cleveland gave up a double to Ruth in the first inning. After that, he honored the Babe with a free pass four straight times. "If Babe got balls somewhere near where he liked to hit them, he would bat .450," Smith said in awe. "He seldom gets a good ball. A pitcher is foolish to give him a good ball."

Such was the respect for Ruth's plate prowess that on June 14, the Browns decided to walk him intentionally—with the bases loaded. Absurd as it seemed, the stratagem worked. St. Louis got out of the jam and won the game, 3–1. The irony is that the Browns pitcher that afternoon, Hub "Shucks" Pruett, had been tremendously successful against the Babe the season before. As a rookie in 1922, Pruett had whiffed Ruth ten times in thirteen at bats. In the lingo of the day, a "cousin" was a pitcher considered easy to hit. In that case, Pruett had grown closer family ties with Ruth in 1923—the Babe already had homered twice off Shucks (so called because the quiet Missouri farm boy never swore). Ruth was truly casting off all the previous season's bad karma.

Late in the month, Bullet Joe Bush shut out the Red Sox at Fenway Park for his tenth victory. That tied both Howard Ehmke, the man he beat that afternoon, and Urban Shocker of St. Louis for the AL lead in victories. The Yanks staff didn't have an anchorman, someone readily identified as the ace. It was a crew of five solid, steady starters. But at the moment, Bush was first among equals.

Leslie Ambrose Bush was from Brainerd, Minnesota. He got his nickname in Missoula, Montana, his first professional stop. While walking the town's dusty streets one broiling hot summer day, he spied a sage hen. He offhandedly tossed a stone at it and plunked the unfortunate poultry right between the eyes, killing it. A nearby policeman asked what he planned to do with the bird. "Eat it," replied Bush.

"That's one expensive meal," said the cop, who fined Bush $25 for killing the hen out of season. The next day's paper noted the incident under the headline "Joe Bush Throws Bullets at Sage Hen." And he was tagged "Bullet Joe" henceforth.

His premier fastball made the nickname a natural one, and Bush tossed enough bullets to catch the eye of Connie Mack, who bought Joe for Philadelphia and used him at age twenty in the 1913 World Series, making Bush the youngest pitcher ever to appear in the Fall Classic. On one of his visits home to Brainerd, the locals presented him with a car to honor his exploits. The young hero got into the roadster and proceeded to accidentally run down and kill a seventy-five-year-old man named Louis Miller. Bush's career went on without interruption.

On August 26, 1916, Bullet Joe walked the first Cleveland Indian he faced. He then retired the next twenty-seven hitters in a row for a near perfect no-hitter. Bush then moved to Boston in time for another World Series appearance in 1918. He was also assigned to chaperone the team's carefree, careless star, Babe Ruth. "Babe carried his money around in rolls of hundreds, fifties, and twenties," Bush later recalled. "Babe would start buying, and as the evening wore on he'd pull out that roll and the bills would start slipping off. One night back at the hotel I returned two hundred sixty dollars he dropped on the floor."

Bush hit upon a tried and true method for hustling the Babe during card games. He would bum a stogie, take a single puff, and toss it on the floor. Ruth would explode. "Those Coronas cost a buck apiece and you're throwing them away!" Thus distracted, the Babe was candy in Bush's hands.

Bush was a supreme bench jockey, with a loud, braying voice and a keen eye for mockable traits. His singing voice, on the other hand, was spoken of fondly in the clubhouse. Bush possessed an excellent baritone. He was also an accomplished ventriloquist. A devoted practical joker, he once was arrested for imitating various animal noises in a restaurant and making them sound as if they were coming from every direction. He always wore a lucky red shirt under his uniform, a heavy flannel he refused to wash or clean. He even kept it in a corner of his locker so it wouldn't mix with his other shirts.

Bush became a success by throwing heat, but he took his career to another level when he added a devastating breaking ball to his arsenal. He was playing long toss with a teammate one day in 1920 when he unconsciously took a funny grip on the ball. It dipped in a crazy manner when he threw it. Bullet Joe had serendipitously discovered a new pitch, an offshoot of the curveball called the forkball. Others have been credited with inventing the pitch in which the ball is jammed between the middle and index fingers and thrown with a snapping movement, but Bush undoubtedly popularized it on the biggest stage. He toyed with it a bit until he felt ready to use it in a game.

The first batter he unleashed it upon was the immortal Ty Cobb. "Cobb swung and missed and demanded the ump inspect the ball," Bush recounted to Lawrence Ritter in *The Glory of Their Times*. "I'll never forget the expression on his face. Then I struck him out and Billy Evans the umpire came out to ask how I threw it. I told him if there is nothing on it, it was none of his damn business how I threw it."

Bush was a solid pitcher before—with the forkball in his repertoire, he was dominant. He won sixteen games in 1921 and might have won thirty in 1922 but missed a full month after badly cutting his finger on a razor blade. Bush settled for twenty-six wins, with a 3.31 ERA.

Those twenty-six wins came in pinstripes, not red stockings. Bush was a key figure in the Rape of the Red Sox, having been dealt to New York before the 1922 season. "It's the greatest Christmas present imaginable," said Bush. He added, "Another good point is that I will have Babe Ruth with me instead of against me." Bush was a primary reason the Yankees got to the World Series despite Ruth's miserable season. But his two losses to the Giants, and the claim that he had eased up to spite Huggins in Game Five, eroded his reputation.

He was doing his damnedest to restore his rep in '23, however. Bush's shutout of Boston came as the Yanks took three of four at Fenway Park, continuing their road prowess. They returned to New York with the surging A's in town. Philadelphia, managed by the legendary, and legendarily lean, Connie Mack was only five games back as they arrived at the Yankee Stadium for a four-game set. Shawkey was sharp in the opener, winning 4–2. The Yanks overcame a rare poor start by Bush to win the second game, 10–9. On the thirtieth, 35,000 came to the Bronx on a Saturday to see Pennock go all the way for his ninth victory, Ruth reach base all five times at bat, and the Yanks win, 6–1, to improve to 42–22, eight games ahead of Philadelphia. "This crucial series has failed to 'croosh'," noted the *Times*. Sad Sam Jones sent Philly limping out of the Bronx on Sunday, July 1, with a 4–0 shutout. In the span of four days, the Yankees had put the AL race in a hammerlock.

22

On June 12, Harry Houdini hung upside down forty feet above Gotham, suspended by a cable from an apartment building. He was bound in a straitjacket. Thousands of onlookers gathered below, stopping traffic as they gaped up at the escape artist wriggling free. Houdini wore a safety wire around one ankle, the result of being slammed against a building by high winds in a similar stunt the year before. He had recently given up on the movie business, saying the "profits are too meager," and was once again performing his escape act in the skies above New York. This time, Houdini extricated himself in under three minutes.

The Giants hadn't had to rely on many dramatic escapes over the first two months. The *Sporting News* put in print what everyone felt: "The Giants are the most powerful ball club ever put together." On the first of June, McGraw's men lived up to the billing by winning their thirty-first game against eleven defeats, humiliating the Phils, 22–8, in Philadelphia, pulling off the rare feat of scoring in every single inning. Pep Youngs drove in seven runs. Only fifteen hundred masochistic Philadelphians turned out to watch the massacre.

The Giants were potent, but their pitching was becoming an issue. Jack Scott suffered a freak injury during pregame warm-ups when a batted ball struck his pitching hand, breaking a bone and shelving him for several weeks. Meanwhile, Jack Bentley was off to a slow start. Bentley was trounced in his debut at Boston, surrendering thirteen hits. It got worse in his second outing. He was pummeled by Philadelphia, giving up six runs and nine hits in two innings. Then he got his first win by "limiting" Philly to eight runs and twelve hits, going the distance in a 13–8 Giants victory. Through May, Bentley went 3–4 and was shelled for sixty-six hits in fifty-two innings of work.

A portion of Bentley's struggles was due to his bizarre, convoluted delivery, one the *Tribune* likened to "a cross between an Einstein theory and a spiral staircase." The effort of tying himself into a pretzel before every pitch tired him out. "When it [gets] to be the seventh inning, I feel the effects," he said. "And yet, I can't seem to pitch without that windup."

The ineffectiveness of his star import worried McGraw. So on June 7 the manager unloaded catcher "Oil" Smith, whom he detested, and pitcher Jesse Barnes to get a Braves pitcher he liked, John "Mule" Watson, along with a replacement catcher, Hank Gowdy. Mule was a typical McGraw pickup, an apparently mediocre pitcher but one who the manager felt would respond to his teachings. Watson was 1–2 with a 5.17 ERA in a limited role in Boston at the time he was dealt, but McGraw took him aside and told him he was now a starter, and an important one at that.

A veteran of the 1914 "Miracle" Boston Braves, Gowdy, like Jack Bentley and Cap Huston, was a war hero. He had been the first major leaguer to enlist and won honors for his bravery at St. Mihiel, the Argonne, and Château-Thierry. After the war, Gowdy went on a public-speaking tour detailing his exploits. He enlisted again during World War II at the age of fifty-three and saw more combat, becoming a major. He ended his tour of duty at Fort Benning,

Georgia, where the baseball diamond, Gowdy Field, is named for him.

The Giants had a relationship with the Braves not unlike the one the Yankees enjoyed with the Red Sox. Whenever the New York side needed a player, Boston was sure to offer one up. McGraw had helped save the Boston NL franchise by convincing his chums to take charge of the team. Indeed, the current manager, Christy Mathewson, was among McGraw's best friends. So when "Big Six" told his former boss that Watson might help the Giants' cause, it wasn't long before the pitcher was headed down the Boston Post Road.

After leaving Philly in flames, the Giants embarked on their first western trip, to Chicago, Pittsburgh, Cincinnati, and St. Louis, baseball's frontier town. The team had played only thirteen times away from the Polo Grounds so far that summer, losing exactly one of those games, to Brooklyn way back on April 20. The epic home stand had allowed the Giants to establish a rhythm and build a working margin.

Arriving in the Windy City, McGraw was greeted by a firestorm of his own making. He had unusually, and rather arrogantly, agreed to pen an article for the *Chicago Daily News* analyzing the strengths and weaknesses of the Cubs. Even in the golden age of baseball and newspapers, even when it came from the Genius Manager, the Messiah of Scientific Baseball, it was a staggering breach of etiquette, a besmirching of the "code" of the game.

McGraw opined that while the Cubs were young and inexperienced, they also lacked "teamwork," and that was mainly due to manager "Reindeer" Bill Killefer. "I have known Bill Killefer since he started out as a young player, and I know that a man of his intelligence would prefer that I be perfectly frank and sincere in my observations," wrote McGraw. "If I were not frank I would not be honest."

McGraw's unusual in-season assessment may have been painful, but it was also accurate. The Cubs were undisciplined, and their fans were impatient with a callow group. The article became a cause célèbre in the Second City and seemed to inspire the team. At 20–23 when the Giants came to town and the article appeared, the Cubbies took two of three from the omniscient John J. Chicago won seven of their sixteen games against the Giants in 1923 and played well the rest of the way, finishing fourth, twelve games over .500.

After the Giants lost the last two games in Chicago, they dropped two of three in Pittsburgh and then were swept four straight by Cincinnati. A defeat by the Cardinals on the seventeenth made it nine losses in ten games. It was the sort of poor form that led McGraw to say, "It's a good thing there is a law against concealed weapons. Otherwise I'd have a gun with me on the bench every day and I'd probably not have any ammo left at the end of the game."

The bad streak coincided with an especially worrisome run of poor starts by McGraw's ace, the elegant lefty Art Nehf. Nehf had won twenty-one, twenty, and nineteen games in the years 1920–22, and after his superb World Series, there was little reason to suspect any falloff. The pitcher started the season by winning five of his first six decisions. But in those wins New York averaged eight runs per game behind him, masking beatings such as the one Nehf took on May 25, when the Phillies scored eight runs off him but lost, or the game earlier in May at the Baker Bowl, when Cy Williams and the Phils lanced him for seven runs in an inning and a third, only to have the Giants score eleven times to take Nehf off the hook.

In June the bats behind Nehf quieted, and he wouldn't win another game until Independence Day.

Pitchers that fit Nehf's description—small lefties who win with guile and not overpowering stuff—are almost always called "crafty." That was Nehf precisely. At 5'9", 176 pounds, Art intimidated no one on the mound. But his competitive spirit and smarts made him one of the more successful pitchers of the early '20s.

Nehf was lazily given the nickname the "Terre Haute Terror"

early in his career—he was born in Terre Haute, Indiana, the hometown of pitching great Mordecai "Three Finger" Brown and Socialist presidential candidate Eugene V. Debs. But fortunately the press caught wind of his fondness for playing the organ, and the "Organist" took over as Nehf's main nom de hardball.

Nehf's father, Charles, was a prominent jeweler in Terre Haute, and Nehf grew up, if not rich, considerably better off than many of his teammates. He studied engineering at Rose Polytechnic (now Rose-Hulman Institute of Technology) but couldn't find a decent paying job, so he stuck with baseball even though he was considered a marginal pro prospect. Erudite and brainier than most players, Nehf sought weighty conversations where he could. The *Los Angeles Times* reported that Art was "more likely to discuss subjects other than baseball with reporters on train trips."

Nehf improved greatly while with Terre Haute of the Central League, to the point that the Boston Braves bought him. He arrived in 1915, the season after the Miracle Braves came from dead last to capture a shocking World Series title. Nehf was a solid if unnotable pitcher for Boston's NL entry, but John McGraw noticed him, especially the way he pitched for the 1919 Braves, a going-nowhere outfit. Nehf beat the Giants twice early in the season, impressing the manager enough to convince him to send four players and $55,000 north for his services.

His fastball was lively enough to keep hitters at bay, but it was Nehf's curve that was his out pitch. He would throw sidearm and sometimes underarm, baffling hitters—they were unable to pick up the pitch in time to hit it hard. And he was an outstanding fielder, cat-quick off the mound and with his glove.

But now in 1923 Nehf hit some icy patches. His curve lacked snap, his fastball lacked verve, his changeup lacked the ability to surprise. Nehf never mentioned injury, although he would be plagued the following season with arm trouble, and he may have felt some strain or tenderness and not said anything about it. After three brilliant campaigns, Nehf would finish 1923 with a mediocre 13–10 record.

McGraw righted the Giants ship in late June. Much of that was due to the welcome sight of the Boston Braves, whom they'd raided, in the opposing dugout. The Giants perennially owned Boston, and they added to the city's miserable baseball summer (the Olde Towne's teams would finish a combined 78½ games out of first place) by taking six straight from the Braves, part of an eleven-game win streak. On the twenty-third, the recently dealt "Oil" Smith expressed his displeasure at going from first to worst, whipping a discarded ball into the Giants dugout, apparently meant for McGraw. His aim wasn't true, and the *Times* noted he "just missed removing the leg of two substitutes and the batboy." Two days later, the Giants scored three in the bottom of the ninth for an 11–10 win over Philadelphia. "The ease and adeptness with which the Giants made their game-rescuing stint made it look almost prearranged," said the *Times*. Clan McGraw finally lost in the last game of June, a 1–0 shutout at the hands of the just-traded Jesse Barnes. Despite the defeat, New York closed the month 4½ games ahead of the Pirates, and 7½ in front of the Reds.

One day during the streak, a woman named Edna Lawson traveled from Los Angeles to New York to visit her friend Van Meusel, Irish's wife. Van was among the leading matchmakers in the city, and she had an inkling Edna might hit it off with Irish's bowlegged drinking companion, reserve center fielder Casey Stengel. Edna and Van went to a game at the Polo Grounds, where they sat behind Blanche McGraw, who was too busy keeping score to chat. Edna was twenty-eight and had never had a serious boyfriend, although on her last trip to New York she had spent some time with a doctor from Brooklyn.

The sawbones never had a chance. "Stengelese," Casey's unique way with the English language, was in its nascent stage—and who could resist it? He called bad players "road apples," and average ones "clerks." "Lobs" were those who left runners on base. Tough guys like McGraw could "squeeze your eyebrows off." Playboys like Ruth were "whiskey slicks."

Stengel himself was no whiskey slick—his face could be generously described as "interesting." But that didn't mean he wasn't charismatic. Casey made an impression on a female writer named Zoe Buckley later in the year, causing her journalistic distance to slip: "We expected to see a loose person of hayfoot, strawfoot awkwardness," she wrote. "But no. Your modern ballplayer is no roughneck. He is trim and immaculate, wears a $90 suit and a camel's hair overcoat. His skin is clear and rosy, his features well cut, his body lithe, with modest bearing but high-proof masculinity."

In June of 1923 Casey channeled his inner Valentino (the real thing was embroiled in a dispute with his studio, Famous Players, and spent the year on a dance tour sponsored by beauty-products manufacturer Mineralava). Stengel took Edna dancing that first night and proposed after two weeks. Edna was attracted to Casey's energy and wit but put him off until after the season. He wrote her and asked after her and marked the days until he could see her again.

The affair lifted Stengel's spirits. It had been a testy, trying season so far. The $75,000 man, Jimmy O'Connell, had taken much of Casey's playing time in center field early in 1923. One day Stengel went down to the Aldine Hotel to drink away his sorrows with writer Frank Graham. After a few slugs of illegal alcohol, Casey muttered that he was through as a player. He wasn't bitter about it, the writer recalled, just factual. Graham reminded him that should the Giants make the World Series, he would probably get some playing time—and some extra cash.

"Yeah, and if I get into a game I'll probably strike out or make a terrible error," lamented Stengel.

"Maybe you'll get a homer," said Graham facetiously.

"If I do, I'll drop dead before I get to home plate," responded Stengel.

A few days later Casey got a chance to play in the City of Brotherly Love. Phil "Lefty" Weinert was pitching for the Phils. Weinert was coveted at one point by McGraw because he was Jewish, and John J. thought he would draw fans in New York. The left-handed Stengel seldom played against southpaw pitchers, but O'Connell was injured and Bill Cunningham sick, so Stengel was in the lineup. Weinert plunked him in the second inning. In the fourth, Lefty came up-and-in on Stengel again, sending Casey sprawling to the dirt. Stengel got up, threw his bat at the startled pitcher, and raced to the mound with violence in his heart.

Casey had studied dentistry before becoming a ballplayer, to the point where his friends called him "Doctor." Calling upon his training, Stengel was doing his best to remove Weinert's teeth. Phillies manager Art Fletcher saw his hurler getting whipped by the smaller Giant and hustled out to pull Stengel off. It took two policemen to wrestle Casey off the field as he screamed curses (mostly anti-Semitic in nature) over his shoulder. NL president John Heydler suspended him for ten days for "gross misconduct."

Such scrappiness won McGraw's heart. Stengel was one of his favorite players for the most basic of reasons: he reminded the manager of himself. This was a paradox, because Stengel was one daffy dude, and McGraw's baseball personality could best be described as *clenched*. Stengel's most notable moment as a player to that point may have come at Brooklyn's Ebbets Field in 1918. Casey was with Pittsburgh after having spent the previous six seasons as a Robin. It was his first game back in Brooklyn. Standing in right field, Stengel noticed a sparrow fly into the outfield wall and knock itself out. Casey, for reasons known only to him, stuck the bird under his cap. When he came to bat the next inning, his former home crowd heavily razzed him. At the same time, he felt the bird coming out of its stupor. So Stengel bowed with a showman's grace to the crowd and doffed his cap, letting the sparrow fly free. The crowd forgot all about the jeering and gave him a standing ovation.

He may have been born in the Midwest, but Casey loved New York City. Legend has it that Stengel was receiving treatment for a bad back in 1921 when word came that he had been traded from Philly to the Giants. Stengel leapt off the massage table and danced a jig. "I thought you had a bad back, dammit," said his manager, Wild Bill Donovan. "Not anymore," replied the gleeful Stengel. His reaction upon reaching Penn Station was to exclaim, "Wake up, muscles, we're in New York now."

He was a gossip, a drinker, a superb dancer, a natural showman. Like Ruth and McGraw, the endless possibility of the New York nightlife appealed mightily to Stengel. "There comes a time in every man's life, and I've had plenty of them," he'd say. He had loved his days spent in the relative hinterlands of Brooklyn, and now he was going back to the city to play the palace: the Polo Grounds. "When you talk about Casey Stengel, you talk about a guy who could stay up all night, drink you under the table, and talk more baseball than any man in history," remembered one former teammate, Charlie Grimm.

Stengel joined up with Frankie Frisch and Irish Meusel to catalog the various insides of New York drinking establishments. They sampled bootleg whiskey and talked the game. They were always ready to play the next day, though—McGraw saw to that. One time the Old Man was laying into a group of players for after-hours carousing. Stengel strolled into the clubhouse, stinking of bay rum, which had been applied by his barber as an aftershave. McGraw didn't care. "At it too, eh, Stengel?" he fumed, and fined Casey $50. "You showed up ready to go or McGraw took your money," Stengel said.

McGraw also hired private detectives to follow Casey and the other night owls on the team. At one point, a shamus reported back to McGraw that Stengel and his buddy Irish Meusel had (briefly) fallen out. When the manager confronted Stengel about it, Casey responded, "I don't like to share a detective with anybody." Even when Stengel stayed in, he liked to help his buddies foil McGraw's curfew checks by pretending to be roommate Hugh McQuillan, calling out in Hugh's tenor, "Here," when the knock came at their door, then switching to his own baritone.

McGraw may have taken a shine to Casey, but he didn't show him any special favors. As the manager had humiliated Ruth during the 1922 Series, he had done likewise to Stengel, pinch-running for his center fielder in the second inning of Game Two. Casey stared daggers at his manager while trotting off the field. "I was so damn mad at McGraw for doing that I couldn't see straight," he said afterward. But he got over it quickly. Blanche McGraw remembered Casey talking long into the night with her husband, making dish after dish of scrambled eggs and bacon. McGraw's cook noticed how his freezer would be depleted after Casey's visits and wondered "how that Mr. Stengel can eat so many peas." McGraw looked upon Casey as a son. The childless manager saw his players as his progeny, and Stengel was all too happy to lap up Little Nap's life lessons. Meanwhile, McGraw wasn't about to admit that any son of his could age, saying of Casey, "He may be old in a baseball sense, but he's the most vigorous old man I ever saw. And he's about as game a fellow as ever lived."

The close relationship didn't help Stengel get off the bench. He had all of nine at bats in June. He sat and watched as Pep Youngs blasted a three-run homer in the eleventh at Braves Field, with the Giants scoring seven times to win a 15–8 slugfest. He grounded out as a pinch hitter in the 11–10 win over the Phillies. And he shook his head while O'Connell rapped out two hits and Bentley turned in his best start of the season in a 6–0 shutout of the Pirates. Still, it was better than being stuck in Philadelphia.

July

23

THE YANKEES SCHEDULE during the month of America's birthday was brutal. Twenty-two of the thirty-one games in July were played away from home, another murderous road trip to rival the May stretch of twenty-two of twenty-five away from the Bronx. It was a roller coaster that would have sunk a lesser assemblage. Instead, New York won sixteen of its road games in July. One factor was the pitching, notably of Bob Shawkey, who won five games in July (he would finish 16–11). Shawkey had broken into the bigs with the A's in 1913 and, until the 1920 rule changes, overwhelmed hitters with his fastball. But "changing conditions" convinced Shawkey to mix in his curveball far more often, to the point that by 1923 it was his primary pitch. It is indicative of his abilities that he won twenty games in 1919 and the same number in 1920 with two different out pitches.

Tall and thin, like many hurlers of the day, Shawkey threw with a hard, almost violent motion, even when he transitioned into breaking balls. The 1928 guide *How to Pitch* explained it thusly: "He puts all his body into his pitching motion and twists himself on his pivot foot long before he lets the ball get away." The author, J. E. Wray, went on to warn his readers that Shawkey's "delivery is not advised for a young pitcher to copy."

Bob was a quiet man, overshadowed by the bigger personalities on the Yankees staff. He worked slowly and methodically on the mound, and likewise studied opposing hitters carefully when he wasn't pitching. He was the team's Steady Eddie—reliable, a hard worker since his teen years in a wooded hamlet deep in the Allegheny Mountains called Sigel, Pennsylvania. Shawkey was in a logging gang by age fifteen, working all day for a buck and two bits. He also served in the navy during the war aboard the battleship *Arkansas,* earning him the nautical nickname "Bob the Gob" ("gob" is slang for "sailor"). He was enormously respected in the Yankees clubhouse, and he took over for Miller Huggins as manager in 1930 after Hug's untimely death.

If the Yankees pitching was stellar, so was the Babe's hitting. Ruth batted .391 during the long trip, shooting him toward the top of the league in batting average, trailing only Harry Heilmann. When his ridiculous walk rate was factored in, Ruth was way ahead in on-base percentage.

Up in Boston, the Red Sox were suffering through their fourth straight abominable season since selling Ruth to New York, en route to a last-place record of 61–91 (with two ties). July was particularly grueling. The Sox played thirty-four games in the month, including a backbreaking nine doubleheaders, most of them on the road. Boston went 11–23 in July, surrendering an unconscionable 232 runs.

They officially bottomed out on July 7. The Cleveland Indians tomahawked them by the incredible score of 27–3. Manager Frank Chance was upset with pitcher Lefty O'Doul's embrace of Beantown's nightlife (not to mention the speakeasies found in other cities), so he left him in to give up thirteen runs in the sixth (all unearned), a record for a single inning. O'Doul took the hint and became a slugging outfielder, and later a successful manager and then restaurateur in San Francisco.

The Sox had been the Team of the Teens, winning four World Series titles in the decade. Those dominant squads of Tris Speaker, Harry Hooper, Duffy Lewis, Stuffy McInnis, and George Herman Ruth seemed very far away by 1923. The man held responsible for turning a championship dynasty into a punching bag, Harry Frazee, sold the Red Sox four days after the massacre in Cleveland. Boston fans heaved a mighty sigh of relief. The Man Who Sold Ruth was out of the picture at last. The *Sporting News,* as pro–Ban Johnson a publication as there was, trumpeted the end of Frazee's reign with an unsubtle headline: "Johnson Elated That Frazee Is Finally Out of Baseball." A group of Ohio businessmen paid Frazee a cool million dollars for the team. They turned over baseball operations to Bob Quinn, a veteran from St. Louis. It took him a decade, but Quinn restored credibility to the Sox before he and the group sold the club to Tom Yawkey.

In all the mythos and hyperbole recounting the sale of Ruth to the Yankees on January 6, 1920, the role of Cap Huston in the deal is usually overlooked. Huston had long thought he could talk Frazee into selling the Babe. After all, the two owners frequented the same drinking establishments, and both loved all the delights that pre-Prohibition New York could offer. Frazee was a Broadway producer first, baseball owner second, and he kept an office just a short stroll from the Yankees offices on 42nd Street. Harry was much the better dresser, much more the ladies' man (he was seldom without a beautiful actress on his arm), and, in his mind, much sharper than Huston. The lyricist Irving Caesar of "Tea for Two" fame once said Frazee made more sense drunk than most people did sober. Huston was more likely to descend into alcohol-induced ramblings. It was a friendship that carried an element of the long con—each man thought he might hustle the other at some point. But it was a friendship, as genuine as could be when cemented by spirits.

Frazee certainly believed no asset was priceless. "Someone asked me if my club was for sale," he said. "What a ridiculous question. Of course it is for sale. So is my hat and overcoat, and my watch. Anyone who wants them can have them at a price. I will dispose of my holdings in the Red Sox at any time for any price." He felt the same way about Ruth, who was holding out for more money (demanding $20,000 when his contract called for $10,000) and had jumped the team on several occasions over financial disputes.

Cap Huston was Johnny-on-the-spot. He swooped in to assure his pal Harry that the Yankees would be happy to pay top dollar to relieve Boston of their talented headache. After all, what are friends for? Ed Barrow, at that point still the Red Sox manager, told Frazee that there was no one on the Yankees roster worth having, so Frazee sold Ruth outright. Barrow also sounded a warning. "You ought to know you're making a mistake," he told Frazee. Frazee, having built himself from nothing into a Broadway titan and baseball owner, believed he knew better.

The Yankees would pay $100,000 for the Babe. Crucially, Frazee agreed to take the money in four $25,000 installments, one straightaway, the others made over the next two years, with 6 percent interest attached. In addition, Ruppert agreed to front Frazee $300,000 in a side deal, with Fenway Park as collateral. In other words, the Yankees might have actually owned the iconic home of their greatest rival had Frazee not repaid the colonel, with interest.

The Boston papers, which relied on the Babe for good copy as much as the New York papers would, ripped the sale. The *Boston Post* wrote: "Ruth is different. He is a class of ballplayer that flashes across the firmament once in a great while and alone brings crowds to the park, whether the team is winning or losing." The papers were filled with loaded terms such as "moneygrubbing" and "Broadway" to connote that Frazee was Jewish—a "fact" that wouldn't go over well with Boston's mostly Catholic population (Frazee was actually Presbyterian). Harry put out a statement defending the move, emphasizing Ruth's leaving the club in 1918. "He is one of the most inconsiderate men that ever wore a baseball uniform," said Frazee. "A team of players working harmoniously together is always to be preferred to that possessing one star who hugs the limelight to himself. And that is what I am after." He noted that Huston and the Yankees had offered $150,000 for Ruth after the 1918 season. Clearly, then, his value was dropping.

Frazee also hinted that New York was receiving damaged goods. "Ruth is taking on weight tremendously.... He doesn't care to keep himself in shape.... He had a floating cartilage in his knee that may make him a cripple at any time." Some in New York actually worried that Ruth wouldn't even be able to play right field as well as the man he was replacing, Sammy Vick. Vick wasn't much of a player, and he was a prodigious eater, to the point where anytime a player tucked into a big meal, it was known as "Doing a Sammy Vick." Ruth, of course, would prove superior to Vick in that respect as well.

Huston would also play a critical role in getting the slugger to sign a new deal with the Yankees. Ruth's initial reaction to being sold down the Boston Post Road was clinical. "I am not surprised," he said. "When I made my demand for twenty thousand a year, I had an idea they would choose to sell me rather than pay the increase, and I knew the Yankees were the most probable purchasers in that event." Privately he wasn't thrilled at the prospect of relocating to New York from Boston. He bitched about the Big Town's cost of living. "New York is so goddamn expensive," he said. "Hell, a taxi ride costs a dollar and seventy-five cents and a show on Broadway is five bucks. Who in hell can pay those prices?"

Miller Huggins immediately went to California, where Ruth was vacationing, to talk contract with his new star. He came home without an agreement—from the first he and Ruth didn't see eye to eye. Til Huston took over as primary negotiator with the Babe, and the two sides quickly agreed. Twenty thousand for 1920 it would be. Huston emerged as the owner who would talk turkey with the slugger. His open, fun-loving side appealed to the Babe, unlike the standoffish Ruppert. Ruth had fun with both of them upon signing. Cap warned Ruth that although he didn't mind paying him the huge salary, it came with caveats: the Babe had to lay off the booze and the women. Ruth replied, "Look at you! Too old and fat to have any fun. And that goes for him too," the slugger exclaimed, pointing to Ruppert. Ruth then nodded over at Huggins, who was hiding in the corner. "As for that shrimp, he's half dead right now."

Huston would become fast pals with his highly paid star. Cap saved Ruth's hide during his first spring as a Yankee in 1920, going into the stands to rescue the Babe from a heckler who had pulled a knife on the Sultan. Out of appreciation, or more probably because he recognized a fellow partyer, Ruth socialized regularly with the owner and often traveled south to spend a couple of winter weeks at Huston's hunting preserve on the Georgia barrier isles.

The passage of time would doom the sale of Ruth to New York as one of sport's most colossal blunders (Frazee would later ask cabdrivers and strangers on the street what they thought of Harry Frazee and laugh when the expletives flew), but at the moment of the move, it wasn't at all clear that that would be the future result. Ruth's power was obvious, but no one could have foreseen the humongous numbers he would put up — thanks in large part to the rule changes that had yet to be announced. Ruth in Boston was hardly a disciplined hitter and was vulnerable to left-handed pitching, and right field at Fenway Park was not nearly as inviting as it would prove to be at the Polo Grounds and later at Yankee Stadium. In his entire career, Ruth never once homered into the right-field bleachers at Fenway Park. And Frazee wasn't obfuscating when he pointed out the Babe's physical deficiencies.

Tellingly, despite the outcry from the Boston press and most of the Sox fans, not one of the players spoke out against the sale of Ruth. Even Waite Hoyt, who liked to say later that after Ruth's sale he "went around insulting Boston officials so they would trade me, preferably to the Yankees," remained mum at the time. The truth of the matter was that the Yankees had taken a large, expensive risk in acquiring the Babe.

Huston and Ruppert were unafraid of risk, as their bet on the new Stadium was proving. In both cases, the gambles paid off—hugely.

Before leaving on the rail tour of the American League, the Yanks had swept eight straight at home against Philly and Washington. The signal game of the home stand was played on July 3. In the eleventh inning of a 1–1 game against the Senators, Ruth made a spectacular catch to rob Goose Goslin of a hit. In the process, the Babe knocked himself unconscious. Team doctors and a couple of volunteers who were called in from the Yankee Stadium grandstand circled Ruth. Finally it was decided that, in their best medical opinion, the cure for Ruth's possible concussion was a glass of water to the face.

Ruth came around, wondering why his head and chest were dripping wet. He then ended the game in the fifteenth by launching his sixteenth home run of the season over the right-field fence off George Mogridge, who had pitched all fifteen innings (as did Bullet Joe Bush for New York—indeed, it was a different time). Roughly a thousand fans poured onto the field to greet Ruth at the plate after the homer, his most dramatic of July.

Bob Meusel was emerging as the team's second-best hitter. On the Fourth of July, the Yankees swept a doubleheader against Washington, 12–6 and 12–2. Meusel had five hits and six RBI in the two games. The spree put him over .300 as he took the league lead in RBI from Pipp, with sixty. Meusel was slugging fifty points higher than Pipp as well. Meanwhile, the day before, the Giants beat the Phils, 4–2, at the Baker Bowl. Irish Meusel knocked in all four runs on two homers, his sixth and seventh of the season. It was a typically productive couple of days for the slugging brothers Meusel.

Ballplayers of the '20s called good conversationalists "barbers." Bob Meusel was not a barber. To the contrary, he often went days without uttering a word. He was called "Silent Bob" or "Languid Bob" when he wasn't being called "Long Bob" in reference to his 6'3" frame. One time Irish returned from a long road trip to the apartment the brothers shared. Bob rose, grabbed his bags, and left on a road trip of his own. No words passed between the two siblings. Bob may have been silent, but that didn't mean he was shy — he was almost as big a carouser as the Babe. He was described in one New York paper thusly: "A strange, cloistered gentleman is Mr. Meusel, impervious to gibes, threats or criticism. He moves through life in solitary splendor."

Irish, on the other hand, was friendly — downright ebullient. He was three years older than Bob but wasn't nearly the physical specimen. Bob was tall and leanly muscled, with a rocket for an arm. Irish was only 5'11", 178 pounds, with a popgun for an arm. Decades later fans still talked about a throw he launched virtually sideways into the right-field grandstand at the Polo Grounds. One time Irish and McGraw were standing in front of a hotel when a homeless man with an arm missing approached. "Pardon me, sir, I had the misfortune to lose my arm and —"

"On your way!" roared McGraw. "Irish ain't got it!"

Emil was more of a grinder, a good hitter but not a feared one. Bob was capable of amazing things. Bullet Joe Bush recalled a game in Detroit when Bob was fast asleep in the bullpen and was called upon to pinch-hit. He woke up, shambled to the plate, and tripled to win the game.

Bob didn't work very hard, at least to the naked eye. The 1923 *Reach Guide* felt that "only a rather lazy and listless manner prevents Meusel from being one of the greatest stars of the game.... He is erratic in the field, careless on the bases, and at times totally indifferent." But he *had* worked hard to get his arm under control. As a minor leaguer in California, his throws bounced crazily due to the spin he put on the ball. So he learned to hit his target on the fly, even the distant catcher. He could also be roused into violence, unlike Irish — he once attacked Ty Cobb with a bat after getting beaned on what he thought were Cobb's orders.

Irish started his career with three decent seasons in Philadelphia, where he used an interlocking grip on the bat, like a golfer's. In 1921 he was traded to New York, a deal onlookers thought would help bring Bob out of his shell. The Meusels moved in together in Washington Heights. Publicly, Bob continued to restrict his vocabulary to "hello" and "good-bye," but he was voluble at home. He, his wife, Edith, and Irish and Van enjoyed games of bridge and long dinners together.

Throughout the InterCity Series, the brothers ignored each other as they ran to right field after every half inning. But it was during the World Series, when fraternal bonds might have been torn asunder, that the two were closest. "We'd go home after each Series game in '21–'23 and we'd sit down and rehash the games," recalled Irish. "The guy whose team had won that day would have himself a good time bragging and the loser would have to stand for some ribbing. Bob and I had some good times."

After sweeping the Sens in front of 45,000 fans at the Yankee Stadium on Independence Day, the Yankees headed for Grand Central Terminal and an express train west, with a 47–22 record, 11½ games in front. The Stadium didn't sit idle with the Yankees out of town, however. On July 24, lightweights Benny Leonard and Lew Tendler held the eagerly anticipated rematch of their epic bout from the previous year. Sixty-five thousand fans (including Babe Ruth — the Yankees spent their off day in New York before heading to Philly to wrap up the road trip) packed the house. It was the first title fight ever held in the Yankee Stadium, kicking off more than a half century of memorable fistic action in the ballpark.

Leonard and Tendler were both Jews, and their rematch (the former earned a controversial decision in 1922) electrified the city's large Hebraic population. The Jewish diaspora that had swelled the Bronx descended on the Stadium, while seemingly the entire Lower East Side crammed the subway system for the ride north. Leonard was born (as Benjamin Leiner) and raised on those streets and was known as the "Ghetto Wizard" as a result. "Lefty" Lew Tendler was an interloper from Philadelphia—he may have been a member of the tribe, but for this night, it was a warring tribe.

Cap Huston had planned for this event—the vault under second base was easily brought to ground level with a minimum of fuss. Cap attended the fight as a fan, gazing down upon the realization of his multisport dream. But he didn't share in the huge profits from the evening—roughly half a million in ticket sales. Leonard took home $140,000 as the convincing victor, peppering away at the overmatched Tendler in a way he hadn't been able to do the summer before.

Fight time was ten p.m., so this was the first night event in Stadium history. Major Birmingham, now the chief engineer for the Stadium (with Cap Huston gone), established a lighting system for the bout, a "glaring white pool" over the ring as well as an intricate system of klieg lights on the surrounding grandstand and red lights marking the exits. The *Times* described the scene: "The big stand looked like a Leviathan at anchor, with white lights shining from each tier like the deck of some liner, and the red lights peeping out from the portholes." The evening went off without a hitch. "Let it be said that Tex Rickard [the famous fight promoter] in his best moments never surpassed the arrangements last night," opined one reporter. The massive throng was helped home by color-coded searchlights that directed them to the different subways and avenues leading away from the Stadium, the first time such a system had ever been used. The crowd handled the inaugural nighttime disembarkation of the Stadium with ease, thanks in part to the new lights.

Yankees pitcher Carl Mays had told the press in May that he longed to become a professional boxer. He even had a planned, if fanciful, schedule, one that started with heavyweight tomato can Floyd Johnson and envisioned Carl duly whipping the rest of the division until he got his shot at Jack Dempsey. Mays's size (185 pounds) and sulfurous personality gave the career change some credence, although the only punches Mays had been known to throw had been at teammates.

Come July 17, Mays desperately wanted to slug Miller Huggins.

Carl had been born in extreme poverty in a backwater Kentucky hill town called Liberty. He often had to hunt and kill his own dinner, although the family was too poor to own a gun. He carried a pocketful of rocks and would whip them at squirrels, killing them with a single shot. Carl became so adept at the practice that he could deliberately bean the squirrels so as not to bruise the meat.

As an adult, Mays recollected accounts of his hard-knock childhood without rancor, but otherwise he was an angry, unpleasant person. The tragic killing of Ray Chapman with a pitched ball on August 16, 1920, at the Polo Grounds had helped neither his disposition nor his public image. The 1921 World Series–fix suspicions didn't help either, nor did his tangential but public role in the Black Sox investigation—Mays was thought to have tossed a few games for cash here and there, though nothing was proven. His personality ensured he didn't get the benefit of the doubt.

Huggins's anger over the 1921 Series and Mays's role in the loss had not subsided. It was merely shoved deep in the manager's intestinal tract. Now, during an endless western trip, it was thrust back up again.

Hug had kept Mays buried on the bench, starting him only four times to that point. "Why would I use him—I'm winning an easy pennant without him," said the manager. One time in Boston, Mays wondered aloud to a group of writers why he hadn't been used much. Huggins was within earshot, and he responded quizzically, "Hey, Carl, you're still with the team?"

On July 17 Mays finally started another game, against the Indians. After a decent first few innings, he tired and got walloped by the Forest City Crew. Huggins let him twist in agony. Despite having plenty of rested arms to turn to, the Yankees manager kept sending Mays out to absorb more punishment. He went the distance, allowing thirteen runs on twenty hits in a lopsided loss. Pipp and Scott, disgusted, refused to finish the game in protest.

Afterward, when asked why he didn't change pitchers, Huggins replied, "He told me he needed lots of work, so I gave it to him."

A week later, Mays got some solace. He started against his personal pigeons, the A's. Mays had beaten the Philadelphians an amazing twenty-three consecutive times, dating back to his days with the Red Sox. The Yanks trailed, 2–1, going into the eighth but scored eight times over the final two innings, including a massive three-run shot by Ruth (the ball left Shibe Park and landed on the roof of a house across 20th Street). Mays got the victory, his twenty-fourth in a row over the hapless A's, tying the record for most wins over a team by a hurler, set by Giants great Christy Mathewson against the Braves. It was one of only five victories for Mays all season.

The day after Mays's historic win, the Yanks drew ten thousand fans to Shibe Park in the second of a four-game set. New York's dominance of the AL was having a deleterious effect on attendance throughout the league, except in Philly, where the "Homicide Row" regularly drew big crowds when they came to town, helping to keep a teetering franchise solvent. Trailing 4–0 in the eighth, the Yanks erupted for a four spot to tie the game, the big blow being Aaron Ward's three-run triple. An inning later, the Babe drew his third walk of the game, his hundredth of the season, and scored on a groundout to win it for New York, 5–4.

The following day, July 26, in brutally hot weather, the Yanks tripped Philly again, 4–3. After the contest, Waite Hoyt was granted permission by Hug to return to the Big Town a day earlier than the rest of the team to prepare for his start against the White Sox two days hence at the Yankee Stadium. After sweeping the A's in the fourth game, the Yanks took a train back to New York. Carl Mays found Hoyt and told him, "Babe says not to talk to you anymore." Ruth was peeved, not because the affable pitcher had left the team but because he hadn't asked *Ruth* for permission. Who the hell did Waite think ran this show anyway? The Babe apparently thought his bid to become player-manager was somehow successful. His teammates quickly abandoned the edict, but Ruth, not usually one to hold a grudge, amazingly froze out Hoyt for nearly two full years.

Hoyt, who was quick to forgive Ruth and welcome back his company, would later speculate that the heat had gotten to the Babe. Ruth may have been hotheaded during the brutal summer months, but when the syndrome turned literal and his melon started to steam, he would run to the dugout and pull a fresh head of cabbage from a water cooler. He would tear off a leaf and tuck it under his cap to cool him off.

Cooling off was hard for all players in those days before air-conditioning truly civilized the country. Traveling on a long trip west, as the Yankees had done, was a punishing endeavor. The trains were slow, hot, and crowded. The hotels could be worse. The Yankees generally stayed in premier lodging, but even five-star hotels were roasters during summer nights in St. Louis, Cincinnati, or Chicago. Players often hauled their mattresses onto balconies and sometimes to nearby parks to sleep alfresco. Lou Gehrig would often soak his hotel sheets in cold water to beat the heat at night, a practice that made his knees and ankles ache as he aged.

Ruth and his teammates didn't get much of a break traveling to and from the train depot either—teams in the 1920s generally walked to the hotel upon arrival and carried their own bags (though not their equipment). Depending on the itinerary of their trip, the players' body clocks could be thrown off. New York, as well as Boston, Chicago, Philadelphia, Pittsburgh, and Cincinnati, adhered to daylight saving time during the summer, while Cleveland, St. Louis, and Washington did not. Team officials often had to remind the players to adjust their watches.

And train travel carried risks. In December 1923, Wild Bill Donovan, the manager replaced by Miller Huggins in 1917, was killed riding the 20th Century Limited en route to Chicago. Donovan was managing the New Haven minor-league team at the time. He had just swapped berths with team president George Weiss because his bed was uncomfortable. The train wrecked in Forsyth, New York. Weiss escaped with a back injury and would go on to preside over the Yankees dynasty of the '40s and '50s. Wild Bill was not so fortunate.

Despite the occasional danger and discomfort, train travel was an essential part of baseball in 1923. The players bonded on the railroads, engaging in marathon games of pinochle, bridge, blackjack, and poker (the Yankees mostly eschewed poker, and the Babe was an inveterate bridge player). Waite Hoyt brought hearts to the Yankees train rides upon joining the club. The writers and even the conductor held standing invites to join in games. The "Negro" porters often kibitzed but were pointedly not allowed to sit down and play.

The teams usually commandeered several cars on a charter basis, including berths for the newspapermen (the teams paid for their tickets in those days, which helps explain the hagiographic coverage that dominated the sporting press). There was a dining car offering generally mediocre fare, and a smoking car, which wasn't the only place where smoking was permitted but was more a fancy name for the lounge car.

Players roughhoused up and down the aisles, talked baseball in small groups, and sang in the smoking car while someone played piano or harmonica. Sports pages were strewn everywhere, and some players, like Hoyt or Nehf, even read books to while away the hours. Aaron Ward started the Yankees on a brief but intense crossword-puzzle craze. Mah-jongg played an outsize role on trains populated by the Philadelphia A's, who took to the game with such fervor that in 1927 Connie Mack would blame it for his team's failure to keep pace with the Yankees in the pennant race (Ruth and Gehrig apparently having little to no role).

One of Ruth's favorite hobbies was to rampage up and down train cars, taking straw hats off the heads of anyone who wore one after Labor Day and punching out the insides. It was a common prank among ballplayers, but Ruth took it to a new level. One time a team-mate named Mike McNally, having seen his straw boater destroyed by a blow from the Babe, filled Ruth's hat with eggs and condi-ments. Ruth put it on, covering his clothes with goop. Unfortu-nately the Babe had to appear in court that day, as a witness against an Italian truck driver who had smashed into Ruth's parked car. It was very warm, and the goulash began to ferment, causing an unholy stench. Finally Ruth offered to pay the Italian man's fine just to get home and change suits.

The Babe never took a train trip without hauling along his new toy, the phonograph, and a couple dozen records. On this western trip in the summer of '23, some of the songs Ruth and the Yankees listened to included Billy Murray's "Yes! We Have No Bananas" and "That Old Gang of Mine"; "Felix the Cat" by Paul Whiteman and His Orchestra; "Cut Yourself a Piece of Cake (And Make Your-self at Home)" by Billy Jones; and Van & Schenck's huge hit "(Noth-ing Could Be Finer Than to Be in) Carolina in the Morning." Country, or hillbilly, music broke into the mainstream in 1923, thanks to a Georgian named "Fiddlin' John" Carson who sold half a million copies of his recordings, including "The Old Hen Cackled and the Rooster's Going to Crow."

A favorite leg of every journey west was the trip departing St. Louis. Before embarking, the players would stop off at the Anheuser-Busch brewery (despite the fact that, in the Yankees' case, the team was owned by a rival brewer) and any of several favored barbecue shacks near the train station, load up on beer and ribs, and gorge themselves as the train sped east. The players would sit out on the boxcar and whip ribs and beer bottles at the passing telegraph poles.

Food was always on the players' minds. In the early days of the Huston-Ruppert ownership, the team picked up all meals, regardless of cost. But after two rookies shared a princely $15 breakfast at the Brunswick Hotel in Boston, a $4 per diem was instituted. Mark Roth, the traveling secretary, would hand out the money to the guys first thing in the morning. The Babe, of course, was renowned for his appetite. "How about putting some lamb chops around that steak for trimmings?" he liked to say. Writer and novelist Paul Gallico once observed on the subject of the Babe: "There was a time when he was undernourished and sometimes starving. No man who goes hungry ever quite forgets it." Some people, however, like Waite Hoyt, thought Ruth exaggerated his food consumption in public for effect, especially as he got older.

Rookies and second-stringers usually were lumped in their own Pullman at the rear of the train, known throughout the game as the "Syracuse Car." The nickname stemmed from the New York Giants' practice, when playing exhibition games in the college town, of clumping the players who seldom got on the field into a separate car and ordering it decoupled—the rest of the team would chug on to the next town for an off day while the substitutes took on the Syracuse nine.

On the trains and in the hotels, the players mixed with the average travelers and fans. Ruth, of course, was an unmistakable presence and drew huge crowds wherever he went. His teammates were more fortunate. Guys like Pipp and Dugan were able to hold forth in the dining car or the hotel lobby for hours, and they weren't always recognized as ballplayers. Wally and Jumpin' Joe were not merely "barbers"—they were prominent stylists. A favorite gag the two played was to get an unwitting stranger to talk about how the Yankees could improve their performance in the field. The players would convince the fan to approach Miller Huggins, peacefully smoking his pipe across the lobby, with his theories of better baseball. They then would laugh as Hug turned beet red at the intrusion.

The country that the teams traveled through was rapidly changing as the postwar slump faded and everyone chased the American dream of success. The late teens had been a time of angry, often violent protest of wage inequity and horrific working conditions, leading to widespread strikes, terrorist activity against capitalist interests, and an overarching crackdown against Communist "agitators." By 1923 the country had been mostly pacified, for better or worse. Consumerism and abundance were now seen as uniting influences on the country. Everyone, regardless of politics or regional background, could agree that upward mobility and disposable income were worth pursuing. It was the American dream as defined by Til Huston: to make enough money to be able to pay someone else to do the hard labor.

Poverty was still rampant in rural areas, especially Appalachia and the Deep South. But unlike the prewar United States, most city inhabitants now lived in a dwelling that averaged one room per person and provided heat, electricity, running water, and an indoor toilet. The average annual income was $1,236, a wage that allowed a comfortable if hardly swank lifestyle. Unemployment was plummeting, thanks to the growing manufacturing centers. This took place despite a wave of immigration that ballooned the national population to 106.5 million people (6 million lived in New York City).

The great migration of African-Americans from the South to the urban North, mainly New York and Chicago, was well under way. More than 200,000 blacks moved to New York City between 1917 and 1925. Towering apartment blocks that housed the swelling populace dominated the skyline. As the Yankees and Giants rumbled west, the landscape changed utterly—rarely was a building half as tall seen anywhere except Chicago. Much of the land was still being farmed and hadn't yet been converted into suburbia.

What any player looking out his train window would have noticed was the growing ubiquity of the automobile. Half a million new cars hit the American road between the end of the war and the stock-market crash. Trains were still the preferred method of travel, but mainly because the roads had yet to keep up with automobile production. A U.S. Army motorcade, including a young lieutenant colonel named Dwight Eisenhower, required more than two months to cross the country just four years earlier, in 1919, and highway and road construction was still in its nascent stage. Cities, especially New York and Detroit, were choked with traffic due to the paucity of drivable streets. The major roadways that would become the feeders to the Yankee Stadium—the Major Deegan Expressway, the FDR Drive, and the George Washington Bridge—didn't exist. A few miles from the field, the Bronx River Parkway was being built in Westchester County. Elsewhere, much of the country remained unpaved. Dust and mud were unavoidable facts of life.

Worse, the cities, especially New York, were death traps for pedestrians and autoists alike. In the first three months of 1923, 217 people were killed in New York auto accidents, after 765 perished in 1922. A *Daily News* study found that lax laws handcuffed police: they could do nothing to prevent reckless drivers from flying around slow streetcars, changing lanes at will, or blasting through dangerous intersections. Only a few roads were outfitted with traffic signals.

The carnage spurred a series of new laws aimed at curbing the death toll, and in other areas progress was taking giant strides. The "closed" car, such as the Stutz Six Sedan and the Cabriolet, was turning automobiling into an all-weather, year-round pleasure. "One does not have to go back very far to remember the day when motoring, like oysters, had its special seasons," said Lee Eastman, president of the Auto Merchants Association, in the fall of 1923. That day was drawing to a close.

Overhead, two U.S. Army lieutenants made the first nonstop cross-country airplane flight in 1923. It took twenty-seven hours to get from Long Island to San Diego in a Liberty monoplane T-2. The brand-new weekly magazine *Time* felt "ultimately, no business will be able to afford any but airmail; no businessman any travel but air travel." In January the first helicopter flight was made in Dayton,

Ohio. The bizarre contraption managed to hover in place four feet above the ground. And as the Yankee Stadium opened in April, a young army lieutenant named Charles Lindbergh was in Americus, Georgia, buying his first plane. Never having soloed before, he nearly crashed it on his first takeoff, revealing only then that he held no pilot's license. Fortunately for Lindbergh, in 1923 a pilot's license wasn't required to buy an airplane.

Perhaps the most notable advancements came in the realm of sound. Three days before opening day at the Yankee Stadium, a set of short films ran before the silent feature at the Rivoli Theatre on 49th Street. The shorts were accompanied by audio of the actors talking, a brand-new development that would shortly revolutionize the cinema industry just as Babe Ruth had the National Pastime.

Portable turntables and phonographs were new phenomena, but they were catching on fast. Phonograph production was up to about 200,000 sets in 1923, and by decade's end there would be five million sold annually. And radio broadcasting stations, numbering fewer than ten in 1921, had undergone a boom. By mid-1923, roughly six hundred stations broadcast programming, a chaotic blend of music, local news, and individuals sponsoring events needing publicity. And come that autumn, there would be baseball on the air—the volume and quality of which would trump any sports broadcasting that had come before.

24

In early July, starting Giants shortstop Dave Bancroft fell ill with pneumonia. The future Hall of Famer wasn't the player he had been. At thirty-two, he found that his quickness and defensive abilities were eroding. Still, Bancroft was hitting .323 when he got sick, and his replacement didn't figure to help the team much.

McGraw turned to rookie Travis Jackson, the kid whose defensive play had been so atrocious in the minors. Now he was to be thrown into the crucible of a pennant race in New York City, under the most exacting manager the game had ever known. But McGraw believed in Jackson and, more important, believed that the manager himself had been able to mold a solid infielder out of the shy Arkansan.

Jackson got off to a rocky start. Sixteen errors in six weeks didn't endear him to Giants fans. But McGraw stuck with him, bolstering the kid's confidence whenever he faltered. Jackson rewarded his manager with a strong showing at the plate. Upon taking the shortstop job, he notched a hit in eleven straight games and had another fifteen-game hit streak in August. Jackson also wowed fans and the press alike with his powerful throws to first, wielding an arm that "appears to have a steel spring concealed up his right sleeve." The Giants maintained both a winning record (26–18) and their NL lead while Bancroft was out. And McGraw was so taken with Jackson that he kept him at shortstop, moving the recovered Bancroft to second and Frisch to third. Heinie Groh, the hero of the 1922 Series, was scuffling. He too was aging (approaching thirty-four in the summer of 1923), and his bottle bat wasn't getting the job done: he was hitting in the .270s, with little power—only four home runs. McGraw started to sit him during the hot summer, hoping to preserve Groh for the stretch run. Conversely, after hardly playing in June, Stengel seized the center-field job in July, rewarding McGraw by hitting .348 with ten RBI and eight extra-base hits.

Meanwhile, despite the Giants' fast start, the Pirates were not going away. One reason was the continuing struggles of Jack Bentley. The Giants survived a rough start in the opener of a five-game series with Pittsburgh on July 10, winning 9–8 in ten innings despite Bentley being strafed for thirteen hits and seven runs. Four days later, the Pirates ripped Jack for four runs in an inning and two-thirds en route to a 10–1 romp. Pittsburgh stayed within 4½ games of the Giants with the win.

The National League was proving tougher for the New York entry than the American League was for its counterpart. Despite preseason predictions of a five-team contest, the Yankees were making a mockery of the pennant race. In mid-July, the Yanks and Giants had virtually the same record—but the Yankees held a double-digit lead on Cleveland, while Pittsburgh and Cincinnati stalked the Giants. The Reds too had caught fire, thanks to star pitcher Adolfo Domingo de Guzman Luque, or Dolf Luque, the "Pride of Havana."

A light-skinned Cuban with a long nose, thin face, and blazing blue eyes, Luque had played in the Negro Leagues before he was told that he was "white enough" to pass in the majors. He signed with the Miracle Braves in 1914 and would stay in baseball for twenty-one seasons. McGraw knew Dolf well from his winters in Cuba, where on many occasions El Orgullo de Habana pitched while El Mono Amarillo watched. Luque's Cuban team in the winter of 1923 was considered one of the greatest to ever play on the island, featuring the "Black Wagner," John Henry Lloyd; the "Cuban Ruth," Cristóbal Torriente; and "El Maestro," Martin Dihigo — Hall of Famers all.

Luque was a tough hombre. His manager in Brooklyn, Wilbert Robinson, told a story about Dolf throughout his baseball life. Luque was a Dodger in the mid-'30s, and an enemy heckler kept yelling, "Lucky Luque!" in his direction. Dolf told Robinson that he was going to punch out the guy if he didn't shut up. Robinson responded, "Aw, come on, Dolf, he paid his way in, let him boo." The insult comic in the stands turned his attention on Robbie: "Hey, fat belly!"

"OK, Dolf," said Robinson, "go ahead and clobber the guy." Luque did just that.

He spoke little English but usually managed to get his point across. Once, after a critical error by teammate Babe Pinelli, Luque chased Babe around the clubhouse with an ice pick. Brushed back by pitcher Tiny Osborne, Dolf flung his bat at the mound in response. He once pulled a gun on an umpire. In later years, as his English improved, he became a pitching coach, teaching Sal "the Barber" Maglie everything he knew about pitching inside, if not about firearms.

Luque was 10–1 with a 1.24 ERA heading into July, and then he turned it up a notch, winning seven of eight games in the month, six of them complete. He beat the Giants, 5–3, in the Polo Grounds on July 8 (despite giving up a home run to Highpockets Kelly, one of only two that Luque would allow all season), twirled a three-hitter against the Phils on the twelfth, then started and won both ends of a doubleheader in Boston on the seventeenth. By comparison to his Beantown heroics, two wins over the Robins in a four-day stretch a week later seemed a pretty ordinary feat, but the second victory pulled the Reds to within 4½ games of the Giants and tied them with Pittsburgh. McGraw was particularly annoyed to see Luque do so well, as the Reds had offered him to New York before the season. The Little Napoleon hadn't wanted the fiery Cuban, fearing he would be too difficult to control.

The National League race got closer still. On the twenty-sixth of July, the Cubbies scored four in the ninth to shock McGraw's men at Wrigley Field, while the Pirates pulled out a twelve-inning thriller at home against Boston, and the Reds crushed the Robins, 9–2. On the twenty-seventh, it was Cincy's turn to claim victory in twelve innings, while Pittsburgh won easily. The Giants were idle, and suddenly, somehow, the lead was down to three games. The next day Pittsburgh inched to 2½ back when the G-men split a doubleheader and the Pirates beat the Braves, 3–1, to complete a five-game sweep.

On the thirtieth, the Pirates hosted New York in a doubleheader at Forbes Field for the first two games of a five-game set, the biggest series of the season to date. Two years earlier, the squads had played a key five-game series in August, with the Pirates ahead by a fat seven games. In the opener, after exhorting his team that they could "beat these bums. Stay close every game and we'll win!" McGraw had done the unthinkable: he let Highpockets Kelly swing on a 3–0 pitch. The pitcher, knowing McGraw never, ever let his men swing away with such a count, grooved a fat one down Broadway, and Kelly hammered it for a grand slam to win the game. The Little Round Man strutted into the clubhouse after the victory, crowing, "If my brains hold out, we'll win!" New York swept all five and went on to speed past the Pirates to capture the flag.

This time, McGraw's brains took part of the day off. Up 4–0 behind Jack Scott, heading into the ninth inning of the first game, the Giants let the Pirates rally for five runs to steal the contest. The key play came on a Baltimore chop infield hit by Johnny Rawlings, the tormentor of Babe Ruth the previous October. He had been dealt to Pittsburgh in the off-season, and here he was, not only haunting his old mates but doing so via the play his old manager had invented. Between games, McGraw started to let his team have it, a good old-fashioned browbeating from the master, when suddenly he stopped and muttered, "Aw, forget it," and left the stunned players in silence. It might have been his greatest stratagem of the season—the Giants sent home early the 32,000 who had been celebrating after the opener, crushing Pittsburgh, 17–2, in the nightcap.

New York won two of the next three to take the pivotal series and send the Pirates to four games back. The Iron City Boys never fully recovered from the blunting of their momentum. But meanwhile Pete Donohue won his sixteenth of the season for Cincinnati, 3–0 over the Phillies, to keep the Reds three off the pace. Cincinnati was primed for an August showdown with New York at intimate Redland Field.

August

25

Just as the NL race started to heat up, tragedy overshadowed baseball. In early August, while the Giants were taking the rubber game against Pittsburgh behind Mule Watson, and Cincy's Pete Donohue was dominating Philadelphia, and the Yanks were beating Cleveland, 4–2, before 15,000 at the Stadium, President Harding was on his deathbed.

The president was popular, but his underlings had been doing their damnedest to discredit his administration. The worst was yet to come. The Teapot Dome scandal and other corruptions weren't yet public knowledge and would come to light only after Harding's death. But the president knew enough that in his final weeks he cried out in frustration, "I have no trouble with my enemies, but it's my damn friends that keep me walking the floor nights."

Eager to escape DC for a while, Harding had headed west on a "Voyage of Understanding." He became the first president to visit Alaska, but while traversing south across British Columbia he fell ill from food poisoning. His health worsened, and by the time Harding's retinue reached San Francisco, the president had developed pneumonia. He appeared to improve, but on the evening of August 2, as his wife was reading to him, Harding suddenly keeled over and died, not three years into his term. Rumors would swirl for decades that he had committed suicide over Teapot Dome and other scandals that his Ohio pals had foisted on the nation, or that he was the victim of a coup led by his wife. Mrs. Harding had refused an autopsy, leading to hothouse speculation.

While Calvin Coolidge was sworn in as the thirtieth president of the United States, baseball took the day off. Landis immediately canceled all games on August 3, and he also called off action one week later, August 10, on the day of Harding's burial, which would be the last time both leagues canceled their schedule for any reason other than work stoppages until September 11, 2001.

When play resumed on August 4, the Giants were in Cincinnati to tangle with the second-place Reds. McGraw loved the Queen City. It was one of his favorite venues for postgame entertainment, with preferred hangouts including the Peruvian Club, Curly's Place on Delhi Turnpike, and especially the Laughrey Club. He would gather up old pals and newspapermen and drink beer by the Ohio River, wolf down sausages with Limburger cheese on rye bread, and stay up till the wee hours, singing favorites like "Three O'Clock in the Morning" or "Off to Philadelphia" or "Dear Old Pal of Mine." That didn't mean the pugnacious Muggsy couldn't find a fight in the heavily Germanic city. For example, after one win in Cincy in 1919, McGraw yelled at the crowd, "We beat you today, and we can't wait to get out of the Home of the Huns!" A nearby policeman, presumably a son of the fatherland, rushed at McGraw and took a swing at him. He missed, connecting with Prince Hal Chase, who decked the flatfoot in return. Despite the fall of one of their brethren, the mounted police swooped in and saved the New Yorkers after a mob of fans stormed over the fences and went after McGraw and Chase.

Four years later, McGraw angered Cincinnati fans again when his team blasted Luque, 14–4, in the opener en route to sweeping a five-

John McGraw ponders his next stratagem, omnipresent bat by his side. The manager used different grips on the stick to signal his players. (National Baseball Hall of Fame Library, Cooperstown, New York)

The ever serious and sober Casey Stengel. (National Baseball Hall of Fame Library, Cooperstown, New York)

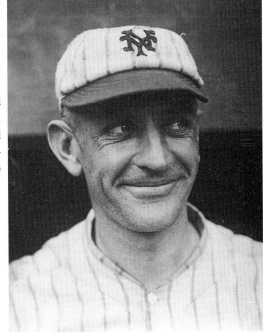

The Babe and Yankees co-owner Til Huston and their steeds for the day. This photo is unrelated to the Yankee Stadium rodeo of August 1923. (Transcendental Graphics / theruckerarchive.com)

The Babe shakes hands with President Warren G. Harding before an April 1923 game at the Stadium. In a command performance, Ruth hit a home run to delight the president. Harding would pass away in August, a fervent baseball fan to the end. (National Baseball Hall of Fame Library, Cooperstown, New York)

Before they became the heart of Murderers' Row, Ruth gives some pointers to new teammate Lou Gehrig in June 1923. (Transcendental Graphics / theruckerarchive .com)

Days before the World Series that would pit the two rivals in mortal combat, McGraw and Ruth amazingly shared a Giants dugout for an exhibition game against the Baltimore Orioles. The Babe played despite a gimpy ankle and hit a colossal home run while wearing a borrowed jersey. (National Baseball Hall of Fame Library, Cooperstown, New York)

Graham McNamee: the first star of sports broadcasting. McNamee is calling Game Two of the 1924 World Series from Griffith Stadium in Washington, DC. No photos of his debut at the 1923 Series exist. (Library of Congress)

The mythmakers of the New York press in a group shot at the Polo Grounds. Fred Lieb is sitting, second from left. Next to him, from left to right, are Damon Runyon, Bozeman Bulger, Sid Mercer, and Grantland Rice. The man sitting on the ground is concessions king Harry Stevens. (National Baseball Hall of Fame Library, Cooperstown, New York)

Fans line up early to purchase bleacher-seat tickets before Game One of the 1923 World Series, the first Fall Classic game in Yankee Stadium history. (Library of Congress)

McGraw and Yankees manager Miller Huggins before the start of the 1923 World Series. (National Baseball Hall of Fame Library, Cooperstown, New York)

The comedy duo of Al Schacht and Nick Altrock attempt to lighten the mood before the Series starts. (National Baseball Hall of Fame Library, Cooperstown, New York)

"Go, Casey, go!" Casey Stengel slides across home ahead of the tag to complete his stunning inside-the-park home run to win Game One for the Giants. (National Baseball Hall of Fame Library, Cooperstown, New York)

The Babe crosses the plate after hitting his monster home run in Game Two, the first of two he would hit that afternoon. The homers paced the Yankees to their first Series win against the Giants after eight defeats. (National Baseball Hall of Fame Library, Cooperstown, New York)

Yankees pitcher Herb Pennock lies on the ground after getting beaned by Jack Bentley in the fourth inning of Game Two. Pennock would recover and get the victory. (National Baseball Hall of Fame Library, Cooperstown, New York)

Casey 2, Yankees 1: Casey Stengel touches home after hitting his second game-winning homer of the World Series, this one in Game Three. The Giants won, 1–0. (National Baseball Hall of Fame Library, Cooperstown, New York)

Ruth contributed as much with his legs as with his bat, here executing a perfect hook slide in Game Five, an 8–1 Yankees romp, as the Yanks seized control of the Series. (National Baseball Hall of Fame Library, Cooperstown, New York)

game series that sent the Reds tumbling to eight games out. Cincinnati went down so meekly that suspicion of foul play was rife. *Collier's Eye,* a noted sporting sheet considered the *Wall Street Journal* of gambling men in the 1920s, put the suspicions into print, accusing Reds players Pat Duncan and Sam Bohne of taking $15,000 to throw the series New York's way. The article was taken seriously enough that the players were summoned to a meeting in New York with NL president John Heydler. But both convinced the authorities of their innocence, pointing out that they combined to hit .294 in the series, not great but hardly proof of dumping games. They also sued *Collier's Eye* and won a settlement.

If McGraw thought or dared hope he was rid of Cincinnati, he was mistaken. After the Giants debacle, the resilient Reds ripped off thirteen wins in fifteen games to reinsert themselves into the pennant chase. The inspiration may have been the finale of the Giants series in Cincinnati, when tensions exploded. Luque was getting razzed heavily on the mound, "taken for a ride" all the way to Havana and back. The fiery Cuban suddenly halted midpitch, raced to the New York dugout, and punched Casey Stengel square in the mouth. Stengel claimed innocence in mocking Luque. He also admitted ruefully that he "was the most likely suspect."

Pep Youngs, who was at bat, chased after Luque and seized him from behind. The Reds infielders belatedly arrived in the now-full dugout, and a donnybrook broke out. A flying wedge of police managed to haul Luque off and break up the fight, but when star outfielder Edd Roush slipped through their ranks to go after Youngs, chaos reigned again. Luque managed to wrest free, grab a bat, and chase after Stengel, whose aging legs found new life while running from the angry Cuban. Both players were finally tackled, ejected, and taken to their respective clubhouses.

The display of team unity pumped up Cincinnati. The Reds hopped on a train east, marched to the Polo Grounds, and turned the tables on the Giants, minus the fisticuffs. The Reds took four of five from Clan McGraw, with Luque and Donohue winning once each. Eppa Rixey, an "attenuated and cadaverous left-hander whose playing livery fits him with the same exactness with which a bologna skin harbors its innards," in the judgment of Paul Gallico, beat the Giants twice. Despite his 6'6" height, Rixey got hitters out not with power but with craft. He enjoyed rubbing it in on the batsmen. "How dumb can the hitters in this league get?" he asked a reporter. "I've been doing this for *fifteen* years. When they're batting with the count 2–0 or 3–1, they're always looking for the fastball. And they *never* get it."

McGraw was forced to use fourteen pitchers in the four losses. His dicey staff was coming undone. Hugh McQuillan was hit hard twice in the series. He was only a middling pitcher during his career, but he did happen to possess one of the greatest pickoff moves of all time. McGraw sometimes brought him in to close games simply to pick off opposing base runners. Sometimes McQuillan never even pitched to the batter. Making the move more astounding was the fact that Hugh McQ was right-handed—thus he didn't rely as much on deception as on timing and accuracy. Unfortunately, he wasn't as accurate when throwing to the plate, and he developed such a good pickoff move by necessity—there were often runners on base against him.

Luque himself had gotten the series flowing for the Reds by hammering a home run off Handsome Hugh in the opener. Marshall Hunt of the *Daily News* saw the blow as vengeance wreaked—"There were wrongs to be righted! *Caramba!* He was the man to do it! *Cristo!*"—for the brannigan in the Giants dugout eleven days earlier.

The 1923 Giants could be outhit and outpitched, but they were seldom outfielded—the team committed the fewest errors in the NL, with 176. Only the Yankees were better, with a mere 144 all season. The series with the Reds was a notable exception for the Giants. During the 5–2 Cincy victory in the finale on August 18, Pep Youngs made a hash of an easy play in right that opened the door for a big Reds inning. In the ninth, as the Giants tried to rally from a three-run deficit, Edd Roush made a spectacular grab in center field, and threw the ball to first to double-off Irish Meusel. The rally died, the Reds won, and McGraw steamed.

Pittsburgh came to town next, and Pep Youngs won the opening game of the set for New York with a stirring dash around the bases in the twelfth inning, an inside-the-park homer that brought hundreds of fans onto the field after Pep bounced headfirst across the plate. But the "Smoky Town Crew" beat Art Nehf once again on August 20, 3–1, as Johnny Morrison won his eighteenth of the season. Morrison, whose "jug handle" curveball was among the most devastating pitches in baseball, would win twenty-five games for the Pirates in '23. Nehf had beaten Pittsburgh twelve straight times during 1921–22, but his downturn was severe enough that now even Pittsburgh could best him with regularity.

McGraw was fit to be tied. He scrambled his lineup before the rubber game, putting Bancroft back in the leadoff spot, and O'Connell, his "posterior flattened from weeks of constant contact with an inhospitable bench," in center field. McGraw tried everything, "remolding, repatterning, rebuilding, enlarging, and embellishing" his lineup—to no avail. Pittsburgh won, 9–5, to take the series. McGraw had used no fewer than seventeen players. In the *Daily News,* Hunt advised McGraw to have his pitchers "play the infield, to prevent wasting energy warming up to relieve."

The Giants' lead was down to 3½ games. The team was off the following day, so McGraw vented his pent-up ire at his home in Pelham, where he and Blanche kept dogs, horses, and several lovely gardens. Away from the park, McGraw wanted nothing to do with baseball, and he turned to Blanche to avert his mind. "When I come home from the baseball grounds I want to forget all the anxieties and worry of the day's work," he explained. "So she takes my mind off it, keeps me interested in other things, and the next day I go back refreshed and ready to meet the demands that are placed upon my judgment."

Only a total of 15,000 fans pushed through the Polo Grounds turnstiles to witness the two dispiriting losses against Pittsburgh. But 22,000 came out on Thursday, August 23, for a suddenly critical doubleheader against St. Louis. The Cards were a mediocre 58–58, fifteen distant games behind the Giants and limping through a twenty-game road trip, but they were not to be trifled with, given the presence in the middle of the lineup of Rogers Hornsby, the "Rajah," a brilliant hitter and second baseman whose elite talent was matched by his poisonous demeanor. Hornsby had a mind-boggling 1922, becoming the only player ever to bat .400 and hit forty homers in a season. He was also as mean as a snake, a "liturgy of hatred" who confessed to Fred Lieb that he was a member of the Ku Klux Klan.

Hornsby's psychopathy was driven not only by racism but by an all-consuming drive to win. That single-mindedness came to the fore in the third game of the four-game set in New York. Irish Meusel had won the opener for the Giants with a homer in the bottom of the ninth after his team blew a 6–1 lead, and in the nightcap the Cards put seven runs on the board in the second inning against Rosy Ryan to ease to victory. McGraw used five different pitchers in the contest. On Friday, the crucial third game was a taut affair. The Giants seemed to be in control, ahead 4–1, when the Cards scored three in the top of the ninth off McQuillan to send the game to extra innings. In the fourteenth, Frisch lined a single into the gloaming to knock in the winning run, giving the Giants a pivotal 5–4 victory.

Earlier in the game, Hornsby had reached third base with one out. The count on the batter, Heinie Mueller, was three balls and a strike. Manager Branch Rickey called for Mueller to take the pitch, which he did — right down the middle for strike two. Disgusted at his manager's lack of aggression, Hornsby threw up his hands and cursed loudly. It was a clear-cut case of a player "showing up" his manager. Hornsby was stranded at third after Mueller and the next hitter were retired.

Hornsby showered after the game but didn't cool off. He complained loudly to Cardinals catcher Ed Ainsmith that Rickey didn't want to win badly enough. Rickey, still incensed by Hornsby's lack of respect on the field, overheard and charged into the steaming spray, fists flying. The two were separated, but when Hornsby unleashed a volley of vulgarity at Rickey, the manager came at the Rajah once more.

Today, a clubhouse fight between two titans of the game would be enormous news, but the press mostly buried it at the time, though one sportswriter, lampooning Rickey's erudition, wondered: "What is the advantage of a college education, if our leading college men are to settle things as angry wolves settle them?" Hornsby got his revenge by taking himself out of the lineup for almost the entire month of September, milking a skin rash that wouldn't have benched a more motivated player.

McGraw, by contrast, was the picture of grace and calm, especially when the Giants beat St. Louis again on August 25 behind Mule Watson. The Reds and Pirates won too, to stay 3 and 4½ games back, respectively. Then Chicago came to the Polo Grounds for a three-game set beginning on Sunday, oddly enough to modern eyes. The Cubbies led, 3–1, entering the bottom of the ninth. With one out, O'Connell smacked his sixth homer of the year to make it a one-run game. Kelly flew out, but Jackson scratched out a single off Chicago starter Vic Aldridge. McGraw sent the "Next Ruth" up to pinch-hit.

Bentley was struggling as a pitcher, although he had sorted a few things out and was 10–7 after the horribly slow start. But as a hitter, he was earning the $65,000 transfer fee. His batting average was .414 entering the game — his prowess had led McGraw to start using him as a pinch hitter in mid-July. He had rapped a double in his first appearance and was 5–11 in the role. Now he batted for catcher Frank Snyder and launched a shot into the right-field bleachers to deliver a stunning 4–3 win for Clan McGraw. It was his lone homer of the season. The 30,000 at the Polo Grounds went bananas, with hundreds streaming onto the field to congratulate Bentley, who hightailed it to the faraway clubhouse in center field as soon as he touched home. The *Daily News* ran his photo the next day with the caption "Well Worth It!"

The Giants won their fourth straight the next day and ended August with a record of 80–47, with a four-game lead over Cincinnati. The Pirates lost four in a row to close the month and sat six back as the season entered its final furlong.

26

IN THE LAST two weeks of June, Ruth went eleven games without a homer, a shallow wadi that drew comment only because of the high standard he set when it came to the long ball. For his career, the Babe homered roughly once every eleven at bats, so going eleven whole games without a dinger qualified as a severe power outage for the Sultan of Swat.

So Ruth did what ballplayers often do when confronted with a slump—he switched bats. Sure enough, on July 2 at the Stadium, he launched his fifteenth home run in the very first inning, collecting three hits and four RBI on the afternoon. The Babe decided to stick with the new bat for a spell.

It was nicknamed the "Betsy Bingle," and it cost $6 rather than the standard $2. That was because Betsy was an assemblage of four pieces of wood glued together. The sideways grain allowed the batter to always have the sweet spot pointing in the right direction. The long bat was also lighter than Ruth's usual lumber. The Babe had clubbed two long homers with the bat in an exhibition game, and now the superstitious Bambino decided he liked it. He certainly liked the bat's moniker. Alliterative double *B*s were a common motif with the Babe's bats. "Black Beauty" and "Big Bertha" were other sticks in his bat bag. He ordered up a half dozen.

A colorful former player named Sam Crawford made the Betsy Bingle. Sam was born in Wahoo, Nebraska, so his nickname, "Wahoo Sam," wasn't much of a leap. Crawford was one of the foremost sluggers of the dead-ball era, teaming with Ty Cobb in the Detroit outfield to lead the Tigers to several pennants (the two rank 1–2 on the all-time triples list). Sam was a mentor to Cobb, and the Georgia Peach credited Crawford with turning him into one of the greats. But the two men fell out, with Cobb feeling that Crawford was jealous that a bigger star was on the team. Crawford, for his part, claimed he stopped liking Cobb because Ty was a cheapskate.

Crawford ended his major-league career in 1917 but felt he could still hit. So he went west to Los Angeles, a favored site for reinvention, and for several seasons starred with the minor-league L.A. Angels. Forty-three years old in 1923, Crawford was home in Nebraska deciding on an offer from USC to manage its baseball team when he crossed paths with Ruth during the Babe's barnstorming tour of the Great Plains. Wahoo gifted the Sultan one of his own bats, a stick that Crawford had been using in the Pacific Coast League and was hoping to market. It was the Betsy Bingle.

The bat had sat in the back of the locker room, unused and forgotten, until Ruth felt the need to change his mojo. He went on a tear for the next six weeks, smacking .390 with six homers when word came from Ban Johnson that the AL president wanted to examine Ruth's new lumber. On August 11 the Babe dutifully brought the bat across the river to Johnson's midtown Manhattan office.

Coincidentally Detroit, Crawford's old team, was in town to play the Yanks. But perhaps it was not happenstance. A complaint had been filed with the league about Ruth's bat, spurring Johnson's sudden interest, and though he was never named, it was strongly suspected that Ty Cobb was the protester. Ruth and Cobb, the Cain and Abel of baseball's first half century, were not speaking in 1922–23. Cobb had long antagonized Ruth. When the Babe would approach Cobb on the field before games, Cobb would loudly ask, "What smells?" Ty was jealous of Ruth's immense popularity, while Ruth was prickly and impatient with those who didn't come to praise him. "Cobb is a prick," Ruth said. "But he sure can hit." During a game in '22, Cobb had yelled to Ruth, "If you were on my club, I'd hit you over the head with a bat." After the season, Cobb salted Ruth's wounds, saying he had predicted his downfall.

Ten days after the Babe turned in his bat, on August 21, a circus of a press conference took place, with Johnson carefully weighing and inspecting the wood in a scene that may have inspired a similar one in *The Natural* (in the film, Roy Hobbs's tryout as a nineteen-year-old rube takes place in 1923). Unlike "Wonderboy," however, the "Betsy Bingle" was ruled illegal. "Only one-piece bats will be allowed from now on," read Johnson from a statement.

Huggins filed an appeal.

I can see no reason why Johnson would bar the Crawford model bat. The rules simply state that the bat must be round, made entirely of wood, and conform to certain dimensions. The new bat used by Ruth is made of hard wood and is perfectly round. The rules do not state that the bat be made of one piece of wood. Ruth's bat is not a trick bat, but simply an improvement on the old style. A four-piece bat is much stronger than a one-piece affair and of course has more driving power.

It didn't do any good. Johnson claimed it was the glue that held the wood together that made the bat illegal.

But the Colossus of Clout wasn't the game's greatest slugger because of any bat. With Ruth, the swing was the thing. "I swing as hard as I can," he explained. "In boxing, your fist usually stops when you hit a man, but it's possible to hit so hard that your fist doesn't stop. I try to follow through in the same way." He used the enormous 48- to 54-ounce "wagon tongues" because they allowed him to build tremendous momentum on the follow-through, though some, like Harry Heilmann, thought Ruth would have been devastating with a lighter bat, like the Betsy Bingle. Casey Stengel doubted that it mattered. "He could've used his sleeve, or a rolled-up copy of the *Police Gazette*. Wouldn't have made a bit of difference."

Cobb was often asked to explain his rival's success, which he did as though preparing a dissertation on the subject. He told F. C. Lane that Ruth could develop his hard-swinging style because he had been a pitcher. "A pitcher is not expected to hit. Therefore, he can follow his own system without managerial interference. As a pitcher he took a tremendous cut at the ball. At first he was awkward.... Gradually he gained confidence, experience, and knowledge of pitchers." When that happened, in the words of Wes Ferrell, a long-time hurler for the Indians and Red Sox, pitching to the Babe became "like looking into the lion's jaw."

Of course, Cobb was firmly on McGraw's side when it came to denigrating the brutish baseball that Ruth played. "Given the proper physical equipment—which consists solely in the strength to knock a ball forty feet further than the average man can do it—anybody can play big-league ball today. In other words, science is out the window." The Babe didn't argue that his way lacked refined technique. "Pick a good one and sock it" was his method. "I get back to the dugout and they ask me what I hit and I tell them I don't know except it looked good."

His mighty blows captured the imagination of a populace, and it wasn't merely the number of home runs—with Ruth, the distance, the arc, the *sound* of his shots were singular and unique. Writer Heywood Broun mused that if new baseballs could talk to one another, they'd say, "Join Ruth and see the world." When normal mortals hit homers, fans fought to catch the ball. When the Babe clubbed one, people were reported to have scurried as if from an incoming mortar shell.

"Baby is going to hit one today," he frequently boasted, even when the opposing pitcher was throwing darts in warm-ups, and he usually backed up the big talk. He did comic double takes when he swung and missed, staring at his bat in mock disbelief, as if there were a hole in it someplace. He was perfectly aware of his talents and why people responded to them. "They'll tell you the science of line shots is what counts. But that's all baloney. What counts is socking that ball and giving it a ride."

Ruth sure socked the ball in the fortnight after giving up the Betsy Bingle.

On August 12, the Babe punished Cobb and the Tigers with a single, double, and home run. The Yankees then went west for a dozen games in St. Louis, Detroit, Chicago, and Cleveland. The Babe warmed up for the trip by blasting three home runs during an exhibition game in Indianapolis on the fourteenth. On the seventeenth, against the Browns, Ruth once again singled, doubled, and homered. At Chicago the next afternoon, he went 3–3 with five RBI, including his thirtieth double and thirty-second homer. After Johnson confiscated his four-piece bat, Ruth hit safely in twelve of fifteen games in August, at a .480 clip, with four homers and eighteen RBI.

During a stultifying game in Chicago on August 20, a comical episode broke the heat-induced doldrums. A small dog burst from the Comiskey Park stands and broke straight for Ruth, who was playing left field that day. The game wasn't halted, perhaps because the Yankees were wrapping up a 16–5 victory and no one wanted to delay its ending. Ruth began to play with the dog, chasing it, running from it. Just as the Babe hurled his glove at the dog in mock anger, Sox first baseman Earl Sheely hit a liner right at him. Ruth reached up and caught it bare-handed. The episode was emblematic of the Babe's stellar defensive play in 1923.

While the Yankees were out west, the west came to the Yankee Stadium.

Long before the start of baseball season, while icy winds swept across the canyons of Manhattan and the snow piled in drifts and turned brown, visitors to Times Square had seen a strange series of ads. They featured an automobile radiator mounted with a large pair of steer horns. Curious city slickers read the fine print with interest: TEX AUSTIN'S RODEO — COMING IN AUGUST.

Tex Austin, the King of the Rodeo, was born in St. Louis in 1886 with the decidedly unfrontier name Clarence Van Nostrand. At age twenty, Clarence blew town and lit out for the prairie, adopting the Lone Star name Tex Austin and telling folks he was raised on a cattle ranch near the Texas-Mexico border.

He was taken by the sport of rodeo and, lacking any discernible talent in the saddle, became a promoter. He papered much of Texas with his recruiting brochure, which assured skeptical riders that "he always pays 100 cents on the dollar. He plays no favorites. No one ever bought, stole or ran away with a title at one of Tex Austin's contests."

Tex was too ambitious for his namesake state to contain him. Convinced that rodeo's future lay in expanding its demographic beyond its core audience — who traveled to events on horseback — Austin shot for the moon, creating the Madison Square Garden Rodeo in New York in 1922. It immediately became the sport's premier event, overshadowing even Cheyenne Frontier Days, thanks to Tex's penchant for paying $25,000 in total prize money and top dollar to the winners. He also invaded Chicago and would even bring his show to the newly built Wembley Stadium in London in 1924 (the Brits were flabbergasted by the gruff, tobacco-chewing riders — especially the gruff, tobacco-chewing female riders).

Austin's pièce de résistance came in August of '23 — hiring the Yankee Stadium for a colossal rodeo. He doubled the Madison Square Garden prize money, offering $50,000 to lure the best cowboys and cowgirls that the West had to offer. Travel expenses weren't provided. Austin's literature explained why, in a speech John McGraw could have written:

If you do your part, your share in the gate receipts should take care of your expenses; if you think you are good there is no excuse for your not being here; if you really are good here is the place it will pay you to prove it.

All the greats were eager to prove it: Pinky Gist, Yakima Canutt, Roy Quick, Ike Rude, Powder River Thompson, Bonnie McCarroll, Bonnie Gray, and the great Soapy Williams. Fabled broncos such as Mystery, Nose Dive, and Peaceful Henry (he wasn't) were brought in to test the riders' mettle, not to mention to taste the Yankee Stadium outfield.

In addition to "Bronk" riding, skills such as calf roping, steer riding, and trick riding were on display. Also steer bulldogging, which *Time* magazine helpfully explained to the uninitiated as "diving from horseback to the horns of a wild steer and throwing it by the application of human leverage to the sweeping horns."

Here was Cap Huston's multisport dream fulfilled. Some four hundred animals were quartered under the Yankee Stadium grandstand. A huge mat made of cocoa was laid down over the infield and part of the outfield in order to protect the ground from so many cloven hooves. The track surrounding the field was used for relay races on horseback. Tickets for the daily events were $2 or $3, depending on how close to the bustin' one chose to sit. It was, as *Time* described, "the greatest primitive spectacle of the struggle of man against beast that the laws of our land permit." It was a drama to match the 1922 World Series, when McGraw had wrestled the bestial Ruth down and hog-tied him.

The Yankee Stadium rodeo was the first and only of its kind held at the House That Ruth Built. Austin lost control of his rodeo empire a few years later and moved to New Mexico, where he pioneered the cattle drive as the kind of tourist attraction seen in the film *City Slickers,* with city folk paying to live a piece of the Old West. Then, upon being told he was going blind in 1938, Austin committed suicide.

September

27

As the West left the Bronx, the Yankees returned to an early fall chill and the permeating smell of horseshit. Neither bothered the team, as they treated September as the winning marathoner does the final lap around the Olympic stadium track. The Yanks won only eight of fifteen on the final western swing of the season. But the Indians were little better and still trailed far behind the Hugmen by 12½ games entering September. The Yanks took three of four from the Senators to open the month, and went on to win twenty-two of their final thirty-four games.

Perhaps the best player on the team in September was Waite Hoyt. He and Artie Nehf had locked up in three memorable pitchers' duels in the 1921 Series, and both had pitched well in 1922. Then both had been struggling for much of 1923. Hoyt's improvement cheered Yankees fans, who had watched the Schoolboy muddle through a rough summer. His ERA climbed a full run, to just shy of four runs per game in late June, but slowly Hoyt came around, refining his curveball and relaxing more on the mound. His ERA dropped. In late August, Hoyt was suspended for brawling with umpire Brick

Owens, and the time off seemed to clear his head. When he returned, he tossed six consecutive complete games, winning five.

Waite Hoyt's nickname, the "Schoolboy," or the "Schoolboy Wonder," reflects the fact that he signed as a fifteen-year-old and was forever the youngest-looking kid in the clubhouse. His other nickname was the "Merry Mortician," in honor of his studying to be an undertaker (his father-in-law owned a funeral parlor, and Hoyt occasionally picked up a dead body on his way to the Stadium, pitched, and then delivered the corpse to the funeral home). "Merry Mortician" was appropriate for his moods too—a bipolar contradiction of aristocratic reserve and flip jocularity, sometimes in the same half inning.

Hoyt was born in Brooklyn in 1899 and attended Erasmus Hall High School. Big for his age, at 6' and 165 pounds, he overpowered varsity players who were three years older. He threw six no-hitters in high school, once striking out twenty-four batters, and he went 31–2 for the Dutchmen. Inevitably, John McGraw caught wind of the outerborough pitching phenom and signed him at the age of fifteen. A photo of Hoyt from the time captures a sullen youth glaring at the camera. McGraw was struck more by his control and easy, fluid motion than by his demeanor. But after exactly one appearance with the Giants in 1918, Hoyt was dealt by McGraw to Boston for Earl "Oil" Smith, a move the manager came to regret. In 1921 Waite went to the Yankees and averaged seventeen wins per season in the decade.

He was good-looking, a ladies' man, and despite his youthful appearance he fit in well with the hard-drinking, night-crawling culture of the Yankees. His father, Ad Hoyt, was a well-known vaudeville minstrel singer (and a friend of McGraw's) who raised Waite to sing and dance. Waite regularly appeared in a performance called "A Battery of Fun." One night he danced with burlesque star Sally Rand at Reisenweber's cabaret at Columbus Circle—in full uniform—before a packed audience of six hundred. Ad was on the bill too, singing "Ol' Man River." Afterward the senior Hoyt said happily, "I used to go to the theater and hear, 'There goes Ad Hoyt and his son.' Tonight I heard, 'There goes Waite Hoyt and his old man.'"

Waite drove his owner, who called him "Hoytz," mad with worry, because he had the audacity to regularly pitch in tight games. "Hoytz, the others win 10–0 or 10–1, but not you—you have to win 2–1 or 3–2," complained Ruppert. Hoyt refrained from back talking to his boss, but he was less forgiving to others who he deemed unprofessional or mediocre, especially umpires. He once excoriated ump George Moriarity from the mound, yelling, "You're out of your element. You should be a traffic cop so you could stand in the middle of the street with a badge on your chest and insult people with impunity."

Hoyt went on to become a popular broadcaster with the Cincinnati Reds, famous for telling rain-delay yarns about the Babe. He had a million of them and collected a few in a short book called *Babe Ruth as I Knew Him*. Hoyt recognized the obvious, that the Babe was the tide that lifted all boats in baseball, and he and all other players were the beneficiaries. He always urged players to "thank God, thank Mommy, thank Daddy—and thank Babe Ruth."

Hoyt's background in the dramatic arts helped him with Miller Huggins, who used to plead with his team to "act like Hoyt" instead of getting soused every night. Waite was out there living it up as hard as or harder than the rest of the fellows—he was just more skilled at sobering up, or acting sober when Hug was around. Years later, Hoyt would admit he was an alcoholic, "a damn good one," and become a high-profile member of Alcoholics Anonymous.

It seemed the entire team had gone through at least a few of the twelve steps, as though inspired by Ruth's off-season abstinence. The hard-partying bunch that stumbled through the 1922 season and World Series had sobered up. Not entirely, of course—these were still drinking men, and Prohibition really only affected the rubes out in farm country. Liquor was available on just about every street corner in New York City, having been trucked in by a flourishing group of gangsters. The feds had punted on trying to keep the city dry early in the year, and the local constabulary was either paid off or at the end of the bar putting away drinks poured from unlabeled bottles. The new Prohibition director of New York, Palmer Canfield, said despairingly, "I am not carried away by any false enthusiasm. There is no figurative sponge that can dry up New York State overnight."

Ruth ignored many laws of civilized society, but the one he flouted with most contempt was Prohibition. Booze, in staggering amounts, is a key cog in the Ruthian myth. Indeed, a significant portion of his popularity was the sense that here was a man doing great things on the athletic field despite copious drinking, thus making a mockery of the abstinence movement's rhetoric. The immigrant class that swelled the nation's tenements felt (with some justification) that Prohibition was largely a war against the poor. They were among Ruth's biggest fans.

In 1923, though, most of the Yankees had throttled back on brazen public drinking. After games, they eschewed the fancy nightclubs in Manhattan, often choosing a quieter evening of steaks and a couple of beers at the Dutchman's, a place near the Stadium off the Grand Concourse. Sometimes the players bought their steaks uncooked and brought them home for dinner.

As for the Babe, he generally preferred drinking at the Ansonia—where a deli down the street would deliver kegs of beer and cases of rye and scotch to Ruth's suite on demand—or at friends' homes, because his fame brought him trouble in saloons. In 1921 he got into an argument in a New Jersey bar with a man who followed him in his car, cut him off, and put a gun to his head. Ruth's buddy and teammate Harry Harper drove up and, seeing that his friend was about to get his head blown off, tried to run down the assailant. When the gunman dove to avoid Harper's car, Ruth knocked the weapon from the man's hand.

The incident didn't keep the Babe from crossing the river to New Jersey. In 1923 Ruth mainly avoided the bright lights, preferring to motor across the Hudson with a friend or two (and just as often alone), find a quiet club, and lay low. Many nights had more songs than drinks, in keeping with his winter regimen. Ruth would locate a place with a piano and belt out tunes until the wee hours. He would then scoop up that night's female companion and head home, waking the next day just in time to go to the Stadium.

The Yankees' wives busied themselves with more occult distractions. A fortune-telling craze broke out among the ladies in early September. Ruth devoted one of his ghostwritten columns in the *American* to his own journey to an oracle, made after Helen got some "good news" from a visit. " 'The cloud is lifting,' " Ruth said the woman told him while reading his palm, a difficult feat with all his batting calluses. " 'You are very happy. You are on your farm. Everything is different from what it was after the World Series last year. In the very first game [of the Series] you made a home run. In the same game you made another homer and it won the game.' "

"I'm hoping that old gypsy knew what she was talking about," the Babe "wrote."

28

THE GIANTS BEGAN their September with mediocre play before poor crowds. The defending champs split the first eight games of the month against Boston and Philly, roughly averaging a puny 6,000 fans during the midweek games. In 1923 the Giants drew a paltry (by their standards) 820,780 fans, still easily the most in the NL but a steep falloff from the previous seasons — about 125,000 fewer than the year before. The expansion of the Polo Grounds had not had the desired effect, while the success of the Yankee Stadium ate away at McGraw's insides, and his box office.

McGraw was as much a promotions man as a baseball man, and he was always looking for ways to get more paying customers through the gates. One way to accomplish this was to schedule as many Sunday games as possible. The first legal Sunday game in New York wasn't held until 1919. It came at the Polo Grounds, as the Giants played the Phillies before a packed house, instantly validating the new law (championed by Jimmy Walker). In the fifth inning of the game, however, a brawl erupted between Giants teammates Rube Benton and Art Fletcher over a missed signal from McGraw. Casey

Stengel, then with the Phils, laughed about the fight years later. "Before the game, Fletcher comes over to our dugout and says, 'Mac says he don't want any trouble today. He has a tip that agents from the Sabbath Society are in the stands, looking for something they can squawk about. So let's just have a nice, peaceful ball game.' So we say all right, we will play that way if they will, and the first thing I see is Fletcher and Benton rolling on the bats!"

Despite the rhubarb, Sunday baseball was a major success, and the cities that didn't allow it, like Philadelphia and Boston, were at a major financial disadvantage. The discrepancy also made for some crazy scheduling. A typical example was a game played on September 9. The Giants had wrapped up a three-game series against Philadelphia the day before and were on the way to Boston for Monday's contest. But a single game was shoehorned in on Sunday afternoon before the Giants departed for Massachusetts.

As close as Ebbets Field was to Manhattan, it wasn't an easy journey in 1923. The Brooklyn–Manhattan Transit Corporation had just risen from the ashes of the bankrupt Brooklyn Rapid Transit Company, and the city would soon undertake a major expansion of subway lines between the boroughs, but in 1923 only a handful of stations were open. Paved and unpaved roads mixed haphazardly. A writer with the *Times* who accompanied the Giants described the trips as "arduous and fruitless explorations in a region that makes the old stomping grounds of Stanley and Livingstone seem like Maiden Lane by comparison." The Giants, apparently exhausted by the journey, lost 6–3.

Even with McGraw cramming in as many Sunday games as possible, and despite the team's excellence, attendance still lagged at the Polo Grounds. McGraw harbored a fantasy of bringing another superstar to New York, one that would trump Ruth. Not just any star, mind you. A six-pointed star—a Jew.

In 1923 Jews totaled more than a quarter of the city's population. Boxing was a reliable draw, as the Tendler-Leonard fight had shown.

Baseball would be even better, a daily draw rather than a one-off. "A home-run hitter with [a Jewish] name in New York would be worth a million," McGraw told the *New York Tribune*.

But one didn't seem to be in the offing. The 1920s were the era of the "Tough Jew," ruffians who unapologetically punched, shot, and bootlegged their way out of poverty. But it was also a time when Jews began to assimilate by more peaceable means. This was the first generation of American Jews to point their sons toward respectable positions that weren't open to the immigrant wave from Eastern Europe. Consequently the period of major Jewish participation in sports was coming to a close. Prospects once steered toward baseball were becoming white-collar professionals instead. McGraw explained the phenomenon bluntly to John E. Wray of the *St. Louis Post-Dispatch*: "Jews stay out of baseball because there isn't enough money in it." Wray thought intolerance was the reason, as well as the "natural tendency of the race to play a lone hand."

But McGraw turned loose his vast network of scouts, and one, Dick Kinsella, did flush some game far from the concrete jungle, in Kansas of all places. A young, powerful slugger was tearing up the Class C Southwestern League playing with the Hutchinson Wheat Shockers. His name was Mose Solomon.

If it all seemed too good to be true, it was. Solomon was too green for Class C ball, much less the New York Giants. Yes, he had powered forty-nine homers that summer and batted .421, but that was against local farm boys. Then there was his glove. It was made out of kugel. Solomon committed thirty-one errors at first base in Hutchinson before the desperate Shockers coaching staff put Mose out in right field, where he was, if possible, even worse. Solomon was a player born too early. He would have made a good designated hitter, like Ron Blomberg, the Jew who was the first DH when the American League adopted the rule in 1973. Nevertheless, a desperate McGraw, disconsolately scanning the empty seats at the Polo Grounds, figured it was worth the risk—after all, he had forged a fielder out of Travis Jackson, who had been equally abysmal in the field down on the farm. And Solomon was eager to escape flyover country and return to New York, where he was born (although he spent his teen years in Columbus, Ohio, the son of a successful scrap-metal dealer).

So on September 9, Erev Rosh Hashanah, Jewish New Year's Eve, McGraw introduced the newest Giant to the press. "We appreciate that many of the fans in New York are Jews, and we have been trying to land a prospect of Jewish blood," McGraw said. "However, we haven't seen many around." This one cost McGraw a pretty penny, as he had to outbid other clubs who caught wind of the manager's interest in Solomon. *If he's good enough for McGraw, he must be good* went the thinking among rival clubs.

"McGraw Pays 50K for Only Jewish Ballplayer in Captivity" read a headline in the *Boston Advertiser*. The *Sporting News* thoughtfully added that Solomon "has verdicts in several fistfights to his credit, having found it necessary to fight his way through because of reflections on his ancestry as a Jew."

A good-looking, muscular kid (at age twenty-two, Mose was 5'9", 175 pounds), Solomon instantly became the most talked-about player in town. He was dubbed the "Rabbi of Swat" before his first at bat. To the Jewish community of New York, it was as though a combination of Abraham and King David had descended in their midst, wearing a form-fitting uniform. Invitations to dinners and High Holiday functions deluged Solomon. He was set up with the daughters of prominent Jews. Local religious leaders often asked him merely to walk around Jewish neighborhoods, shaking hands and giving batting tips to the kids. In that dizzying month of September, Solomon was out almost every night, meeting his responsibility to the community. Even if he was good enough to be a major leaguer, the meshuga schedule prevented vitally needed practice.

Solomon rapidly turned cynical. When several offers of marriage came in, "Hickory Mose" told Dick Kinsella that Dick should look up the records of the women and see how much each was worth. At season's end Solomon would marry a wealthy woman from Waterbury, Connecticut, named Gertrude Nachmanovitz.

Mose wore the Giants uniform, but McGraw didn't dare play him, especially in the pennant-race crucible. A couple of other rookies got a little playing time ahead of Solomon—Bill Terry and Hack Wilson, a pair bound for Cooperstown. Attendance indeed shot up, but the Jews in the crowd hooted McGraw for not playing their boy.

Solomon finally saw some action on September 30, the final regular-season game at the Polo Grounds, against the Braves. Reported the *Tribune:* "As that appropriate line, 'Solomon playing right field for New Yawk,' wafted over the Polo Grounds from the announcer's megaphone, the voices waxed jubilant. It was, 'Oh, you Mose!' and 'We're with you, Solomon.'"

Mose looked overmatched at the start, striking out on the first three pitches he saw in the bigs and popping out weakly the next two trips. But he came up in the tenth inning of a 3–3 game, and the "Hebraic Hitter" lashed a double over third, knocking in Frisch with the winning run.

The New York minyan went bananas. Unfortunately there were no more home games for McGraw to profit from, so Mose didn't see the field again until the season finale at Brooklyn. He started in right, went 2–4 with a pair of singles, and made "an inglorious muff," according to the *New York American.* The Brooklyn crowd cheered louder for Solomon of the enemy Giants than for their own Robins.

McGraw wanted to keep Mose on the roster for the Series—not to play but as a gate attraction. When Solomon found out he wouldn't be paid, he went home to Columbus to play what passed in those days for pro football. McGraw was outraged. No one, not even a Jewish golden goose, defied him like that, especially a kid who couldn't catch the ball with a butterfly net. Mose was sold to Toledo and never made it back to the bigs.

Five years later, McGraw, still searching for that elusive Jewish

Babe Ruth, worked out a strapping local kid from Monroe High in the Bronx. McGraw's expert judgment was that "Henry [better known as Hank] Greenberg has been scouted by the Giants, and will never make a ballplayer." Greenberg, of course, would power fifty-eight homers in 1938, make the Hall of Fame, and set the standard as the greatest Jewish ballplayer until Sandy Koufax took the mound.

29

As the mid-August sun beat down relentlessly on Sportsman's Park in St. Louis, the four thousand in attendence were lulled into a stupor by the slow pace of the game between the Yanks and Browns. The contest the day before had wrapped up in a tidy 90 minutes, and the game the next day would take only 1:45 to complete. On this punishingly warm dog day, however, the game droned on for nearly two and a half hours, despite being a pitchers' duel won by Herb Pennock, 3–1. The reason for the tortoise-like pace was Browns hurler Dave Danforth. It was Danforth's first game back after a suspension for discoloring the ball in violation of the game's new "clean ball" rule. In protest of the suspension and what he felt was an absurd rule change, Danforth continually asked for new balls throughout the game, due to dirty spots only he could see. He demanded fifty-eight balls in nine innings. As a result, the action slowed to a crawl.

When it came to major-league pitchers, Danforth was merely the most outspoken, as all hurlers uniformly hated the rule. Some fans agreed. *Baseball Magazine* felt "the game has been losing its attractiveness to the older devotees of the sport, and is gradually losing its popularity with the newer generation of patrons who consider the game merely as a more or less thrilling amusement, and are ignorant of or without regard for its finer points and scientific possibilities." The *Tribune* noted that "dyed-in-the-wool lovers of the game want something done to steer baseball toward better pitching."

Ban Johnson did something. After Danforth's symbolic display of outrage, Johnson ordered that AL umpires were to keep slightly discolored or smudged balls in play. Not coincidentally, there would be several no-hit and one-hit games pitched in the Junior Circuit in the season's final few weeks.

In Philadelphia on September 4, Sad Sam Jones cracked a wide smile after no-hitting the A's, 2–0. Oddly, Jones didn't strike out a single batter, despite a crackling curve that lived up to his other, more accurate nickname, "Horsewhips." Ruth went hitless in the game and fell one point behind Heilmann for the batting-average race. The Babe would never lead Heilmann again. He had more fun later in the day, playing in a twilight charity game for the Kensington, Pennsylvania, Ascension of Our Lord Club. The club was in financial straits, so Ruth paid a visit that in a single evening wiped out the $6,500 debt the club owed. He played first base and scored his team's only run in a 2–1 loss to a team called the Lit Brothers. Ruth appeared to have hit a game-winning home run on a massive blow to right field. The assistant pastor yelled, "That ball has cleared our parish!" But since the unusual layout of Kensington Park placed the right-field bleachers only two hundred feet from home plate, all balls hit over the fence were ruled doubles. So the huge throng, including the two thousand fans watching from the railroad tracks beyond the park, saw Ruth stranded at second as the game ended. When it was over, the pastor asked how he could repay Ruth. "Say, Father, are you kidding me?" was the Babe's reply.

Three days later, on the seventh, the A's were no-no'd again, this time by Howard Ehmke of the Red Sox. Howard was a string-bean sidearmer with a nasty curve. "Ehmke's arm is about as large as a bill-clerk's wrist," wrote F. C. Lane in *Baseball Magazine.* "He is so long and bony that one is led to strain his ears to hear him rattle when he walks." Ehmke mastered the art of throwing with such an angular windup that the batter couldn't possibly follow the ball out of his hand.

So it was on that day in Philadelphia. The *Philadelphia Public Ledger* reported: "Ehmke's zippy crossfire came out of the shortstop's chest like bad news from a Gatling gun." By rights, the no-hitter was broken up in the seventh, when A's pitcher Slim Harriss hit one to the wall in right for an apparent double. Trouble was, he missed first base and was ruled out. In the eighth, a liner off Frank Welch's bat was bobbled in left. Originally it was ruled a hit, but the scorer changed his mind after loud protests from the crowd. And Ehmke went into the record books.

Sad Sam and Ehmke dueled four days later, on September 11 at the Yankee Stadium, and but for another controversial scoring decision, Ehmke would have beaten Johnny Vander Meer to immortality by fifteen years. Whitey Witt led off the first inning with a bounder to third. Howard Shanks, an outfielder forced by injuries to take over third base for the day, booted it in what appeared to the crowd to be a clear error. After the game, Shanks admitted, "I knew it was an error when I made it." But official scorer Fred Lieb somehow thought it a single. The crowd hooted at him all game, as did other writers ("Oh, Fred, you *must* change that," said Bob Boyd of the *Evening World*), but Lieb stood by his decision, as did Landis when it was appealed to his office. Ehmke set down the next twenty-seven Yankees in order—a perfect game, minus that first batter. But history records it as merely a one-hitter. Ehmke had come that close to consecutive no-hitters.

Umpire Tom Connolly, who had worked Ehmke's no-hitter on the seventh and gotten the pitcher to autograph a baseball that day, was an ump for this game as well. He went to the Red Sox clubhouse after the game and had Ehmke autograph another ball, telling him, "If you didn't pitch a no-hit game today, I shall never live long enough to see one." Ehmke had to settle for his twentieth win of the season. In a horrid year for Beantown baseball, September had some bright moments beyond Ehmke's brilliance. On September 8, Sox outfielder Ira Flagstead threw out three Yankees on the base paths in a single game. Two days later, first baseman George Burns pulled off an unassisted triple play. And on the twenty-ninth, Waite Hoyt and Sox hurler Jack Quinn were the pitchers in a game that finished in an amazing one hour and three minutes. Incredibly, it was hardly a pitching masterpiece—the final score was 5–4, Boston.

Apparently, given their futility against Ehmke, the Yankees needed another hitter. So they called up "Biscuit Pants." After pummeling the Eastern League, Lou Gehrig was back on the roster as a replacement for Pipp, who badly sprained an ankle stepping off a train. Gehrig was far more comfortable than he had been during his summer tour of duty in the Bronx. In six games at the end of September, "Larrupin' Lou" went 10–20 with a homer and nine RBI. His first home run in the majors came on September 27 at the "Bijou of the East," Fenway Park. Gehrig started for the first time, batting cleanup behind Ruth, a combination that would terrorize baseball for years to come. Gehrig's homer was a four-hundred-foot shot to right field off Wild Bill Piercy.

He was also winning over his teammates. On September 26, Gehrig came in for Pipp in the seventh inning at first base. Bullet Joe Bush was on the mound, chasing his nineteenth win of the year. He hollered at Huggins, "Don't put that damn clown out there at first! This game may not mean anything to the team, but it means a lot to me. That guy will gum it up!" The manager ignored him and winced as Gehrig botched a bunt, allowing a run to score.

"Ya stupid college punk!" fumed Bush. "Where's your brains, dummy?" Bush was still grumbling in the dugout when the Yankees batted in the eighth inning, trailing Detroit, 3–0. Ruth was yet again walked intentionally to load the bases. Gehrig came to the plate. "Don't send this kid up there," Bush said to Huggins. This time, Hug was vindicated, as Gehrig drove the first pitch he saw off the right-field wall, plating three runs to tie the game.

Between innings, Bush apologized—his way. "Look, kid, you may not be so hot with the glove, but you can pound the ball." Alas, there was little Gehrig could do after Bush gave up five runs in the tenth inning and lost, 8–3. Bullet Joe would have to wait a few more days for his nineteenth (and final) win.

By then, the AL pennant race had long since been decided. Also decided was the Most Valuable Player Award. The MVP vote came two weeks before the end of the regular season. Ruth received notice of the honor on September 20, hours before the Yanks beat St. Louis, 4–3, to clinch the AL pennant for the third straight season. The Babe went out and produced a typical game for that season: he tripled in a run, scored a run, and walked twice in four trips to the plate. Nothing fancy—just outstanding, winning baseball.

Amazingly 1923 was the only time Ruth captured the MVP, due to the odd rules governing the prize at the time. It wasn't awarded by today's standards until 1922, and perhaps due to fear of a Bambino monopoly, a rule was inserted that stated a player could win it only once. Unsurprisingly Ruth didn't get it in '22 (George Sisler did), so the '23 award was his first and only. One writer in each of the eight baseball towns in the league voted; Ruth was the unanimous winner, getting all eight first-place votes. Eddie Collins of the White Sox nipped Heilmann for second place. There was no National League MVP awarded in 1923 (Dazzy Vance of Brooklyn would win the inaugural NL MVP in 1924).

Ruth used the opportunity to stroke the New York press, as he did so often and well: "I think I know how much I appreciate the vote given to me by the baseball reporters.... After all that happened last year this prize would never have been possible without the way the New York writers acted since. I said at the [Elks Club] newspaper dinner I wanted their help, and all I asked for was a fair chance. They certainly gave me both, and I'll try hard in the future."

For winning the MVP, Ruth was awarded a gold medal, and a plan was announced to inscribe his name under Sisler's in a monument to baseball that was to be constructed in Washington, DC, at the cost of $100,000. In a rare moment of bureaucratic budgetary discretion, the monument was never built.

30

WHILE THE MOSE Solomon passion play evolved, the Giants tried to fight off the pesky Reds. The McGrawmen did just enough to keep their noses in front of pitching-rich Cincinnati, which lacked the firepower to take full advantage of the Giants' indifferent play to open September. At hitter-friendly Wrigley Field, New York's bats turned anemic, with the Giants scoring just three runs in two days, losing both games. Then, Stengel was injured when he cut his heel on either a broken soda bottle or the base of the outfield wall. Bruised and fumbling, the Giants saw their lead dwindle to four games with thirteen to play. On the sixteenth, they were in clear need of a win to reverse the negative momentum.

Fortunately for New York, Cubs manager Bill Killefer, the same man McGraw had criticized in print in June, went with a rookie pitcher, Nick Dumovich, who would quit baseball after this, his only season. This game eased that decision. The Giants scored single runs in each of the first six innings. They were matched by six from the Cubs, led by Hack Miller, who slugged three doubles and a triple off Jack Scott. In the seventh, the visitors upped the pace, scoring four times to seal the win, with Irish Meusel's two-run homer being the decisive blow.

The critical victory had nearly been abandoned in the eighth inning. With New York winning, 10–6, Youngs threw out Cubs shortstop Sparky Adams as he attempted to stretch a single into a double. Umpire Charlie Moran made the call on a close play, and all hell broke loose at Wrigley. First one soda bottle, then two, then a dozen flew from the stands in Moran's direction. The Wrigley faithful seemed to have better arms than most of the Cubs as they targeted the helpless ump. Ironically the incident came one year to the day that the Yanks' Whitey Witt was knocked cold by a thrown bottle in St. Louis. Due largely to the Cubs-Giants game, after 1923 glass soda bottles were never again sold in parks across the majors.

Moran sought shelter in the Giants dugout (perhaps not the wisest decision), at which point the mob got ugly. Hundreds and hundreds of missiles were launched from the crowd, and police were called out to form a phalanx in front of the Giants bench. McGraw, being McGraw, leaned out at one point and waved to the crowd, then ducked back in.

Judge Landis happened to be at the game, and he turned toward the crowd and shook his cane at the mob. That did little to quell the riot. After fifteen minutes, the storm blew itself out, and the game eventually was finished. McGraw and his team needed a police escort from the field, and armored cars led them back to the hotel.

There was fighting at the Polo Grounds too. Two days before the Chicago riot, the second titanic boxing match of the year had taken place at the Giants' field. Jack Dempsey outslugged Luis Firpo in a legendary brawl that featured nine knockdowns in the first round alone. Near the end of the first stanza, the "Wild Bull of the Pampas" knocked the "Manassa Mauler" clear out of the ring, a moment famously captured in a painting by George Bellows. A 1950 poll would declare that instant the most dramatic in sports in the first half century. Dempsey, despite gashing his head on a reporter's typewriter (Babe Ruth sat in shock two rows back—"I thought Jack was coming to shake hands with me," Ruth joked afterward), was shoved again into the ring and knocked Firpo out in the second round. The Giants took the fight as a good omen. In four prior championship bouts in 1923 held at the Polo Grounds, the title belt had changed hands. Dempsey's retention of the heavyweight belt cheered the heavyweights in the dugout, who planned on keeping their crown as well.

The mayhem in the Windy City touched off a six-game winning streak for the Giants, during which they averaged nine runs per game. Highpockets Kelly blasted three home runs in a 13–6 rout of the Cubs, followed by a 10–4 clubbing of the Cards. The Giants then removed Pittsburgh from the pennant race, sweeping three at Forbes Field. Pittsburgh's manager was Charlie "Jolly Cholly" Grimm, a friendly, gregarious man—in many ways the polar opposite of McGraw. Led by Grimm, the Pirates dugout at times morphed into a hootenanny, with players singing and playing guitar and harmonica during games. McGraw, naturally, found such behavior revolting. After putting the harmonizing Pirates down for the third straight game, McGraw yelled at Grimm, "You can't sing your way to a pennant in this league!"

That left the Reds, and Cincinnati was the next stop for McGraw's team.

The Reds had the league's best staff, with Luque, Donohue, and Rixey all winning twenty-plus games. But their batting order cried out desperately for someone to take the load off Edd Roush, the Hall of Fame center fielder who stood out like a Monet among art-school students. That Cincinnati had stayed in it this long with the far deeper Giants was testimony to both the team's tenacity and the inconsistency of McGraw's pitching staff.

On the twenty-fourth, Donohue ended the Giants winning streak with his twenty-first victory of the season, 6–3, as Boob Fowler had four RBI for Cincy. The Reds were now three behind, with six games left. Tuesday's matchup on the twenty-fifth at Redland Field became the make-or-break contest of the season. It was Cincy's last head-to-head shot at the Giants.

The Reds felt good about their chances, with Luque, their ace, on the bump. Dolf was 26–7, and his opponent, Mule Watson, had started the season with the execrable Braves and had never been near a start as vital as this one. Weeks earlier, Watson had crumbled under the stress of the pennant chase, getting impossibly drunk and missing a game. McGraw suspended him indefinitely, but such was the state of the staff that a group of players went to the Little Napoleon and took the unprecedented step of asking the manager to reinstate Watson, as he was sorely needed. McGraw, seeing their point, called him back to the team.

Against the Reds, Mule was touched early. George Burns, who used to wrestle with Jim Thorpe before games during his years in New York (he was traded in the deal that brought Groh to Coogan's Bluff), led off with a single and gave his former manager a sarcastic wave from first. The next batter, Jake Daubert, doubled Burns home, and just like that it was 1–0 Reds.

The capacity crowd of 20,010 was howling, but Bancroft, Meusel, and Youngs quieted them with key hits. The Giants tied it in the second and scored twice in the third to lead, 3–1. Luque and Watson were in control after that, and the score remained 3–1 until the bottom of the ninth. With two out, the Reds' Babe Pinelli, who would go on to a long career as an umpire after his playing days were over, singled in a run to make it 3–2. That brought up the potential winning run, Boob Fowler, the hero of the day before. McGraw, pacing in the dugout, took a few steps toward the mound as if to replace Watson, then thought better of it. "I liked Mule's chances against Fowler," he explained later. It didn't make much sense on the face of it—a tiring hurler in a tough spot against the man who had knocked in four runs the day before. And McGraw put no value on the complete game—Claude Jonnard was ready to relieve, as he had done often during 1923.

But the manager went with his gut and was rewarded. Watson got two quick strikes, then jammed Boob with a fastball, popping him up to end the game. The Little Napoleon had done it again. The Reds were out of time. Days later, the Giants clinched the NL flag for the third straight season. They would finish 95–58, four and a half games ahead of Cincinnati. McGraw was now just four victories away from achieving his ultimate goal.

October

31

On October 1, the Giants got their first close-up look at the concrete behemoth across the river, holding a two-hour practice at the Yankee Stadium. McGraw groused that Tex Austin's recent rodeo had torn up the outfield, but he was happy with the condition of the infield. When asked about his team's chances in the upcoming clash with the Yankees, McGraw answered with a steely, "We're looking forward to the Series getting under way." The Giants held another workout in the Bronx the following day, a session eyed closely from the stands by rivals Jones, Shawkey, and Pipp. Pipp hobbled about on a cane, his ankle heavily wrapped. He told reporters he had just given the ankle a "bake out" under the heat of an electric lamp and was confident he'd be able to play in the Series.

Then came a game and a circumstance that seem utterly bizarre to the modern eye. On October 3, an exhibition game pitted the minor-league Baltimore Orioles against a combined team of Yankees and Giants at the Polo Grounds. Wearing an ill-fitting Giants uniform borrowed from Jack Scott—and taking orders from John McGraw—was Babe Ruth. Incredibly, with a World Series that promised to border on the homicidal starting in exactly one week, the signature personalities were on the same side in a meaningless exhibition game. Even more amazing—Ruth had rolled his right ankle getting off a train (the same way Pipp had) in Boston a few days before. Indeed, the *Tribune* noted, "Ruth was pretty lame and limped back and forth at his various duties. He looked as if his foot needed a rest between now and Series time." A superstar playing hurt in a meaningless exhibition days before the biggest set of games in his career? And sharing the dugout with his archrival and main nemesis? Ruth never thought twice about it. The contest benefited former Giants owner John T. Brush, who was battling dementia, and Ruth lent his name to help the gate, as he did countless times for causes great and small throughout his career.

McGraw was careful to keep his signs generic and not give anything away to the enemy in his midst. Ruth wasn't paying attention anyway—as he "wrote" the next day in the *New York American:* "In Major League Baseball we don't go pussy-footing before a 'big event,'" a touching naïveté that McGraw would have mocked. Ruth certainly didn't pussyfoot around during the game, blasting a monster home run clear out of the Polo Grounds, spurring an easy 9–3 win over the Orioles. "And he'll hit a few here next week!" yelled a fan, one of five thousand in attendance. "Just getting the range, that's all." Apparently, Ruth was intent on playing his way to health. "The left one hurts more than the right one does now," he said with a sly grin after the game.

The Yankees still had four regular-season games left, against the A's (early-October dates were kept open to play makeup games that were rained out). The MVP not only played in all four games but went berserk, crushing A's pitching to the tune of nine hits in fourteen at bats. He also hit three more homers and had nine RBI. Ruth was even intentionally walked with the bases empty, "taking the free pass to absurd new extremes," said the *Tribune.* The last home run came on October 7, the final day of the regular season. Ruth crushed a two-run bomb off Slim Harriss of Philadelphia for his 41st of the season, and the 238th of his career to that point. The Yankees lost the season finale, 9–7, but finished 98–54, taking the AL by an astounding sixteen games. Many of the Giants came out to watch at least one of the final contests. They got in for free, which didn't help the lowly attendance take any. "They were nearly half of those there," according to one report.

The smattering of fans pushed the Yankee Stadium gate to 1,007,066 on the season. That was about 19,000 fewer fans than had paid to watch the team play in the Polo Grounds the year before. The Yankees' easy run to the pennant explains the decline to some degree. The team also played better away from home. Their road record was an awesome 52–24, six games better than the 46–30 mark they put up in the Yankee Stadium. The team scored slightly more and had a few additional hits on the road than at home, though they hit considerably more homers in the Bronx, 62–43. Ruth was the exception to that trend—twenty-two of his forty-one homers came away from the House That Ruth Built.

As Ruth feared, the Polo Grounds was actually a better hitter's park, at least for him, than the Stadium nicknamed after him. He knew it too, complaining that if he had played the full season in Manhattan, he'd "have hit eighty home runs." Of his Yankee Stadium homers, all but four were hit to right or right-center field— the rest were inside-the-park home runs, including three late in the season: one on a misjudged fly ball to center, the others lined smashes to the deepest reaches of the Stadium. All his other numbers were better in the Bronx, however, so there was clearly something he liked about hitting in his new home.

Conversely the Stadium suited the Yankees pitchers just fine. The staff led the AL in ERA, strikeouts, complete games, hits allowed, and victories. Going into the Series, Messrs. Jones, Bush, Pennock, and Shawkey provided the Yanks' main advantage when matching up with the Giants.

In early October, the commissioner of health for New York City, Dr. Frank Monaghan, decided to examine for himself the phenomenon that was Babe Ruth. He put a nearly naked Babe through a hard physical workout and examined him closely, seeking to understand his gifts. The good doctor found Ruth's mind to be "exceptionally alert" and that Ruth's heart rate, after a vigorous "fifteen-minute workout with dumbbells," was a quite healthy 74. "I went over a body that I could honestly, from a medical and physical standpoint, say is close to perfection," raved Dr. Monaghan.

Ruth's play in 1923 was close to perfection as well. His forty-one home runs tied Philly's Cy Williams for the major-league lead. He might have won the home-run title outright (as he did eleven times in his career) but for Major League Rule 48, which said that balls that cleared the fence in fair territory but landed foul were to be ruled foul balls. The rule, which was changed to its current model in 1930, cost Ruth six homers in 1923, five of them away from the Yankee Stadium. Additionally, had it not been for what *Baseball Magazine* called the "intentional pass evil" (Ruth was walked purposefully an estimated eighty times—no exact count exists), he surely would have added to his homer total.

His 131 RBI edged Tris Speaker by one, with Irish Meusel leading the NL with 125. Heilmann of Detroit did best Ruth by ten points in batting average, .403 to .393, thus denying the Babe the Triple Crown. Ruth also led the majors in runs scored, walks (his 170 stood as the all-time single-season record until Barry Bonds broke it in the early years of the new century), on-base percentage, slugging percentage, OPS (which combines on-base and slugging percentages), and various other more complex metrics, such as Pete Palmer's Batter-Fielder Wins, which estimates how many more wins a player provides for his team when compared with an average replacement. In Ruth's case, it was 10.1—had a C-rated player taken Ruth's place on the 1923 Yankees, the Hugmen would have won eighty-eight games, not ninety-eight. Ruth threw out twenty-one runners from the outfield and stole seventeen bases. In 1923 the Babe was a five-tool player extraordinaire. He had a couple of flaws: he led the majors in strikeouts, as he did five times in his career, and he was thrown out stealing an astounding twenty-one times. The concept of the game's greatest slugger attempting thirty-eight steals and being unsuccessful 55 percent of the time is a baffling one. Apparently some aspects of Scientific Baseball were appealing even to the Big Brute, just as McGraw seldom complained when one of his Giants went deep, even though he felt "the game far more interesting when the art of making scores lies in scientific work on the bases."

Soon after, sportswriter Walter Camp, the "Father of American Football," the man who had outlined many of the rules and stratagems of pigskin, assessed Ruth, using metaphors that advanced, as the game had, from the pastoral frontier to the modern industrial nation:

> Today he ranges over the right field territory like a shaggy buffalo endowed with the legs of an antelope; he throws to the bases with bullet-like speed and accuracy; he slides on a close play with all the abandon of an express train trying to make up lost time, and at bat he crashes his terrific home run to right field, crosses a wary infield with a delicate bunt, or shortens his grip and pokes singles and doubles to any field.

In short, he was a complete, dominant player in 1923.

Ruth's regular season was greeted with huzzahs from the same press that had so quickly turned on him the year before. The *Sporting News* forgave and forgot: "He's the greatest ever; his name and deeds will echo through the ages." The *Daily News* labeled him the

"Persevering Babe," adding, "In other years his team meant nothing to him; if he hit a homer now and then he was fulfilling his obligation to his employers, he thought. This season Babe has had his heart and soul in his work." Even Joe Vila praised his "outstanding" contributions at the plate and in the field.

Ruth had proved to the doubters that he was the game's greatest player and that there was much more to him than merely crushing balls over distant fences. He had come through for his team in games large and small. He had shown one and all that he could stay clean and relatively sober throughout a season and had won back the "dirty-faced" kids he had apparently lost the year before.

But there was still a gaping hole in his pin-striped résumé. Without a World Series win as a New York Yankee, there would be a loud "Yeah, but..." at the end of any mention of his fight back from the depths. And Ruth would have to do it in the big city in order to vault into the game's pantheon.

32

On a warm spring day back in May of 1923, a man named Graham McNamee was serving his required jury duty in midtown Manhattan. During his lunch hour, instead of joining his fellow jurors for a sandwich, McNamee on the spur of the moment strolled a few blocks to the offices of AT&T. As he entered, he could hear a loudspeaker in the lobby of the building blasting the programming of AT&T's New York City flagship radio station, WEAF (660 on the AM dial, the forerunner of WNBC).

McNamee was two months' shy of his twenty-fifth birthday when he brazenly walked into the station manager's office and asked for a singing audition. Impressed by McNamee's baritone voice, the manager offered him future work but couldn't promise anything, as the station's opera programs were booked at the moment. McNamee responded that he would be happy to work as an announcer. Surprised at the request—it seemed unlikely that anyone knew enough about radio to *want* to be such a thing in the spring of 1923—the manager agreed to find McNamee some work.

The eager young man did it all around the station—answering

phones, opening and closing pianos for the players, escorting unac-
companied ladies home after programs, and, yes, doing some singing and announcing. He was paid a grand sum of $50 a week for the
grunt work, barely enough to buy a radio.

Graham McNamee was born in Washington, DC, and raised in
St. Paul, Minnesota. His father was a successful lawyer, but the time
he spent away from the family led to a divorce. His mother held
high hopes for her only son, and in 1920 she moved with Graham to
New York. A stage mother of Ruthian proportion, she wanted
McNamee to pursue a career as an opera singer. Toward that end,
she enrolled Graham in voice lessons and accompanied him to
auditions.

"Breaking in is next to impossible as a newcomer," wrote McNamee
of his early experiences in the Big Town, but Graham found some
success as a singer, debuting at Aeolian Hall and eventually getting a
nice notice in the *Times:* "Anyone who sings the aria 'O Ruddier
Than the Cherry' from Handel's *Acis and Galatea* with such admira-
bly flexible command over the 'divisions,' with such finished phrasing and such excellent enunciation as McNamee showed, is doing
a difficult thing very well indeed." He also found his wife, soprano
Josephine Garrett, in one of the opera companies he joined.

But opera left McNamee unfulfilled. He preferred to speak rather
than sing and had an obvious gift for the language and for using his
voice to capture mood and moment. He figured his opera background would get him in the radio front door, but he dreamed of
becoming an announcer.

In this dawn of radio's existence as a medium, the announcers
were mostly engineers whose sole duty was to introduce the musical
acts and get out of the way. McNamee took the art form to a new,
unprecedented level. From the start he imbued high drama into even
the most mundane of announcements. He would sprint to the studio
to achieve a breathless tone in his readings. He even smiled at the

microphone as though he were talking to an individual listener at the other end.

McNamee was introduced to Sam Ross, WEAF's program director. Ross had listened to McNamee and thought his command of dramatic inflections perfect for a new and promising area of broadcasting—sports. In late August, the program director gave McNamee his first sports assignment, calling the Harry Greb–Johnny Wilson middleweight championship fight (Greb won an easy decision at the Polo Grounds). Graham did well enough accounting for the jabs and crosses that Ross figured he could handle balls and strikes.

At that moment the only person who could claim to put "sports broadcaster" on his tax return was Major J. Andrew White, a dandified NBC employee who wore pince-nez spectacles with a ribbon dangling from the frames. White called the earliest boxing matches on radio, including the Jack Dempsey–Georges Carpentier fight in July 1921, the first sporting event to be carried live on the airwaves. White also called the astounding Dempsey-Firpo fight at the Polo Grounds. He was confused by the intense action, yelling out, "He's up! He's down! He's up!" over and over, without ever identifying exactly *who* was up or down. McNamee, who would instantly become White's chief rival, felt there was plenty of room for improvement in the nascent field.

The World Series made its radio debut in 1921. Most fans still "watched" the Series on Play-O-Graphs, large boards set up in prominent city locations that carried the score, inning, outs, and sometimes even cardboard cutouts of players that were pushed around the bases according to the action on the field. Few fans possessed radios. Westinghouse fed stations WJZ in Newark and WBZ in Springfield, Massachusetts, with the first broadcast made live from the World Series. It wasn't anything that would have made Marconi proud of his invention.

A radio engineer turned pioneering sportscaster named Harold Arlin was the main voice. He had called the first rudimentary games on Pittsburgh station KDKA in 1920. He was better known, if he was known at all, for interviews with players that were occasionally heard on Westinghouse stations. One of his more forgettable subjects was the usually talkative Babe Ruth, who encountered an epic bout of stage fright. "I introduce him and this garrulous guy, he can't say a word," remembered Arlin.

Only the opening game of the '21 Series was broadcast. Arlin gave updates after every half inning, recapping the action. At the Polo Grounds, a reporter named Sandy Hunt passed along the play-by-play via telephone to another broadcaster named Tommy Cowan, who then re-created the action. Cowan "sat atop...a building in a tiny shack" in Newark in order to ensure clear transmission. It was hardly an earth-shattering broadcast, but in the aftermath, it was clear to all that baseball and radio worked well—the game could be easily visualized in the mind.

In 1922 the range of the World Series broadcast expanded to include more stations in New England and as far south as Baltimore. Virtually overnight, it seemed, the medium had grown by leaps and bounds. By the time of the Giants-Yankees rematch, sixty million radios had been sold in the United States. Floyd Gibbons and Lowell Thomas became national figures by reading the news on the radio in the early '20s. Singers such as Guy Lombardo and Rudy Vallee and the mysterious Silver Masked Tenor became stars by belting out tunes over the airwaves. The cheapest and most popular set was a Radiola model that cost $25 (roughly $575 today). During the World Series, the company advertised baseball as a reason for buying a radio for the first time, giving away score sheets with some purchases.

Grantland Rice was hired to add to his duties as a *Tribune* sportswriter by providing play-by-play. A Radiola ad in the *Tribune* trumpeted the paper's involvement in the radio venture:

Hear the crowd roar at the World Series games with Radiola. Grantland Rice, famous sports editor of the *New York Tribune,* will describe every game personally, play-by-play, direct from the Polo Grounds. His story, word by word, as each exciting play is made by the Yankees or Giants, will be *broadcasted* [italics theirs] from famous Radio Corporation–Westinghouse Station WJZ.

It was the first example of media synergy in sports history. The *Tribune* put a boxed notice of the coming broadcasts on the front page for two weeks before the Series. It and other papers held listening parties in their building auditoriums, free to the public. Groups of fans were reported to clump around sets during the games. The *Times* estimated the radio audience for Game One of the '22 Series at five million.

What that mass audience heard was of cleaner fidelity than the year before, helped by the fact that no other stations in the tristate area went on the air during the broadcast of the games. Unfortunately the content wasn't much better. As a radio performer, Grantland Rice was an excellent writer. He often said nothing for painfully long stretches and limited most of his calls to simply "Strike one . . . ball one . . . strike two, foul . . . ground out to shortstop." The brief descriptions were made in Rice's atonal, unmistakably southern voice. The sportswriter admitted afterward, "The broadcast officials wanted me to keep talking, but I didn't know what to say." One listener wrote in to complain: "I would hear the crowd let out a terrific roar, and it seemed ages before I knew whether it was a single or a three-bagger." Fortunately, perhaps, Rice worked only the first three games of the Series, including the tie game. After that, he claimed his newspaper duties left him too busy to announce the game, and WJZ abandoned the Series and turned elsewhere to entertain its listeners.

Nevertheless, the response to the concept of baseball on the radio was overwhelmingly positive. The *Times* captured the feeling: "The cheers which greeted Babe Ruth when he stepped to the plate could be heard throughout the land. And as he struck the ball, the shouts that followed indicated whether the Babe had fanned or got a hit even before the radio announcer could tell what happened." Radio stores were packed with people who wanted to listen to the game over this wondrous new instrument. They often left with a set. One New Jersey man claimed two thousand people had jammed into his storefront to listen over a loudspeaker.

The radio sets of the time bore little resemblance to the radios we now know, or even to the radios that every household possessed during the golden age of the medium in the 1930s and '40s. The early-'20s models were wallet-sized crystal sets consisting of a wire coil and an extremely thin wire strand known as a "cat's whisker." The user moved the whisker to touch various points on the crystal, which tuned in different stations and frequencies depending on where it was touched. The method was prone to accidental slippage, and dead spots were plentiful. But when a station came in clearly, it was heaven for the listener, who often donned headphones to augment the sound clarity. To hear a far-off Babe Ruth connect over such a contraption must have seemed a miracle to fans of the day.

A generation of future announcers came of age listening to the crystal sets while under tables or behind chairs. Vin Scully, the famous voice of the Dodgers for over half a century, recalled lying on a pillow at his boyhood home in Washington Heights and listening to games, lost in reverie. Don Dunphy, one of boxing's most prominent announcers, would listen to events and relay them to the rest of his family, getting an early training in play-by-play.

Imagine, thought Sam Ross, if a professional broadcaster describing the events with some dramatic flair could augment the experience of listening to the roar of the crowd. *That* would be a powerful combination. So when WEAF was granted permission by Commissioner Landis to broadcast alongside WJZ, Ross assigned his new "sportscaster," Graham McNamee, to the 1923 World Series.

The problem was that McNamee knew little about baseball. Phrasing, inflection, building the drama—these he understood inherently. The rules and strategy of the game, not so much. So Ross decided to hire a writer of his own, W. O. McGeehan of the *Times,* to handle the play-by-play and let McNamee get his feet wet. Graham agreed to the security blanket, noting, "The baseball enthusiast is even more exacting than the fight fan."

AT&T laid "special land wires" connecting the station to both the Polo Grounds and the Yankee Stadium, as well as to radio stations as far north as WMAF in South Dartmouth, Massachusetts, and south all the way to WCAP in McNamee's hometown of Washington, DC. The increase in range and quality of the broadcast was significant. It was like taking a layer of Saran Wrap off the microphone into which the announcers spoke. The sound of their voices came through much clearer, as did the galvanizing noises made in the background.

Here's how the newspapers carried WEAF's programming schedule for October 10, 1923:

11 AM Playing the Health Game by Clara Tebutt
11:20 AM Writing for the Movies by Mrs. Frances Patterson
11:50 AM Market reports
1:30 PM World Series Play by play
4:00 PM Milton F. Rehg, baritone, with piano and soprano

Much to the disappointment of Mrs. McNamee, her son, Graham, was to be heard during the 1:30 broadcast, not singing on the 4:00 show. McGeehan sat in the press box, handling the action by a phone wired to a room next door, where McNamee sat in front of a saucer-shaped microphone. An engineer crouched behind him, ready to fix the inevitable technical issues.

McNamee opened the broadcast of Game One with what would become his standard first line: "How do you do, ladies and gentlemen of the radio audience? I am Graham McNamee." He would go on to utilize that opener, and his patented sign-off—"This is Graham McNamee. Good night, all"—for the next ten years.

At first, McNamee was forced to remain mostly mum, merely coaching McGeehan on his craft between innings. As soon as McNamee got the chance to use his voice and his personality, however, it became apparent that the writer was second banana to this new and gifted announcer. McNamee talked constantly, using his instant catchphrase "Wheeee!" incessantly to describe big moments. Despite a bit of a backlash from fans complaining that McNamee obviously didn't know what the hell he was talking about (sample sentence: "The next ball is a strike"), he did so with such verve and panache that the broadcast was a hit. The handwriting was on the wall in vivid Magic Marker. McGeehan lasted until Game Four, at which point McNamee took over by himself, and the writer was scarcely missed.

When asked about his technique, McNamee responded, "You must make each of your listeners, though miles away from the spot, feel that he or she too is there with you in the press stand, watching the pop bottle thrown in the air, Gloria Swanson arriving in her new ermine coat; McGraw in his dugout, apparently motionless, but giving signals all the time." McNamee did just that, adeptly. He may not have been a McGraw when it came to the rule book, but he was a master at dramatizing the action. And like most of the audience, he was especially taken by the Bambino. "When Babe Ruth batted," he said, "I was almost too engrossed to speak."

At one point during a Series game, McNamee dropped a thermos of coffee on himself, ruining his suit. He mentioned it on the air and got scores of letters in response. Clearly he was on to something. After the Series, WEAF received more than seventeen hundred letters praising McNamee's work, an extraordinary number given the relative paucity of the listening audience.

Over on WJZ, J. Andrew White was broadcasting the Series as

well, peering down at the action through his armless eyeglasses. White and McNamee initiated the first electronic media feud. The former thought Graham's histrionics and dramatic description of the action unbecoming to a professional. McNamee mocked White's stolidity and lack of enthusiasm. The battle was a rout—McNamee was the people's favorite, and his style caught on. White would leave radio for an executive position a few years later.

In 1926 WEAF and WJZ became corporate cousins, under the banner of the National Broadcasting Company. NBC's new president, Merlin Hall Aylesworth, was asked to name radio's greatest asset. He replied, "Graham McNamee."

McNamee would become the most recognized radio personality in New York, and by extension the United States. His excitable calls of every World Series through 1932; the Rose Bowl; and numerous important boxing matches, including the famous 1927 "Long Count" fight between Jack Dempsey and Gene Tunney, made him a household name and a cult hero. He was profiled in national magazines and appeared on numerous billboards, making McNamee's face as recognizable as his voice. He would drive his sizable Cadillac up and down Broadway, giving the thumbs-up to fans calling out to him, to waving traffic cops, to adoring women.

Even during the days of his widest appeal, he was criticized for taking a certain license with the action in front of him. "I don't know which game to write about, the one I saw or the one I heard Graham McNamee announce," said Ring Lardner after a particularly theatrical performance at a World Series game.

"I will freely admit to being an entertainer first and a broadcaster second," McNamee said. But it was his magnetic persona that helped grow an inchoate medium to brave new heights. George Hicks, who followed McNamee as a well-known announcer for NBC, said of Graham's technique, "He was the first great ad-lib personality. He threw away the script. He was a showman. He had to make mistakes. You wouldn't knock Laurence Olivier for taking liberties with a part. Graham was in the same class—he was an artist." In the 1930s McNamee would also become the narrator of Universal Pictures newsreels, making his voice instantly recognizable around the world.

Heywood Broun later observed of McNamee, "He has been able to take a new medium of expression and through it transmit himself—to give it vividly a sense of movement and of feeling. Of such is the kingdom of art."

33

ON OCTOBER 9, the Yankees held a short team meeting to prepare for the Series. It devolved into a Miller Huggins burlesque, as he unleashed a storm of invective at the Giants while simultaneously pumping up the Yanks, insisting they were the best team in the city and would prove it, starting the next day. As he spat and sputtered, Hug stripped off his sweatshirt, uniform, and two shirts, ending up hopping around the clubhouse in only an undershirt.

It was an unusual display of histrionics from the Mighty Mite, who ordinarily swallowed his emotions. Huggins might have felt more secure in letting loose, thanks to a new one-year contract to manage the team in 1924, signed in the week before the Series. There would be no lingering questions about Hug's status hanging over the team as they prepared to tangle with their archenemy. Ruppert talked up his manager during the informal press conference announcing the deal: "Huggins knows baseball and is one of the keenest students in the game....He is real modern and quickly adapted himself to the change in the style of play brought about by the lively ball. As for discipline, there will be no back talk and no laying down on him. Watch Huggins in the coming Series."

One man whom neither the press nor anyone else would be able to watch in the Series was Lou Gehrig. His September run had announced him as an impact player. The Yankees wanted Gehrig on the postseason roster as insurance and possibly to replace the crippled Pipp. Judge Landis said that was all right by him so long as the opposing manager consented.

Unfortunately the "opposing manager" was John McGraw. John J. still smarted over Gehrig choosing school over the Giants in 1921. Not one to drop a grudge, especially when it meant giving a hated opponent an advantage, McGraw nixed the deal. "These are the hazards of baseball," he said. "The rules are quite clear. If the Yankees have had an injury, that is their tough luck."

Celebrities and ordinary joes alike crushed into the city in anticipation of the Series. The "Line of Bright Lights," Broadway, teemed with people into the wee hours, and restaurants and hotels were forced to turn away customers. At the Yankees offices at the Stadium, Ed Barrow was deluged with ticket requests. He installed three separate phone lines on his desk, and all three trilled ceaselessly as the Series approached.

The reserved seats went quickly. It was a new era in America, dubbed the "Golden Age of Sport" by Grantland Rice. Disposable income was going to recreation, and paying top dollar to see the big game displayed an unmistakable status. The ballpark was a place to be seen. The *New York Post,* in 1923 not yet the tabloid that offered screaming headlines like "Headless Body Found in Topless Bar," captured the zeitgeist:

The bustle, the excitement, the hustling around for tickets, the jam of the crowds, the privilege of unrestrained cheering and jeering—all come under the heading of relaxation. The American likes to relax, and the harder it comes the better he likes it.... The man on the street has become very extravagant about his amusements. When it comes to big sporting events, the public likes to pay and pay and pay.

Press headquarters were once again at the Commodore Hotel at 42nd and Lexington Avenue, next door to Grand Central Terminal. Shuttle buses delivered the writers to Harlem and the South Bronx. The New York reporters hosted a mammoth group of out-of-town press—in all, more than two hundred sportswriters crammed the Commodore pressroom. One of them, nervously hanging back from the group, was future Ruth biographer Tom Meany. Meany was at his first Fall Classic, covering the action for the *Brooklyn Daily Times*. He would be an integral part of New York baseball for four decades, passing away in 1964 while handling publicity for the fledgling New York Mets.

Amid the loud clattering of Underwood #5 typewriters were four writers generally considered at or near the top of the heap. Grantland Rice, Damon Runyon, Fred Lieb, and Heywood Broun had amazingly all met at the Polo Grounds on opening day 1911 as freshmen writers about to tackle the top job in sports—covering John McGraw and the New York Giants. A dozen years later, their expertise and potent, if purple, prose separated them from the large pack.

As you might expect, Damon Runyon was from Manhattan—Manhattan, Kansas, that is. His first name was Alfred, but an editor at the *New York American* dropped it. Covering John McGraw and the city's boxing world during Prohibition inspired Runyon and propelled him to later fame deciphering the slicks of Broadway for the world beyond the Hudson River, most famously in stories that became the hit Broadway show and film *Guys and Dolls*. Before he gave the world Nathan Detroit, Runyon covered the Detroit Tigers.

Grantland Rice of the *Tribune* was a southern gent, from Murfreesboro, Tennessee. Rice was so devoted to his craft that once, when his press pass was lost before a game, he bought a ticket, climbed into the stands, and wrote his story with his typewriter balanced on his knees. He was sport's primary mythmaker during the Roaring '20s, deliberately setting out to make the Ruths, Dempseys, and Tildens larger than life. His most famous story, in which he coined Notre Dame's backfield the "Four Horsemen," is about football, but baseball was his favorite sport.

Heywood Broun was a member of the Algonquin Round Table, a jolly, tubby Harvard dropout whose shambling demeanor — Alexander Woollcott once compared him to an "unmade bed" — belied his sharp wit and intelligence. He had been a theater critic for the *Telegraph* before getting the baseball assignment and approached sports as he did plays, peppering his copy with reviews of the artistic performances on the field. He moved to the *Tribune* and then to the *World,* where he wrote his widely read column "It Seems to Me" after 1921. In 1923 Broun published *The Sun Field,* perhaps the first novel to use baseball as a microcosm of America, or at least the New York version of the game. One of the book's central figures is a strongly built baseball star whose lone weakness is "a fast blonde on the outside corner of the ballpark." Broun called him "Tiny Tyler," but he's very plainly based on the Babe.

As for Lieb, the writer who coined the term the "House That Ruth Built," he would cover the game for nearly seven decades. Lieb was less of a wordsmith than the others but a much more dogged reporter, and he would be present, Zelig-like, at virtually every big moment on and off the field until Watergate.

These men, plus other writers such as John Kieran, Marshall Hunt, W. B. Hanna, Ring Lardner, Joe Vila, Paul Gallico, Dan Daniel, Ford Frick, Westbrook Pegler, and Bozeman Bulger, formed the heart of a press corps that had outsize power in the days before radio developed and television was invented. They shaped public opinion of every facet of the sport. Aside from the few thousands who attended the games, the press were the sole witnesses to the on-field heroics, and as they traveled with the teams, they got to know the players and managers intimately. They were storytellers, heirs to a grand tradition of mythmaking.

Ruth was something different to each of them. To Runyon, the voice of the Broadway slick, he was the Big Town personified. To Gallico, Hunt, and the people's paper, the *Daily News,* he was the up-from-nothing kid who used his great talent to stick it to the swells. To Rice, he was King Arthur, a subject worthy of epic poems. To Broun, he was a canvas upon which to project his social concerns and wit. To the straightforward baseball man Lieb, he was simply the best player Lieb had ever seen.

The main exception to the Ruth worship was Joe Vila of the *Sun.* Vila was a proponent of Scientific Baseball and a McGraw man, and he disliked the home run and the high-scoring game it had foisted upon purists like him. Mostly he disliked the Bambino, whom Vila considered a blowhard and a phony (Joe was hardly the only writer to dislike Ruth—Frank Young of the *Washington Post* was a longtime critic, for example—but most of the others weren't based in New York).

During the 1921 Series, Vila had written that the Babe was "faking" his arm injury because he couldn't handle the pressure of the World Series, or perhaps he was merely hungover. Facing a player about whom one has written negatively is part of being a sportswriter. It's an aspect of the gig not taught in journalism school. Vila was rudely introduced to that particular facet of his job, in the form of an incensed, 220-pound Colossus of Clout. Ruth was ruled unfit for Game Six of the Series, and before the game marched directly toward the press box, his stare punching a hole through Vila. The Babe shouted at the writer and raised his arm as if to strike. In defense, Vila grabbed the only weapon he had handy—his typewriter. But Ruth merely rolled up his sleeve to show Vila his wounded wing and dared the *Sun* to photograph it for the front page. That didn't happen, nor did Joe apologize, but he did spend much of the game peeking over his shoulder at the glowering Babe.

The writers, with occasional exceptions, were highly educated in fields outside sport and were men of the world. Many were war veterans, others spoke several languages, and all seemed to have the collected works of Shakespeare and *Bartlett's Familiar Quotations* with them in the press box. John Kieran of the *Times* was typical, an expert on the Bard who read Latin and Greek, spoke fluent French, and was an ardent bird-watcher. He took his binoculars everywhere, even when golfing with the Babe. One time Ruth rolled in an eagle from long range only to see Kieran staring through his field glasses at a blue heron in a nearby mangrove. "Look at that fucking so-and-so!" Ruth exploded. "I make the best fucking shot of the season and that dumb SOB's looking at some crazy bird and didn't even see it!"

The arrival of the Babe in New York had captured the imagination of these accomplished professionals, and many of the best switched from covering the Giants to covering the Yankees. It was as though the decade or so they spent following the Giants had been an apprenticeship, and now they were ready to become master craftsmen. They recognized a good story when it launched baseballs into orbit in front of them, and John McGraw and the Giants slid deep under Ruth's immense shadow. The press still liked McGraw personally, and certainly his and the Giants' successes were lauded. But the writers were in the hero-crafting business, and there was room for only one media megafaun—and that was Babe Ruth. Every move and utterance they caught (on the field, that is) was passed along to the readers, whose demand for more Babe was unquenchable. To the writers, John McGraw was still just another dispenser of baseball pabulum. He may have been charming at night, but during the day McGraw didn't give the reporters much to work with. The Babe was the Greatest Story Ever Told, and Lord, the writers worked to capture every detail. As Lieb wrote: "With the exception of King David of Israel, whose slingshot knockout of Goliath is recorded in millions of Bibles printed in hundreds of languages, Babe Ruth is the most publicized athlete who ever lived."

Even though Ruth made better copy, most in the press favored McGraw in the upcoming battle. "The Giants are more resourceful in a short critical jam . . . steadier hitters, faster on the bases," thought W. B. Hanna. He also thought the Giants held the edge in right field. "Youngs is just about as dangerous as Ruth at the bat," he wrote. "More so probably in a short series."

Runyon felt the Giants' edge was less physical and more mental:

McGraw uses a species of psychology on Ruth in these games. McGraw knows Ruth feels the weight of responsibility on his shoulders. McGraw knows that Ruth, realizing what the public expects of him, is wildly eager to live up to expectations, to his great reputation, is apt to be strained, nervous, over-anxious when he steps to the plate. McGraw has his pitchers pitching to Ruth as if he were an ordinary hitter, pitching calmly, fear-lessly, giving him pitching he MUST hit at.

Perhaps the fact that the pitchers show no great respect for his slugging reputation is highly disconcerting to Ruth. Any man is apt to be somewhat taken aback when he finds a low valuation placed upon his ability.

Syndicated writer John Foster summed up the coming contest: "McGraw will try to manipulate [the Babe] so that he will look like a mere pawn on the World Series chessboard. It is up to Ruth to show whether or not he is a king."

Unlike the press, the roster of celebrity experts found no consensus as to what team would win. Songwriter George M. Cohan stuck with his buddy McGraw: "Honest to goodness, I think the Giants will win it." Florenz Ziegfeld agreed: "John McGraw has demonstrated that he is the greatest manager in baseball, and his team this year is as great as any he has ever directed." Walter Catlett, an actor who would have a big role in *Yankee Doodle Dandy,* nevertheless picked the Giants. "John McGraw and the Giants will surely win." Famous dames, on the other hand, favored the American Leaguers. For example, Fanny Brice, who inspired the Barbra Streisand vehicle *Funny Girl,* said, "I pick the Yanks. Babe Ruth will be at his best, and I believe he will show that he can still make home runs." So did the first lady of the American theater, Marilyn Miller. "The Yankees will win. I am certain Ruth will be a big factor."

The World Series

34

WEDNESDAY, OCTOBER 10, dawned clear and bright, and the temperature was a mild sixty-two degrees at game time — which umpire William Evans, eager to avoid any brush with twilight after the tie-game debacle of 1922, guaranteed would be two p.m. "to the second."

A startling phenomenon greeted Stadium employees when they reported for work the morning of Game One. About twenty people were already lined up at the ticket booths, having queued overnight to ensure admittance. No one could recall having seen such a thing before. The first man in line, a Brooklynite named Arthur Yarish, spent the night perched on a wooden box, gazing enviously at the man behind him, Martin Belasco of the Bronx. Belasco had thought to bring a roll-away bed and blanket with him and snoozed through the long wait.

When the unreserved tickets went on sale at ten a.m., fans from all forty-eight states were on line, as well as baseball enthusiasts from Mexico, Canada, and Cuba. One man traveled from Manila to New York to see the game, a journey of some ten thousand miles. Many,

many more were turned away or could not even get to the park. Interest in the game ran so high that the *Times* was forced to plead with fans to refrain from calling for score updates, as the paper did not want its phone system paralyzed.

In all, 55,307 fans would enjoy the afternoon sunshine at the Yankee Stadium, eager to see the first-ever World Series game in the new building. Curiously, the team didn't make standing-room tickets available, as it had on opening day, which would have swelled the gate past 60,000. Tickets for this monumental event in New York sporting history cost $6.60 for box seats; $5.50 for lower grandstand reserved seats; $3.30 for upper deck, mezzanine, and unreserved seats; and $1.10 for the bleachers, or "sun seats."

Dignitaries turned out in force, from business tycoons J. P. Morgan, Harry Payne Whitney, and Harry Sinclair, to artistes like George M. Cohan, opera tenor John McCormack, and actor Louis Mann, to sportsmen like Jack Dempsey, chess champ A. D. Lasker, and dozens of baseball players and execs. Surprisingly Cardinals manager Branch Rickey sat in a box next to his star player, Rogers Hornsby, even though the two men had exchanged blows only weeks earlier.

The papers assessed in acute sociological detail the average joes who came out, especially the bleacher dwellers. Rowdy, intense fans, forerunners to today's infamous "Bleacher Creatures," occupied right field, where the Babe worked. Before the game, an argument between a "colored" Yankee fan from Harlem and a white Giants fan from Newark occasioned a barrage of rolled-up newspapers thrown at both fans. Several policemen had to step in to quell passions. Left field sported a more genteel lot. One fan was overheard translating Latin prose, and many had the audacity to read books while awaiting the first pitch.

The center-field denizens were portrayed as simply odd. The *Tribune* reported on one Henry Stovack, of Albany, who had lost his left leg but got around quite well on his brand-new crutches. So sanguine was Stovack about the Yankees' chances to win that he had bet said crutches. A fellow handicapped friend identified only as

"Bull" was to win them if McGraw's men were victorious. Bull put up five hundred cigarettes on every game. "If the Giants win more games than the Yankees, I lose my walking sticks," said Stovack. "But I'm thinking I'll smoke all winter on Bull."

Such were the men of the bleachers—and they were almost uniformly men. One estimate had fewer than 150 women in attendance, making Game One the "largest stag party ever staged out of doors." Some blamed the long lines at the ticket windows and the relatively few reserved tickets sold ahead of time. After all, ladies, as the *Tribune* noted, "don't like to stand in line." One well-dressed flapper was scared out of the bleachers by a chorus of offers to make room for her. But the few distaff fans in the house knew their baseball. One was triumphant in a wager on Ruth's batting average for the season. Her spoils? Three boxes of peppermints.

Otherwise, according to the *Times,* it was a true melting pot, where "western farmers and eastern bankers, newsboys and college students, actors and athletes, rich and poor, old and young, all mingled together in the amphitheater where the gladiators fought."

Entertainment for the fans before the game was provided by the Seventh Regiment Band, in an encore performance of opening day, and by the comedy team of Nick Altrock and Al Schacht. Ed Barrow had spent the week before the Series negotiating with the two Washington Senators coaches, who made an extra buck with pregame routines such as "tightrope-walking" the foul lines and re-creating famous boxing matches. After some tough bargaining, Barrow signed Altrock and Schacht to perform before Game One.

Both men had been major-league pitchers. Schacht was signed by Washington after he anonymously sent clippings of his minor-league performances to Senators owner Clark Griffith. On the clippings Schacht scrawled, "Get this guy," and signed, "A Fan." He won only fourteen games in the majors but ingratiated himself with Griffith and was kept on as a coach. Altrock was more successful. He had a couple of twenty-win seasons to his credit. He too was friendly with

Griffith, and the owner responded by not only keeping him around as a coach but letting Altrock pitch occasionally over a period spanning twenty-plus seasons—a transparent ploy to allow Nick to claim he had played in five different decades.

But it was as the "Clown Princes of Baseball" that Altrock and Schacht left their mark on the game (years later, Max Patkin would swipe the act and make it a solo). In time, the duo would become baseball's answer to Martin and Lewis—right down to the bitter distaste the partners held for each other. Once close friends, the pair fell out badly, seldom speaking except when performing. The dispute dated to a drunken evening, when Altrock supposedly called Schacht a "Jew kike bastard." Thus the pair's comic aping of the Dempsey-Firpo fight before the game held dark overtones—their friends wondered when one partner would "mistakenly" slug the other.

Cap Huston spent the morning of the first game taking his daily constitutional at the Englewood Country Club, a few miles northwest of the Stadium in New Jersey, after which he headed to the park. Huston sightings were infrequent at games after he sold his portion of the Yankees, but there was no way he would miss the first World Series in his beautiful new stadium. Cap spent most of his time before Game One drinking coffee from Harry Stevens's large spread in the Yankees offices, studiously avoiding his former partner, Ruppert, who otherwise was a genial host, presiding over his guests as though hosting a large party. In effect, he was. Commissioner Landis spent a full hour at the buffet, wolfing roast-beef sandwiches and baked chicken. He needed to build up his strength—Landis threw out the ceremonial first pitch before the game.

At field level, while the band marched and Schacht and Altrock pretended to slug each other, press photographers and movie cameramen were engaged in a terrifying, vertigo-inducing climb up long ladders to their perches. The men shot from "birdcages"—scaffolding hung from the mezzanine floor so as not to impede the sight lines. There was one behind and above either dugout. While their famous writing brethren yukked it up over sandwiches and bootleg whiskey in the warmth of the owner's suites, the techies hauled heavy equipment up to the gods, "where one little error is a putout for eternity." The *Tribune* noted wryly: "As an architectural triumph the conceit is a masterstroke but scarcely a sound risk for an underwriter."

They looked down on a sporting green that had mostly recovered from Tex Austin's cowboy crucible. "Squads of garden manicurists worked all day and all night on the playing field," reported the Associated Press, "and this morning there were only a few spots in the turf to show where the cowpunchers had helped the steers and broncos tear up the sod several weeks ago."

Down in the Giants clubhouse, uniformed players arrived in clumps of twos and threes, having changed clothes across the river and taxied to the Bronx. The stroll across the water had not offered their manager a clear answer to the question of the day. McGraw sat in his office, puzzling over which of his pitchers to start. The lack of reliable starters that had plagued the Giants all season troubled the manager, not to mention the sharps, who made the Yankees slight favorites due to their superior moundsmen. Even hours before the game, McGraw wasn't sure who would start the all-important opener.

Publically, McGraw stood behind his pitchers:

In my opinion, the opposition was a good deal stiffer in the NL this year, and our pitchers should be rated accordingly. . . . I realize that Ruth has had a great year, and that he may be a considerable factor in the Series, but we had that danger the previous two Series, and we came out on top. Last year we had what competent judges called a poor pitching staff, but we had good pitching when we needed it. This year, the pitching staff is at least twenty percent stronger, and certainly the rest of the team has not fallen in strength.

But McGraw struggled to ascertain a starting rotation for the Series. Art Nehf, the little lefty, seemed the obvious choice for the opener, based on his prior big-game success, and the press seemed certain McGraw was simply being coy in not naming him until the final hour. In fact, the manager preferred not to name starters in advance, revealing later that he liked his pitchers to "get a good night's sleep" unburdened by the knowledge of a big game the next day. But more to the point, Nehf's disappointing season had soured McGraw on his ace. So John J. pulled a fast one. He tapped Mule Watson as his surprise choice.

The pick revealed McGraw's confidence, if not arrogance, in his team's ability to whip the Yankees. After all, he had snuffed Ruth and the potent Yankee attack for seven consecutive Fall Classic games, and nine of twelve contests overall, and his confidence in doing so again was sky-high. Winning Game One with Watson on the hill would not only give his team a leg up but strike a devastating psychological blow to his enemies across the diamond. *It's World Series time, boys,* the start of Watson seemed to say. *McGraw Time is here. You might as well surrender now.*

Watson may have had McGraw's confidence, but he didn't display much of his own: the Yankees' first turn at bat in a World Series game at the Stadium resulted in a run. The Babe made his initial appearance in the bottom of the first, "greeted with respectful silence where last year he was jeered and booed from all sides," reported the *Times*. Ruth reached on a fielder's choice and scored on a two-out double by Meusel, who was batting cleanup, with the gimpy Pipp dropped to fifth in the order. Watson slapped his glove against his hip in anger. Then Whitey Witt dumped a two-out single in front of Stengel in center field in the next frame, and quickly the Yankees led, 3–0. The cheers that accompanied the run-scoring hits rolled across the massive yard like thunder. It appeared the Yankee Stadium came with instant October mystique.

McGraw wasn't one for fate, however. He reamed out his club as they trotted in after the close of the bottom of the second. The fear the Little Round Man could instill in his club was as impressive as the way the team responded to his tongue-lashings.

Hoyt, the Yankees starter, had cruised through the first two innings, the only notable moment being a deep fly by Casey Stengel. Ruth scampered up the embankment and gloved the shot, causing Stengel to complain, "He ain't an outfielder, he's a robber!" Now in the third, however, Hoyt showed signs of shakiness right away, giving up a hit and a walk to the first two Giants batters. Sensing the vaudevillian's sudden stage fright, the Little Napoleon went all out with moves. He pinch-hit for Watson, ending his surprise-starter experiment after two innings. He ran for the slow-footed Gowdy, and when Bentley singled in Watson's stead, McGraw ran for him too. All in the third inning!

A force-out at second with the bases loaded off the bat of Bancroft scored the Giants' initial run of the Series. With one in and runners at the corners, Hoyt mistakenly went into his windup. The speedy Bancroft immediately took off for second, stealing the bag easily. Heinie Groh, picking up where he left off after tearing the cover off the ball in the '22 Series, smacked a shot down the first-base line, where Pipp would have been holding Bancroft on. The two-run triple tied the game and chased Hoyt after a mere two and a third innings. Frisch greeted reliever Bush with a single to make it 4–3, Giants.

It was vintage McGraw. Few managers then or now would have had the courage and the self-belief to go all-in only two innings into the World Series. But McGraw had seen, with eyes conditioned over three decades to discern pitchers losing their command, that Hoyt was vulnerable. And he went for the jugular, removing his starter and using three men off his bench while much of the crowd was still finding its way inside. Once again, McGraw's dugout maneuvering was dizzying the Yankees.

Ruth flew out to start the third. The Sultan had been trying to yank virtually everything to right, and McGraw's pitchers took advantage, throwing changeups and slow curves outside. There was no video for the Babe to inspect between at bats, no hitting coach to get in his ear and give him guidance. His teammates would no sooner offer Ruth batting tips than give stalking advice to an African lion. The Babe was on his own, and with every failure, McGraw and the Giants turned up the volume on the taunts, nothing personal this time, just repeated reminders of Ruth's utter incompetence.

Finally, Ruth adjusted at the plate. With one out in the fifth, he waited on a curve from Watson's replacement, Rosy Ryan, and drove it the other way, down the left-field line. Irish was shading far over toward center, the idea that Ruth might show patience and discipline at the plate never occurring to him. As the ball rolled and rolled, Ruth steamed to third, engaging in a bizarrely long slide, what Rice described as a "twenty-foot hook slide."

It was a hit, *finally* a hit. But even what should have been a clear positive moment became tinged with failure. Meusel followed the triple with a bloop into short center field. Frisch got a jump on it and made a nice running catch on the grass for the second out. Ruth, aggressive as always on the base paths, saw the Flash heading away from the infield and decided to tag up and head for home. Frisch uncannily threw it perfectly to the plate without setting himself and nailed Ruth at the plate by five feet.

So in the span of a minute or so, the Babe's long-awaited batting success against the Giants had been undone. "Nice going, Big Monk!" yelled McGraw, his voice clearly heard over the hushed throng. The score remained 4–3, Giants. As Percy Hammond put it in the *Herald*, "The Colossal Babe smote mightily, and safely traversed ¾ of the arena, only to be cut down on the threshold of his destination, and to be left there, a soiled, undone and disconsolate hero."

Frisch's perfect throw was emblematic of the game after the Giants seized the lead—the Yankees attacked and attacked, while the Giants' superbly trained defenders parried. An even more scintillating defensive play frustrated Ruth again in the seventh inning. Bush, who had relieved Hoyt and supplied not only excellent pitching but two hits, singled, and Jumpin' Joe Dugan tripled him home to tie the game at four. Ruth strode confidently to the batter's box, needing only a fly ball to put his team in front.

Since Ryan had entered the game, McGraw's instructions to him had been, thought the *Tribune,* "brilliant and constant." Now McGraw gripped his bat and signaled to Ryan to start the Sultan with his usual dish, a big looping curve that Ruth took for a ball. But then the manager uncharacteristically called for a fast one, and Ryan left it a little over the plate. The Babe whacked a screaming one-hopper down to Highpockets Kelly at first, one that "left a trail of smoke and flame in its wake." The rangy first-sacker dove flat out to his left and knocked down the ball. He scrambled into foul ground to retrieve it, whirled, and threw a bullet home to nail the sliding Dugan.

Kelly's play was sensational, one some observers called the finest Fall Classic fielding play ever seen. Ruth stood at first base, exasperated. When Meusel flew out to end the inning, the game was amazingly still tied at four, and the Yanks were shaking their heads in the dugout.

Their frustration mounted in the eighth. Pipp, starting despite his gimpy ankle, was picked off second base after McGraw called for a pitchout, a development that caused Pipp's father, sitting near press row, to "about swallow his tongue." Huggins would later comment acidly that his main regret from the game was that Pipp was just healthy enough to play. Schang followed the baserunning gaffe with a clean single, one that would likely have scored Pipp.

The game remained tied into the ninth. With two outs and extra innings looming, Stengel wobbled to the plate to face Bush, who had reached six and a third shutout innings of relief on the afternoon, his forkball tying the visitors in knots. Since Frisch's single back in the third inning, Bullet Joe had allowed but two singles, one by Stengel. Bush and Casey were actually close friends, having roomed together on a trip to Japan during the off-season. Now the shadows lengthened as the "Brainerd Meteor" glared at the Giants outfielder, their friendship put on hold for the moment. Bob Meusel, aware of Stengel's penchant for slicing balls down the left-field line, was unusually close to the stripe. Witt in center didn't slide over to compensate.

Bush worked to a full count on the Giants center fielder. Then Stengel slapped the payoff pitch into left-center. It wasn't hit particularly hard—Fred Lieb would remember that he started to mark Stengel for a single in his scorebook. But following the advice of Wee Willie Keeler, Stengel had "hit one where they ain't." Meusel was hugging the line, and Witt was miles away. The ball shot to the distant fence like it was on roller skates.

Stengel, on thirty-three-year-old knees that were never that spry to begin with, hustled around the bases as Witt chased his hit. As Stengel rounded second, Dugan noticed a strange sound emanating from the Giant. "You could hear him yelling, 'Go, Casey, go! Go, Casey, go!' to himself above the noise of the crowd. It was the damnedest thing." Witt finally reached the ball and flipped it over to the rifle-armed Meusel, who pegged one to the cutoff man, Ernie Johnson (who had replaced Scott), in short left. As Stengel staggered around third, he never thought about stopping.

Casey wore a sponge in his left shoe to cushion the heel he had injured in Chicago, and as he hit the final straightaway, it popped free from his cleat. Many fans thought Stengel had thrown a shoe and began to laugh despite the tense situation. Casey too thought he had burst a tire and covered the last ninety feet in a limping, shuffling approximation of a run. He resembled a contestant in the latter stages of the dance marathons that were starting to sweep the nation. Johnson fired a one-hopper to Schang at home as Stengel stumbled the final steps. The ball kicked high in the air. Casey slid in, angling for the outside edge of the plate, just as Schang caught the ball and slapped the tag down—too late. Stengel had completed an inside-the-park home run, giving the Giants a 5–4 lead.

The team poured out of the dugout and pummeled Stengel in celebration. "Half a dozen Giants rushed forward to help Casey to his feet," reported Damon Runyon, "to hammer him on the back, to bawl congratulations in his ears as he limped unsteadily, still panting furiously, to the bench where John J. McGraw, the chief of the Giants, relaxed his stern features to smile."

Had Stengel's dash come at the Polo Grounds, thus ending the game, it would have been even more dramatic and perhaps better remembered today. As it was, the Yanks still had three outs to play with. Ruth was due up fourth in the bottom of the ninth, but he never got to bat. Bush led off the inning with a grounder to third, which he almost beat out—he was ejected for arguing the decision too vehemently. Dugan skied one to left with two out, and Meusel battled the setting sun for a moment, raising the briefest of hopes that he might lose it, setting the stage for a dramatic Ruth appearance at the plate. But Irish gloved the ball, and Ruth dropped his huge bat in the on-deck circle and trudged to the clubhouse.

The Giants had won, *again.* Impossibly, despite all the pin-striped chances to win, the Giants' combination of excellent defense, timely hitting, and derring-do on the bases had proven decisive. The National Leaguers had now won eight consecutive Series games over their Gotham foe. The great Bambino could chop trees into sawdust and terrorize AL pitchers till kingdom come. But when faced with the brilliance of McGraw and the superiority of NL ballplayers, Ruth and his Yankees, no matter what ballpark they called home, crumbled every time.

Percy Hammond summed it up best: "Mentally Mr. McGraw's boys are to Col. Ruppert's as post-graduates are to freshmen.... 'Get away from here,' Mr. McGraw seemed to say, 'this is no place for a *Yankee.*'" Ring Lardner piled on: "It was a game that could only have been lost by one team in the world—the Yankees."

The Yankee clubhouse was a somber one. "The players dressed silently and morosely," reported the *World*. They knew they had let a winnable game slip away. One reporter thought that "through their gloom beamed a spark of determination and confidence." He must not have been looking at Huggins, who was beet red with anger, or Schang, who was near tears. Bush said of his game-losing pitch, "I threw it just as hard as I could. He crashed it good and plenty." The Babe was calm. "I swore off a lot of things this year," he said. "One was to make World Series alibis."

Down the hall, the Giants were a giddy group. Stengel cheerfully pointed out the bruises he sustained in the celebration at home plate. "Here is where Jack Bentley congratulated me. This [red spot just below the knee] is best wishes from Hank Gowdy. I feel a lump behind my ear where Frisch wished me long life and happiness. Thank heaven Jim Thorpe isn't with this team anymore." The celebration was a movable one—the Giants had to go back to the Polo Grounds to change into their civilian clothes, left behind at the dictate of their rancorous manager.

In the sporting press, the general consensus was that Game One of the 1923 World Series was as great a contest that had ever been played. McGraw's machinations, the cut and thrust of the Yankees bats against the Giants gloves, and the scintillating running stumble around the base paths by the least likely of heroes turned the game into what we would today call an "instant classic." That it took place in such a grand and glorious new sporting palace added to the drama.

The deciding play, Stengel's inside-the-park homer, turned into an iconic one, in large part thanks to Runyon's write-up in the *New York World* the following day:

This is the way old "Casey" Stengel ran yesterday afternoon running his home run to a Giant victory by the score of 5 to 4 in the first game of the World Series of 1923. This is the way old "Casey" Stengel ran running his home run when two were out in the ninth inning and the score was tied, and the ball still bounding inside the Yankee yard.

This is the way—

His mouth wide open.

His warped old legs bending beneath him at every stride.

His arms flying back and forth like those of a man swimming with a crawl stroke.

His flanks heaving, his breath whistling, his head far back, Yankee infielders, passed by old Casey Stengel as he was running his home run home, say "Casey" was muttering to himself, adjuring himself to greater speed as a jockey mutters to his horse in a race, saying "Go on, Casey, go on."

People generally laugh when they see old "Casey" Stengel run, but they were not laughing when he was running his home run home yesterday. People—60,000 of them, men and women—were standing in the Yankee stands and bleachers up there in the Bronx roaring sympathetically, whether they were for or against the Giants.

"Come on, Casey!!"

The warped old legs, twisted and bent by many a year of baseball campaigning, just barely held out under "Casey" Stengel until he reached the plate, running his home run home.

Then they collapsed.

The play and Runyon's finely wrought description made Stengel almost as famous across the country as Ruth, if only for a moment. Everywhere, fans recounted the perfectly placed hit and Casey's unlikely circumnavigation of the base paths, while kids imitated the limping, gasping dash for the plate, yelling, "Go on, [insert name here], go on!" All winter, Stengel himself was asked to re-create his mad dash, sliding across living rooms and saloons around Kansas City and New York.

While everyone was calling his dash one of the game's greatest moments, Casey himself stayed grounded. The next day he told a reporter, "Baseball's a business. Some of us are plugging sorts, like bookkeepers, and some are plungers, flying high, doing wonderful things by spurts, then plunging. . . . I've had a pretty checkered career. They call me superannuated now. I'm thirty-three. I'm no wonderful runner and I wouldn't expect to set the Mississippi River afire with my brains. I guess I'm a bookkeeper that had a lucky day."

There was one negative for Stengel: after the season, when he was trying to persuade his girlfriend, Edna Lawson, to marry him, her father wondered why Edna would marry such an old man. Edna had to bring Casey to meet his future father-in-law to reassure him that while Stengel may have been old by baseball standards, he was still young enough to marry.

Not only did Stengel now rival the Babe in renown but he had eclipsed him on the diamond as well. The Giants led the series, 1–0, and with play shifting to the Polo Grounds for Game Two, there was little reason to believe the Little Napoleon and his Giants were headed toward anything but a third straight championship.

35

Thursday, October 11, was gloomy and overcast. Rain threatened to fall on upper Manhattan for much of the afternoon but held off. Instead, a "pale, speakeasy sun" tried to push through the scudding clouds. There was no wind, and the championship flags flying over the Polo Grounds hung limp. The teams had agreed to play without any off days, so Ruth and McGraw had little time to dwell on the twists and turns of Game One before heading to Coogan's Bluff for Game Two.

The threatening weather didn't keep more than 40,000 fans from swelling the grandstands, 40,402 to be exact, a new attendance record for the Polo Grounds. In the box seats, Major August Belmont, eponymous owner of the Long Island racetrack, talked up the coming match race between Zev, the scrappy American Thoroughbred, and Papyrus, the English champion, one week hence. Few gave the Yankee upstart a chance against the purebred, imperious champ, but Zev would win going away, delighting what the *Tribune* called "the largest turnout by members of society in the history of this country."

Thomas Meighan, matinee idol of Broadway turned silent-movie star, created a stir when he walked through the grandstand to his seat near the press box, where he sat with George Ade, well-known humorist and playwright. Ade's specialty was chronicling the immigrant experience in the big city. Meanwhile, Colonel Ruppert escorted his eighty-four-year-old mother to the Polo Grounds. It was, amazingly, the first time she had seen a game in person.

Those who weren't lucky enough to procure advance tickets could call upon Jacob's Ticket Office, at 50th and Broadway in the Hotel Normandie (or "call Fitz Roy 4188-89-90"). Ticket brokers like Jacob could accommodate the less fortunate with marked up seats for the Series, or perhaps he could interest you in a ticket for the Army–Notre Dame game, or even a grandstand spot for the Zev-Papyrus match race?

In Game Two, McGraw again eschewed Nehf and went with Handsome Hugh McQuillan as his starter. Pennock took the ball for the Yanks. It was a pressure-packed situation for the Knight. The left-hander had been brought over by Huggins to balance out the righty staff, and although the Giants featured a squadron of switch-hitters, they were considerably more potent against righties. Over the course of the regular season, the Giants had hit only .247 against southpaws, compared with .285 against righties. So Pennock had an advantage, but his postseason experience was limited to three measly innings of relief way back in 1914 with the Athletics. He was normally at home on his country estate in Pennsylvania by now, instead of preparing to take the hill in a must-win scenario against the two-time defending champions.

The press tracked each World Series game's first pitch as a supposed harbinger of the game's results. McQuillan's initial offering was a beauty of a slow curve that froze Ward for a called strike. By the superstition of the day, this boded well for McGraw's men. Unfortunately for John J., Babe Ruth wasn't paying attention to folklore.

Ruth walked in the top of the first, putting two on with one out, but McGraw's leak-proof infield came up big again, turning a double play on a Meusel grounder to short. Bob's brother, Irish, smacked a home run in the second to offset one by Ward in the top of the frame, so the game was tied at one when Ruth came up to lead off the fourth.

The Babe was now 8–37 in eleven Series games against McGraw and the Giants (his arm injury scratched him from two games in 1921), a measly .216 average, with but a single home run. In Boston, Ruth had been a dominant postseason force on the mound. But here in the big city, the Great Bambino had been coming up small. The press pointed out his ineptitude, which could not be ignored. But he wasn't subjected to modern-day talk radio and Internet-style hazing, which would surely include the words "choker," "overpaid," and "not a real Yankee." For all the Babe's gargantuan accomplishments during the 154-game preamble, he had been a Big Apple Bust (the new appellation for the city had been coined by John J. Fitz Gerald in the *New York Morning Telegraph* earlier in the year) when it counted — in the World Series. Ruth was running out of chances to do something clutch and to defeat McGraw in a meaningful game.

Giants bench jockeys rode Ruth from the moment he appeared in the on-deck circle. Before the game, McGraw, when asked by a reporter (who apparently hadn't been watching the Series) if the manager would pitch to Ruth, let loose a cackling yelp. "Why *wouldn't* we pitch to Ruth? I've said before and I'll say again, we pitch to better hitters than Ruth in the National League." Until the fourth inning of Game Two, few could disagree.

Handsome Hugh started the Babe with two wide ones, then threw a fastball up around Ruth's neck. The Colossus of Clout swung and missed with "comic ferocity and ineptitude," as Heywood Broun wrote in the *New York World*.

Snyder peeked into the dugout to see what McGraw wanted for the 2–1 pitch. As Broun put it, "McGraw scratched his nose to indicate 'Try another one of those shoulder-high fastballs on the Big Bum and let's see if we can't make him break his back again.'"

So Hugh hurled in another high hard one, and the Babe swung

with the same force. This time, however, he connected with what the *Tribune* called "a wallop that sounded like a barrel of crockery being pushed down the stairs." The ball rocketed high and far beyond the right-field roof, more than 300 feet off the ground, a blast later estimated at 475 feet. A police officer patrolling outside the Polo Grounds picked up the rolling ball and pocketed it. Lardner wrote: "If anybody had been riding on the ball they could have gotten on the Elevated [train] without climbing the stairs." It was an epic blast, one deserving of the appellation "Ruthian." And with that, two years and twelve innings' worth of postseason frustration fell off Ruth's back. Even McGraw was moved. He later called it "one of the heftiest swats I have ever seen in my life." He surely felt a twinge of unease as the ball sailed onto the avenue, a precognition that perhaps things might be different this time around.

The Yanks led, 2–1, and before the fourth was done, they added another, sending McQuillan home for the afternoon. When Ruth came up in the fifth, Jack Bentley was pitching. This time, McGraw stuck to ordering slow curves, but Bentley's didn't bend like so many previous ones to the Babe. Ruth swung over it a little but got plenty of the ball, enough to send it on a low line over the right-field wall. In just two at bats, he had doubled his home-run total from the previous thirty-seven. The forty thousand fans in attendance let loose with a gasp, then an appreciative roar—such was the effect of Ruth's long ones on even enemy crowds. Of course, there were plenty of Yankee fans at the Polo Grounds that afternoon. Now there were some new ones.

After the game, a stunned Bentley was razzed by Nehf and Scott about Ruth's shot. When asked how best to pitch to Ruth, the "Next Babe" answered, "I suggest a change in direction—throw the ball to second base."

Suddenly the Yanks had lost their "dazed, schoolboy appearance" and played with a strut. Staked to a 4–1 lead, Pennock was confident and in control. He handcuffed the mighty Giants lineup with a similar combo of curves and changeups McGraw had used against the

Babe. Pennock had his biggest trouble with Bentley, who drilled him in the back with the first pitch he threw. Herb groaned "loud enough to be heard in the dollar seats," according to the *American,* and stayed crumpled on the ground for several minutes, surrounded by sympathetic players. Finally the Knight of Kennett Square got up and walked slowly to first. Then he returned to the mound and continued to keep the Giants off balance.

Only in the sixth did Pennock find trouble. As an airplane circled slowly over the Polo Grounds, its pilot getting a free look at the action, the pitcher was touched for three straight singles to make it 4–2. With Frisch at second and Youngs at first, Irish Meusel hit a grounder to short, and as Ward tried to turn two, he was taken out, courtesy of a Pep Youngs flying body block. It was textbook McGrawism: "Do anything you can get away with." Even the partisan Giants' crowd booed Youngs's impersonation of a linebacker. Amazingly NL umpire Bob Hart let the play go without comment.

Cunningham was playing in Stengel's stead in center field, but he couldn't replicate Casey's magic at the plate, hitting into a double play that ended the threat.

Cunningham was due up again in the eighth with two on and two out, but McGraw sent the veteran Hank Gowdy to hit for him, even though Stengel remained available. McGraw preferred a righty batter against the lefty pitcher to seeing if Casey could replicate his Game One heroics. Gowdy had starred in the 1914 Series for the Miracle Braves, but this time Pennock retired him on a soft fly to center.

The defining moment of the day came in the ninth. Ruth sauntered to the plate with two out and a runner on second. If ever a situation called for an intentional walk, it was this. But McGraw was not the type to admit defeat so easily. "The Old Guard dies, but never surrenders" is how Broun assessed the situation. McGraw ordered Bentley to pitch to Ruth, who launched yet another deep fly, this time toward the distant right-center-field fence. Stengel, now in to play defense, managed to run it down just in front of the wall, where, he later said, he "felt the hot breath of the bleacherites as he caught it." Just a hair to the right, and it would have been the first three-homer game in Series history. "I hit that last one harder than the other two," said Ruth.

Pennock set down the cowed Giants in order in the ninth, and the Junior Circuit New Yorkers had at last bested their former landlords. "That was the greatest game you ever pitched, Herbie!" Ruth exclaimed to his friend after the final out. The Series was level at a game apiece. Ring Lardner's sarcastic column the following day was headlined "Yankees Finally Win; Landis Doubts Legality." It was indeed a victory an eternity in coming, and one hard to believe for many witnesses. McGraw, for one. He closed the clubhouse to the press for thirty minutes after the game and gave the team "skull practice," a euphemism for going over the fundamentals at top volume. Berating, exhorting, demanding—McGraw did a little of everything.

The writers competed with one another over which of them could best capture the day's monumental turn of events. Grantland Rice and Heywood Broun were the clear winners. Rice noted: "Last fall they hammered [Ruth] into the dust and sat upon his neck....His debasement was complete, a blighted being with a batting average of .118. But the ancient slogan still rides down the ages—Ruth, crushed to earth, will rise again."

Broun compared the defiant, defeated McGraw, hammered and humbled by Ruth's power, to Macbeth and Ulysses S. Grant ("I'll fight it out on this line if it takes all summer"). Recalling McGraw's dismissal of Ruth before the game ("Why *wouldn't* we pitch to Ruth?"), Broun wrote: "Ere the sun had set on McGraw's rash and presumptuous words, the Babe had flashed across the sky fiery portents which should have been sufficient to strike terror and conviction into the hearts of all infidels. But John McGraw clung to his heresy with a courage worthy of a better cause." Broun capped his story with his famous coda/prophecy.

"The Ruth is mighty and shall prevail."

36

THE TEAMS RETURNED to the Yankee Stadium for Game Three. Once again, McGraw had his team change in Manhattan and cross the river into the Bronx in full uniform. As he traveled across the Macombs Dam Bridge, the game's foremost tactician had to be replaying Game Two in his head. Sure, it was easy to write off a single loss, even to a hated rival. This was baseball, and McGraw would lose 1,948 games (and a record twenty-eight World Series games) before his long career was over. Nothing to worry about.

But it was the way the Giants lost. Getting shut down by Pennock was fine. Losing because Meusel or Pipp or another of the Yanks hitters had a big day—no problem. But losing to a shattering display of Behemoth Ball by the Big Bam? Intolerable.

Had McGraw read the city's score of morning papers, he would have seen not only recounts of the Babe's heroism but instant advertisements capitalizing on the Ruthian display. "Yesterday's home runs weren't all at the Polo Grounds—we hit a few out ourselves" was a typical example, copy used for an ad pushing overcoats for the Rogers Peet Company.

Nevertheless, as he approached the Stadium shortly after eleven in the morning, McGraw cracked a little smile. He still had an ace to play—Art Nehf. The little lefty thrived in pressure situations. Sure, during the long campaign he had let down, but McGraw was confident he would regain his mojo on the big October stage. To McGraw, Nehf was the antithesis of Ruth, a quiet performer who came through in the clutch. "Hoosier Art" had his work cut out for him. In addition to the revivified Ruth, he would be opposing the Yankees' winningest pitcher, Sad Sam Jones. That the Yanks could throw a twenty-one-game winner in Game Three was the surest sign of their mound depth.

Friday, October 12, was Columbus Day, and McGraw had to fight his way through the massive crowds that had turned out early. The holiday, combined with Ruth's dramatic turnabout, had an electric effect—62,430 fans found their way into the park. "Every crevice of the huge Yankee Stadium was filled," reported the AP. Another 20,000 were turned away but milled about the Yankee Stadium in the vain hope of deliverance inside. There was seemingly a cop for every fan. At one point, a throng of ticketless fans rushed the gates, only to be turned back by a determined cordon of police. The *Times* described the chaos as it might have the fighting in the just-ended Russian Civil War: "Men and women...were running as if panic-stricken...at the booths. [They] fairly fought for admission. Clothes were torn, hats were knocked away...the police pulled and hauled against the wild onslaught of the crowd." One paper wrote: "If the battling and embittered colonels...had built for 100,000 fans, the place would have been filled just as easily." The *Post* noted: "The comeback of the Yanks and the rejuvenated Ruth worked New York up to a pitch of excitement which is somewhat unusual in a city of Gotham's sophistication."

The Macombs Dam Bridge was the scene of a terrible traffic snarl of "battered taxicabs, elegant limousines, touring cars, streetcars, sightseeing buses and just plain flivvers" that the *American* reported backed up well onto the 155th Street Viaduct. An estimated 10,000 fans stood on a small hill beyond the left-field fence. Roofs of nearby apartment houses were covered with people, even though none were within a block of the Stadium. Any tree, streetlamp, or pillar that could be scaled was, by fans desperate for a glimpse of the action. Subway employees watched from a "dead" train conveniently parked overlooking the Stadium.

Among the massive crowd lucky enough to gain entry was Jacob Ruppert's mother, who was "signed to a contract for the rest of the Series" after proving to be a good-luck charm for her son's team in Game Two, as well as the one star who could match Ruth for wattage—Charlie Chaplin. The silent-movie actor wore a black derby that he doffed to well-wishers, revealing graying hair.

The huge throng showed their pleasure by creating a relentless din, starting when Ruth smacked several towering homers in batting practice. "Ruth finally had arrived as a ball-punching World Series hitter...and the fans caught on," wrote one reporter. A howling roar greeted the players as they took the field and didn't let up for nine taut innings. Stadium ushers, decked out in red coats and caps, struggled to keep the stands peaceful as the taut pitchers' duel went on.

After a puzzling, frustrating, disappointing season, Artie Nehf was justifying McGraw's confidence in him. Ruth touched him for a soft single in the first, but Nehf recovered to get the next seven hitters in a row. In the fourth, Dugan led off with a double. The Babe strolled to the plate. The crowd quivered with excitement. Nehf had hamstrung Ruth with ease in 1922. But the massive drives the Babe had hit the day before were fresh in the memory of both manager and pitcher. Nehf delivered an "unintentional" intentional walk, throwing four straight balls well out of the strike zone. Ruth stared into the Giants dugout, pointed at McGraw, and laughed at him.

The Yanks had two on and no out, and the fans thought a bunt in order. Huggins agreed, even with his cleanup hitter, Meusel, at the plate. Hug signaled for a sacrifice, but Meusel ignored him and swung away, bouncing into a double play that had the crowd boo-ing. Pipp then grounded out, leaving the game scoreless.

In the following inning, the fifth, it was Jones who hit into a double play with two aboard. And in the sixth, Nehf restored order to his skipper's universe. Accompanied by bellowed insults after every pitch, Artie the Organist looped in three slow curves that Ruth swung on and missed by a considerable margin.

Meanwhile the Giants couldn't touch Sad Sam. Working quickly, as usual, he didn't allow a base runner the first time through the order. Frisch bunted for a hit in the fourth to dash dreams of the first World Series no-no, but two cans of corn stranded the Flash. The NLers put two runners on in the sixth, but Jones jammed Pep Youngs badly enough to shatter his bat, killing the rally.

The taut contest was scoreless as it headed to the seventh. Barely an hour and twenty minutes had passed, and already it was crunch time. Tension gripped the huge crowd. A scoreless game this late favored McGraw and his small-ball style. But all it would take for victory was a single jolt of power from the Babe.

There came a jolt of power, all right, not from George Herman but Charles Dillon. With one out, Stengel faced Jones, having lined out hard and walked in his two plate appearances. He took a ball and fouled one off. Ruth and the Yankees may have heard an ocean of insults from the Giants dugout, but they were no slouches in the epi-thet department either. Now they unloaded on their favored target, Stengel, about his age, his overly dramatic trip around the bases in Game One, his floppy ears, and his general clownishness. While Stengel had delivered the decisive blow in the opener, it was seen as a fluke, the result of improper positioning and Providence. The last thing the Yanks expected was a repeat, and they let Casey have it.

Stengel was well known to struggle with good changeups, and Jones's was giving the Giants fits. Sad Sam got a strike on a change-up, then came high and tight with a fastball, forcing an angry Sten-gel to duck away. The 2–2 pitch was a screwball, not a changeup.

Jones would later say he was mistaken in going away from his money pitch, but he wanted to surprise Stengel. What was a surprise—shocking, even—was what Casey did with the pitch, launching it on a straight line over the right-field fence. It skimmed over the wire separating the bleachers from the players for the game's first run.

Stengel's Game One inside-the-park shot was accompanied by a wall of sound from the Yankee Stadium throng. This time, there was stunned silence as the Giant circled the bases at a much more leisurely pace than he had forty-eight hours earlier. Casey looked toward the men who had been hurling invective at him moments before and flicked his nose several times, a common insult at the time that essentially meant "Stuff that right up your rear end."

Ruppert was apoplectic and left his front-row seat, desperate for someone, *anyone,* to right this outrage. Unfortunately the only person of influence he could find was a man disinclined to help—Ban Johnson. Johnson's hatred of McGraw went back a long way, but he had fallen out with Ruppert as well over a legal battle in 1919 that brought Carl Mays to the Yankees. Ban sat with a smug smile as the colonel demanded Stengel be severely disciplined or suspended—*something.* When the beer baron finally ended his soliloquy, Ban looked up at him and paused, enjoying the moment. Finally Johnson gave him a firm response: "I'll think about it."

Ruth for his part was hardly miffed. "I don't mind it," he said. "Casey's a lot of fun." Unlike after Game Three the year before, there would surely be no angry visit to the Giants clubhouse this time around. Landis took a dimmer view of Stengel's insult but not much dimmer—the judge fined Casey $50 and warned him that his postseason check would be confiscated if he were to misbehave again. When Ruppert complained, Landis explained his decision with a comment that echoed down through baseball history.

"Casey Stengel just can't help being Casey Stengel."

It was the first time in Series history that a scoreless tie had been broken by a home run. Stengel's blow had put the Giants in front, but the Yanks still had plenty of time to do something about it. Third baseman Heinie Groh robbed Scott on a bouncer to his left with two men on in the seventh. Groh, playing despite a painful "rupture," or hernia, next dove all out to rob Dugan of a sure hit in the eighth. Despite Groh's sterling play, the situation was tricky for Nehf in the eighth. Ruth lugged his heavy bat to the plate with a man on first and two out. McGraw had several options. Relieve Nehf—but the pitcher had been brilliant all day. Intentionally walk Ruth—but McGraw would rather have cut off a limb than give in to the Big Monkey. Pitch to Ruth as usual—but the brace of big flies the Babe had mashed the day before gave the Little Napoleon pause.

The conundrum was settled by Nehf, who threw a quick pitch to Babe before McGraw could think about a substitute hurler. Then Artie did as he had done in the fourth—give Ruth four balls well out of the danger zone and deal with Meusel while saving his manager some face. It worked like a charm, as once again the dour slugger failed to come through, popping harmlessly to center to end the threat. Ruth spat furiously at the ground as the ball was caught but held his tongue—something he had been unable to do in 1922. He took out his frustration on Nehf, saying after the game, "I was all set to break up the old game in the eighth but Nehf wouldn't get close enough for me to reach with a broom."

The Yanks went out in the ninth, but not quietly. Aaron Ward struck out, then turned and confronted Frank Snyder, the catcher, accusing him of tipping his bat with his glove just as Ward was starting his swing. It was an act of interference typical of McGraw's hazy relationship with the rule book. Ruth galloped onto the field, positive of the infraction, and a "near-riot" ensued at home plate. Ward later said Snyder was a serial tipping offender. Nothing official was done, and the game ended moments later, a 1–0 Giants win to give the NLers a 2–1 lead in the Series. The two teams got together in the common runway that led to the clubhouses and nearly came to blows. "What the boys are saying to each other...could never be printed in 'The Youth's Companion' or 'The Christian Advocate,'" reported John Kieran in the *Herald*.

Charlie Chaplin called it "the finest baseball game I have ever seen." Stengel entertained reporters with his bravado. "That's two for Stengel, and one for the Yankees," he crowed. Meanwhile, his father, Lou Stengel, ran out onto the streets of Kansas City, yelling, "My boy Charley hit another home run!" The Yankees were subdued, in particular Pipp, who had reinjured his ankle while sliding and was dubious about his availability for the remainder of the Series. Lou Gehrig would have been a nice card for Huggins to play, but McGraw had seen to that.

The Giants manager enjoyed a happy journey back to the Polo Grounds with his team. As the jubilant club changed into their civvies in Manhattan, McGraw leaned back in his chair in the small office he kept off to the side of the main locker room, content. He gibed easily with reporters, convinced that his coveted third-straight title was in hand. "Class will tell," he said over and over. "We are now enjoying a fine advantage and should come through nicely, as I have always believed we would from the start. The hardest part of the road has been passed and we will have smoother running from now on."

37

DAVID LLOYD GEORGE, the popular and recently deposed prime minister of England, arrived via steamship in New York to much fanfare on the morning of Saturday, October 13. As he was ushered to a waiting auto, someone shouted, "Who do you like in the Series?" Lloyd George merely smiled, unfamiliar as the Welshman was with the offshoot of rounders that so captivated the colonials.

Lloyd George had last visited the United States in 1921, and for the city's baseball fans, not much seemed different on the morning of this new visit. The Giants were still on top, John J. McGraw was still the Lord of New York Baseball, and the Bambino was no match for Muggsy. Yes, Ruth had finally snapped out of his Fall Classic funk, but there seemed little doubt that the Giants would win two more games and another championship.

One Giants fan who liked their chances was Charlie Chaplin. For Game Four he sat with Meighan in Box 105 of the Polo Grounds grandstand. Fans called out to him throughout: "Make a funny face for us, Charlie!" "Have you got your mustache with you?" The press also noted a sharp increase in the number of women attending the game, for reasons left unexplained.

Home-field advantage had been nonexistent so far, the visiting squad winning all three games. Jack Scott, McGraw's miracle man of 1922, was the Giants' Game Four starter. The tobacco farmer—the "former plodding plowman from a North Carolina one-store town," in the words of the *Daily News*—had been the best pitcher on the team since his return to baseball, going 24–9 as a Giant in a season and a half despite his hand injury earlier that summer. And no one in upper Manhattan had forgotten his Game Three shutout in 1922, exactly one week shy of a year ago. Bob Shawkey would get the ball from Huggins. He had been strafed in the '21 Series but had a good start in a losing cause in '22. Shawkey pulled on his uniform over his hallmark red sweatshirt and went to work.

Scott stuffed the Yanks in the first, including a biting breaking ball that caught Ruth looking. But in the second, he fell apart. Pipp and Ward stroked clean singles. Schang then laid down a sacrifice bunt, and Scott booted the easy pickup. Everyone was safe. Everett Scott then singled in a pair, sending the unrelated Jack Scott out of the game and across the street, where he spent the rest of the day hiding out in a restaurant, unable to face McGraw, the man who had given him a new lease on life the year before.

Rosy Ryan came in and proceeded to dump gasoline on the fire. A sac fly from Shawkey made the score 3–0. Witt doubled home Scott for another run. Ruth walked with one on and one out, and this time Meusel made the Giants pay, tripling over his brother's head for two more runs. That made it 6–0, and McGraw's hook was overdue. McQuillan became the third pitcher of the inning.

The Yanks tacked on a run in the third and another in the fourth when the Babe walked and scored yet again. It was 8–0, and McGraw, red-faced in shame and rage, barely looked to the field. A Ruth error and an inside-the-park dinger from Youngs gave those among the 46,302 (another new Polo Grounds record) who bothered to stay to the end some late thrills, but it was all cosmetic. The final was 8–4. Five Giants pitchers had thrown an exhausting 161 pitches all told. "It was a bad game for a good team to lose," was the postmortem from McGraw.

"We've chased every right-hander they've got," retorted Huggins from the loud Yankees locker room. The Series was tied at two.

Charlie Chaplin was still sanguine about the Giants' chances. "I'm sure they will win in the long run, although the Yankees looked awfully strong today," said the Little Tramp. "I'm sorry that I had to see Mr. McGraw defeated in the last contest I shall witness in this Series, for I am going back to California tomorrow."

McGraw himself wasn't nearly as confident. That night, the manager sullenly drank beer after beer at his sybaritic Waldorf suite, surrounded by friends and family. There was one rule: no one was to discuss baseball. The "Giant Beard of Strategy" needed a rest. Earlier, someone had asked McGraw if he thought Ruth was better than Pep Youngs. "The feller regretted the question," said one of McGraw's pals. Despite the edict, Marshall Hunt thought it his duty to approach the manager and ask about the next day's combat.

"Throw him out!" roared McGraw. "He's touched on a sore subject!" John J.'s brother-in-law gave Hunt the bum's rush, and the reporter found himself in the hallway. He also found himself banned from the Giants' traveling party for 1924. The stress was getting to Big Jawn. But Hunt had the last laugh in the *Daily News,* writing that he had no need to follow the team around, as he had seen "enough pitching changes [in the Series] by McGraw to satisfy for life."

Sunday, October 14, dawned cold and misty. The gray skies did little to discourage hordes of fans from gathering in the South Bronx, pressing to gain entry into Game Five. While several dozen fans had waited overnight to line up for tickets for the first game, some three thousand were now on line at dawn, and many more had slept in the hundreds of cars parked haphazardly in the lots, streets, and alleys surrounding the Stadium. Autos crammed into any available space on the sidewalk—perpendicular to adjoining cars or blocking traffic. One reporter counted license plates from ten different states. Hundreds of bonfires lit the area, warming the hopeful fans against the autumn chill. The collective smoke added to the morning murk.

The ticket booths opened at ten a.m. Fans on line were fed by dozens of instant, unofficial vendors who sold coffee, hot dogs, peanuts, and milk, along with blankets, coats, and hats. Two seventeen-year-old Yankees fans fronted the line. A half hour after the metal gates rolled up and the windows opened, all remaining seats had been sold.

Game Five was only the fourth World Series game played on a Sunday and of course was the first such game contested in the Yankee Stadium. The official attendance was immense—a reported 62,817, breaking the record set in Game Three two days earlier. Almost as amazing was the huge throng that was turned away at the gates—at least 35,000 fans, with some estimates putting the unlucky ones shut out of the action at an astounding 50,000. Police barricades were set up miles from the Stadium, urging fans to turn around well before the jammed blocks around 161st Street and River Avenue. Tickets were going for as much as $25 apiece.

The masses ensured that the total receipts through five games would crack the $1 million mark. The Stadium was proving a boon for the wallets of not only Colonel Ruppert but also all the players and officials associated with the Series. Their share of the take was bound to be higher than ever before.

Once again, the cream of New York's social set made the trip out to the palatial new Stadium. The newest "It Girl," actress Marilyn Miller, was in attendance, as was Jack Dempsey, fully recovered from the slugfest with the Wild Bull of the Pampas.

Before the game, McGraw and Huggins met with Landis to determine the site of Game Seven. Today, the All-Star Game decides home-field advantage in the Series, a setup that is widely criticized. Imagine if matters were determined as they were in 1923— mid-Series, by the flip of a coin. The commissioner produced a quarter from his pocket, John J. called heads, and the coin landed on tails. Game Seven, the deciding game of this epic World Series, would be played at the Yankee Stadium, if necessary.

McGraw remained calm to the press, but his insides were raging. Control was everything to the Little Napoleon, and events were rapidly slipping from his grasp. The coin flip may have set him over the edge—*Imagine leaving such a thing to the fates!* But it was his pitching that left him truly frazzled. "I haven't the least idea about who will start for us tomorrow," he had said in the wake of the Game Four beating, and his options were limited. The staff had been adequate enough to get the Giants through the National League pennant race, but in the crucible of a short series, not one was trustworthy, save Nehf. Now, another hiccup—after McGraw chose Mule Watson as his hurler of choice, Mule took ill in the hours before the game. McGraw turned to Jack Bentley. His lack of enthusiasm was palpable.

McGraw couldn't make his pitchers throw strikes, so John J. sought to achieve mastery of the situation in other areas. Before the game began he engaged in a long and loud argument with the umpiring crew, insisting that Ruth was breaking the rules by stepping out of the box after each pitch and should be called out. It was a desperate gambit, and the men in blue rejected it out of hand. Yet this was quintessential McGraw. He could no longer stomach watching idly while his pitchers tossed away the World Series, so he picked a fight with two prized enemies: the umpires and Babe Ruth. He felt so good afterward that he went into the clubhouse and singed his team with an insult-laden tirade. If the Giants were to lose this game, it wouldn't be because McGraw had done nothing to prevent it. One reporter twisted

Émile Coué's new mantra to describe the manager's state of mind: "Every day, in every way, Mr. McGraw gets madder and madder."

The *Times* captured his frustration: "It looks as if the Series has resolved itself into a battle between Ruth and McGraw. Ruth has all the advantage. He can act where McGraw can only direct. With all his baseball genius, the Little Napoleon must do everything secondhand."

Unfortunately for the defending champs, no gambit could prevent a virtual repeat of the day before. The Yankees demolished Bentley right away. Joe Dugan's father had presented him with a new bat before the game, and Jumpin' Joe used it to collect four hits on the afternoon. His single in the first started a three-run rally. Meusel tripled in two runs with a screaming line drive to left that barely missed being a home run.

Irish turned the tables on his brother and tripled himself, albeit to center, and came home to score to make it 3–1, but in the bottom of the second, the roof fell in on the Giants. With two aboard, Dugan hit a sinking liner that Stengel dove for and missed. By the time the ball was retrieved, Joe had circled the bases, and it was a 6–1 game. The Yankees gleefully reminded Casey that he was now responsible for an inside-the-park home run for each team.

Ruth came up and smashed a two-hopper that Kelly knocked down but couldn't hold. Unfairly, the play was scored an error. Frisch was handed an even more egregious error later in the inning. Pipp chopped one past the mound, and Frisch's throw appeared to beat Ruth to the plate. But the Sultan of Sliding executed a perfect fadeaway slide, touching the back corner of the plate with his toe, and was called safe. Fred Lieb was the official scorer, and his ruling of E-4 was greeted with disbelief in the press box.

Bentley was long gone by this point. When McGraw came out to yank him in the second inning, a fan yelled, "Start them two at a time—that way we won't have to wait for the change later!" Jack Scott, who had lasted just a single inning the day before, came in to relieve Bentley. Dugan led off the fourth against Scott. Just as Jack was ready to deliver, Dugan called time, then yelled out to Scott, "Hey, Scotty—pull in your ears. You look like a loving cup out there!" He then proceeded to line a base hit.

By the time Meusel knocked in Dugan with the Yankees' eighth run, the Giants had given up sixteen runs in twelve and a third innings. The nickname "Bronx Bombers" wouldn't replace "Ruppert's Rifles" until the 1930s, but for the first time in World Series play, either appellation fit. It was a team effort. Ruth was 2–5 with three walks and reached on an error in the span—part of every rally, but hardly a one-man wrecking crew. It was telling, however, that after Ruth flied out deep to center in the eighth inning, the huge crowd filed out. Most had stayed through the rout merely to see if the Babe could hit another homer.

The final score was 8–1. At last, the home team had won a game. The Giants had managed only three hits off Bullet Joe Bush, all from Irish Meusel. " 'Bullet Joe' Bush Baffles Sluggers of the McGraw Clan with Slow Fork Ball," reported the *Atlanta Journal-Constitution*. It was a nice present for Bush on the date of his wedding anniversary. Meanwhile, the Yankees' lineup suddenly seemed unstoppable. McGraw had no answer. He had been hailed as a genius while calling the pitches that stymied the Yanks in 1922. Now his hated rivals were blasting his selected pitches all over two different parks. They had bashed out twenty-seven hits in two games.

Brainy baseball was taking a beating. "When intellect collides with ash manipulated by thick and freckled wrists," wrote Rice, the mighty win. The Yankees' "reply to the Mental Urge was a salvo of 14 hits...leaving Mental flat on its writhing back." The champs were in shock. "Silently the players trooped into the clubhouse after their trip by taxi from the Yankee Stadium," reported the *Times*. "And as silently they discarded their playing uniforms and donned street clothes."

McGraw had few arrows left in his quiver. His old ace and flatmate Christy Mathewson wasn't going to walk through the club-house door to save the day. The current Giants moundsmen had to come up big. It would be up to the one hurler McGraw could rely on to prevent the title from changing hands and keep McGraw's pride intact.

"You can bet there will be a seventh game," the manager told the skeptical throng of reporters in the Giants clubhouse on his way out the door. "Arthur Nehf will see to that."

38

THE BALL TRACED a high parabola, arcing over the distant fence. The large green number "435" sat far below, painted on the fence where the right-field stands began their curve toward center, a once formidable figure now mocked by the satellite hurling far overhead. It soared and soared, carrying completely beyond the area where baseball was being played.

Despite its name, polo was never played at the Polo Grounds. The original park, built in 1876, had been home to polo matches, and the name was thereafter given to any place the Giants called home. But just beyond the baseball fences was Manhattan Field, where polo was occasionally still played. A thriving cricket green got more regular use. It was here that the ball, bruised from its lengthy travels, crash-landed, scattering a surprised group of West Indian cricketers.

The man who had launched this artillery shot stood briefly back at home plate, well over five hundred feet distant, his body corkscrewed with the effort of providing escape velocity for the ball. Then, as if shaken from his reverie by the mammoth roar of the crowd, Babe Ruth remembered that he needed to make a trip around the bases, and he set off on his pleasurable jog.

It was the first inning of Game Six, and Ruth had just broken two records with the blast: most home runs in a World Series (3), and most career World Series homers (4), records that "stood out like a redheaded man at an Italian picnic," in the estimation of *Baseball Magazine*. It was a fitting blow for an assault on the game's historical ledger. A curveball from the enemy's ace had hung just enough in the danger zone, and the sport's most feared slugger of all time had hammered it to jelly, sending it on a curve of a different sort, entirely out of the park. Had the contest ended right then and there, few would have gone home disappointed.

But the remarkable day had only just begun.

A cold, misty rain fell on and off throughout the afternoon, and the attendance dropped appropriately—only 34,172 passed through the turnstiles. Some opted to listen to Graham McNamee's lurid, breathless descriptions of the action on the radio in auditoriums throughout Manhattan, including in the *Times* and *Tribune* buildings.

It's likely the gloom that had set in among Giants' supporters held the figure down as well. The bashing at the hands of the potent Yankees lineup seemed likely to continue, Art Nehf or no Art Nehf. Ruth's presence in the middle of the order was providing comfortable shade for the likes of Meusel, Dugan, and Pipp, and there wasn't an easy touch in the entire starting nine.

That didn't mean that the Little Napoleon was about to give in. His team was still the two-time defending champs and would be until the final out of a fourth loss. This was the message McGraw delivered in the clubhouse, at top volume and containing an encyclopedia of blue language. It was a classic Johnny Mac stem-winder. If he was to be dethroned today, in his home park, by his hated former tenants turned crosstown rivals, led by a hulking baboon that had defaced the beauty of his chosen game—if this was really going to happen on this murky Monday, then by God, McGraw was going to go out at the top of his lungs.

The manager would have had every confidence in Nehf and his ability to extend the Series to a deciding seventh game. He had been brilliant in Game Three and had won the clinching games (always the hardest to win) of the previous two Series. Even the pair of games Nehf lost in the '21 Classic were the result of poor run support, not of the Yanks' hitting him hard.

So one can easily picture McGraw choking down his bile when his October ace was taken deep (*very* deep) by the blasted Bambino. Right as the curtain was going up too—half the paying customers were probably still looking for a place to sit. Scientific Baseball had once again had its microscope smashed by the Babe's Big Bertha.

Pennock got the start for Huggins's team, and right away it was clear that the slender Knight wasn't as surgical as he had been in Game Two. Three consecutive singles evened the game in the bottom of the first. A two-out hit by Cunningham scored Frisch in the fourth, giving the Giants the lead. An inning later, Snyder smacked a low liner that cleared the left-field wall, making it 3–1. And the fantastic Frisch tripled and scored in the sixth.

The Flash was doing it all. In the fourth, he turned in a candidate for the defensive play of the Series, sprinting out to right field and diving to snag a bloop off Dugan's ash. "His speed was so great that he ran out from under his hat, and with his hair blowing, finally leaped forward to take the ball on a miracle catch that swept the crowd up with a stand-shaking uproar," wrote Rice.

Meanwhile, Nehf was dominating. Shaking off Ruth's power displays far easier than his manager was ever able to, Nehf got to work making the vaunted Yankees lineup look foolish. After a one-out safety in the second, Artie didn't allow another hit through the seventh inning. The only base runner in that spell was Ruth, who set yet another Series record in the process, drawing his eighth walk (all quasi-unintentional). Nehf retired eighteen of nineteen hitters, including a strikeout of the Babe in the seventh, as the Hugmen were "rolled back as some mighty cliff would roll back the summer surf." The Yankees remained hopeful, muttering on the bench, "We can get to him, we can get to Nehf." The press was inclined to read this as proof of the improved morale on the team, compared with the quitters of '22.

Ward began the top of the eighth by popping meekly to first, making it nineteen of twenty retired by Nehf. Then, as Rice wrote, "with the startling suddenness of a simoon across the Indian Ocean," the game changed. Schang finally got the pinstripes a hit, a clean single to left. Scott did likewise. Fred Hofmann was called in from coaching first base to hit for Pennock, and he walked on four pitches. Just like that, the bases were loaded. The *Tribune* set the stage: "The crowd was a seething cauldron of riot and action, great stuff for a mob scene picture of the French Revolution."

Huggins then pulled a trick from the McGraw playbook, hitting for Witt with a pitcher, Bullet Joe Bush. Nehf seemed shaken, for he threw four more consecutive wide ones, forcing in a run to make it 4–2, Giants. That was enough for McGraw. He pulled Nehf from the game, replacing him with Rosy Ryan. Nehf walked slowly off the field, head bowed, face buried in his glove. It had been a shockingly swift demise for the classy twirler. The *Tribune* said it all: "Nehf's last stand was one of the tragedies of sport. From the heights of the conqueror he had dropped within three minutes to the rocks below, as if fate had pushed him from the ledge just as he was crossing the final gap." *Baseball Magazine*'s description used similes that its readers were more apt to understand: "For 16 [World Series] innings Nehf was as tight as the coat on a frankfurter and then he collapsed like a busted accordian."

Nehf had gone south so rapidly that Ryan was not even tossing warm-up pitches when McGraw told him to get in the game. Unsurprisingly the cold Ryan promptly walked Dugan on four more pitches, forcing in another run. That made twelve consecutive balls thrown by Giants hurlers, an astounding loss of control at the worst possible time. McGraw, whose staffs never gave up the most walks in the league during his long career, who hastened to rid his teams of fast but inaccurate pitchers, whose every action as manager was in the name of control, had been undone by a bout of wildness by two of his most reliable pitchers. Worse, the score was now 4–3, the bases were still loaded, and practically sprinting to the plate to hit was George Herman Ruth.

Up in the WEAF radio booth, Graham McNamee was milking the drama for all it was worth. It was a seminal moment in the long and storied history of baseball on the radio. Listeners far from New York could hear the exultant roar of the crowd as Ruth strode to the batter's box. The immediacy of the moment could not be matched by newspaper accounts.

No recording of McNamee's call exists, but McNamee remembered the Babe's monumental at bat years later. "Then came the thrill of all time, all World Series' and all sports," he wrote. "Babe Ruth stepped up to bat. One hit would mean victory for the Yanks, and for them the Series. It was another 'Casey at the Bat,' and the stands rocked with terrific excitement." Ruth, brought to his lowest ebb on this very field one year ago, now had the opportunity for one more grand redemption, against the very opponent who had humiliated him.

However, Ryan wasn't interested in playing his seemingly foreordained role in the drama. He was a little looser now, and it showed. Ryan threw a big, slow curve, which Ruth cut on hugely and fouled off. From the bench, McGraw next called for a changeup, which Snyder dutifully relayed to Ryan. But the Irishman crossed up his manager, either because he had confidence in his curve or because he simply misread the sign. Either way, McGraw swallowed his anger when the Sultan almost fell over after swinging and missing at the looping offer from Ryan. The third pitch was a ball outside, making the count 1–2.

Now Snyder trotted to the mound with a message from the dugout: "The Old Man says to throw the next one in the dirt."

"Into the dirt?" asked Ryan.

"Yeah," said Snyder. "Throw it at his feet. The Old Man says he will swing at it no matter where you throw it. Put everything you have on it, but throw it right at his spikes."

The Babe, "alone amid the alien corn," as Keats would have noted had he been in the press box, didn't change his expression as he waved his heavy lumber once, twice, then rested it casually on his shoulder, waiting for his chance to strike. Ryan pinched off the pitch at the moment of delivery, increasing the snap but taking away some of the distance. The ball came in faster than the earlier curves, looking more like a slider. The pitch broke down, as Ryan had been ordered to make it do.

The Babe was swinging his mace like a Visigoth and found only "empty October air." He had missed the pitch in the dirt (indeed, it bounced off the plate) by nearly a foot.

Ernest Thayer, the sportswriter who penned "Casey at the Bat," in which the mighty Casey lets down the Mudville nine by striking out to lose the game, was from Worcester, the same rugged city that gave the world Wilfred Patrick Dolan "Rosy" Ryan. It's unlikely either the Giants pitcher or the thousands in the stands were aware of this literary irony. But the Polo Grounds rocked as though the game were over. Mighty Ruth had struck out!

"Broken and dejected," the Sultan skulked back to the Yankees dugout, where no one met his gaze, although Huggins uncharacteristically gave him a reassuring pat on the shoulder. That single strikeout now threatened to undo an entire season's worth of success and rehabilitation of the Babe's image. "There is no crown so great that in a twinkling it can't be changed into the hollow horns of a derided goat," wrote Rice.

"John McGraw took the biggest chance of his historic life," remembered McNamee.

He ordered Ryan to pitch to Ruth. The crowd faded into a blurred background. Cheering became silence. Ruth lashed out at the first ball. Ruth hurled his weight against the second. [Here McNamee either ignores or forgets that Ruth took a ball outside.] Ruth spun at the third. Ruth shuffled back to the dugout, head hung low. The picture of dejection.

The biggest thrill passed when the great Babe fanned. Time's phantom flits into oblivion in moments like this. I was a dripping rag draped over the microphone.

In his ghostwritten column the next day, Ruth remembered the terrible moment. "After I made that third swing I felt like phoning for a reservation for one of the benches in City Hall Park. Had I taken my shoes off after going back to the bench I believe my heart would have fell out of my sox [*sic*]."

The Yanks trailed by a run and two were out, but the bases were still loaded.

And there was Meusel to be reckoned with. Long Bob hadn't played that well in the Series, batting just above .250 to this point, but he led the team with six RBI and had a reputation for icy professionalism at the crucial moment. "Meusel has no psychology in his makeup," reckoned the *Daily News*. "He is an athlete with no feeling." Ryan had just completed the biggest strikeout of his career, one that would live on in baseball history—provided he retired the dour cleanup hitter from California.

Alas, Ryan had "pitched his soul away" in striking out the Babe. Meusel bounced the first pitch he saw back through the box. In the Giants dugout, the team reacted as though they were out of the inning. But Ryan flailed hopelessly for it and turned in horror as the ball bounded just to the left of second base and cleanly into center. With two outs, pinch runners Hinkey Haines and Ernie Johnson scored easily, pumping their arms in ecstasy, putting the Yankees ahead.

Then the Giants' defense, their towering strength suddenly turned

Achilles' heel, failed them. Center fielder Cunningham uncorked a mighty heave to third to try and gun down Dugan, but his throw sailed wide of Groh. Dugan skipped home with the fifth run of the inning, and, amazingly, the Polo Grounds scoreboard now read:

YANKEES 6

GIANTS 4

The two RBI (none was awarded for Dugan's run due to the error) gave Meusel eight for the Classic, a Series record to join his predecessor at the plate. For all of Ruth's home runs, no hit was bigger in franchise history to that point. His single became known as the "$50,000 blow," as that was the monetary difference between the winning and losing shares for the two teams.

No one was happier in the visiting dugout than Ruth, and not just because he went through cash faster than any ten of his colleagues. No, fortune had smiled on the Babe, for now his strikeout with the bases full would be a mere footnote to history rather than a defining moment in his already checkered postseason career.

The Yankees were giddy, but there was, of course, still the small matter of recording six more outs before the (illegal) booze could flow. With Pennock out, Hug asked Sad Sam Jones to bring the Yankees home. In the bottom of the eighth, Pep Youngs touched Jones for a single, and with two out, the Giants fans turned all hopes to their power star—Stengel. Could this "mighty Casey" equal Ruth with a third Series homer and tie up this already legendary game?

"Horsewhips" Jones sent in one of his sharp breaking balls, and Stengel popped up in foul ground wide of third. Dugan salted it away to dash the dreams of the Coogan's Bluff faithful. An inning later it was all over when Jack Bentley became the second pitcher to pinch-hit in the game. He tapped a roller to second, and when Pipp gloved Ward's easy toss, the Yankees were champions for the first time in franchise history.

39

HAPPY CHAOS REIGNED in the visitors' clubhouse, where the players shivered after hours in the damp chill (as the *American* put it: "For all who said it would be a cold day when the Yankees could beat the Giants—it was"). Pipp lit a cigar. Ruth uncharacteristically did not. The Babe bear-hugged Meusel, yelling words of praise (and, no doubt, thanks) in his ear. Cries rose up across the room: "What are we now? Champs!" "This is the day, boys!" "Who do we gotta beat next year?" Despite the nation's bylaws, real beer flowed freely, courtesy of the Jacob Ruppert Brewery. Hair was mussed, hugs were exchanged, and someone threw an armful of baseball bats across the room, forcing several men to leap over the skittering wood.

Ruth yelled for quiet and stood on a rubdown table to give a short and awkward tribute to his manager. It professed a love and respect from soldiers to field general and was likely written for him by one of his admirers in the typing class. Ruth then awarded Huggins a diamond ring, a gift from the team. Quietly, embarrassed by the fuss, Huggins stood on a chair, muttered his thank-yous, and drifted over to Ruppert, who was shaking hands merrily. He had had a difficult time making it from his box to the locker room after the final out, as fans surrounded the ecstatic colonel to offer congratulations.

Sad Sam Jones approached Ruppert and reminded him of a transaction from earlier in the season. Jones was an avid rabbit hunter on his Ohio farm, and he had asked for one of Ruppert's purebred beagles to assist in flushing out game. Sad Sam assured his boss that in exchange the Yankees would win the World Series for him. The colonel smiled and said, "You were right, you were right."

Ruth drifted over to Pennock and gave him an enormous slap on the back, one that nearly severed the scrawny pitcher in half. If Ruth was the dramatic lead actor of the Series, then Pennock, with two wins and a save, performed the key supporting role. The *Reach Guide* of 1923 actually named the Knight as its World Series MVP, noting: "Nowhere in all the annals of the World's Series will the vigilant reader find that a twirler of such meager physical structure has performed in the manner of the young man who rides to the hounds at Kennett Square."

There was more jewelry to be handed out. The commissioner's office gave each Yankee a gold watch, and Ruppert announced he would see to it that a gold fob was added to every one. More important to the players were the dollars they would receive as champs. The winners' share was $6,143.49 each, a huge sum for everyone but Ruth and by far a new Series record. The losing Giants didn't make out too badly, receiving checks for $4,112.88, also a new mark. It was only $400 less than many of the same players had made for winning the 1922 Series.

Among those splitting some of the Yankees' spoils were Phil Schenck, the old-time Highlanders groundskeeper; mascot Eddie Bennett (Ray Kelly was a little young for his share, though Ruth made sure his parents got a handsome bonus); trainer Don "Doc" Woods; and, even though he wasn't allowed to play in the Series, Lou Gehrig. Despite the windfall, Gehrig would take an off-season job as an office clerk with New York Edison. The Giants gave $1,500 to pinch runner Dinty Gearin, who made a single appearance in the Series. Mose Solomon, the "Rabbi of Swat," got nothing.

The huge attendance figures in the new and expanded parks brought the players these princely bonuses. The total attendance of 301,000 broke the old record by more than 30,000, despite the Series being only six games. The gross income from the ticket buyers was well in excess of a million dollars, $1,063,815.00 to be exact, making for a players' pool of $368,783.04. The gate was up more than $400,000 from the 1922 Series.

The press returned to the Commodore Hotel later in the afternoon to write their stories for papers from Maine to California. The men were in various stages of typing, calling in their stories, or partaking in spirits when they all rocketed to attention and grabbed a notebook. For there was Tillinghast L'Hommedieu Huston striding purposefully toward his happily grinning ex-partner, Colonel Jacob Ruppert.

It was the first time the two men had shared anything like a civil conversation since their breakup. In the wake of victory, however, they were like brothers, shaking hands and clapping each other on the back in what was clearly a staged event. Til's hearty laugh shook the windows of the Commodore as he congratulated Ruppert. Then, when he was certain the press mob was ready, pencils poised, he spoke of his ex-partner: "We disagreed, yes, but they were always the honest disagreements of opinion between men with pronounced views or policies. I am as happy tonight as if I, and not Jacob Ruppert, were sole owner of the Yankees."

Colonel Ruppert was conciliatory as well. "We have had differences in the past, but not the sort of differences that many have thought," he insisted. When asked for a follow-up statement, he gave a simple one.

"I am the happiest man in America."

To his lasting credit, McGraw was outwardly classy in defeat. "I just can't seem to get that third straight [Series] victory," he said outside the clubhouse after the game. McGraw stared into space, his thoughts miles away. Then he snapped out of his reverie. "The best team won," McGraw told a hushed group of reporters. "There is no disputing that....I'm going to shake hands with everybody connected with the Yankees from Colonel Ruppert down to the batboy. They played a great game against a good team, and nobody should begrudge them their victory. My hat is off to them."

He strode into the delirious Yankee clubhouse, seeking out Ruppert and Huggins, and, as promised, shook their hands. However, the batboy wasn't so honored, and neither, it should be noted, was Ruth.

The Giants offense had been stymied. Dave Bancroft was miserable in the leadoff spot, getting a mere two singles in twenty-four at bats. The ineptitude, and Travis Jackson's presence, led McGraw to dump Bancroft on the Braves the following season. Other members of the "$100,000 infield" were equally anemic. Kelly and Groh both sported matching .182 batting averages in the Series (and Heinie did not feel moved to update his vanity license plate afterward). Only Frisch excelled, hitting .400 and making several standout plays in the field.

But it was pitching, the Giants' weak link all season, that had come back to haunt the team at the most pivotal juncture. Nehf's collapse represented the season in microcosm. "Wise observers beholding the recent overthrow of the Giants did not trouble to ask why the Yankees won" went one recap. "On the contrary, they ventured the query, how, with such a pitching staff, did McGraw ever win a pennant?"

Back in the losing team's clubhouse, Nehf was devastated. He sat in front of his locker, weeping. McGraw reappeared and put an arm around his shoulder. "Never mind, Art. Don't take it so hard. It wasn't your fault....I wish I had left you in there."

"I was gone, Mac, I couldn't pitch anymore."

"You could have struck Ruth out. He was so crazy to hit I could have struck him out myself. And you would have stuck that ball Meusel hit into your hip pocket." McGraw glared at Ryan, who looked down. "That's what cost us the ball game, a lousy cheap hit through the box." Nehf was one of the best fielding pitchers in the National League; Ryan was not nearly as slick with the glove.

Suddenly McGraw turned from enraged to ebullient. "But the hell with it! I would have given anything to win this Series, but I guess it wasn't in the cards." The manager loved Nehf, the way the small man battled and his coolness under duress, this afternoon being the exception. Inwardly McGraw was fuming. But he made a show of accepting defeat philosophically for the sake of Nehf and the rest of the team, whom he vowed to return to the top the following season. Later, he would hang his head on Blanche's shoulder and cry.

McGraw could hardly be blamed for his pitchers' inability to throw strikes or slow the powerful Yankees lineup, but as he had received an outsize amount of the credit after the great successes in '21 and '22, he ate most of the blame now. He had called every pitch from the bench, after all. And those pitches worked to much less effect this time around. As McGeehan wrote in the *Times:* "Investigators of psychic phenomena must take note of the fact that Mr. McGraw's hypnotic powers work only on Mr. Nehf this year, and that after seven innings either Mr. McGraw's current exhausted or he burnt out the fuse."

The press who the year before had tripped over themselves crediting Jawn J.'s genius for the Giants' success now turned on a dime and mocked Scientific Baseball and its greatest champion. "This World Series was generally recognized as a combat between the thinking power of John J. McGraw and the baseball agility of the Yankees," wrote Westbrook Pegler. "Now that it is over and the Yankees have won, it is rumored that McGraw strained a tendon in his medulla oblongata in winning the first game of the Series."

Graham of the *Journal,* who was as close to McGraw as any newspaperman, said the loss devastated the manager just as much as or more than the previous season's victory had delighted him. "He never wanted to beat anyone quite as much as he wanted to beat the New York Yankees in that series," Graham wrote. "It seared him to know that while conquering the world he had lost New York.... His old friendship with Ruppert and Huston was dead. He hated the Yankees and made no bones about it.... It was a rough and acrimonious series."

Graham, Lieb, and other writers made it a point to swing by the Waldorf that night to check in on what they assumed would be a devastated Little Napoleon. "The least we can do is to drop in and sit up with the body," Graham figured. But since so many other people felt similarly, a great party erupted. Even Yankee stalwarts Dugan and Pipp stopped by to pay respects. They said they were glad to have won but regretted having to beat the great McGraw. They wound up having many drinks in McGraw's suite, even though they were expected at Ruppert's brewery for what the Dugan vernacular referred to as a "Come all yez."

The victory party at the brewery was raucous, as years of frustration and bitterness were forgotten. "It seemed everybody who ever expressed a wish that the Yankees would win the Series trotted in while the boys were munching and gargling," reported the *Daily News*. "All training rules...were knocked flatter than the Giants pitching staff." Ruppert was effusive in his praise of his skipper, the man the *Times* called "the managerial misfit of 1921–22, [but] the oracle of this one." The Knickerbocker Kingpin asked the assembled revelers to "give credit to Miller Huggins. He made the team what it is, and he can have a job with me as long as he wants it. The Yankees played the kind of ball I knew they could play. It took lots of faith to keep a brave front in the last two years, but I always felt that Huggins and the players would justify my confidence in them."

It is a truism in sports that the latest game, series, or achievement is instantly regarded as the best ever, with fantastic feats barely a decade old slipping down the memory hole. But it is inarguable that the Series left the likes of Lieb, Rice, and Lardner flush with pleasure. The *Trib*'s "World's Series of 1923 Reaches Mark for High Grade Playing Never Achieved in the Past" was a typical summation of the Series. So Colonel Ruppert's ultimate take on his team's first championship is understandable.

"When the Yankees did win a World's Series," he said, "it was the greatest one that was ever played."

Epilogue

AFTER HIS TRIUMPH in the World Series of 1923, Babe Ruth's first order of business was, of all things, to buy life insurance. It truly was a changed Babe—that winners' share was burning a hole in his pocket, and instead of it jumping out at the first speakeasy or cat-house he chanced upon, he put it into a security blanket for his family. Ruth called his pal Harry Heilmann of the Tigers. Heilmann's salary was about one-fifth of Ruth's, so like most players, he augmented his pay with an off-season job. Heilmann sold life insurance, although not very successfully. His lack of ability in closing deals would lead him to a different career when his playing days were over. He became a longtime radio broadcaster for the Tigers.

Thanks to Ruth, Heilmann had one of his best days in the insurance business, selling the Babe a $50,000 policy. "Ain't he a hard-boiled gent?" asked Ruth. "He beats me out of the batting championship, then takes a wad of money out of my vest pocket. If I beat him in the batting race next year I'll try this insurance trick and see if it works both ways." Helen and Dorothy were named beneficiaries.

Not that the Babe had turned into Holy Joe. He hosted a grand bash the night after the Series at the Hunter Island Inn in Pelham Bay Park, not far from McGraw's home. Needless to say, John J. wasn't in attendance, though Irish Meusel and Casey Stengel made appearances. There were reports of bacchanalia and epic drunkenness throughout the North Bronx and neighboring Westchester County. But before he could get into any trouble in New York, Ruth set off on a $1,500-a-game barnstorming trek through small towns in upstate New York and Pennsylvania, including flyspecks on the map such as Hornell, New York, and Mahanoy City, Pennsylvania.

Typical of the trip was a stop in Wilkes-Barre, Pennsylvania. Ruth arrived at five a.m., plowed through a massive breakfast, visited a sick child, set the local record for home-run distance during batting practice, went 3–5 with a home run during the game while playing all nine positions, including catcher, attended a pair of banquets in his honor, signed practically every scrap of paper in town—and somehow found the energy to go out and stalk some deer late at night. Then an overnight train to the next town, where Ruth did it all over again.

It was in Scranton, a city that the Babe always enjoyed visiting, that the Ruth women nearly collected on the insurance policy the Babe had just purchased. When the final out of the day's exhibition game was recorded, a tsunami-sized human wave rolled toward Ruth, eager to touch the great man. Ruth turned and ran for the ramparts but tripped and fell. Thinking he was playing around, a group of children piled on top of the Babe, nearly suffocating him. Fortunately some police officers managed to extricate him from the same "dirty-faced" kids he had let down the year before.

The Babe had what he most desired, and most needed—a World Series triumph as a Yankee. His stat line from the Series certainly reads impressively. There were the record three homers and the eight walks. He hit .368, with seven hits (two singles, a double, and a triple in addition to the round-trippers—the Babe hit for the Series cycle). He slugged an even 1.000—nineteen total bases in nineteen at bats. Throw in a .556 on-base percentage, and his OPS hits a ridiculous 1.556, or more than 150 points higher than his '21 and '22 Series *combined*. Only in 1928 would he have a finer postseason at the plate, statistically speaking. It was the exclamation point to an exceptional season.

By dethroning the Giants, the Yankees and their bashing style vaulted past Scientific Baseball and accelerated its decline. It was a game more and more for the "moneyed class," and these weren't baseball purists. The new breed of fan cared little for Scientific Baseball and its patient, cutthroat style and were thrilled by the power game. The notion that runs could come quickly and in great number mirrored their expectations in business, in the markets, in life. Hitting and running and stealing and spiking—McGrawism— were for the birds. Totally wet. The Ruthian scene was the one people wanted to be part of.

It was also the first day of the rest of New York baseball's life. Seemingly overnight, the upstart Yankees had gone from entertaining but lightweight second citizens to the kings of New York. As the *Times* reported: "Ruth showed that the Giant supremacy could be broken down. Leading the way himself, he showed that the Giants were not invincible, that their pitchers could be hit, and that John J. McGraw's strategy, while superb, was not invincible." The Giants were suddenly passé, yesterday's news. In his memoir *For 2¢ Plain,* the writer, newspaper publisher, and Giants fan Harry Golden summed up the new reality: "The Giants represented...old New York that was still a man's world before the advent of the League of Women Voters; the days of swinging doors, of sawdust on the barroom floor, and of rushing to the growler." Ruth and the Yankees were the future. They were no passing fad—they were here to stay. They were aviation, not flagpole sitting. The Giants didn't transform overnight into losers; they simply weren't the top of the heap anymore.

It was as much a self-inflicted wound by the Giants as it was an

Act of Ruth. As Frank Graham wrote years later: "The New York Giants in 1923 were blinded to everything save their own seeming advantage in the struggle with the Yanks, lightly brushing off the lost revenue of pushing out the Yanks and therefore creating a monster north across the river." In the long term, Ruth was ephemeral, his impact on the Giants and their attendance figures inevitably limited by time. But by reacting with anger, jealousy, and shortsightedness, McGraw and the Giants sealed their own fate. It is likely Ruppert (with or without Huston) would have built his team its own stadium in time. But the Giants pushed the Yankees into creating a juggernaut, marrying the biggest star in the country with a grand edifice to display him. Had McGraw (and Stoneham) not acted in such a knee-jerk fashion to the Babe's instant popularity, they might have withstood the Ruth phenomenon and delayed the construction of Yankee Stadium until Ruth was near or at the end of his career.

Instead, the Stadium became a cash cow that enabled Ruppert to keep the Yankees on top for the rest of his life, and far beyond. The colonel plowed profits into scouting areas of the country often beyond the means of other clubs, particularly the West Coast. The franchise won six more World Series titles and seven AL pennants in the next fifteen seasons under his stewardship. Ruppert lived to see Prohibition repealed as well. He died in January 1939. When the Babe came to see him on his deathbed, the colonel refrained from calling him "Root" for the first time. He called him "Babe." Ruppert is buried at Kensico Cemetery in Valhalla, New York, in Westchester County, not far from the final resting place of Lou Gehrig.

Cap Huston settled roughly halfway between New York and Havana. He had moved into a mansion on Butler Island, one of the barrier islands he treasured, off the Georgia coast. Huston also continued to spend a good chunk of time at Dover Hall, the hunting estate he owned in nearby Brunswick, Georgia. Many in baseball, including Ruth, made annual winter pilgrimages down south to hunt, fish, and drink with Cap. The Babe once shot a sickly cow, thinking it an elk. Ty Cobb, true to his reputation, refused to sleep in Ruth's cabin, braying, "I have never slept under the same roof with a nigger, and I'm not going to start now in my own state of Georgia."

Huston often threatened to buy his way back into the bigs, but the closest he came was a stake in the minor-league Atlanta Crackers. He died of a heart attack at his desk on Butler Island in 1938.

Cap's old enemy Miller Huggins had gotten the last laugh. After the championship of 1923, the press that had scorned him now sang his praises, saying the victory "illustrates the value of perfect team play, combined with submission to managerial authority and discipline." The Mighty Mite was, for a brief moment, the toast of the Big Town.

Sadly, the health problems that dogged Huggins throughout his career worsened as his successes mounted. The Yankees won three straight pennants and two titles in the years 1926–28, but Huggins suffered from a variety of ailments throughout. Then, in 1929, he came down with erysipelas, a skin infection caused by streptococcus bacteria. Even then, it wasn't a death sentence, but Huggins's numerous issues weakened his immune system, and he dwindled rapidly. He passed away on September 25, 1929, at age fifty. The American League canceled its games on September 27 out of respect; the viewing of his casket at Yankee Stadium drew thousands of tearful fans. He was inducted into the Baseball Hall of Fame in 1964. The very first monument erected in the far reaches of the Yankee Stadium outfield was to Hug.

Ruth was shocked by Huggins's death. He could hardly speak, breaking down in tears in the clubhouse and at the funeral. He finally managed to say, "You know what I owe him. You know what I thought of him. I cannot realize yet that we won't have him with us again on the bench." Nice words, if a little hollow—Myrtle Huggins told Fred Lieb that Ruth had taken five years off Miller's life.

Huggins lived to see the first refurbishment of the Yankee Stadium.

In 1928 Colonel Ruppert hired L. M. Neckermann & Son to add seven new sections to the upper decks in left field. The expansion cost $400,000. Hug was gone by the time of the next project, in 1936–37. Neckermann was struggling under the crushing weight of the Depression when Ruppert brought the firm back to expand the right-field grandstand by six sections and to replace the wooden areas of the Stadium with concrete and steel. For $850,000, the project added roughly 10,000 seats to the Stadium and made center field's "Death Valley" not quite so vast, as the acute angles of the outfield walls were smoothed into a sloping curve. A postwar expansion plan to increase capacity to 100,000 was never implemented, but in the winter of 1945–46 there were more changes to the interior, such as the replacement of the concrete backstop with fencing.

With that, the Yankee Stadium remained essentially unchanged until the 1970s, when a major refurbishment sent the Yankees back to the home of an NL crosstown rival, this time the Mets and Shea Stadium, for two years — 1974 and 1975. The Stadium got a massive overhaul. One hundred eighteen columns were removed, improving sight lines but detracting from the Romanesque elements of the original. The frieze was replaced by a replica that circled the wall atop the bleachers. The field was lowered, the seats made plastic, the monuments taken out of play, and the mammoth batting background, aka the "Black," added to dead center field. In all, the changes left some to consider the Stadium an entirely new edifice.

Jacob Ruppert and Til Huston's dream palace died entirely when the Yankees moved to a new $2.3 billion Stadium built across the street ($1.2 billion came in the form of taxpayer subsidies). Little by little, the old Stadium was taken apart. By mid-2010, there was barely anything left of the original House That Ruth Built.

After the '23 Series, once John McGraw recovered from what amounted to an Irish wake, he departed on a European vacation with Blanche. While in Paris, he announced that the Giants would play the Chicago White Sox in a tour of Europe, exposing the Continent to the National Pastime. The McGraw who dined at the finest French restaurants in the City of Light was fifty—not exactly decrepit even by 1920s living standards, but he was an *old* fifty. His face was deeply lined from years in the sun, his jowls deep set, his brow in a permanent furrow. His waistline was thicker than ever, his hair whiter than ever. And in a candid moment after the Series, McGraw was forced to admit his favored style of play had become anachronistic. "With the ball being hit all about the lot the necessity of taking chances on the bases has decreased....A manager would look foolish not to play the game as it is....There is no use sending men down on a chance of stealing a bag when there is a better chance of the batter hitting one for two bases or maybe out of the lot."

McGraw and the Giants made it back to the World Series in 1924, losing to the Washington Senators. It was the final pennant of his storied career. Ruth would go on to win four more pennants and three more rings, team with Lou Gehrig to form the heart of the 1927 Yankees—generally considered the best team in history—and reset his own home-run records for a single season and for a career.

John McGraw's home-run hero in the '23 Series had been Casey Stengel. One would think his excellent play, and McGraw's fondness for his pupil, would keep Casey in New York for a while, but McGraw never let personal feelings determine his roster. He dealt Stengel to the Braves soon after the Series. Casey looked on the bright side. "Well, maybe I'm lucky," he said. "If I'd hit three home runs McGraw might have sent me clear out of the country."

Stengel, of course, landed on his feet. In a historical irony he got the job Babe Ruth wanted most—manager of the New York Yankees. It was a development as unlikely at the time as Casey's inside-the-park homer was in 1923, but it was as successful. Using the principles learned at the foot of McGraw, such as platooning and regular use of relief pitching, he piloted the great Yankees dynasty of the 1950s, turning what had been a colorful career into a Hall of Fame one. In 1962 he helmed the first incarnation of the New York Mets, the team created to fill the National League vacuum left in the wake of the Giants' and Dodgers' departure for California. That would have made New Yawk Jawny happy.

To the last, McGraw and the new style of play just didn't mix. In 1930 he told a reporter:

> This lively ball is hurting baseball. I think the club owners ought to get together on it. I suppose six out of eight teams in each league would like to see it go. It has taken the confidence out of pitchers. The ball is so lively that fielders cannot handle it and throw it to the plate. Bunting is gone—the ball is too lively. And baserunning has disappeared. The public liked that. Those plays were always close.

In June of 1932 an ailing McGraw handed over management duties to Bill Terry, who had blossomed under McGraw into a Hall of Fame first baseman. McGraw's final official act as manager was a fitting one—filing a protest against old enemy Bill Klem. "To the end he was faithful to his truculent creed," noted the *New York World-Telegram*. McGraw stayed around to consult for home games. He made one last appearance in uniform as the NL manager during the first All-Star Game in July 1933.

Less than a year later, on February 25, 1934, a month and change shy of his sixty-first birthday, McGraw died of uremia in suburban New Rochelle, New York. There were tributes from all over baseball. The most lasting came from Cornelius McGillicudy, aka Connie Mack: "There has been only one manager, and his name is McGraw."

For several years, both while still in pinstripes and after his playing days came to an end, Ruth angled to become manager of the Yankees, only to be rebuffed repeatedly by Ruppert ("Manage the Yankees? You can't even manage yourself," the owner reportedly said). Even when the Babe expanded his search to the rest of the majors, none of the owners whose wallets had fattened greatly from Ruth's accomplishments would throw the aging slugger a bone. It appeared that the bill was coming due—after years of Ruth behaving as though he were bigger than the game, he was now being painfully made aware that once the home runs stopped he was just another ex-jock. Salaries had shot up thanks to Ruth, and the owners didn't forgive him for it. It didn't help that his superabundance was now awkwardly out of step with a country suffering under the Great Depression.

Ruth was so desperate to stay in baseball that he signed on with the lowly Boston Braves in 1935, assuming he would be made manager. But he had been given the runaround by Braves ownership, who wanted Ruth in the field to attract some more fans to the park. In a foreshadowing of the fate of another New York baseball legend, Willie Mays, who would hang on too long, Ruth played two desultory months with the Braves before quitting the game.

The Babe paid a worse price for all those cigars. He was diagnosed with throat cancer in 1946, although the press refused to use the "c word" in reports on Ruth's condition. Ruth passed away on August 16, 1948, at the age of fifty-three. When news of the Babe's death came, the Yankees were playing their old nemesis, the Giants, in a midseason exhibition game back across the river at their old home, the Polo Grounds.

Tributes flowed in from across baseball and across the world. But words written by the inimitable Damon Runyon after the Babe's heroics in Game Two of the 1923 World Series still applied a quarter century later. "When you are a very old man," Runyon told his readers, "you can tell your children of the player of your time who was so great they ran separate stories in the paper of his daily doings.

"They will not believe you, of course."

Acknowledgments

This book was mainly written in three places: the Decatur (Georgia) Public Library and two coffee shops in downtown Decatur—Java Monkey and Dancing Goats. I wish to thank the staffs at all three, in particular the two coffee shops, whose employees were kind enough to overlook the fact that I don't actually drink coffee and thus was far from an ideal customer. The staff at the Atlanta-Fulton County Public Library was also helpful. And, of course, this book wouldn't have been possible without the assistance of the fine folks at the New York Public Library, in particular the staff in the Microforms Section.

January may not seem the ideal time to visit the ancestral home of the summer game, but I spent several glorious days comfortably ensconced in the bosom of the A. Bartlett Giamatti Research Center at the National Baseball Hall of Fame in Cooperstown, New York. While driving snow piled up outside, I remained warm, transported to a place where it was always perfect baseball weather (at least until I broke for lunch). The library staff—Freddy Berowski, Gabriel Schechter, John Horne, and fearless leader Tim Wiles—were gracious and ever helpful, whether advising about obscure questions on bygone hardball events or where to find a decent slice of pizza within walking distance. Many thanks, gentlemen.

My path from television producer to writer has been an interesting one. I wish to thank the many fine editors who were willing to print my work and improve it at the same time. They include Chris Suellentrop, who agreed to run my very first piece for Slate.com (I snail mailed it to him from Asia—by some miracle it saw the light of day), and his successors Bryan Curtis and Josh Levin. Kevin Jackson, Jay Lovinger, Josh Dean, Bill Brink, Will Leitch, Alexander Belenky, Dean Robinson, Brent Cunningham, and Aaron Schatz, thank you as well.

Several published authors helped point the way for me, either by offering advice or answering questions. Jeff Pearlman started the process by giving me a well-timed boot in the bottom. Jonathan Eig, Jane Leavy, Michael MacCambridge, Ray Robinson, and Michael Weinreb also graciously passed along their experiences, even though many were busy getting their own books written and to market. And two friends who also happen to be accomplished writers (and so much more), Alan Schwarz and Gary Imlach, provided long and greatly appreciated insight into the writing method.

Several writers, historians, and experts were always willing to add a little more depth and nuance to the narrative. My thanks to Dom Amore, Marty Appel, Bill Burgess, David J. Halberstam, Bill Jenkinson, Christopher Klein, Norman L. Macht, Amber Roessner, K. Jacob Ruppert, Stuart Shea, Steve Steinberg, and Kim van Alkemade.

My editor at Little, Brown, John Parsley, has been a champion of this book from the beginning, and his powerful devotion to it has helped me immensely. John's ability to improve the narrative with the deftest of touches, as well as calmly talk me off ever higher rooftops, was a gift beyond measure. His assistants William Boggess and Sarah Murphy were welcome support as well. Karen Landry kept me from looking like an idiot by catching my numerous errors of spelling, fact, and grammar. She cannot be thanked enough, especially because as a Red Sox fan she had a powerful incentive to sabotage this project from within. Heather Fain and Elizabeth Garriga worked wonders in the publicity department. Thanks also to Reagan Arthur—had I known when we were teenagers, and she was my stepsister Jill's best pal, that Reagan was to become such an industry honcho, I'd have spent much more time sucking up to her. Better late than never.

Many moons ago, while a fresh-faced young college student at Syracuse University, I would attend the annual nearby New York State Fair with my close friend and roommate, Benjamin Wolf. His cousin would also be at the fair, accompanied by whatever farm animal his family deemed prizeworthy that season. He would slip away from the stalls and join Benjy and me to drink beer, check out the surprisingly high-quality bands that played the fair, and engage in various other age-(in)appropriate activities.

Amazingly, said cousin, aka Farley Chase of the Waxman Literary Agency, would become my agent and prove as adept at navigating the Byzantine alleyways of the big-city publishing world as he was the dirt and hay-strewn pathways of the state fair. He instantly plucked the precious gem of a marketable idea from the free-flowing river of my imagination and helped make this book happen in countless other ways great and small. And as a fellow Yankees diehard, Farley can always be counted on for a sympathetic ear when the time comes to vent about pitching changes and ticket prices.

The aforementioned Ben Wolf not only brought Farley and me back together as partners in publishing but has been a great and true friend since those callow days of youth. He has also provided a reliable staging ground for my research ventures to the big city, a service more valuable and appreciated than he can possibly imagine. And he lives close enough to Yankee Stadium that we can be back home after games while Frank is still belting out "New York, New York." Thus huge thanks are due to Ben; his wife, Nicole; and his darling son, Sashi Binh, for their hospitality. David, Franca, and Benjamin

Kraft have likewise consistently put a roof over my head and a hot meal in my belly on my trips north, so thanks to them as well.

My oldest friend, Mark Sternman, and I met and bonded over baseball as fourth graders back on a distant playground in Westchester County. Through Strat-O-Matic; fantasy baseball; the ups and downs of Rodney Scott, Ellis Valentine, and Delino DeShields; and all-too-infrequent trips to Fenway and the Bronx for actual live action, we have remained tight thanks to the game. Unsurprisingly, Mark was an invaluable aid to this project, reading several drafts, offering tips and pointing out errors of fact and conception, and heading down to the Boston Public Library when the situation required some eyes on the ground in Beantown. Having a close friend who doubles as a baseball encyclopedia isn't strictly necessary for writing a book of this nature, but it sure helps. I count myself lucky for his friendship of three decades and counting.

Most of all, I wish to express my gratitude to my family—my mom, Judith Weintraub, for instilling the love of books and reading at such a young age (although she probably never meant for me to be engrossed by *Jaws* as a seven-year-old); my dad, Arthur Weintraub, whose ardor for baseball may have been forever cooled when Bobby Thomson broke his heart but who surely passed along the sports-loving gene; my brother, Mark, the true writing talent in the family; his wife, Laura, and their kids, Kayleigh, Jack, and Ryan, whom I love as my own; and most especially to my beloved wife, Lorie Burnett, my best friend and first editor, without whom none of this would be possible; and Phoebe and Marty, who hopefully will understand one day why Daddy seemed a bit distracted for the past year and a half.

Notes

Preface

Ellington himself lived in a tony row house in Sugar Hill during the Harlem Renaissance, as did W. E. B. DuBois, Thurgood Marshall, and Adam Clayton Powell.

The Harlem River Speedway was originally built for carriage horse racing before the rise of the automobile demanded its name be changed to Harlem River Drive.

One remaining trace of the Polo Grounds still exists. A staircase dedicated to John T. Brush remains mostly intact. It connected Edgecombe Avenue up on Coogan's Bluff with the Harlem River Speedway, where the Polo Grounds ticket booths were a short stroll away. The dilapidated staircase is part of Highbridge Park and is slated for restoration under Mayor Michael Bloomberg's PlaNYC 2030 project.

The "Top Hat and Bat" logo is not to be confused with the interlocking *NY*. The Yankees wore several different designs on the team caps, settling on a solid navy cap with the interlocking insignia in 1922. In 1917 the team removed the interlocking *NY* from the jersey, and it stayed off until 1936. The Babe never wore an interlocking *NY* on his jersey as a Yankee.

The "Top Hat and Bat" logo design concept was long thought to be the brainchild of a man named Harry "Lon" Keller. According to popular history, Keller, an illustrator who often worked for the Yankees, was asked by then co-owner Larry MacPhail to draw up the logo before the 1947 season for the team's publications. He wasn't credited, nor did he think to ask for a copyright. That left the door ajar for a recent counterclaim by the family of a man named Sam Friedman, who say that it was Friedman who first drew the logo. According to the *New York Times,* Friedman is said by his descendants to have scrawled the design on a cocktail napkin at the "21" Club for a different Yankees co-owner, Dan Topping.

Introduction

There are other stories about the origins of the nickname "Babe," but what matters is not how the nickname was first used but rather its utter perfection. In the words of Fred Lieb: "Babe went as naturally with Ruth as ham goes with eggs."

Ruth, of course, had more nicknames than any player ever. The "Sultan of Swat" and the "Big Bam" are well known. Lesser-known monikers include "His Ball Mauling Majesty," the "Caliph of Clout," the "Harlem Catapult," the "Titan of Thump," the "Wizard of Wallop," the "Swattingest Swatter of Swatdom," and simply "Zeus."

At the Ansonia Hotel, they still talk about Ruth's time living there. Although the exact location of his room is lost to history, one sales rep told me (perhaps facetiously) that she tells all prospective new tenants that the room they are looking at was the Babe's. The description of the Ansonia is informed by personal observations I made when visiting the gem on the Upper West Side. By the late '20s, several Yankees would call the Ansonia home, including Herb Pennock, Tony Lazzeri, and Mark Koenig.

The "House That Ruth Built" is actually a play on the Mother Goose nursery rhyme "This is the House That Jack Built":

This is the house that Jack built.

This is the malt
That lay in the house that Jack built.

This is the rat,
That ate the malt
That lay in the house that Jack built.

This is the cat,
That killed the rat,
That ate the malt
That lay in the house that Jack built.

And so on for several more verses.

Chapter 1

The tale of the construction worker who tossed a good-luck charm into the pit over which the Yankee Stadium was built was brought back into the public eye for a brief moment during the construction of the new Yankee Stadium, across the street from the refurbished old barn. A workman named Gino Castignoli tossed a jersey into the new Stadium site. However, his intentions were evil, as the jersey was that of David Ortiz of the Boston Red Sox. The Yankees jackhammered the shirt from under the construction pile and donated it to the Jimmy Fund, the longtime pet charity of the Red Sox. It raised $175,100 at auction.

Drumming up offense wasn't the only reason for the banning of the spitball. The terrible influenza epidemic of 1918 that killed roughly half a million Americans (and an estimated twenty-five to thirty million worldwide) had a profound effect on the country, and baseball was no different. Emergency sanitary rules were enacted in the wake of the "Spanish Lady," and the prohibition against pitchers licking their fingers before gripping the ball was an offshoot.

Chapter 2
Anyone curious about the finer details of the Yankee Stadium can examine the original blueprints, as I did, many of which are available from private sellers online.

Chapter 3
Arnold Rothstein's legendary pool match with Jack Conway is worthy of its own book. Conway was a billiards champ from Philly who came to the Big Town and called A.R. out. Over thirty long hours, Rothstein bested his challenger and collected some $4,000 in bets. The men wanted to keep playing, but McGraw stepped in and ended the match, growling, "If you don't want to sleep, some of the rest of us do."

An anecdote showing the sway Rothstein held over the Giants, and Stoneham in particular: On the night of August 8, 1920, Rothstein placed an emergency call to Stoneham demanding some $300,000 to cover unexpected losses at a gaming house Rothstein operated. Stoneham pulled the cash from his vault in his Nelson Avenue mansion and delivered it to the Big Bankroll, whose nickname was inappropriate on this evening, at least. However, by the time Stoneham arrived with the dough, Rothstein's fortunes had changed, and the money wasn't required. But the owner of the Giants didn't think twice about delivering the humongous sum to a nefarious character in the dead of night.

Chapter 4
The acceptance of Change Order #9 meant the bleachers leapt from being roughly 10 percent of the overall budget to roughly 20 percent.

Change Order #10 also was a doozy. It ordered several boiler rooms, offices, and an elevator shifted from the easterly, first-base side of the Stadium to the westerly, third-base side. Unfortunately much of the concrete footings, columns, and trusses were already in place on the third-base side, and this largely unnecessary order meant that work had to be redone from scratch.

Chapter 5
Frank Graham, in *The New York Giants,* thankfully transcribed the account of Ruth's ill-conceived invasion of the Giants clubhouse for posterity. It also appears in a slightly different form in Robert Creamer's *Babe: The Legend Comes to Life.*

Ruth's negative reaction to being labeled as partly black was a sign of the times. Rapidly changing societal structures resulted in a slew of racial disturbances in the early '20s. Perhaps the most notorious incident took place in January 1923. The Florida backwater town of Rosewood was the scene of a spasm of racial violence, resulting in at least half a dozen lynchings and all of Rosewood being burned to the ground. The spark for the race riot were unconfirmed whisperings that a white woman had been assaulted by a black drifter.

With regard to Rice's quote about heroes being "made and wrecked in a single Series," modern Yankees fans will recognize a familiar echo—the postseason failures of Alex Rodriguez from 2004–07.

Chapter 6

Ruth and Meusel returned from their 1922 suspension for illegal barnstorming in May. Thirty-eight thousand turned out at the Polo Grounds for Ruth's first game back, on May 20 against St. Louis. The Browns won, 8–2, and the Babe went 0–4. The most dramatic moment of the game came before Ruth's second appearance at the plate. Til Huston and one of his favorite drinking buddies, sportswriter Jimmy Allison, appeared in the press section with a bottle of illegal whiskey—an almost daily occurrence, despite the law of the land. Just as a hush fell over the throng in anticipation of Ruth's at bat, the bottle slipped from Allison's pocket to the concrete floor with an outsize crash. Half the ballpark, including Ruth and the home-plate umpire, turned toward the sound. Huston remained stone-faced while Allison blushed. The rest of the writers roared with laughter.

Some of the Babe's teammates also had a sour season in 1922. At many points during the season, players squared off in fistfights, including Carl Mays against catcher Al DeVormer, DeVormer against fellow catcher Fred Hofmann, and Waite Hoyt duking it out with his much smaller manager, Miller Huggins.

Ruth may have stolen McGraw's thunder as New York's foremost sportsman-about-town, but he couldn't touch the Little Round Man as a vaudevillian. As early as 1912, McGraw was touring with the B. F. Keith circuit, pulling down more than any other act, around $3,000 a week, tax-free. He would follow Odiva the Goldfish Lady onstage and tell baseball stories while dressed in his Sunday best. Later, he honed the act to an explanation of the scientific elements of the game, appearing onstage with a blackboard, diagramming stratagems like it was the first day of spring training. The monologue was fittingly called "Inside Base Ball." "With the aid of a diagram, he revealed the hitherto carefully guarded secrets of inside baseball as perfected by the Giants" went one review. Pretty dry stuff compared to the dancing bears and midget circuses that were the stuff of the circuit, but since McGraw's genius was considered nonpareil, the act socked them in.

The infamous Elks Club dinner got plenty of ink from the multitude of sportswriters who were there. Accounts vary on exactly who said what, but a consensus was formed by reading the various stories and takes on the evening.

Details of Ruth's illegitimate daughter with Juanita Jennings come from an interview with Linda Tosetti, Ruth's granddaughter, on the *ESPN SportsCentury* profile of Ruth.

Chapter 7

Wee Willie Keeler hit 'em where they ain't to the tune of a lifetime batting average of .341. Somewhat surprisingly, despite playing for nineteen seasons, Keeler fell sixty-eight hits shy of the three thousand mark.

Both the NL Baltimore Orioles and the minor-league version owned by Jack Dunn are unrelated to the modern-day Baltimore Orioles, who began play in 1954 when the St. Louis Browns moved to Charm City.

John McGraw liked to talk about his psychological warfare affecting the outcome of games. He particularly liked to describe a game (perhaps apocryphal) against the Cardinals in St. Louis. The Giants trailed by five runs in the top of the ninth. Two men reached, and another single followed, one that would have easily scored the runner from second—but McGraw waved the runner back to third even as he was headed home. "Now why did I do that?" he asked any reporter, player, or fan who asked about his methods. "I'll tell you why. Because I wanted those bases loaded. I knew what effect that would have on the pitcher." Sure enough, according to McGraw, the hurler came unstrung. The Giants scored six times and pulled out a victory.

Chapter 8

The Babe never did hit one into the "Bloody Angle," nor did he give up an inside-the-park homer as a result of a crazy bounce. Pitcher Bullet Joe Bush was the first Yankee to slice a homer into the small area of seats. The Bloody Angle was eliminated after the 1923 season, as home plate was moved up fifteen feet and the foul line redrawn to take the area out of fair territory.

The running track was incorporated into the standard warning track we are familiar with today during the 1937 refurbishment of the Stadium.

The origin of the phrase "out in left field" has other possibilities. Some think it refers not to the fans in the bleachers but the left fielder at the Yankee Stadium, who likewise was farther from the action than the right fielder, though not so drastically, depending on his positioning. Another theory is that right-field fans used the phrase pejoratively for their left-field brethren not because of the distance but because anyone who bought a seat so far away from the great Babe was crazy.

Football made its debut at the Yankee Stadium in 1925 with the Army–Notre Dame game. The Stadium would see many memorable gridiron moments, including Knute Rockne's "Win One for the Gipper" speech before Notre Dame met Army in 1928, and the consensus "Greatest Game Ever Played"—the 1958 NFL championship game, won in overtime by Baltimore over (ironically enough) the New York Football Giants.

Chapter 9

There are several versions of the cigar-stub story, with varying roommates and numbers of cigar stubs. Both the New Orleans train incident and the Detroit hotel incident are related in Fred Lieb's *Baseball as I Have Known It*. Lieb is blunt but unapologetic about the fact that reporters, including him, covered up many of the Babe's extracurricular antics.

For many years, a rumor persisted that Ruth once hung his manager by the ankles over the side of a train platform while the locomotive was going full speed. No proof ever emerged to back this up, and both player and manager denied it ever happened—although Claire Hodgson, Ruth's second wife, said that it did. The tête-à-tête in Huggins's billet in the spring of 1923 may have been the genesis of the "Throw Miller from the Train" story—the Babe was certainly mad enough to at least consider tossing Huggins into the landscape.

Chapter 10

Scott's record of 1,307 consecutive games played lasted until August 17, 1933, when Gehrig passed him on the way to 2,130.

Joe Dugan had mediocre numbers for 1923—.283 batting average, seven homers, sixty-seven RBI. He did score 111 runs and played a strong third base, committing just twelve errors in 146 games.

Chapter 11

The moniker "$100,000 infield" had been applied before to sterling quartets, most famously the Philadelphia A's of the early 1910s. The unit included Stuffy McInnis at first base, Eddie Collins at second, Jack Barry at shortstop, and Frank "Home Run" Baker at third. In today's dollars, they would have to be called the "$2 million infield," a figure that now would barely pay for a decent utility player.

Stengel's hiring as manager of the Yankees in 1949 was greeted as something of a joke, in large part stemming from Stengel's prior stops as skipper. He managed Brooklyn from 1934–36, furthering the "Daffiness Boys" legend and averting attention from the fact that the team finished sixth, fifth, and seventh under Stengel. In 1938 he was hired by the Boston Braves and suffered through six more seasons of fifth-place or worse finishes. In his final season in Beantown, 1943, Stengel missed the first two months after being run over by a taxi and suffering a broken leg. Sulfurous *Boston Record* columnist Dave "the Colonel" Egan nominated the cabdriver as the man who did the most for Boston baseball that season.

Jimmy O'Connell was banned for life after supposedly approaching a Phillies shortstop named Heinie Sand and offering him $500 in exchange for easing up in a series against New York late in 1924. Landis found out about the alleged bribe within twenty-four hours, and O'Connell was summoned to his office. The young, naive Giant explained that he had merely been the bagman—the plot started with Pep Youngs, Highpockets Kelly, and Frankie Frisch, along with coach Cozy Dolan. The players firmly denied the allegation. Cozy gave a more modern answer: "I can't recall." Dolan and O'Connell were kicked out of the game for good. The three future Hall of Famers were exonerated.

Chapter 12

The *Lusitania* was torpedoed by the U-boat *U-20* off the Irish coast on May 7, 1915— 1,198 people were killed. The incident helped spur the U.S. entry into World War I.

McGraw's bet on his Giants to win the World Series in 1905 was commonly known at the time. Obviously such a wager would not have been allowed even before Judge Landis's tenure as commissioner, but in 1905, so long as McGraw wasn't betting against his team, there was no outcry.

McGraw was ejected 131 times from games as manager. Bobby Cox broke that record in 2007 and finished his career in 2010 with 158, although it should be noted that behavior that earned an early shower for the Atlanta manager would have been laughed off in McGraw's day. And Cox never organized a mob to attack an umpire, as McGraw is said to have done in Alex Chadwick's *The Illustrated History of Baseball*.

Larry Doyle was involved in one of the more blatant blown calls in World Series history. In 1911, the same year he uttered his famous "It's great to be young and a Giant" line, Doyle came home with the winning run in Game Five against Philadelphia on a sacrifice fly. Doyle's slide plainly missed home plate, but umpire Bill Klem, a frequent target of McGraw's ire, on this day gifted one to the Giants. The A's won the Series regardless.

William Fallon, aka the "Great Mouthpiece," was the quintessential amoral defense attorney, the punch line to the joke "Is he a criminal lawyer? Yes, very." Fallon represented hundreds of alleged murderers, gamblers, rumrunners, and other shady sorts during his colorful career, perhaps most notably Arnold Rothstein, whom

Fallon called "Ol' Massa Mind." Rothstein almost certainly arranged for Fallon to defend his pal McGraw.

Chapter 13

The Gordon Highlanders Regiment fought all over the world in the name of the Crown. Its soldiers were primarily recruited from the northeast of Scotland, hence the name "Highlanders." The unit lost some 28,000 men during World War I.

The Giants went 20–8 while playing at Hilltop Park in 1911 and drew large crowds, including 22,000 to see Christy Mathewson best Brooklyn, and another 20,000 for a doubleheader on May 30, again against the Superbas (as Brooklyn was nicknamed then—there was a popular entertainment troupe called Hanlon's Superbas, and when the unrelated Ned Hanlon took over as manager of Brooklyn, the press trotted out this new name for the team), the final games they played uptown before heading back to Harlem and the refurbished Polo Grounds.

The Polo Grounds that burned down in 1911 was the third park to have the name—the original Polo Grounds was at 110th Street, between Fifth and Sixth Avenue, and the second edition was in the southern hollow of Coogan's Bluff, later to be named Manhattan Field. Thus the postfire, best-known edition of the Polo Grounds is actually Polo Grounds IV.

Chapter 14

"Harvard Eddie" Grant played for the Giants from 1913–15, a light-hitting infielder whose main claim to fame was his erudite yelling of "I have it!" rather than the grammatically incorrect "I got it!" when a pop-up was hit to him. His memorial plaque in center field was in play and read:

In Memory of Capt. Edward Leslie Grant / 307th Infantry–77th Division / A.E.F. / Soldier-Scholar-Athlete / Killed in action / Argonne Forest / October 5, 1918 / Philadelphia Nationals / 1907–1908–1909–1910 / Cincinnati Reds / 1911–1912–1913 / New York Giants / 1913–1914–1915 / Erected by friends in Baseball, / Journalism, and the Service.

Grant was mortally wounded in the Argonne Forest while leading a mission to try to find the famous "Lost Battalion" (a combined unit of five hundred U.S. soldiers of whom roughly 60 percent were killed, wounded, or captured during fighting in the Argonne). The plaque was laid on Memorial Day, 1921. It can be seen in the famous highlight of Willie Mays making his over-the-shoulder catch of Vic Wertz's shot in the 1954 World Series. After the Giants' final game in New York in 1957, the plaque was stolen and a curse was ascribed to Eddie Grant, as happens when franchises go any significant length of time without winning a championship. In July 1999 the plaque (or perhaps a prototype of the original—the truth is unclear) was discovered in an attic of a private residence in Ho-Ho-Kus, New Jersey, and donated to the Baseball Reliquary. In a perhaps related story, the Giants won their first championship since 1954 in 2010.

After Game One of the 1922 World Series, McGraw and Giants majority owner Charles Stoneham dropped by the press room at the Commodore Hotel on 42nd and Lexington to have a drink with the newspapermen. A bull-faced guard refused them entry, however, as they did not have the proper button required for admittance. "I own the Giants!" roared Stoneham. "I paid for half this setup!" It was true—the teams floated the boat for the press, a fact that explains a good deal of the soft coverage considered the norm in the '20s. Colonel Ruppert happened to be in the room and vouched for his rivals. "Orders are orders, but I thought everybody in New York knew John McGraw," huffed Stoneham.

Lord Mountbatten was a well-known sportsman, but his trip to the Polo Grounds for the World Series isn't among his more publicized exploits. In October 1922 the future final viceroy of India was honeymooning with Lady Mountbatten in the United States, staying at the Ritz-Carlton and being feted by the New York "Four Hundred"—the cream of Gotham society since the gilded age and the Astors— prominent citizens such as General Cornelius Vanderbilt III and his wife, who hosted Mountbatten in Manhattan. A baseball game was decidedly down-market for British nobility. But McGraw and Ruth, whose outsize personalities were so very un-British, held Mountbatten spellbound.

Chapter 15

According to attendance figures given in the box scores—which, as evidenced by the opening day shenanigans, need to be taken with a grain of salt—the Yankees averaged 26,250 for the first eight-game home stand in April.

According to baseball historian Bill Jenkinson's research, Ruth's homer in front of President Harding traveled an estimated 480 feet.

In just twelve games in April, Ruth walked sixteen times.

Chapter 16

Cy Williams played under the following managers in Chicago: Frank Chance, Johnny Evers, Hank O'Day, Roger Bresnahan, Joe Tinker, and Fred Mitchell (yes, all three of the immortal trio "Tinker to Evers to Chance"). And in Philly: Pat Moran, Jack Coombs, Gavvy Cravath, Wild Bill Donovan, Irvin "Kaiser" Wilhelm, Art Fletcher, Stuffy McInnis, and Burt Shotton.

The teams Williams toiled for between 1912 and 1930 finished 11½, 13½, 16½, 17½, 26½, 24, 26, 47½, 30½, 43½, 35½, 45½, 37, 27, 29½, 43, 51, 27½, and 40 games out of first, a mind-blowing average of 31 games behind for his career. Despite the unending losses, Williams was the National League's all-time home-run hitter until 1929, when Rogers Hornsby surpassed him.

Two others had hit three home runs in a game before Cy Williams did it, a namesake and a teammate, and both in 1922. Ken Williams (no relation) of the St. Louis Browns hit the hat trick on April 22 against the White Sox, and on September 15, Phillies rookie catcher Butch Henline hit three dingers against the Cardinals. Ruth would not hit three homers in a regular-season game until 1930, well after his prime home-run years. However, the Babe twice hit three homers in a World Series game, in 1926 and in 1928. In all, Ruth accomplished the feat four times, including once while playing for the Boston Braves in the twilight of his career. Four homers in a game is the record, held by several players. The first to do it was another Yankee slugging great: Lou Gehrig, in 1932. He did it on June 3, the same day that McGraw retired from managing, overshadowing Lou's feat.

Frank Frisch was elected to the Hall of Fame in 1947 after recording the highest career batting average for a switch-hitter, at .316. Pete Rose, by comparison, shattered Frisch's record for hits by a switch-hitter but posted a career average of .303.

Brooklyn's lone sustained run of good play in 1923 came in late May and early June, when the Robins made a brief run at the Giants. The catalyst was a multitalented player named Jimmy Johnston. Flexible enough to play several positions, Johnston was a solid if unspectacular hitter over his thirteen-year career. In mid-1923, however, he went berserk at the plate, with three or more hits in six straight games. Unfortunately for the Robins, star outfielder Zack Wheat, who was hitting over .400 in late June, severely sprained an ankle and missed two months. Any dreams of a subway pennant race went down when Wheat did.

Chapter 17

Everett Scott wasn't much of a hitter throughout his career, making the fact that he played so many consecutive games more remarkable. In 1923 he posted his career high for homers with six, but his OPS didn't break .600, and he got worse in 1924 and 1925. Midway through '25, the Yanks had seen enough and waived their iron man. The Senators, apparently still moved by the ceremony for Scott's one thousandth straight game, claimed him. Scott was dropped by the Sens, the ChiSox, and the Reds within a year before getting the hint and calling it a career.

Being the captain of the Yankees didn't carry quite the weight in 1922 that it would for Thurman Munson and Derek Jeter. Indeed, Ruth's punishment was less symbolic than financial—the captain received an extra $500 a year in exchange for such duties as carrying the lineup card to the home-plate umpire.

Chapter 18

The story of Wilbert Robinson's ill-fated stunt catch of a dropped "ball" from an airplane is part of baseball lore and has been told in many places, with some of the smaller details differing. The tale as it appears in the narrative contains only confirmable details.

Catching balls dropped from high places was a brief craze that enveloped Ruth as well. One day during the 1923 season, Bob Meusel tossed balls to Ruth off the roof of a thirty-story building in midtown. The Babe caught one on the third try.

Chapter 19

The construction of the Coney Island boardwalk required 3.6 million feet of timber and 7,700 cubic yards of concrete, thus rivaling the scope of the Stadium project, at least in those areas.

Chapter 20

George "the Sizzler" Sisler was a standout at the University of Michigan, where his first baseball coach was Branch Rickey.

Some reports about just how dramatic Gehrig's first batting practice was may have been embellished after Lou became the great "Iron Horse." In Ray Robinson's biography of Gehrig, he writes that just as the newcomer was flailing miserably during batting practice, a group of students from Columbia who had slipped into the stands to watch (there was no security presence, this being 1923) started cheering for Lou. "Show that big guy, Lou—he's not the only one who can hit it out of the park." According to Robinson, the show of support relaxed Gehrig, and he proceeded to hit well. "Attaboy, Lou—Babe knows he's got company now," yelled one of the Columbia crew after Gehrig's hitting display was finished. When I talked with the gracious author, ninety-one years young, Robinson recalled the source of this aspect of the story being Frank Graham's bio of "Larrupin' Lou." For some reason I remain dubious about this part of the scene, and I needed to make cuts someplace, so I excised it from the narrative.

Ruth's penchant for forgetting names is legendary, as is his calling everyone "Keed," even longtime teammates. Less known is his catchall name for train porters: "Stinkweed."

Ruth's "Bellyache Heard 'Round the World" was almost certainly not a bellyache induced by eating too many hot dogs, but as with many aspects of the Ruth legend, its precise truth is as hard to pin down as mercury. Some posit it was a severely torn groin, others a sexually transmitted disease, still others that he fell ill from ingesting rudimentary performance-enhancing drugs (in this case, the performance in question being sexual, not athletic). The reality will likely never be known for certain.

A 2010 study in the *Journal of Neuropathology & Experimental Neurology* suggested that Gehrig might have contracted ALS from brain trauma, most likely from the same sort of beaning that felled Pipp.

Chapter 21

Pep Youngs's three triples in a game tied the modern record—a player named Bill Joyce had hit four triples in a game in 1897 while playing with the Giants. Major leaguers have hit three triples in a game forty-six times since 1900, including Miller Huggins in 1904 while playing for the Reds.

Youngs was inducted into the Hall of Fame in 1972. Some believe it a classic case of a player whose career was cut short and who thus didn't attain the lifetime numbers generally associated with enshrinement, but was so outstanding in his limited time in the show that he had to be included. Others think it a case of the Veterans Committee voting in an old crony who was well liked but undeserving of Cooperstown immortality.

Chapter 22

One night in August 1922, McGraw was having dinner at the Lambs Club with concessionaire Harry Stevens, his songwriting buddy George M. Cohan, and Judge Emil Fuchs, the Giants' team attorney. Braves owner George Washington Grant was there too. McGraw saw him and told Cohan, "You've always wanted to buy a team. Grant's is for sale." Cohan laughed the remark off, saying he would stick to his brand of entertainment. McGraw then turned to Fuchs. "Why don't you buy them?" Emil shocked his companions by answering, "Sure." He insisted on Christy Mathewson being his manager, and a short time later, the Braves had new ownership—one in the sway of McGraw.

The article McGraw wrote criticizing the Cubs appears in the *Chicago Daily News* on June 7, 1923. "Cubs Lack in Teamwork, Says McGraw" was the inflammatory headline.

Another key to the Cubs' surge was the strange case of Charlie Hollocher. The shortstop was an overnight sensation back in 1918, a good fielder from the streets of St. Louis who modified his batting stance one day and suddenly became another Honus Wagner. There was no Rookie of the Year Award in those days, but Hollocher would surely have won it in 1918, leading the NL in hits and total bases while playing a slick short. A tough lefty named Ruth, however, stymied the pint-size wonder in the 1918 World Series.

By 1922 Hollocher was among the best shortstops in the league, leading the circuit in
fielding average while walloping out a .340 batting average, the highest at the position since the incomparable Wagner. But in January 1923, Hollocher complained of
stomach pains. He was laid low, although an examination by doctors revealed nothing obviously wrong. Hollocher missed the first month of the 1923 season, not
appearing in a game until May 11 at the Polo Grounds. All seemed fine as he hit .342
in sixty-six games. The Cubs won more than they lost in the stretch. Then, on
August 3, Killefer found a note on his desk at Wrigley Field:

Dear Bill—
Tried to see you at the clubhouse this afternoon but guess I missed you. Feeling
pretty rotten so made up my mind to go home and take a rest and forget baseball
for the rest of the year. No hard feelings, just didn't feel like playing anymore.
Good luck.
As Ever,
Holly

Hollocher returned to St. Louis and submitted to a battery of medical tests, which found
nothing wrong. He sat out the rest of 1923, and the Cubs never threatened the Giants
without him. He was cleared to play in 1924, returning with some fanfare in May.
The *Chicago Tribune* reported optimistically: "The X-ray plates of Charlie Hollocher's stomach have definitely determined that there is nothing organically wrong
with the star shortstop." But Hollocher lasted only seventy-six games before jumping the team again, this time never to return.
The pain was obviously real to Hollocher, but no diagnosis was ever made that explained
his agony. The tale came to a disturbing end in 1940, when Hollocher killed himself
with a shotgun blast to the throat. His wife told police he had been complaining of
stomach pain of late.
Art Nehf had a good statistical season in 1924, going 14–4, but pitched only 171 innings
(down from 268 in 1922) as he battled arm soreness. His effectiveness continued to
dwindle, and after Nehf's two appearances with the 1926 Giants, McGraw sold him
to Cincinnati.
Boston's horrific 1923 on the diamond came as little surprise to Sox manager Frank
Chance, who told a reporter before the season that his club would definitely finish
last. He was correct.
Casey Stengel's first nickname wasn't "Casey" or "Doctor" but "Dutch," as in "Deutsch,"
in honor of his German heritage.
Another version of the Stengel-to-New-York story had him drinking in a saloon when
McGraw reached him by phone, telling Stengel to get to New York the next day. Casey
was so excited (goes the tale) that he raced to the train station and arrived that afternoon.

Chapter 23
Lefty O'Doul wasn't even the losing pitcher despite giving up thirteen runs in an inning
on July 7. Boston's starter that day, Curt Fullerton, gave up eight runs in three
innings to take the loss. Sadly for the Sox, the 27–3 drubbing was the first game of a
doubleheader. In the nightcap, the Indians once again beat Boston, though by a
more face-saving 8–5 score.

After finding himself as a hitter, O'Doul had an incredible season at the plate while with the Philadelphia Phillies in 1929. He hit .398 with 32 homers, 122 RBI, and 152 runs scored. His 254 hits set an NL record that was tied by New York's Bill Terry in 1930 but never broken.

O'Doul's restaurant still operates in San Francisco's Tenderloin District, and a small bridge that spans McCovey Cove outside AT&T Park in San Francisco is named for O'Doul.

The Carl Mays deal that sparked the sequence of events that led Ruth to be sold (and the Yankee Stadium to be built) resulted in an imbroglio that divided the American League into two warring camps: the "Insurrectos," a group that fought with Ban Johnson (who tried to halt the Mays trade) and that included the Yankees, the Red Sox, and, for reasons unrelated to the Mays deal, the Chicago White Sox; and the "Loyalists," or the other five teams. Johnson waged a protracted war against the Insurrectos, in particular with Frazee—the Sox owner spent a fortune in legal costs due to various suits Johnson levied against him. That inspired Frazee's thirst for liquidity more than did his Broadway empire, although there is no doubt he kept one hand on Broadway even while he was in Boston. The legend that pins the sale of Ruth to the Yankees on Frazee's desire to raise funds to produce the show *No, No, Nanette* barely hints at the truth. Readers interested in a thorough deconstruction of the events surrounding the Mays and Ruth transactions should read Glenn Stout and Richard A. Johnson's *Red Sox Century.*

The sale of Ruth was unquestionably a debacle for the Red Sox, but it should be pointed out that they finished sixth in the AL in 1919—with the Babe in the lineup.

According to Colonel Jacob Ruppert's great-grandnephew K. Jacob Ruppert, Harry Frazee's great-grandson Max is not only friends with the Rupperts but a diehard Yankees fan.

Ruth was a superb pitcher in Boston. He set a record for consecutive World Series scoreless innings, 29⅔, a mark that stood until 1960. From 1914–18, Ruth, with a sterling 2.09 earned run average, was well on his way to a Hall of Fame career as a pitcher, despite the fact that he tipped off his curveball by sticking out his tongue during his windup. It wasn't until years later that Ruth was informed of his "tell."

Huggins may have failed to sign Ruth during his trip to California in the winter of 1920, but he did sign a slugging outfielder—Bob Meusel.

With regard to Huston and Ruth's tight relationship being a boon to salary negotiations, here is more evidence: Before the 1923 season, Huston upped Ruth's salary to $50,000. Ruth wanted to make it $52,000, as he always wanted to make "a grand a week." Huston supposedly agreed to flip a coin for the extra two thousand and was good to his word when the Babe won the toss.

Ruth took some abuse for the size of his contract. His response: "It isn't right," he said. "A man ought to get all he can earn. A man who knows he's making money for other people ought to get some of the profit he brings in. Don't make any difference if it's baseball or a vaudeville show. It's business, I tell you. There ain't no sentiment to it. Forget that stuff."

Some accounts have 1924 as the year Ruth took the glass of water to the face to revive him from unconsciousness—it is possible that there were two separate incidents. The lack of proper medical care is an often overlooked facet when arguments are made comparing modern-day players to those of Ruth's era. For example, Ruth almost certainly wouldn't have been forced to miss so much time during the 1921

Series had modern antiseptic spray been available. Instead, the strawberry on his arm that he suffered while sliding became infected, and he nearly lost the use of it.

Ruth's homer in the fifteenth to beat Detroit was his most dramatic of July, but his most massive blast of the month came in an exhibition game in Grand Rapids, Michigan, a prodigious shot that cleared the scoreboard by fifty feet, landing in a distant tree. Half a century later, reserve pitcher George Pipgras still talked about the homer in awestruck tones.

Benny "the Ghetto Wizard" Leonard is one of the great, if unheralded, lightweights of all time. *The Ring* magazine put him at number eight on its list of the top fighters of the twentieth century. His first fight with Lew Tendler, in New Jersey on July 27, 1922, was a bruising battle that Tendler clearly won, according to most ringside accounts. But New Jersey law stated that the champion could lose his title only via knockout, so Leonard kept the belt. Benny worked on solving Tendler's lefty style for a year and pummeled him in the rematch. Despite Tendler's brilliance as a fighter, he never could get past Leonard to win a championship.

The story of Mays hurling the beanball that resulted in the death of Ray Chapman of Cleveland, still the lone on-field death in major-league history, is tangential to the events related in this book, but it is fascinating and is well told in Mike Sowell's *The Pitch That Killed.*

Another favored Ruth hobby on train trips was to celebrate important wins by tearing the shirts right off his teammates' torsos. His fellow Yankees weren't necessarily enamored of this behavior—unlike Ruth, they couldn't afford to order dozens of tailored shirts at a time, as the Babe did regularly.

Chapter 24

Here are the details of Luque's amazing feat in Boston, when he started and won both ends of a doubleheader: In the opener, Luque pitched six innings, giving up two runs and five hits. He left after the Reds scored four in the top of the seventh, and Eppa Rixey pitched the final three innings for his first (and only) save of the season. In the nightcap, Luque went all the way, even though the Reds led, 9–0, after six innings. Dolf surrendered five runs in the final three innings but still got the win comfortably. Luque was 15–2 when the long day was over. It is safe to say that something like that will never be seen again.

Chapter 25

"Prince Hal" Chase spent his final season, 1919, with McGraw and the Giants, but he is best known as one of the first stars in Yankees franchise history, playing while the team was still the Highlanders. The Babe himself called Chase the best first baseman ever, a judgment admittedly made before Lou Gehrig established himself. Hal was also involved in numerous corruptions, large and small. Following the 1919 season, he was effectively blackballed from the game after NL president John Heydler received evidence that Chase had been paid by gamblers to fix games. Chase was never formally banned from baseball by either Heydler or Landis, but no team dared sign him, considering him to be tainted goods.

McGraw was particularly sensitive to gambling accusations, and an incident from 1922 hadn't helped. With the Giants closing in on the pennant, talented but troubled pitcher "Shufflin' Phil" Douglas, in an alcoholic haze, wrote a bizarre letter to a friend of his, a player on the St. Louis Cardinals named Les Mann, stating that he was sick of McGraw (who had hired a former player to keep tabs on Phil and had recently fined the star hurler $100) and would do whatever it took to deny him the flag—for a price.

I want to leave here but I want some inducement. I don't want this guy [McGraw] to win the pennant and I feel if I stay here I will win it for him. If you want to send a man over here with the goods, I will leave for home on [the] next train. I will go down to fishing camp and stay there.

Unfortunately the recipient of the letter, Les Mann, dropped a dime on Douglas, turning the letter over to Branch Rickey, who forwarded it on to Landis. The judge wasted little time in banning Douglas from the game for good.

In late August Charles Stoneham was indicted for mail fraud and perjury in relation to the fraudulent dealings of two bucket shops (more commonly known as "boiler rooms" today) that Stoneham swore under oath he didn't own. The grand jury disagreed. His lawyers kept him out of jail, but Landis forced Stoneham and McGraw to immediately sell their betting interests in Cuba—the casino and the track. The decision gutted McGraw—he relished the bon-vivant status the gambling palaces bestowed upon him in Havana, so different from his stern taskmaster image in the States.

As for Stoneham, he merrily flaunted Landis's order to dissociate himself from the criminal element. Rumors flew that he would be forced to sell the team (with a natural buyer close by—Til Huston), but Stoneham held his ground. Arnold Rothstein still made regular appearances in his box at the Polo Grounds. William Randolph Hearst's New York American launched a long series of articles aimed at bringing the Giants owner down, but the power of the press proved limited in this case.

Wilbert Robinson loved to talk about McQuillan's ability to pick off runners and swore he was present on several occasions when Handsome Hugh was inserted into games just for that reason, not to pitch to batters.

Precise details of Hornsby's brawl with Branch Rickey are difficult to find, given that the incident was buried for weeks. Lee Lowenfish does a good job of tracking the fight in his bio Branch Rickey: Baseball's Ferocious Gentleman.

Hornsby had a messy history with Rickey, and with McGraw as well. The Giants attempted to acquire the pugnacious hitter as early as 1921 but were unable to do so. Hornsby partly blamed Rickey for his not being dealt to a city with such fabulous horse tracks (gambling on the ponies was the Rajah's main vice), and the two were at loggerheads for much of their time in St. Louis. Cards owner Sam Breadon fired Rickey in 1925, at which time Branch sold his stock holdings in the team to, of all people, Hornsby. Hornsby also took over as player-manager and led the Cards to a World Series title, besting the Yankees in 1926. But that winter he demanded far more than the one-year, $50,000 contract being offered, and in response, Breadon dealt his World Series hero to the Giants in exchange for McGraw's problem star Frank Frisch. Hornsby refused to sell his stake in the Cards unless he could be guaranteed a large profit, and the NL didn't allow him to play for New York while owning a piece of St. Louis. So the two teams and NL president John Heydler raised a $66,000 kitty to buy off Hornsby to complete the deal.

In New York, the two domineering personalities clashed immediately. Hornsby and McGraw both attempted to get away from the park in order to gamble on horses as much as possible—otherwise they fought over everything. Hornsby spent much of the season filling his teammates' ears with lectures on how McGraw was doing everything wrong. The Rajah hit .361, but when a sizable number of Giants went to Charles Stoneham and vowed never to play with Hornsby again, another trade was inevitable. Hornsby was dumped on the Braves, who could always be counted upon to do New York's bidding, for two nonentities, catcher Shanty Hogan and outfielder Jimmy Welsh.

Chapter 26

The press at the time openly speculated that Cobb was the one to drop a dime on Ruth and his Betsy Bingle, but no proof was ever proffered.

"Wahoo Sam" Crawford was the first player ever to lead both leagues in home runs (NL in 1901, AL in 1908). Ed Barrow, his manager for two seasons, said of Sam, "There was never a better hitter."

The Cobb-Crawford feud took an interesting turn after Cobb's death in 1961, when a reporter found among Ty's papers several letters written to influential baseball men campaigning for Crawford's induction into the Hall of Fame. Sam had been elected for immortality in 1957, apparently unaware of his enemy's efforts on his behalf.

Cobb and others thought that because Ruth started out as a pitcher, managers allowed him to hit for power rather than precision, but Bill James, the great baseball analyst and historian, calls such claims "bullshit—he hit that way because he was Babe Ruth, and he was deeply convinced that the rules did not apply to Babe Ruth."

If you want to know more about the brief but extraordinary history of New York City rodeos and Tex Austin, check out *Time* magazine from June 25, 1923, and August 20, 1923.

Chapter 27

"Government Abandons Attempt to Police City" read the headline in the *Daily News* of April 1, 1923, in a story detailing the inability of the feds to rid the city of illegal alcohol. It was not an April Fools' joke. The state Prohibition enforcement agencies continued the Sisyphean task of trying to keep New Yorkers from taking a drink.

Chapter 28

Two years before the passage of the law that allowed Sunday baseball in New York City, McGraw had been arrested for staging a game on the Sabbath. On Sunday, August 19, 1917, the Giants hosted the Reds in a game at the Polo Grounds. Christy Mathewson reluctantly pitched for New York—he was opposed to playing ball on the Sabbath, but McGraw convinced him to start on the grounds that the proceeds from the gate would benefit the U.S. Army. Fred Toney shut out the Giants, and after the game McGraw and Mathewson were hauled downtown by the cops. The Sabbath Society, a group based upon keeping any fun out of the holy day, had sworn out a complaint against the two Giants. The magistrate dismissed the charges with a quickness that seemed to foretell the coming of Sunday ball in New York.

Mose Solomon's name is often misspelled as "Moses" or "Moe," but the proper name is "Mose."

Chapter 29

The scoring decision that cost Howard Ehmke a second-straight no-hitter calls to mind the kerfuffle over umpire Jim Joyce's blown call at first base that cost Detroit's Armando Galarraga a perfect game in the summer of 2010.

Here are the full results in the 1923 AL MVP vote:

	PLAYER	TEAM	POS.	1ST PLACE VOTES	TOTAL
1	BABE RUTH	NY	OF	8	64
2	EDDIE COLLINS	CHI	2B	0	37
3	HARRY HEILMANN	DET	OF	0	31
4	WALLY GERBER	STL	SS	0	20
4	JOE SEWELL	CLE	SS	0	20
6	CHARLIE JAMIESON	CLE	OF	0	19
7	JOHNNY BASSLER	DET	C	0	17
8	CHICK GALLOWAY	PHI	SS	0	13
8	GEORGE UHLE	CLE	P	0	13
10	GEORGE BURNS	BOS	1B	0	8
11	HOWARD EHMKE	BOS	P	0	7
11	MUDDY RUEL	WAS	C	0	7
13	ROGER PECKINPAUGH	WAS	SS	0	6
14	URBAN SHOCKER	STL	P	0	5
15	JOE JUDGE	WAS	1B	0	4
15	MARTY McMANUS	STL	2B	0	4
15	KEN WILLIAMS	STL	OF	0	4
18	BUCKY HARRIS	WAS	2B	0	3
18	JOE HARRIS	BOS	OF	0	3
20	JOE HAUSER	PHI	1B	0	1
20	WALTER JOHNSON	WAS	P	0	1
20	CY PERKINS	PHI	C	0	1

The absence of Bob Meusel, Sad Sam Jones, Wally Pipp, and other Yankees is due to the fact that the team chose to nominate only Ruth for the award. Thus they weren't on the ballot, and the writers could not vote for them. In this writer's opinion, Heilmann deserved second place, and Tris Speaker of Cleveland, who as player-manager refused to nominate himself, deserved third place.

There was no National League MVP at the time. With the additional absence of the Cy Young Award, Dolf Luque of Cincinnati clearly would have deserved the MVP, ahead of Frankie Frisch and Cy Williams.

Chapter 30

Reports vary on the cause of Stengel's heel injury, and the man himself wasn't sure either.

Reports also vary widely on the number of fans who squeezed into the Polo Grounds for the Dempsey-Firpo fight. The most plausible number is 82,000, which would dwarf any throng at the Yankee Stadium that year. Stoneham and the National Exhibition Company reported gate earnings on the fight at $1,188,603, a massive haul that speaks mainly to Dempsey's popularity.

Claude Jonnard would lead the league in appearances and saves (retroactively figured, since there was no such animal as the save stat in 1923), with forty-five and five, respectively. Teammate Rosy Ryan started fifteen games but also relieved often, with four saves. He matched Jonnard with forty-five appearances.

The George Burns who played outfield for Cincinnati is not the same George Burns who starred for the Boston Red Sox and collected the first hit in Yankee Stadium history. The National League Burns was a hugely popular member of the Giants before being dealt to the Queen City—after the trade, a "George Burns Day" was held at the Polo Grounds to honor the crowd favorite. The "other" George Burns was a very good player on several teams, including the Indians, where he won the 1926 MVP Award. Neither are to be confused with the cigar-chomping comic star of *Oh, God!* and *The Sunshine Boys*. That George Burns was born Nathan Birnbaum and claimed to have taken his stage name from the ballplayers. Appropriately for the sake of this narrative, Burns met his wife and stage partner, Gracie Allen, in 1923.

Chapter 31

In the exhibition game against the Orioles, Ruth homered in his third at bat. His first two times up, he struck out and was hit by a pitch—facing a heralded young prospect listed in the box score as "Groves." It was actually Lefty Grove, who went on to win three hundred games as one of the greatest southpaw pitchers in baseball history.

Here are more details of the Babe's homers in 1923: He slugged more homers—ten—against St. Louis than against any other team. Elam Vangilder of the Browns surrendered three of them to become the pitcher taken deep most often. Eight of Ruth's dingers were at Sportsman's Park in the Arch City, by far the most of any venue outside the Yankee Stadium. Due to the extreme road trips and home stands, Ruth's home-away splits have long streaks—for example, the Babe didn't hit his third homer at the Yankee Stadium until June 8. He hit nine straight on the road before slugging five at home, then eight more away, five more at home, and four away before finishing with seven of eight at the Stadium. Thirty of the forty-one came against right-handed pitchers. July was his most prolific month, with ten homers, followed by May, with nine. As he hit more homers on the road, it follows that the plurality of his shots came when he was playing left field, not right—twenty-one to thirteen. He hit four while playing center field, and another three while "resting" at first base. For his career, despite the fact that Ruth is identified in the public imagination as a right fielder, he hit but 342 of his 714 homers while playing in right. Two hundred eighty-nine came while he was in left field.

According to research by Ruth home-run scholar Bill Jenkinson, the Babe whacked ten shots in 1923 that exceeded four hundred feet at the Yankee Stadium and didn't leave the park. Conversely, only five of his Bronx home runs were "cheap shots" into the short porch in right. Jenkinson estimates that Ruth hit twenty-one blasts of four hundred feet or more in 1923 that didn't go as home runs due to the configurations of the various parks.

So where does Ruth's 1923 season rank on his list of accomplishments, or the all-time list, which amounts to the same thing? Ruth's 1927 season is first among legends, due to the sixty homers he slugged that season, but 1920 and 1921 were better—as was 1923. Perhaps the best way to judge a player's offensive value is by adding on-base percentage to slugging percentage, resulting in a sum shorthanded by baseball fans as OPS. Ruth's OPS in those seasons:

1920—1.379
1921—1.358
1923—1.309
1927—1.258

When adjusted for park dimensions, 1923's performance slips into a tie with 1921's, as the Yankee Stadium actually turned out to be a slightly worse hitter's park for Ruth than was the Polo Grounds. Considering that the Babe won a title in 1923 despite the immense pressure surrounding him to perform well after the disaster of 1922, a case can be made that '23 was Ruth's finest overall season.

Chapter 32

When asked shortly before his death in 1942 what his most memorable moment at the mike was, McNamee chose the Babe's "called shot" of 1932.

McNamee was inducted into the Sports Broadcasting Hall of Fame in 1984.

Crystal radio sets were phased out in favor of more powerful factory-built models in the 1930s but enjoyed a brief renaissance during World War II, when it was discovered that the Germans could pinpoint transmissions from standard army radios but not jerry-rigged crystal sets (called "foxhole receivers" during the war). Even today there is a subset of hobbyists devoted to building and using the crystal sets.

Chapter 33

In 1911 Fred Lieb had just started with the New York Press and was breathless with excitement at working in newspapers. The Press was based in New York's short-lived answer to Fleet Street, a newspaper row in the shadow of the Brooklyn Bridge that included the Press (headquartered at 7 Spruce Street); the Tribune, the Sun, and the World (all on Park Row); and the German-language Volkszeitung, which had a higher circulation than all but the largest dailies. Lieb and Runyon met in the Polo Grounds press box that spring day in 1911 when Runyon strolled over, extended a hand, and said, "Hello, I'm new here too."

Another member of the "Class of '11," Grantland Rice, had perhaps too much southern honor for his own good, handing over a small fortune to a friend before heading off to fight in World War I. When he returned from the war, Rice discovered his friend had lost the entire wad on bad investments and had committed suicide.

Heywood Broun's novel The Sun Field, with a wonderfully informative introduction by Darryl Brock, was reissued by Rvive Books in 2008 and is a must-read for any baseball or literature fan.

Here is proof that the New York Post was a radically different paper in 1923: one headline that ran during the World Series read, "How the Domestic Servant Problem May Be Solved."

Chapter 34

Full play-by-play accounts of the World Series of 1923 can be found at Retrosheet.

Ray Robinson, the author of *Iron Horse* and many other baseball books, first started going to games at the Yankee Stadium in 1928. He recalls that most often he sat in the right-field bleachers, the lair of the rowdiest fans, and the combination of the distance and the huge cloud of tobacco smoke that invariably settled over the field made judging balls and strikes from that vantage impossible. Nevertheless, Robinson recalls, fans in right field bet on the outcome of nearly every single pitched ball, despite the large sign at the rear of the bleachers that read: BETTING PROHIBITED.

Some reports claim that in the first inning of Game One, a Giants player, likely Casey Stengel, threw a bar of soap to the mound, a reference to Waite Hoyt's ad contract with Lifebuoy. This definitively happened in the 1921 Series between the teams, and the incidents may have been confused. It's also possible it was a running joke. As it cannot be rigorously sourced for 1923 as well, I decided not to include it in the narrative.

Jim Thorpe, the famous football player and Olympian, played baseball for the Giants on three separate tours of duty between 1912 and 1918, none of them particularly successful. He was better remembered in New York baseball circles for his ability to best any member of the Giants in wrestling.

The small discrepancy between Joe Dugan's overheard "Go, Casey, go!" and Runyon's "Go on, Casey, go on!" can be chalked up either to Runyon mishearing Dugan's description after the game or to Runyon's feeling that the inclusion of the extra words made for better copy.

Chapter 35

The 1923 game between Army and Notre Dame was scheduled to be played at the Polo Grounds, but the Giants' appearance in the World Series forced the contest to be moved to Ebbets Field in Brooklyn. Notre Dame won, 13–0.

Rice, in writing "Ruth, crushed to earth, will rise again," riffed on a line by William Cullen Bryant, who wrote in the poem "The Battle-Field" that "Truth, crushed to earth, shall rise again." Broun, in writing "The Ruth is mighty and shall prevail," used similar wordplay, deleting a *t* from the Latin "magna est veritas et praevalebit," or "truth is mighty and shall prevail," a verse from the Book of Edras in the Latin Vulgate Bible. As noted in the narrative, these were men whose scope of knowledge went far beyond the box scores.

Ruth barely missed hitting three homers in Game Two of the '23 Series. In 1926 he would become the first player to do so in the World Series, clubbing three at his favored slugging ground, Sportsman's Park in St. Louis, as the Yanks buried the Cardinals, 10–5, in Game Four. They would lose the Series, however, when the Babe was thrown out stealing to end Game Seven. Ruth would provide a carbon copy in 1928, when he hit three homers once again in Game Four at Sportsman's Park against St. Louis. This time, however, the Yankees swept the Cardinals. In all, Ruth would hit fifteen homers in forty-one World Series games. The 1922 Series was the only one in which he was wearing a Yankees uniform and didn't hit at least one home run.

Chapter 36

Stengel's nose-flick had a World Series antecedent. During the 1912 Series between the Giants and the Red Sox, Fred Snodgrass (later to make the infamous "$30,000 muff" of a fly ball in the deciding game) had thumbed his nose at vociferous fans in Fenway Park who had been insulting his parentage, questioning his sexual orientation, and alleging various encounters with area dens of iniquity. After the nose-flick, outraged Boston mayor John Fitzgerald, aka "Honey Fitz," charged onto the sporting green in full finery (top hat and striped pants) and demanded Snodgrass be arrested. A squad of Boston's finest backed him up and made across the diamond toward the astonished Giant. Snodgrass explained to the coppers that he had merely been flicking a fly from his nose. The police, now hearing it from the same fans who had been tormenting Snodgrass, retreated, pulling the esteemed mayor back to his seat.

Chapter 37

David Lloyd George, who had led England through the war and done so much to shape postwar Europe, was toppled from power due to a scandal involving the selling of peerages and titles for money, which was to be used to form a new liberal political party. Stanley Baldwin, a conservative, was the British prime minister in October 1923.

Readers surprised by the whipsaw reactions to Ruth's and McGraw's performances after every game should note that the media in 1923 was not unlike the media of the early-twenty-first century—knee-jerk, eager to make grand proclamations after every game, if not every at bat, and proven wrong so often as to be comical.

The practice of flipping a coin to decide the site of World Series games ended after 1924. John McGraw lost the toss again that season, with the result that Game Seven was played in Washington, DC. The Sens won at home. McGraw was also on the wrong end of one of the other two coin flips that actually mattered, in 1912—the Giants played at Boston and lost (1909 was the other season it happened). In 1925 the leagues decided to rotate home-field advantage.

The nickname "Bronx Bombers" was an offshoot of the "Brown Bomber," the press moniker for heavyweight champ Joe Louis. It is surprising, then, that the pre-Stadium Yankees (or the Giants) weren't known as the "Manhattan Maulers" as a tribute to the "Manassa Mauler," heavyweight champ Jack Dempsey.

Chapter 38

Frisch lost his Giants cap racing to make a sensational catch on the center-field grass at the Polo Grounds. Another pretty fair player named Mays would make a habit of doing the same three decades hence.

Graham McNamee's remembered description of Babe Ruth's dramatic bases-loaded at bat mistakes one detail—even had Ruth come through with a hit, the Yankees wouldn't have won the Series just yet; it was only the top of the eighth inning.

At the time the book was completed, the Yankees' 1923 championship was the first of twenty-seven won by the Yankees. It is a figure far ahead of any franchise in American sports. For the Yankee haters out there, it should be noted that the Yankees have also lost more World Series—thirteen as I write this—than any other team.

Chapter 39

A few sources mention that Miller Huggins accepted his gift of a diamond ring from the Babe while stark naked, a detail I didn't find particularly credible (or aesthetically pleasing), so it was excised from the narrative.

While McGraw and Ryan himself felt Rosy could have fielded Meusel's "$50,000 blow," some press accounts of the hit describe it as a smash that landed near or past second base and thus was practically unfieldable by a pitcher following through with his windup.

Herb Pennock had to make do with the *Reach Guide* MVP, for there was no official Series MVP Award handed out, nor was a luxury car presented to the recipient, standard practice today. The Knight's two wins and 3.63 Series ERA were good, but Ruth still has to be considered the MVP, despite his strikeout with the bases full in his final at bat of the Classic.

The winners' share for the Yankees was originally put at $6,160.46 but was retabulated by the commissioner before the checks went out, cutting $16.97 from each Yankee's take. The haul was worth roughly $78,000 in today's dollars. By contrast, for winning the 2009 World Series, each Yankee took home just over $350,000.

McGraw may never have won three straight World Series, but he did lose three in a row, from 1911–13, two to the A's, one to the Red Sox. On the other hand, the Giants won four straight NL pennants from 1921–24. In the ensuing ninety-plus years, no National League team has even won three in a row, save the wartime St. Louis Cardinals, who captured three flags from 1942–44 in a severely depleted sport. The Gashouse Gang didn't do it, or the Big Red Machine, or the Boys of Summer, or the nicknameless Phillies that fell just short in 2010.

Epilogue

The Society for American Baseball Research bio of Dover Hall, Til Huston's Georgia estate, makes for fascinating reading. It can be accessed at http://bioproj.sabr.org/bioproj.cfm?a=v&v=l&bid=2583&pid=19624.

British actress Fanny Kemble, whose book on slavery persuaded parliament not to side with the Confederacy during the Civil War, was the original owner of Huston's mansion on Butler Island.

The first expansion of the Yankee Stadium was part of Osborn's original design and was considered "Phase II" of the construction plan.

Many experts refer to the post-1976 Stadium as "Yankee Stadium II," reflecting the massive changes in design and scale that were undertaken. But *Green Cathedrals,* the bible of ballparks by Philip Lowry, makes no such distinction.

McGraw's defeat in the 1924 Series was as unlucky as the loss in 1923 was bitter. The Giants led the Washington Senators, 3–1, in the eighth inning of Game Seven, but a ground ball to new Giants third baseman Fred Lindstrom hit a pebble and bounced into the outfield, tying the game. The contest went to the twelfth inning, when another bad-hop grounder got past Lindstrom to score Muddy Ruel with the Series-winning run.

Stengel's line about being traded away after his slugging heroics in the 1923 Series has also been reported as "If I'd hit three homers, [McGraw] would have traded me to the Three-Eye League." All agree that he did say upon departing for Boston from the city that he loved, "The Paths of Glory lead but to the Braves."

The new Yankee Stadium seats 52,235, including standing-room patrons, and is considerably more intimate than the original park. During its inaugural season of 2009, the new Stadium was deemed too home-run friendly, an ironic charge given the creation myth of the original Stadium. In another irony, some believe that the old Stadium was the cause of wind tunnels that aided home runs across the street in the new park. In 2010 the original Yankee Stadium was mostly torn down, thus ending the cyclonic effect, and the home-run rate dropped considerably. A simpler explanation may lie in the fact that home runs and scoring declined in 2010 throughout baseball.

Of course, the first season in the new Stadium had something in common with the first season in the original Stadium: in 2009, as in 1923, the Yankees won the World Series.

McGraw's protest against Bill Klem as his final baseball act is noted in Joe Williams's article announcing McGraw's retirement in the *New York World-Telegram* of June 4, 1932, but it does not say precisely why the protest was lodged.

Sources

I have spent much of my adult life gleaning information from others through the interview process. Since there was no one I could talk to in person about Babe Ruth, John McGraw, the 1923 season, or any of the events that take place in the narrative, I relied extensively on secondary sources, primarily from newspapers and magazines.

As it turns out, that was a gift beyond measure. What might have been an ordeal of squinting at microfilm became the pleasure of reading the great Grantland Rice, Damon Runyon, Heywood Broun, John Kieran, Ring Lardner, and many, many more. These were the men who reported on the "Golden Age of Sport," and I owe them gratitude for doing so with such verve, wit, and style. Newspaper accounts from these contemporary sources form the backbone of the narrative.

Here are the newspapers I consulted: the *New York Times, New York Post, New York Daily News, New York American, New York Journal, New York Herald, New York Tribune, New York World, New York Sun, Bronx Home News, Washington Post, Boston Globe, Atlanta Journal, Chicago Tribune, Chicago Daily News, Los Angeles Mirror, Los Angeles Times.*

Certain periodicals also were key, starting of course with the *Sporting News,* of which I consulted numerous issues between 1920 and 1924. Others included the 1920–24 issues of *Baseball Magazine,* the 1922–24 *Reach Guide,* selected issues of *Literary Digest,* early issues of *Time* and *The New Yorker,* the 2009 *New York Yankees Media Guide* and 2005 yearbook, and the "Yankee Stadium First Fifty Years" pamphlet, issued by the Bronx County Historical Society.

There were many key online sources, none more important than Retrosheet (www.retrosheet.org). The website is a project of the Society for American Baseball Research (SABR), of which I am a proud member—it has cataloged the box scores of virtually every game in baseball history dating back to the nineteenth century. There are also play-by-play logs from most seasons (albeit not 1923, except for the World Series), game-by-game results, daily and yearly statistical splits, and an ocean of other information, some of it valuable, some of it ephemeral, all of it pleasurable.

SABR also maintains an ongoing Baseball Biography Project (bioproj.sabr.org) that limns the lives of hundreds of players both great and obscure. Many of these proved useful.

While I got the original idea for this book while leafing through *Total Baseball*—the most complete hardball encyclopedia in print— Baseball Reference (www.baseball-reference.com) is the handier online version. Baseball Library (www.baseballlibrary.com) and Baseball Almanac (www.baseball-almanac.com) were other excellent reference points. Ballparks of Baseball (www.ballparksofbaseball .com) is an excellent resource for annual attendance figures. A website devoted to Waite Hoyt (www.waitehoyt.com) provided details from the Merry Mortician's life.

The Baseball Hall of Fame in Cooperstown, New York, provided invaluable clip files on most of the dramatis personae, along with numerous hard-to-find books and answers to many questions. A pair of episodes from the ESPN SportsCentury series, profiling Ruth and Casey Stengel, also helped.

The Babe has likely been written about more than any other sports figure, and this book owes a large debt to the writers who have tackled the immense, sprawling life of Ruth. Robert W. Creamer's *Babe: The Legend Comes to Life* is the Babe Ruth of Babe Ruth biographies. Leigh Montville's recent *The Big Bam* is a worthy successor to the crown. One of the joys of writing this book was discovering older, less-known Ruth books, such as Marshall Smelser's *The Life That Ruth Built* and Robert Smith's *Babe Ruth's America*. The Babe himself put out some (ghostwritten) books. *Babe Ruth's Own Book of Baseball* was a delightful jewel plucked from obscurity, in particular its gold mine of '20s-era baseball slang.

Charles Alexander's *John McGraw* remains the major work covering Muggsy's picaresque life. I was fortunate to discover the prolific if sadly forgotten writer Frank Graham. His midcentury histories of the Giants, Yankees, McGraw, and Stengel were invaluable and fun. Creamer's bio of Stengel was also important, as was Maury Allen's *You Could Look It Up*. The great Bill James (along with his faithful companion Rob Neyer) provided not only much information through their work but inspiration, especially James, to a baseball-loving teenager growing up a few miles from Yankee Stadium in suburban New York. Donald Dewey and Nicholas Acocella's *New Biographical History of Baseball* provided numerous snappy anecdotes and facts about players great and small. Joseph Durso, Harvey Frommer, and Jim Reisler have gone to the Yankees well often in their careers; their works helped greatly. Ruth researcher Bill Jenkinson has done yeoman duty investigating nearly every one of Ruth's dingers, including those hit during exhibitions and barnstorming tours. His *The Year Babe Ruth Hit 104 Home Runs* is a must for any Ruth fan. Burt Solomon's epic *Baseball Timeline* is a joy (and a feat) to pick up. And any baseball book recounting this era has to refer to the great interviews conducted by Lawrence Ritter in his majestic oral history *The Glory of Their Times*.

I also wish to recognize Harry Swanson, a true scholar of the construction of the Yankee Stadium. In 2004 he put out an apparently self-published manuscript with the unwieldy title *Ruthless Baseball: Yankees Purified by Fire Stadium Construction*. It is a treasure trove of info about the building of the Stadium. If, for example, you wish to peruse a complete list of subcontractors employed by White Construction on the project, this is the source for you. This book would be infinitely poorer without Swanson's work.

Bibliography

Alexander, Charles. *John McGraw*. New York: Penguin Books, 1988.

———. *Our Game*. New York: MJF Books, 1997.

———. *Ty Cobb*. New York: Oxford University Press, 1984.

Allen, Lee. *The Hot Stove League*. Kingston, NY: Total Sports, 2000.

Allen, Maury. *You Could Look It Up: The Life of Casey Stengel*. New York: Times Books, 1979.

Anderson, Chris. "Wally Pipp: A Son's Tale About the Start of Gehrig's Consecutive Games Streak." Pipp's boy talks about the beginning of Lou Gehrig's streak at the expense of his father. http://www.heraldtribune.com/article/20090422/ARTICLE/904221026?p=4&tc=pg (accessed September 4, 2010).

Appel, Marty. "Secrets of Yankee Stadium." 2008 Major League Baseball all-star game official program, July 15, 2008.

———. "Yankee Stadium Story." *Yankees Magazine,* July 1991.

Berg, A. Scott. *Lindbergh*. New York: G. P. Putnam's Sons, 1998.

Biographical Directory of the United States Congress. "Ruppert, Jacob Jr." http://bioguide.congress.gov/scripts/biodisplay.pl?index=R000513 (accessed May 12, 2010).

Bready, James H. *Baseball in Baltimore*. Baltimore: Johns Hopkins University Press, 1998.

Broun, Heywood. *The Sun Field*. New York: G. P. Putnam's Sons, 1923 (Westport, CT: Rvive Books, 2008).

Browning, Reed. *Baseball's Greatest Season, 1924*. Amherst, MA: University of Massachusetts Press, 2003.

Capano, Vince. "The Good Old Days of Beer in New York." http://www.beernexus.com/beerinNYhistory.html (accessed April 5, 2010).

Chadwick, Alex. *The Illustrated History of Baseball*. New York: Booksales, 1995.

Chieger, Bob, ed. *Voices of Baseball*. New York: Penguin, 1983.

Clem, Andrew. "Yankee Stadium." Graphic images of the stadium dimensions over its history. http://www.andrewclem.com/Baseball/YankeeStadium.html (accessed August 12, 2010).

Coffey, Wayne. "Part One: The House That Ruth Built." *New York Daily News Magazine,* April 6, 2008.

Coghlan, Mary Ellen. "The John T. Brush Stairway." Information about the historical marker at the base of the stairway. http://www.hmdb.org/marker.asp?marker=31264 (accessed October 1, 2010).

Cohen, Rich. *Tough Jews*. New York: Vintage, 1999.

Cohen, Stanley. *Dodgers! The First 100 Years*. New York: Birch Lane Press, 1990.

Creamer, Robert W. *Babe: The Legend Comes to Life*. New York: Simon & Schuster, 1974.

———. *Stengel*. Lincoln, NE: University of Nebraska Press, 1996.

Crepeau, Richard C. *Baseball: America's Diamond Mind*. Orlando, FL: UCF Press, 1980.

Curran, William. *Big Sticks*. New York: William Morrow, 1990.

D'Amore, Jonathan. *Rogers Hornsby: A Biography*. Santa Barbara, CA: Greenwood Publishing Group, 2004.

Deford, Frank. "Giants Among Men." *Sports Illustrated,* August 25, 2003.

Dewey, Donald, and Nicholas Acocella. *The New Biographical History of Baseball*. Chicago: Triumph Books, 2002.

Dickey, Glenn. *The History of the World Series Since 1903*. New York: Stein and Day, 1984.

Dickson, Paul. *Baseball's Greatest Quotations*. New York: HarperCollins, 1991.

———. *The New Dickson Baseball Dictionary*. New York: Houghton Mifflin Harcourt, 1999.

Downey, Patrick. *Gangster City: The History of the New York Underworld 1900–1935*. Fort Lee, NJ: Barricade Books, 2004.

Durant, John. *The Story of Baseball*. New York: Hastings House, 1947.

Durso, Joseph. *Baseball and the American Dream*. St. Louis: The Sporting News, 1986.

———. *The Days of Mister McGraw*. New York: Prentice-Hall, 1969.

———. *Yankee Stadium: Fifty Years of Drama*. Boston: Houghton Mifflin, 1972.

Eig, Jonathan. *Luckiest Man*. New York: Simon & Schuster, 2005.

Fetter, Henry D. *Taking on the Yankees*. New York: W. W. Norton, 2003.

Frick, Ford C. *Games, Asterisks, and People*. New York: Crown, 1973.

Frisch, Frank, with J. Roy Stockton. *Frank Frisch: The Fordham Flash*. New York: Doubleday, 1962.

Frommer, Harvey. *Baseball's Greatest Managers*. New York: Franklin Watts, 1985.

———. *Five O'Clock Lightning*. Hoboken, NJ: Wiley, 2007.

———. "Opening Day at Yankee Stadium: 1927." Essay that imparts details about the construction of the Yankee Stadium. http://www.travel-watch.com/yankee1927openingday1.htm (accessed March 3, 2010).

———. *Remembering Yankee Stadium*. New York: Stewart, Tabori & Chang, 2008.

Gallico, Paul. *Farewell to Sport*. New York: Alfred A. Knopf, 1937.

Gilbert, Thomas. *The Soaring Twenties*. Danbury, CT: Franklin Watts, 1996.

Goldman, Steven. *Forging Genius: The Making of Casey Stengel*. Washington, DC: Potomac Books, 2005.

Graham, Frank. *Casey Stengel*. New York: John Day Company, 1958.

———. *McGraw of the Giants*. New York: Putnam, 1944.

———. *The New York Giants*. New York: Van Rees Press, 1952.

———. *The New York Yankees*. New York: Putnam, 1943.

Halberstam, David. *Sports on New York Radio*. Chicago: Masters Press, 1999.

Hano, Arnold. *Greatest Giants of Them All*. New York: G. P. Putnam's Sons, 1967.

Holtzman, Jerome. *Jerome Holtzman on Baseball*. Champaign, IL: Sports Publishing LLC, 2005.

———, ed. *No Cheering in the Press Box*. New York: Holt, Rinehart and Winston, 1973.

Honig, Donald. *Baseball America*. New York: Fireside, 2001.

———. *Baseball When the Grass Was Real*. New York: Coward, McCann and Geoghegan, 1974.

Hornsby, Rogers, and Bill Surface. *My War with Baseball*. New York: Coward-McCann, 1962.

Hoyt, Waite. *Babe Ruth as I Knew Him*. New York: Dell, 1948.

Hynd, Noel. "When the Yankees Beat the Giants in the 1923 Series, a New Era Began." *Sports Illustrated*, November 3, 1986.

Jackson, Kenneth T., ed. *The Encyclopedia of New York City*. New Haven, CT: Yale University Press, 1995.

James, Bill. *The Bill James Guide to Baseball Managers*. New York: Scribner, 1997.

———. *The Bill James Historical Baseball Abstract*. New York: Random House, 1992.

———. "Life, Liberty, and Breaking the Rules." Essay embracing the American scofflaw, including Babe Ruth. Slate.com, September 13, 2010. http://www.slate.com/id/2266750 (accessed September 15, 2010).

James, Bill, with Rob Neyer. *The Neyer/James Guide to Pitchers*. New York: Fireside, 2004.

Jenkinson, Bill. *The Year Babe Ruth Hit 104 Home Runs*. New York: Carroll & Graf, 2007.

King, David. "Ross Youngs." Thediamondangle.com, February 2002. http://www.thediamondangle.com/archive/feb02/rossyoungs.html (accessed August 22, 2010).

Klein, Christopher. "On the Trail of Babe Ruth." Traveling to the Babe's various homes, including his Sudbury farm, Home Plate. ESPN.com, April 11, 2010. http://sports.espn.go.com/travel/news/story?id=5079312 (accessed August 19, 2010).

Krantz, Les. *Yankee Stadium: A Tribute*. New York: HarperCollins, 2008.

Lake, Thomas. "Thumbing His Way Back Home." *Sports Illustrated*, July 26, 2010.

Levitt, Daniel R. *Ed Barrow*. Lincoln, NE: University of Nebraska Press, 2008.

Lieb, Fred. *Baseball as I Have Known It*. New York: Coward, McCann and Geoghegan, 1977.

Liebman, Glenn. *Grand Slams*. Chicago: Contemporary Books, 2001.

Linkowski, Jeffrey. "Yankee Stadium, 1927." Brief history of the stadium. http://www.angelfire.com/pa/1927/stadium1.html (accessed February 21, 2010).

Lipsyte, Robert, and Peter Levine. *Idols of the Game*. Atlanta: Turner Publishing, 1995.

Littlewood, Thomas B. *Arch: A Promoter, Not a Poet—the Story of Arch Ward*. Ames, IA: Iowa State University Press, 1990.

Lowenfish, Lee. *Branch Rickey: Baseball's Ferocious Gentleman*. Lincoln, NE: University of Nebraska Press, 2009.

Lowry, Philip J. *Green Cathedrals*. New York: Walker & Company, 2006.

McGraw, John. *My Thirty Years in Baseball*. New York: Boni and Liveright, 1923.

McNamee, Graham, and Robert Gordon Anderson. *You're on the Air*. New York: Harper and Brothers, 1926.

McNeil, William. *The Dodgers Encyclopedia*. Champaign, IL: Sports Publishing LLC, 2003.

Mead, William B., and Paul Dickson. *Baseball: The Presidents' Game*. Washington, DC: Farragut Publishing, 1993.

Meany, Tom. *Babe Ruth: The Big Moments of the Big Fellow*. New York: Grossett & Dunlap, 1947.

Montville, Leigh. *The Big Bam*. New York: Broadway Books, 2006.

Moore, Thomas F. "Sports Announcer by Accident." *Sports Illustrated,* October 12, 1964.

Morris, Peter. *A Game of Inches,* vol. 1. Chicago: Ivan R. Dee, 2006.

———. *Level Playing Fields*. Lincoln, NE: University of Nebraska Press, 2007.

Mosedale, John. *The Greatest of All: The 1927 New York Yankees*. New York: The Dial Press, 1974.

Murphy, Cait. *Crazy '08*. New York: Smithsonian Books, 2007.

Neyer, Rob. *Rob Neyer's Big Book of Baseball Lineups*. New York: Fireside, 2003.

Neyer, Rob, and Eddie Epstein. *Baseball Dynasties*. New York: W. W. Norton, 2000.

Osborn Engineering Company. *A Century of Progress*. Cleveland: Osborn Engineering Company, 1992.

Pietrusza, David. *Rothstein*. New York: Carroll & Graf, 2003.

Pitoniak, Scott. *Memories of Yankee Stadium*. Chicago: Triumph Books, 2008.

"Profiles: Mister Muggsy." Profile of John McGraw. *The New Yorker,* March 28, 1925.

Rader, Benjamin G. *Baseball: A History of America's Game*. Chicago: University of Illinois Press, 1992.

Reisler, Jim. *Babe Ruth: Launching the Legend*. New York: McGraw Hill, 2004.

———. *Babe Ruth Slept Here*. South Bend, IN: Diamond Communications, 1999.

———. *Before They Were the Bombers*. Jefferson, NC: McFarland, 2002.

———, ed. *Guys, Dolls, and Curveballs: Damon Runyon on Baseball*. New York: Carroll & Graf, 2005.

Rice, Damon. *Seasons Past*. New York: Pranger Publishers, 1976.

Rice, Grantland. *The Tumult and the Shouting*. New York: A. S. Barnes, 1954.

Ritter, Lawrence. *East Side, West Side*. New York: Total Sports, 1998.

———. *The Glory of Their Times*. New York: Harper Perennial, 1992.

Roberts, Russell. *Stolen! A History of Base Stealing*. Jefferson, NC: McFarland, 1999.

Robinson, Ray. *Iron Horse*. New York: W. W. Norton, 1990.

Robinson, Ray, and Christopher Jennison. *Yankee Stadium: 75 Years of Drama, Glamor, and Glory*. New York: Penguin Group, 1998.

Rosenblum, Constance. *Boulevard of Dreams*. New York: New York University Press, 2009.

Roznowski, Tom. "Hometown." Profiles of famous Terre Haute, Indiana, citizenry. http://www.wfiu.indiana.edu/hometown/profiles.htm (accessed July 30, 2010).

Ruth, George Herman. *Babe Ruth's Own Book of Baseball*. New York: G. P. Putnam's Sons, 1928.

Ruth, Mrs. Babe, with Bill Slocum. *The Babe and I*. Englewood Cliffs, NJ: Prentice Hall, 1959.

Schoor, Gene. *The History of the World Series*. New York: William Morrow, 1990.

Seymour, Harold, and Dorothy Jane Mills. *Baseball: The Golden Age.* New York: Oxford University Press, 1971.

Silvia, Tony. *Baseball Over the Air.* Jefferson, NC: McFarland, 2007.

Smelser, Marshall. *The Life That Ruth Built: A Biography.* Lincoln, NE: University of Nebraska Press, 1975.

Smith, Curt. *Voices of Summer.* New York: Carroll & Graf, 2005.

Smith, Robert. *Babe Ruth's America.* New York: Thomas Y. Crowell Company, 1974.

Solomon, Burt. *The Baseball Timeline.* New York: DK Publishing, 2001.

Sowell, Mike. *The Pitch That Killed.* Chicago: Ivan R. Dee, 1989.

Spatz, Lyle. *New York Yankee Openers.* Jefferson, NC: McFarland, 1997.

Spatz, Lyle, and Steve Steinberg. *1921: The Yankees, the Giants, and the Battle for Baseball Supremacy in New York.* Lincoln, NE: University of Nebraska Press, 2010.

"Sport: Voices." Profile of Graham McNamee. *Time,* October 3, 1927.

Stanton, Tom. *Ty and the Babe.* New York: Thomas Dunne Books, 2007.

Steinberg, Steve. "The Curse of the Hurlers." *Baseball Research Journal,* no. 35, 2007.

Stewart, Hope. Huston/Gladhart genealogy chart. Family tree showing Til Huston and Lena Belle Gladhart backgrounds. http://www.hope.stewart.name/genealogy/wc01/wc01_002.html (accessed February 11, 2010).

Stewart, Wayne. *Babe Ruth.* Santa Barbara, CA: Greenwood Publishing Group, 2006.

Stolley, Richard B. *The Jazz Age: The '20s.* Alexandria, VA: Time Life Books, 1998.

Stout, Glenn. *New York Yankees Yesterday and Today.* Lincolnwood, IL: Publications International, 2007.

———. *Yankees Century.* New York: Houghton Mifflin, 2002.

Stout, Glenn, with Richard A. Johnson. *Red Sox Century.* New York: Houghton Mifflin, 2000.

Sullivan, George, and John Powers. *The Yankees: An Illustrated History.* Philadelphia: Temple University Press, 1997.

Sullivan, Neil. *The Diamond in the Bronx.* New York: Oxford University Press, 2001.

Swanson, Harry. *Ruthless Baseball.* Bloomington, IN: AuthorHouse, 2004.

"The Theater: Are You an American?" Report on Tex Austin's rodeo. *Time,* June 25, 1923.

"The Theater: Ride 'Em, Cowboy!" Report on Tex Austin's rodeo. *Time,* August 20, 1923.

Thorn, John, and Pete Palmer, eds. *Total Baseball.* New York: Warner Books, 1989.

Thornley, Stew. *Land of the Giants.* Philadelphia: Temple University Press, 2000.

Toledo, Springs. "The Eighth God of War: Benny Leonard." History of Leonard's ring career. *The Sweet Science,* December 30, 2009. http://www.thesweetscience.com/boxing-article/7572/eighth-god-war-benny-leonard/%29 (accessed September 22, 2010).

Tosches, Nick. *King of the Jews.* New York: Ecco, 2005.

Traub, James. *The Devil's Playground.* New York: Random House, 2004.

Ultan, Lloyd. *The Beautiful Bronx (1920–1950).* New York: Harmony Books, 1979.

Ultan, Lloyd, and Gary Hermalyn. *The Bronx in the Innocent Years, 1890–1925.* New York: Bronx County Historical Society, 1991.

Van Alkemade, Kim. *Orphans Together: A History of New York's Hebrew Orphan Asylum.* Shippensburg, PA: Shippensburg University Press, 2009.

Vecsey, George. *Baseball.* New York: Modern Library, 1996.

Wagenheim, Kal. *Babe Ruth: His Life and Legend*. New York: Henry Holt, 1974.

Wallop, Douglass. "The Babe," from *Baseball: An Informal History*. W. W. Norton, 1969.

Ward, Geoffrey C., and Ken Burns. *Baseball: An Illustrated History*. New York: Alfred A. Knopf, 1994.

White, G. Edward. *Creating the National Pastime*. Princeton, NJ: Princeton University Press, 1996.

White, Shane, and Stephen Garton, Stephen Robertson, and Graham White. *Playing the Numbers*. Cambridge, MA: Harvard University Press, 2010.

Wickes, George. *Americans in Paris 1903–1939*. New York: Doubleday, 1969.

Williams, Peter. *When the Giants Were Giants*. Chapel Hill, NC: Algonquin Books, 1994.

Wukovits, John F., ed. *The 1920s*. San Diego: Greenhaven Press, 2000.

Zoss, Joel, and John Bowman. *Diamonds in the Rough: The Untold History of Baseball*. New York: Macmillan, 1989.

Index

About the Author

Robert Weintraub is a sports columnist for Slate.com and has written for ESPN.com, *Play,* the *Guardian,* Football Outsiders, and many other publications, as well as written and produced for ESPN, Turner Broadcasting, ABC Sports, the Discovery Channel, and dozens of other television outlets. He lives in Decatur, Georgia.